Constitutional Debate in Action
Criminal Justice

H. L. POHLMAN

Dickinson College

◆

HarperCollins*CollegePublishers*

EDITOR-IN-CHIEF: Marcus Boggs
DEVELOPMENTAL EDITOR: Jennifer Goebel
PROJECT EDITOR: Andrew Roney
TEXT DESIGNER: Nancy Sabato
COVER DESIGNER: Kay Petronio
COVER PHOTOGRAPH: Barbara Maslen
PHOTO RESEARCHER: Nina Page
ELECTRONIC PRODUCTION MANAGER: Valerie A. Sawyer
DESKTOP ADMINISTRATOR: Sarah Johnson
MANUFACTURING MANAGER: Helene G. Landers
ELECTRONIC PAGE MAKEUP: RR Donnelley Barbados
PRINTER AND BINDER: RR Donnelley & Sons Company
COVER PRINTER: RR Donnelley & Sons Company

Constitutional Debate in Action: *Criminal Justice*

Library of Congress Cataloging-in-Publication Data

Pohlman, H. L., 1952-
   Constitutional debate in action. Criminal justice / H. L. Pohlman.
     p.   cm.
   ISBN 0-06-500512-0
   1. Criminal justice, Administration of—United States—Cases.
2. Civil rights—United States—Cases. I. Title. II. Title:
Criminal justice.
KF9223 . A7P58 1995
345. 73' 05—dc20
[347. 3055]   94-19168
                                                       CIP

94 95 96 97 9 8 7 6 5 4 3 2 1

To Ken, Jim, Ron, and Don
and the memory of Tony

CONTENTS

P R E F A C E

The standard textbook on constitutional law assumes that the United States Constitution is best understood as a set of Supreme Court decisions. *Constitutional Debate in Action* is a series of textbooks that adopts a different premise without denying the value of the traditional approach. At a minimum, the orthodox casebook insightfully shows how the Constitution, from 1789 to the present, has evolved as Supreme Court justices have transformed constitutional doctrine. Yet, it is indisputable that such a text does not capture all the aspects of the U.S. Constitution that deserve to be considered. It is not, for example, especially illuminating in regard either to the process of constitutional adjudication itself or to the surrounding political context of any particular case. The Constitution is presented as what the justices say it is, but the political and intellectual forces that directly shape Supreme Court decisions are often ignored or deemphasized. The result is that doctrinal sophistication is often purchased at the expense of the student's understanding of the nature of constitutional adjudication. The student knows a lot of constitutional law, but he or she knows less about how and why it has grown. *Constitutional Debate in Action* tries to rectify this imbalance by viewing constitutional interpretation as an institutionalized form of debate by which certain litigants and their lawyers press their political demands and arguments upon the Supreme Court. It is in this fashion, in the wider context of human wants, passions, and values, that judges interpret the Constitution and thereby transform the basic framework of our government and society.

The more political and process-oriented view of the Constitution that is articulated in *Constitutional Debate in Action* has several distinctive features. First, breadth is sacrificed for depth. A case-study approach is used, and therefore each volume explores in depth only five landmark decisions. Second, each chapter begins with an introduction that describes the legal background as well as the political context. Relevant out-of-courtroom discussions of the constitutional issue in question are excerpted and highlighted in "boxes" set off from the text. Newspaper headlines from the period are also included. These materials will help the student appreciate the political context in which the Supreme Court is operating and assess the degree to which political factors are influencing constitutional adjudication.

The series, however, does not ignore the relevant legal arguments. Rather, it gives a great deal of attention to the process of constitutional argumentation by including sources that deserve more attention than traditional casebooks have given to them: the legal briefs filed in landmark cases and the corresponding oral arguments made before the Supreme Court. These materials, if properly presented, are pedagogically useful.[1] First, the adversarial character of the briefs and oral ar-

---

[1]Overly technical discussions and the large number of citations that are often found in legal briefs have been eliminated from the excerpts that follow. In addition, for the sake of producing a readable text, stylistic usages peculiar to legal briefs, as well as small grammatical errors and typos, have been adapted to standard English or corrected. The same policy was followed in regard to the "boxes" and the Supreme Court opinions.

gument awakens student interest. Students want to figure out for themselves which side has the better argument. And, in general, the time spent reading the briefs is time well spent. The adversarial character of the American approach to constitutional adjudication more or less assumes that the best legal arguments find their way into the actual briefs of the cases, and, in the main (though not always), this assumption is borne out by the quality of the arguments found in the briefs.

However, even in the unlikely event that the briefs and oral argument of a particular case are not of the highest caliber, they nonetheless have pedagogical value. As students compare the validity of the opposing arguments, they are, in effect, preparing themselves for what comes next: a critical evaluation of the edited Supreme Court opinion. In each chapter, the opinion follows the briefs and oral argument. The students, in short, have done a lot of thinking about the issues before they have to consider what the Court has said. They are, for this reason, more inclined to analyze, dissect, and digest the opinion than merely to read and summarize it. In this way, reading the briefs and oral arguments not only provides insight into the process of constitutional adjudication but also encourages students to adopt a more critical perspective on the role that the Supreme Court plays in our constitutional democracy. Is it a court of law? Is it a political policymaker? Is it a little of both? *Constitutional Debate in Action* is designed to underline the significance of these questions by including materials that reveal the important but ambiguous role of the Supreme Court.

Each chapter ends with a postscript that briefly describes important developments of constitutional doctrine since the Court decided the landmark case. They are not meant to be comprehensive or detailed discussions. Instead, their primary purpose is to reaffirm the significance of the landmark decision itself. They show how such cases illustrate important moral, constitutional, and philosophical issues that will, in various guises, constantly reappear in our constitutional democracy.

Though *Constitutional Debate in Action* embodies a somewhat novel approach to teaching constitutional law, it is intended not to replace the more orthodox casebook approach but rather to complement it. It is possible to use the series as the main text in a course on American constitutional law, but any particular volume of the series can also function as a supplemental text for a course taught in the traditional manner. The virtue of such a supplement is that it gives students a different perspective from that of the main text. Most casebooks challenge the best students and frequently intimidate the rest. Page after page of abstract and complicated judicial reasoning is often too much for them. A change of pace is at times useful if not necessary. This series was designed with this need in mind. It will enable any class on constitutional law, no matter what major text is being used, to pause occasionally throughout the term to take a closer look—a look from a different perspective—at a landmark case. Such a supplement can improve student morale in a pedagogically valuable way.

The assumption of this text is that constitutional argumentation before the Supreme Court takes place within a broad political context. In many of the cases that come before the Court, litigants representing distinct political agendas press their claims and arguments. However, not just anyone can litigate before the

Court because there are rules that limit access to all courts. Rules governing *ripeness* and *mootness* concern the nature of the "case or controversy" under litigation, whereas *standing* has more to do with the nature of the parties. Courts, including the Supreme Court, will address only "live" controversies. If a dispute has not yet "ripened" or if it has, for whatever reason, resolved itself (become "moot"), then courts—including the Supreme Court—will refuse to hear it. In the same way, the criteria of standing ask whether the litigant has "a sufficient personal interest" in the issue before the Court. Physical injury or economic damage clearly suffices for standing, but courts can deny access to others, not on the ground that the issue is not a "live" one, but rather because the person initiating the suit has not shown that he or she has been sufficiently harmed. The law governing ripeness, mootness, and standing is composed of complicated rules that limit the character of judicial policymaking, including the sort of policymaking inherent in constitutional adjudication.[2] Nevertheless, many litigants representing distinct political agendas satisfy the criteria of these rules, thereby insuring that the Supreme Court plays a political role in the process of constitutional argumentation.

For practical purposes, constitutional argumentation before the Court begins with "the rule of four." Whether the case is coming from the lower federal courts or from a high state court, the party appealing to the Supreme Court must convince four justices to review the case. Throughout most of its history, the Supreme Court has had no lack of cases from which it could pick and choose. At the present time, approximately 5,500 cases are appealed to the Supreme Court each year, and the Court hands down decisions with full opinions in only 120 to 150 cases. Therefore, because the Court has so many cases to choose from, it controls its own docket. Though political and institutional factors at times limit the Court's discretion, it is nonetheless true that the Court decides only those cases that four justices want it to decide.

Once the case is accepted for review, the petitioner (who filed the case at the Supreme Court) and the respondent (who answers) submit their constitutional arguments in written briefs. Soon thereafter both sides present their arguments orally in front of the justices of the Supreme Court. In addition, the Court often permits "friends of the court" (*amici curiae*) to submit briefs and participate in oral argument. These "friends" are individuals, groups, or organizations that are interested in the litigation. The number of *amici* briefs filed varies enormously from case to case and the degree to which they influence the Court is largely unknown. However, the fact that American constitutional adjudication tolerates, if it does not encourage, the participation of interested third parties is not without significance. It highlights the political aspect of the constitutional process.

After reading the briefs and listening to the oral argument, the justices discuss the case at a weekly conference and cast their initial votes. Each justice has one vote. If the chief justice votes with the majority, he or she has the privilege of deciding which member of the majority should write the majority opinion. If the

---

[2]For a more thorough discussion of these rules and others that limit access to courts, see Henry Abraham, *The Judicial Process*, 6th ed. (New York: Oxford University Press, 1993), Chapter 9.

chief justice votes in the minority, then the most senior judge in the majority makes the opinion assignment. However, not all decisions produce a majority opinion. If a majority of the justices decide in favor of the petitioner but cannot agree upon an opinion, the result is a plurality opinion or opinions. Moreover, any justice who agrees with the majority can also write his or her own concurring opinion. Justices who disagree with the majority or the plurality can either join a dissenting opinion or dissent separately.

In short, every individual justice is free to join any opinion or write one of his or her own. Therefore, the initial vote at conference is not decisive. The justices are perfectly free to change their minds. Hence there is often a great deal of fluidity in the voting as justices circulate, revise, and recirculate opinions and dissents. What started out as a majority opinion may end up as a dissenting opinion; a dissent can become the majority opinion. Consequently, the meaning and significance of a decision depends not upon the initial vote but rather upon how the justices vote when the decision (with any concurring and dissenting opinions) is handed down. The more consensus there is on the Court, the more definite the meaning of the decision and the greater its potential significance.

An analysis of a Supreme Court case, including those that follow in this series, requires paying attention to a number of different factors. First, the facts of a case should be noted: who did what to whom, when, why, how, and where. What were the political, social, and economic contexts of the litigation? Second, who are the parties to the litigation: Who initiated the lawsuit against whom? How did the lawsuit fare in the lower courts? Who is appealing to the Supreme Court? Third, what are the legal issues of the case and the arguments on both sides of the question? Which side has the better argument? Why? Fourth, are there any political influences operating on the Court? What are they? Are they permissible influences, or do they undermine the legal character of constitutional adjudication? Fifth, which side does the Supreme Court favor, and what is the breakdown of the vote? How many concurring and dissenting opinions are there? Sixth, how do the different justices justify their respective positions? Which justification is best? Finally, what is your general evaluation of how the Supreme Court has performed in the particular case under consideration?

Keeping these sorts of questions in mind while reading the following chapters, but at the same time keeping them distinct, will focus attention on the relevant issues. The present volume is entitled *Criminal Justice*. It discusses five landmark cases concerning incorporation and the right to a jury trial, police confessions, plea bargaining, the exclusionary rule, and the death penalty. Any number of cases could have been used to explore these important areas of constitutional law. I chose *Duncan v. Louisiana, Miranda v. Arizona, North Carolina v. Alford, United States v. Leon,* and *Gregg v. Georgia* because they reveal, in an insightful way, how the American system of constitutional adjudication involves the constant interplay of politics and law. Other cases, it is true, could probably have served this purpose just as well, but this fact is not overly significant. The underlying assumption of *Constitutional Debate in Action* is that the question of which cases deserve attention is less important than a deeper awareness of the process of constitutional adjudication itself.

Acknowledgments

I want to express my appreciation to Dickinson College for all the support that I received while working on *Constitutional Debate in Action*. I especially thank George Allan, the Dean of the College, along with Susan Nichols, Leon Fitts, Jeff Niemitz, Kim Lacy Rogers, and Sue Norman. The staffs at Dickinson Law School Library and Dickinson College Library, especially Tina Maresco and Natalia Chromiak, also provided invaluable assistance. Tina and Natalia processed my numerous interlibrary-loan requests with cheerful efficiency. I am also very grateful to my students, especially those who took an interest in this project. In particular, I would like to thank Bruce Butler (class of 1990), Cindy Mather (class of 1991), and Michelle Quinn (class of 1991). These students helped me put the initial sample chapter together and were wonderful sounding boards at a time when I was unsure of what exactly I was trying to accomplish. I will always be in their debt. For many hours of typing and proofing that went into this series of textbooks, I gratefully recognize the contributions of Jennifer Williams (class of 1992), Richard Schirmer (class of 1992), Ann Marie Branson (class of 1994), Marc Snyderman (class of 1994), and Tim Grieco (class of 1994). They did excellent work in a job that is as important as it is thankless. Finally, I am happy that I have this opportunity to express my gratitude to my student research assistant, Daniel DeArment (class of 1993). For the past year, Dan has been at my side helping me separate the wheat from the chaff, giving me the benefit of his perspective as a student. In this capacity, Dan gave me many valuable suggestions, especially in regard to the material set off in "boxes" throughout the series. I owe Dan a great deal for all the energy and insight that he has infused into this series. I am also indebted to the Mellon and the Dana foundations for their support of the student work that went into *Constitutional Debate in Action*.

A number of colleagues and friends deserve mention here for tolerating my obsession with this project over the past couple of years. Eugene Hickok, who is a fellow member of Dickinson's Political Science Department, has been an invaluable associate. I have used his books, his ideas, and his time. I want to thank him for all that he has done for me without promising that I will never ask for his help again. Gary Gildin, a member of the faculty of the Dickinson Law School, also patiently suffered my pleas for advice, giving me a number of valuable suggestions. When I was contemplating whether to begin this project, D. Grier Stephenson, from Franklin and Marshall College, gave me the necessary encouragement to get started. Last, I want to thank Victoria Kuhn, my departmental secretary, who put more time and energy into this series than anyone save myself. Never have I seen a person have so much fun working so hard tracking down permissions for copyrighted material. I owe Victoria so much because, as she knows, I would have been buried in frustration and despair by the job that she pursued with efficiency and good humor.

I also want to thank Philip B. Kurland and Gerhard Casper, the editors of *Landmark Briefs and Arguments of the Supreme Court of the United States,* published by University Publications of America. I often used this series while working on my project. It was an invaluable resource. Moreover, the editors and University Publications of America have graciously allowed me to use their designations of which justices asked what questions during oral argument. In my opinion, having the names of justices linked to specific questions is a valuable pedagogical aid, and I am grateful to the editors and the press for letting me use their work. In the same vein, I want to thank all those who gave me permission to use copyrighted material. I use the material because I think, rightly or wrongly, that it will make the difficult task of teaching constitutional law somewhat easier. I am grateful because they care enough about education to give my textbook a chance to make a difference in the crucible of the classroom.

Marcus Boggs, Jennifer Goebel, Andrew Roney, and Paula Soloway, my editors at HarperCollins, have done a wonderful job ushering this project through the various stages of the publication process.

Last, I wish to apologize for the many mistakes that I have made in this series of constitutional law textbooks. I only wish to add, by way of explanation, how difficult it was for me to write and edit these fifteen chapters. Given the publication deadlines, I found it to be very much like trying to square fifteen circles in as many months. The task was one that made for some long days and short nights. I can only hope that the reader irritated with one of my lapses will understand if not forgive.

H. L. Pohlman

Incorporation and the Right to a Jury Trial

DUNCAN V. LOUISIANA
391 U.S. 145 (1968)

✦

Today the right to a jury trial is a *national* Sixth Amendment right. Any criminal defendant in the United States facing the possibility of more than six months of imprisonment upon conviction has the right to demand a jury trial.[1] Not only the federal government but also every state has to respect this right. In the nineteenth century, the constitutional rights of criminal defendants were vastly different. At that time, the Bill of Rights, including the Sixth Amendment, restricted only what the federal government could do.[2] Though certain provisions of the Constitution, such as the ones prohibiting *ex post facto* laws or suspensions of the writ of *habeas corpus*, were applicable to states, the Bill of Rights was not. States could legally violate all the rights protected from federal infringement by the Bill of Rights, including those concerned with criminal justice. Not until the twentieth century did the Supreme Court begin to "incorporate" many of the particular provisions of the Bill of Rights into the Fourteenth Amendment's due process clause, thereby applying them against the states. By this process of *incorporation,* the Court created a national set of substantive and procedural rights.

---

[1] *Baldwin v. New York*, 399 U.S. 66 (1970); *Blanton v. North Las Vegas,* 109 S.Ct. 1289 (1989).

[2] See *Barron v. Baltimore,* 7 Pet. (32 U.S.) 243 (1833).

1

In *Duncan v. Louisiana* (1968), the justices debated the pros and cons of incorporation as they considered whether to apply the Sixth Amendment right to a jury trial against the states. The case concerned a defendant who had been convicted of simple battery after a trial without a jury. He appealed his decision to the Supreme Court, claiming that he had a Sixth Amendment right to a jury trial and that Louisiana had a constitutional obligation to respect his wish to be tried by a jury. Though the jury was an old and sacred institution, it was not at all clear that defendants had a constitutional right to a jury trial. No doubt the Sixth Amendment barred the federal government from denying a jury trial to a defendant who refused to waive the right, but were the states operating under similar or identical restraints? This question depended on the legitimacy of the doctrine of incorporation. *Duncan* is therefore a useful case to examine the role that the Supreme Court has played not only in creating a national set of substantive rights but also in fashioning a constitutional code of criminal procedure.

Evaluating what the Supreme Court has done by incorporating the Bill of Rights into the Fourteenth Amendment's due process clause requires balancing the values of federalism and individual rights. It is obvious that every Supreme Court decision incorporating a provision of the Bill of Rights limits the ability of state legislatures to experiment. Of course, today there is consensus that certain rights are so important that state legislatures should not be allowed to tamper with them. But where should the line be drawn? Despite the value of legislative experimentation at the state level, is every right found in the Bill of Rights equally worthy of being nationalized? In 1932, Justice Louis Brandeis, one of the twentieth century's great defenders of individual rights, gave his estimation of the value of local experimentation:

> Denial of the right to experiment may be fraught with serious consequences to the Nation. It is one of the happy incidents of the federal system that a single courageous State may, if its citizens choose, serve as a laboratory; and try novel social and economic experiments without risk to the rest of the country. This Court has the power to prevent an experiment. We may strike down the statute which embodies it on the ground that, in our opinion, the measure is arbitrary, capricious, or unreasonable. . . . But in the exercise of this high power, we must ever be on our guard, lest we erect our prejudices into legal principles. If we would guide by the light of reason, we must let our minds be bold.[3]

Brandeis is reminding us that the Supreme Court can go too far in the direction of extending and protecting individual rights. By narrowing the range of legislative options, the Court can prevent experimentation and thereby shut out the "light of reason." Is Brandeis correct? Does the value of experimentation have any bearing on whether the Supreme Court should have nationalized the Bill of Rights?

Besides encouraging experimentation, the American federal system fragments political power. There are a number of advantages to such a system of de-

---

[3]*New State Ice Co. v. Liebman*, 285 U.S. 262, 311 (1932), Brandeis dissenting.

centralized political decision making. First, it discourages the growth of a mono-lithic national government capable of as much evil as it is of good. In *Federalist No. 51*, James Madison explained how a large *federal* republic prevents tyranny. First, in a federal system,

> the power surrendered by the people is first divided between two distinct govern-ments, and then the portion allotted to each subdivided among distinct and sepa-rate departments. Hence a double security arises to the rights of the people. The different governments will control each other, at the same time that each will be controlled by itself.[4]

In this fashion, federalism complements the separation of powers. The powers of each state government and the national government are divided and distributed to separate legislative, executive, and judicial "departments." The branches can therefore "check and balance" each other, allowing each government to control it-self. But the federal system permits the governments to control each other, pro-viding Americans with a "double security."

Madison also thought that federalism preserved liberty in a way quite differ-ent from the method of checks and balances. A country that respected the princi-ple of federalism could be much larger than a unitary state. Size was significant because a large country would have a "multiplicity of interests" that would make it very difficult for one faction to dominate and oppress the others.[5] Hence federal-ism prevented tyranny not only by functioning as a vital part of a system of checks and balances but also by providing the political structure for a large and diverse country.

In your view, do Madison's arguments have any relevance to the twentieth century? Do the states check and balance the federal government? Does the size of the United States contribute to the American commitment to individual rights and limited government? Do Madison's arguments have any bearing on the cre-ation of a national set of individual rights, including the rights of the accused? Should state legislatures have the discretion to enact radically different codes of criminal procedure? Do the states confront such different problems that they should have the power to "experiment" in this fashion? Does state control over criminal procedure advance the cause of freedom? Is it possible that a judicially created set of national rights is a step in the direction of tyranny? If so, in what ways?

Another purported virtue of federalism is that it promotes democracy by let-ting people at the local level, not bureaucrats in Washington, D.C., make signifi-cant policy decisions. Is this true? Is it important that people who are most af-fected by an issue be given the authority to resolve it? Does such a system let those who are most familiar with local conditions and realities shape the policies

---

[4]*The Federalist Papers*, ed. Clinton Rossiter (New York: Mentor, 1961), p. 323.

[5]Ibid., pp. 324–325. For a more elaborate explanation of Madison's views concerning the value of large states, see his famous *Federalist No. 10*.

that affect their lives? Do you think Americans would have more political satisfaction if they had more control over their local affairs? Would local control over criminal procedure deepen the American commitment to democracy?

Experimentation, prevention of tyranny, and democracy are the primary values that underlie the American principle of federalism. Their significance must be weighed when evaluating what the Supreme Court has done by nationalizing the Bill of Rights, including the right that will be considered more fully in this chapter, the right to a jury trial. The Supreme Court's twentieth-century nationalization of the Bill of Rights was based on the due process clause of the Fourteenth Amendment:

> No State shall make or enforce any law which shall abridge the privileges or immunities of citizens of the United States; nor shall any State deprive any person of life, liberty, or property, without due process of law; nor deny to any person within its jurisdiction the equal protection of the laws.

At the time of the Fourteenth Amendment's ratification in 1868, there was little reason to believe that the due process clause would become the constitutional vehicle for the creation of a national set of individual rights immune from both federal and state control. After all, an identical clause restricting the federal government had been part of the Fifth Amendment for many years. The way that it had customarily been interpreted hardly anticipated the awesome role that the Fourteenth Amendment clause would play in the twentieth century. For example, in *Den v. Hoboken Land and Improvement Co.* (1856), the Supreme Court said that judges must interpret "due process" by looking to "settled usages and modes of proceeding existing in the common and statute law of England, before the emigration of our ancestors."[6] The clause was therefore a guarantee that imposed on the federal government a limited number of common-law procedures. The federal government could deprive someone of life, liberty, or property only if it followed these procedures. So understood, it was in no way a constitutional basis for a national set of individual rights, whether of the substantive or of the procedural type.[7]

Though the phrase "due process" had a rather limited meaning in the period immediately preceding the Civil War, the clause of the Fourteenth Amendment (1868) that forbade any state from enforcing any law "which shall abridge the privileges or immunities of citizens of the United States" arguably provided the textual basis for a national set of rights. However, in the *Slaughterhouse Cases* (1873), a 5–4 decision, the Court declined to interpret this phrase in a way that would allow the federal judiciary to become the defender of individual rights

---

[6]*Den v. Hoboken Land and Improvement Co.*, 18 How. (59 U.S.) 272, 276–277 (1856).

[7] One notorious exception to the general mid-nineteenth-century view that "due process" was merely a procedural guarantee was Chief Justice Roger B. Taney's infamous decision in *Dred Scott v. Sandford*, 19 How. (60 U.S.) 393 (1857). Taney claimed that the federal law outlawing slavery in certain federal territories deprived citizens of their property without due process of law. At the time, Taney's "substantive" view of due process received little support.

against the states. American citizens, the Court said, had rights as citizens of the federal government and as citizens of the states in which they resided. The "privileges and immunities" clause protected only the former "bundle" of rights, not the latter. The Court then went on to list the kinds of rights that were dependent on federal citizenship. Because the Court's majority could not believe that the Fourteenth Amendment radically changed the relations between the federal government and the states, the list was small and unimpressive. Included were the right to participate in and interact with the federal government, the right of free access to American seaports, the right of federal protection when abroad, the right to use the navigable waters of the United States, and the privilege of the writ of *habeas corpus*.[8] All other rights were dependent on state citizenship and were therefore subject to state control. Thus in 1873 the Supreme Court interpreted the privilege and immunities clause in such a way that it could not provide the basis for a broad set of national individual rights enforced by the federal judiciary against the states.[9]

The dissents in the *Slaughterhouse Cases* bitterly contested the majority's conclusions. For instance, Justice Stephen J. Field said that the majority's view of the privilege and immunities clause reduced it to "a vain and idle enactment, which accomplished nothing, and most unnecessarily excited Congress and the people on its passage."[10] Field envisioned the Fourteenth Amendment as a constitutional shield for a national set of rights enforced by the judiciary against the states. These rights were based on the "natural and inalienable" rights that all "free governments" recognize. Field's dissent therefore anticipated what the Supreme Court was going to accomplish, first by relying on substantive due process and later by relying on the doctrine of incorporation.

However, a decade after the *Slaughterhouse Cases*, in *Hurtado v. California* (1884), the Supreme Court refused to interpret the due process clause of the Fourteenth Amendment in a way that would impose national restrictions on the criminal procedures of states. Hurtado had been convicted of murder after having been indicted by information (an indictment by a district attorney) rather than by a grand jury (the constitutionally required federal procedure). His argument, relying on the customary interpretation of due process, was that indictment by information conflicted with the settled "modes of proceeding" of the common law and for that reason violated the due process clause of the Fourteenth Amendment.

In response, the Supreme Court admitted that if a "mode of proceeding" coincided with the common law, it was within due process, but held that the converse was not true. Some procedures, like indictments by information, were compatible with due process even though they were unknown to the common law. To

---

[8]See *Slaughterhouse Cases,* 16 Wall. (83 U.S.) 36, 79 (1873).

[9]It should also be noted that the majority in the *Slaughterhouse Cases* quickly dismissed arguments claiming that the Thirteenth Amendment and the due process and equal protection clauses of the Fourteenth Amendment constitutionally authorized the federal judiciary to defend a broad set of national rights against the states.

[10]*Slaughterhouse Cases,* 16 Wall. (83 U.S.) 36, 96 (1873).

conclude otherwise, to hold that any procedure not recognized by the common law was not due process, would be "to deny every quality of the law but its age and to render it incapable of progress or improvement."[11] Moreover, the Court said it was unreasonable to claim that due process under the Fourteenth Amendment required a grand jury indictment. After all, if the Court interpreted the due process clause of the Fourteenth Amendment in this fashion, it would make the grand jury provision of the Fifth Amendment superfluous. The due process clause of the Fifth Amendment would already require grand jury indictments, thereby rendering the grand jury provision pointless. But since no constitutional clause should be interpreted to make another meaningless,[12] the Court concluded that the due process clause of the Fourteenth Amendment did impose some restrictions on how states could deprive someone of life, liberty, and property, but they were not identical to the restrictions imposed on the federal government by the Bill of Rights.

The Court discussed an example of a procedure not prohibited by the Bill of Rights that the due process clause of the Fourteenth Amendment would prohibit. If a state adopted a special procedure for a "particular person or a particular case," the Court said it would not qualify as due process, and the federal judiciary would step in.[13] In general, however, deference to state legislatures would be the norm because due process refers to the "law of the land in each state, which derives its authority from the inherent and reserved powers of the State." The state must stay within "the limits of those fundamental principles of liberty and justice," but the "greatest security" for these rights "resides in the right of the people to make their own laws, and alter them at their pleasure."[14]

What do you think of Hurtado's argument that due process had to be equated with common-law procedures? Should the federal judiciary invalidate any criminal procedure of a state that is not sanctified by eighteenth-century common law? Would such a response unduly circumscribe the state's ability to experiment with new forms of procedure? But what of the Court's conclusion that none of the criminal justice guarantees of the Bill of Rights can be applied against the states? Is this an extreme reading of the due process clause of the Fourteenth Amendment? Does it really matter whether the due process clause of the Fourteenth Amendment has a meaning different from that of the due process clause of the Fifth? And finally, does the Court have too high an opinion of state legislatures when it says that the best way to preserve "fundamental rights" is to let people of any particular state "make their own laws, and alter them at their pleasure"?

Hurtado constituted a sharp rejection by the Supreme Court of any sort of uniform constitutional code of national criminal procedure. However, notwithstanding this decision, within fifteen years the Court relied on the due process

---

[11]*Hurtado v. California*, 110 U.S. 516, 529 (1884).

[12]Idem, 534–535.

[13]Idem, 535.

[14]Idem. *Hurtado* was a 7–1 decision. Justice John M. Harlan I, dissented, arguing that the Bill of Rights should be applied against the states. Harlan's policy of "total incorporation" did not receive much support on the Court until *Adamson v. California*, 332 U.S. 46 (1947).

clause to invalidate state socioeconomic regulations on the ground that they were "unreasonable" deprivations of "liberty of contract." In *Allgeyer v. Louisiana* (1897), the Court invalidated a law that prohibited anyone from obtaining insurance on Louisiana property from a marine insurance company that had not complied with state law.[15] In the Court's view, such a law was an unreasonable infringement of the freedom to contract protected by the Fourteenth Amendment. Liberty of contract was a part of the "life, liberty, and property" that the state could not take away without due process. Since the law was unreasonable, it was not in accord with due process.

Allgeyer was an important and controversial case because the Court interpreted due process as a substantive, rather than as a procedural, limitation. Louisiana had not violated fundamental procedures in the way that it had made the law or in the way that it had enforced it. Instead, it had violated a substantive right of individuals by enacting a law that "unreasonably" infringed on the liberty of contract. Accordingly, in *Allgeyer*, the Court did under the due process clause what it had earlier declined to do in the *Slaughterhouse Cases* under the "privileges or immunities" clause. The decision increased the number of national economic rights and sharply expanded the judiciary's role in protecting such rights from state interference.

The high point of substantive due process was *Lochner v. New York* (1905), a case in which the Court invalidated a state law that prohibited bakers from working more than ten hours a day or sixty hours a week[16] The Court often invoked this doctrine in the decades that followed,[17] but it came under heavy attack during the New Deal. The Court abused its power, commentators argued, by injecting a *laissez-faire* economic philosophy into the Fourteenth Amendment's due process clause.[18] The end result, after a bruising battle with President Franklin Roosevelt, was that the Court gradually abandoned the substantive due process doctrine and retired from the socioeconomic area.[19] By the mid-1940s, the Court would no longer invalidate socioeconomic laws of the states on the ground that they violated a national right to contract.

---

[15]165 U.S. 578 (1897). For the origins of the substantive due process doctrine, see *Munn v. Illinois,* 94 U.S. 113 (1877); *Railroad Commission Cases,* 116 U.S. 307 (1886); and *Mugler v. Kansas,* 123 U.S. 623 (1887).

[16]198 U.S. 45 (1905).

[17]See *Adair v. United States,* 208 U.S. 161 (1908); *Coppage v. Kansas,* 236 U.S. 1 (1915); *Adkins v. Children's Hospital,* 261 U.S. 525 (1923); *Weaver v. Palmer Bros. Co.,* 270 U.S. 402 (1926); and *Morehead v. New York ex rel. Tipaldo,* 298 U.S. 587 (1936).

[18]For a more thorough discussion of substantive due process and the events of the New Deal, see H. L. Pohlman, *Constitutional Debate in Action, Volume 1: Governmental Powers* (New York: Harper-Collins, 1995), ch. 2.

[19]See *West Coast Hotel Co. v. Parrish,* 300 U.S. 379 (1937); *United States v. Carolene Products Co.,* 304 U.S. 144 (1938); *Olsen v. Nebraska,* 313 U.S. 236 (1941); and *Williamson v. Lee Optical Co.,* 348 U.S. 483 (1955). Of course, it is arguable that the Court revived the substantive due process doctrine during the 1960s and 1970s when it invalidated state laws (prohibiting the use of contraceptives and abortion) based on a right to privacy.

However, by retreating from the socioeconomic field, the Court did not abandon substantive due process. Even before the New Deal, the Court had already incorporated certain substantive rights found in the Bill of Rights and applied them against the states. Especially important rights that were nationalized in this fashion were the freedoms of speech,[20] of the press,[21] and of religion.[22] Accordingly, though the Supreme Court may have abused its powers in the way that it applied substantive due process in the socioeconomic area, the doctrine of liberty of contract in the early twentieth century bridged the chasm separating the nineteenth-century tradition of judicial passivity in regard to a national set of individual rights and the more modern outlook embodied in the doctrine of incorporation. Though the right to contract was eventually repudiated, the Court's experience applying it against the states prepared the way for the Court's distinctive twentieth-century role: the protection of a set of uniform national rights against both the federal and the state governments.

By incorporating the First Amendment into the Fourteenth Amendment, the Court rejected the *Hurtado* principle that no provision of the Bill of Rights could be applied against the states through the due process clause. Even if the phrase "due process" appeared in both the Fifth and Fourteenth Amendments, and even if the phrase in the Fifth could not possibly be equivalent to other rights listed in the Bill of Rights, the Court slowly and tentatively incorporated certain rights listed in the Bill of Rights into the due process clause of the Fourteenth Amendment.

In *Palko v. Connecticut* (1937), though the Court rejected the argument that the double jeopardy clause of the Fifth Amendment was incorporated into the Fourteenth Amendment, Justice Benjamin Cardozo explained the new understanding of the relationship between the Bill of Rights and the due process clause of the Fourteenth Amendment. He said that due process consisted of the "'fundamental principles of liberty and justice that lie at the base of all our civil and political institutions'" and that they were of the "the very essence of a scheme of ordered liberty."[23] Any state law that violated "fundamental rights" would therefore be invalidated. Such rights, of course, did not have to be mentioned in the Bill of Rights. On the other hand, if a certain right was essential for "a scheme of ordered liberty," it would not be surprising if it were listed in one of the first eight amendments. The due process clause only incorporated fundamental rights, but the Bill of Rights was a good place for the Court to begin its analysis of whether any particular right was fundamental or not.

Cardozo's fundamental rights approach to due process did not, of course, treat all the rights contained in the Bill of Rights equally. There were three options. Such "preferred freedoms" as speech, press, and religion the Court incorporated fully. The federal judiciary would protect these rights from state action to the same degree that it protected them from federal action.

---

[20]See *Gitlow v. New York*, 268 U.S. 652 (1925); and *Fiske v. Kansas*, 274 U.S. 380 (1927).

[21]See *Near v. Minnesota*, 283 U.S. 697 (1931).

[22]*Hamilton v. Regents of the University of California*, 293 U.S. 245 (1931); and *Cantwell v. Connecticut*, 310 U.S. 296 (1940).

[23]*Palko v. Connecticut*, 302 U.S. 319, 328, 325 (1937).

Other rights within the Bill of Rights were partially incorporated. The Court would apply the "core" of the right against the states, but it would not have the same scope as it had against the federal government. For instance, certain forms of double jeopardy might violate the due process clause, but not the kind practiced by Connecticut in *Palko*. After being indicted for first-degree murder, a jury found Palko guilty of second-degree murder, and the judge sentenced him to life imprisonment. Based on a state law, the prosecution appealed, arguing that the trial judge had made several errors. Connecticut's highest court agreed with the prosecution and remanded Palko over for a retrial, at which time he was convicted of first-degree murder and sentenced to death. The retrial, Cardozo argued, was not a violation of due process. All that the state wanted was a trial free from substantial legal error. The retrial was constitutional even though the Fifth Amendment prohibited the federal government from doing what Connecticut had done.[24] In short, double jeopardy was incorporated against the states, but the right against the states did not have the same scope as it had against the federal government.

Finally, Cardozo concluded, there were provisions of the Bill of Rights that were in no way essential to "a scheme of ordered liberty." These rights were completely outside the due process clause. In Cardozo's judgment, the right to a jury trial was one of these nonfundamental rights.[25] Hence in 1937 the Supreme Court's view was that states had no constitutional obligation to respect the right to a jury trial.

The fundamental rights approach to the due process clause of the Fourteenth Amendment reigned supreme without serious challenge until *Adamson v. California* (1947), at which time a debate concerning the meaning of due process erupted on the Court. In this case, Adamson claimed that his murder conviction violated the Fourteenth Amendment because at his trial the prosecution had commented on his failure to take the stand. The Supreme Court, in a 5–4 decision, ruled that what California had done did not violate the due process clause. Even though it would have violated the Fifth Amendment privilege against self-incrimination if the federal government had commented on a defendant's failure to testify on his own behalf, states were free to engage in such a practice because it did not violate the defendant's fundamental right to a fair trial. The Court did not consider the Fifth Amendment privilege against self-incrimination to be fundamental.

In his dissent, Justice Hugo Black articulated a theory of due process that will forever be linked to his name: the doctrine of total incorporation. According to Black, the due process clause of the Fourteenth Amendment fully incorporated *all* the provisions of the Bill of Rights. His argument was twofold. First, he insisted

---

[24]The right to counsel was another example, according to Cardozo, of a right that had different contours depending on whether the federal government or a state government was involved. In *Powell v. Alabama,* 287 U.S. 45 (1932), the Court ruled that no state could convict an indigent defendant of a capital crime without providing him with counsel. However, in *Palko,* Cardozo said that the earlier decision did not turn on how the Sixth Amendment was interpreted. Instead, the ruling was that in the particular circumstances of the case, the defendants could not have received a "fair hearing" without counsel. See *Palko v. Connecticut,* 302 U.S. 319, 327 (1937).

[25]*Palko v. Connecticut,* 302 U.S. 319, 325 (1937).

that the framers intended the Fourteenth Amendment to create a set of national rights equivalent to those that had previously been applicable only against the federal government. The Supreme Court therefore had a constitutional obligation to enforce the Fifth Amendment against the states. Second, he claimed that Cardozo's fundamental rights approach to the due process clause was nothing other than the discredited "natural-law formula" that the Court had used to invalidate socioeconomic laws during the heyday of liberty of contract. The Court should therefore abandon this "subjective" interpretation of due process for the "objective" standards embodied in the Bill of Rights. The discretion of courts would thereby be confined. Laws violating the Bill of Rights would be invalidated, but states would be free to enact all other laws without fear of judicial abuse of power. Finally, there was no reason to fear that total incorporation would confine the states to an "18th Century straitjacket." Since the provisions of the Bill of Rights were not "outdated abstractions" but rather vital principles of continuing relevance, judicial enforcement of them would ensure the preservation of liberty in the United States (see Box 1.1).

In a concurring opinion, Justice Felix Frankfurter defended Cardozo's fundamental rights approach to due process and attacked Black's thesis of total incorporation. First, he denigrated Black's claim that the framers of the Fourteenth Amendment intended to nationalize the Bill of Rights. It would be "extraordinarily strange" for the framers to have used the phrase "due process" to impose on the states the specific rights, liberties, and procedures listed in the Bill of Rights. They would have had to have been either "ignorant of" or "indifferent to" the traditional meaning of the Fifth Amendment's due process clause: "settled usages and modes of proceeding." After all, "due process of law" cannot mean one thing in the Fifth Amendment and another in the Fourteenth. Second, Frankfurter denied that the fundamental rights approach to due process inevitably degenerated into "the idiosyncrasies of a merely personal judgment." To decide if a law violated due process, judges must consider whether it offends those "canons of decency and fairness which express the notions of justice of English-speaking peoples." Though this standard is nowhere "authoritatively formulated," it does not leave a judge "wholly at large" (see Box 1.2).

Which justice has the more justifiable approach to understanding the meaning of due process and the degree to which the judiciary should enforce a national set of rights against both the federal government and state governments? What do you make of the fact that the justices disagreed so sharply about the intentions of those who framed the Fourteenth Amendment or that, ever since this decision, debate has raged in academic circles concerning the historical purpose of the Fourteenth Amendment?[26] Do these historical investigations have any

---

[26]Soon after *Adamson* was decided, Charles Fairman, a prominent constitutional authority, attacked Black's interpretation of the historical purpose of the Fourteenth Amendment. See his article "Does the Fourteenth Amendment Incorporate the Bill of Rights?" *Stanford Law Review* 2 (1949): 5–173. Coming to Black's defense, William Crosskey responded to Fairman's charges in "Charles Fairman, 'Legislative History,' and the Constitutional Limitations on State Authority," *University of Chicago Law Review* 22 (1954): 1ff. For the most recent battle of this war over historical intent, see Raoul Berger, *The Fourteenth Amendment and the Bill of Rights* (Norman: University of Oklahoma Press, 1989); and Michael K. Curtis, *No State Shall Abridge the Fourteenth Amendment and the Bill of Rights* (Durham, N.C.: Duke University Press, 1986).

BOX 1.1

Justice Black on Incorporation

... My study of the historical events that culminated in the Fourteenth Amendment, and the expressions of those who sponsored and favored, as well as those who opposed its submission and passage, persuades me that one of the chief objects that the provisions of the Amendment's first section, separately, and as a whole, were intended to accomplish was to make the Bill of Rights, applicable to the states. ...

... I further contend that the "natural law" formula which the Court uses to reach its conclusion in this case should be abandoned as an incongruous excrescence on our Constitution. I believe that formula to be itself a violation of our Constitution, in that it subtly conveys to courts, at the expense of legislatures, ultimate power over public policies in fields where no specific provision of the Constitution limits legislative power. ...

... [In *Allgeyer v. Louisiana,*] the Court in 1896 applied the due process clause to strike down a state statute which had forbidden certain types of contracts. In doing so, it substantially adopted the rejected argument of counsel in the Slaughter-House Cases, that the Fourteenth Amendment guarantees the liberty of all persons under "natural law" to engage in their chosen business or vocation. ...

The foregoing constitutional doctrine, judicially created and adopted by expanding the previously accepted meaning of "due process," marked a complete departure from the Slaughter-House philosophy of judicial tolerance of state regulation of business activities. Conversely, the new formula contracted the effectiveness of the Fourteenth Amendment as a protection from state infringement of individual liberties enumerated in the Bill of Rights. Thus the Court's second-thought interpretation of the Amendment was an about face from the Slaughter-House interpretation and represented a failure to carry out the avowed purpose of the Amendment's sponsors. This reversal is dramatized by the fact that the Hurtado Case, which had rejected the due process clause as an instrument for preserving Bill of Rights liberties and privileges, was cited as authority for expanding the scope of that clause so as to permit this Court to invalidate all state regulatory legislation it believed to be contrary to "fundamental" principles. ...

I cannot consider the Bill of Rights to be an outworn 18th Century "strait jacket.". ... Its provisions may be thought outdated abstractions by some. And it is true that they were designed to meet ancient evils. But they are the same kind of human evils that have emerged from century to century wherever excessive power is sought by the few at the expense of the many. In my judgment the people of no nation can lose their liberty so long as a Bill of Rights like ours survives and its basic purposes are conscientiously interpreted, enforced and respected so as to afford continuous protection against old, as well as new, devices and practices which might thwart those purposes. I fear to see the consequences of the Court's practice of substituting its own concepts of decency and fundamental justice for the language of the Bill of Rights as its point of departure in interpreting and enforcing that Bill of Rights. . . .

It is an illusory apprehension that literal application of some or all of the provisions of the Bill of Rights to the States would unwisely increase the sum total of the powers of this Court to invalidate state legislation. The Federal Government has not been harmfully burdened by the requirement that enforcement of federal laws affecting civil liberty conform literally to the Bills of Rights. Who would advocate its repeal? It must be conceded, of course, that the natural-law-due-process formula, which the Court today reaffirms, has been interpreted to limit substantially this Court's power to prevent state violations of the individual civil liberties guaranteed by the Bill of Rights. But this formula also has been used in the past, and can be used in the future, to license this Court, in considering regulatory legislation, to roam at large in the broad expanses of policy and morals and to trespass, all too freely, on the legislative domain of the States as well as the Federal Government. . . .

Source: Adamson v. California 322 U.S. 46, 71–90 (1947).

practical value for constitutional adjudication? Should they be the controlling factor in how the due process clause of the Fourteenth Amendment is interpreted? And what of the potential for judicial abuse of power? Is Black correct that the fundamental rights approach to the Fourteenth Amendment invites judges to apply their own personal prejudices? Is Frankfurter's response to this issue either persuasive or adequate? What of Black's doctrine of total incorporation itself? Could it be said that imposing the Bill of Rights on the states in one fell swoop is itself a form of judicial abuse of power? Is Black insincerely using a historical argument to embody into constitutional law his own preference for a national set of rights?

By coming within one vote of a majority in favor of total incorporation, *Adamson* marked the high point of Black's doctrine.[27] Never again did Black's view of the due process clause of the Fourteenth Amendment come so close to becoming law, though the Court continued to expand the set of national rights enforceable against the states, first by using the traditional fundamental rights approach and later by formulating a new doctrine called *selective incorporation*. An example of the former was *Wolf v. Colorado* (1949), in which the Court held that the due process clause incorporated the central core of the Fourth Amendment but not the remedy used in federal courts to enforce the right to be free from unreasonable searches and seizures—the exclusionary rule.[28] By this sort of fundamental

---

[27]In fact, only Justice William O. Douglas joined Black's dissent in *Adamson*. Justice Wiley B. Rutledge joined Justice Frank Murphy's separate dissent that fully incorporated the Bill of Rights against the states but rejected Black's corollary that confined the due process clause to *only* the provisions of the Bill of Rights. Murphy wanted to incorporate all of the provisions of the Bill of Rights but reserve the power of courts to invalidate state laws that violated fundamental rights not listed in the Bill of Rights.

[28]338 U.S. 25 (1949).

BOX 1.2

Justice Frankfurter on Incorporation

... Between the incorporation of the Fourteenth Amendment into the Constitution and the beginning of the present membership of the Court—a period of seventy years—the scope of that Amendment was passed upon by forty-three judges. Of all these judges, only one, who may respectfully be called an eccentric exception, ever indicated the belief that the Fourteenth Amendment was a shorthand summary of the first eight Amendments theretofore limiting only the Federal Government.... Among these judges were not only those who would have to be included among the greatest in the history of the Court, but—it is especially relevant to note—they included those whose services in the cause of human rights and the spirit of freedom are the most conspicuous in our history.... [T]hey were also judges mindful of the relation of our federal system to a progressively democratic society and therefore duly regardful of the scope of authority that was left to the States even after the Civil War. And so they did not find that the Fourteenth Amendment, concerned as it was with matters fundamental to the pursuit of justice, fastened upon the States procedural arrangements which, in the language of Mr. Justice Cardozo, only those who are "narrow or provincial" would deem essential to "a fair and enlightened system of justice." To suggest that it is inconsistent with a truly free society to begin prosecutions without an indictment, to try petty civil cases without the paraphernalia of a common law jury, to take into consideration that one who has full opportunity to make a defense remains silent is, in de Tocqueville's phrase, to confound the familiar with the necessary.

The short answer to the suggestion that the provision of the Fourteenth Amendment, which ordains "nor shall any State deprive any person of life, liberty, or property, without due process of law," was a way of saying that every State must thereafter ... have a trial by a jury of twelve in criminal cases ... is that it is a strange way of saying it. It would be extraordinarily strange for a Constitution to convey such specific commands in such a roundabout and inexplicit way....

... It ought not to require argument to reject the notion that due process of law meant one thing in the Fifth Amendment and another in the Fourteenth.... Are Madison and his contemporaries in the framing of the Bill of Rights to be charged with writing into it a meaningless clause? To consider "due process of law" as merely a shorthand statement of other specific clauses in the same amendment is to attribute to the authors and proponents of this Amendment ignorance of, or indifference to, a historic conception which was one of the great instruments in the arsenal of constitutional freedom which the Bill of Rights was to protect and strengthen....

And so, when, as in a case like the present, a conviction in a State court is here for review under a claim that a right protected by the Due Process Clause of the Fourteenth Amendment has been denied, the issue is not whether an infraction of one of the specific provisions of the first eight

Amendments is disclosed by the record. The relevant question is whether the criminal proceedings which resulted in conviction deprived the accused of the due process of law to which the United States Constitution entitled him. Judicial review of that guaranty of the Fourteenth Amendment inescapably imposes upon this Court an exercise of judgment upon the whole course of the proceedings in order to ascertain whether they offend those canons of decency and fairness which express the notions of justice of English-speaking peoples even toward those charged with the most heinous offenses. These standards of justice are not authoritatively formulated anywhere as though they were prescriptions in a pharmacopoeia. But neither does the application of the Due Process Clause imply that judges are wholly at large. The judicial judgment in applying the Due Process Clause must move within the limits of accepted notions of justice and is not to be based upon the idiosyncrasies of a merely personal judgment. The fact that judges among themselves may differ whether in a particular case a trial offends accepted notions of justice is not disproof that general rather than idiosyncratic standards are applied. An important safeguard against such merely individual judgment is an alert deference to the judgment of the State court under review.

Source: Adamson v. California, 332 U.S. 46, 62–68 (1947).

rights approach, the Court had, by the late 1950s, applied some elements of the majority of the criminal procedures listed in the Bill of Rights, but not all of them.[29]

In the early 1960s, primarily at the urging of Justice William Brennan, the Court slowly abandoned the traditional fundamental rights approach to due process in favor of selective incorporation. The central premise of this doctrine was that not all of the rights listed in the Bill of Rights were applicable to the states. Only those that were "fundamental" were "selectively incorporated." In this sense, selective incorporation respected the value of federalism more than Black's doctrine of total incorporation did. However, one tenet of the selective incorporation doctrine did not favor federalism. If a provision of the Bill of Rights was incorporated into the Fourteenth Amendment, its full scope had to be applied against the states. The right applied against the states had to be equal in scope to the one applied against the federal government. According to Brennan, the Court should no longer enforce provisions of the Bill of Rights more sharply against the federal government than against the states. All incorporated rights were to have equal contours, whether enforced against federal or state action.

In a steady progression of cases in the field of criminal justice, the selective incorporation doctrine produced a uniform constitutional code of criminal proce-

---

[29]For a list of these cases, see Jerold H. Israel, "Selective Incorporation: Revisited," *Georgetown Law Journal* 71 (1982): 285–286.

dure. *Mapp v. Ohio* (1961)[30] overturned *Wolf v. Colorado* and applied the exclusionary rule against the states. In *Betts v. Brady* (1942), relying on the "fundamental fairness" approach, the Court had held that a state had to supply an indigent felony defendant with an attorney only if "special circumstances" made a fair trial impossible existed. Approximately twenty years later, on the ground that the right to counsel was fundamental, the Court ruled in *Gideon v. Wainright* (1963) that the Fourteenth Amendment imposed the same right to counsel on the states that the Sixth Amendment imposed on the federal government.[31] States were obliged to supply all indigent defendants with attorneys in felony cases. In *Malloy v. Hogan* (1964), the Court applied against the states the same rules governing the privilege against self-incrimination that had operated against the federal government.[32] Other rights were similarly added to the evolving set of national rights of the accused.[33]

In the latter half of the 1960s, the Court addressed the issue as to whether the federal right to a jury trial guaranteed by the Sixth Amendment was fundamental and therefore fully applicable against the states. The right to trial by jury was, of course, old and venerable. In 1215, by signing the Magna Carta, King John made it law in England that "no free man shall be taken or imprisoned . . . or outlawed or exiled or in any way destroyed except by the lawful judgment of his peers or by the laws of the land." Though vague, these words sanctified the idea of popular participation in the administration of criminal justice and contributed to the growth of the common-law jury: a group of twelve laypersons whose primary responsibility was to decide the issue of guilt or innocence by a unanimous vote. Included within the Bill of Rights of 1689, the right to a jury trial had become one of the sacrosanct principles of the English constitution. William Blackstone, a renowned eighteenth-century legal commentator, referred to it as a "palladium" of liberty.[34]

Across the Atlantic Ocean, the American colonists cherished the jury as much as their English counterparts. In the Declaration of Independence, one of the charges against King George III was that he had deprived the colonists "in many cases of the benefits of Trial by Jury." Since this was one of the rights for which they fought, the framers included it in the Bill of Rights. In *The Federalist Papers*, Alexander Hamilton commented on the widespread support for this particular right. While those who favored the new federal constitution regarded the jury "as a valuable safeguard to liberty," those who opposed it considered the jury "the very palladium of free government."[35] Later in the nineteenth century, the French observer Alexis de Tocqueville described the American attitude toward

---

[30]367 U.S. 643 (1961).

[31]*Betts v. Brady,* 316 U.S. 455 (1942); *Gideon v. Wainright* 372 U.S. 355 (1963).

[32]378 U.S. 1 (1964).

[33]See *Pointer v. Texas,* 380 U.S. 400 (1965) (right to confront opposing witnesses); *Klopfer v. North Carolina,* 386 U.S. 213 (1967) (right to a speedy trial); and *Washington v. Texas,* 388 U.S. 14 (1967) (right to compulsory process for obtaining witnesses).

[34]Harry Kalven, Jr., and Hans Zeisel, *The American Jury* (Boston: Little, Brown, 1966), p. 7.

[35]*Federalist Papers,* p. 499.

the jury. It was "the most energetic means of making the people rule" and "the most efficacious means of teaching it how to rule well."[36]

Despite this long and illustrious history of the right to a jury trial, critics of the institution began to appear, especially after the turn of the twentieth century. An especially bitter attack appeared in the *American Bar Association Journal* in 1924:

> Too long has the effete and sterile jury system been permitted to tug at the throat of the Nation's judiciary as it sinks under the smothering deluge of the obloquy of those it was designed to serve. Too long has ignorance been permitted to sit ensconced in the places of judicial administration where knowledge is so sorely needed. Too long has the lament of the Shakespearean character been echoed, "Justice has fled to brutish beasts and men have lost their reason."[37]

A more measured and more substantive critique came from Jerome Frank, a federal appellate judge and one of the founders of a school of legal philosophy known as American legal realism. In 1949, he disputed the contention that juries were better than judges at fact-finding. Why should the law follow a procedure that no "sensible business organization" or "historian" would use to decide questions of fact? Frank also pointed out that juries had the *de facto* power to nullify the application of laws to particular cases by acquitting guilty defendants or convicting innocent ones. Though many legal commentators admired this characteristic of juries, Frank condemned it. Why should "a twelve-man ephemeral legislature, not elected by the voters," be "empowered to destroy what the elected legislators have enacted or authorized"? Indeed, jury nullification was especially troubling because most juries released guilty defendants not because of the harshness of the law but because of the impact that irrelevant facts—"the artful lawyer," "the poor widow," "the brunette with the soulful eyes"—had on the jurors' prejudices. Frank's conclusion was that jury trials were incompatible with the "rule of law" (see Box 1.3).

After Frank's attack on the jury, commentators came to its defense, but none was as formidable as a distinguished English judge by the name of Sir Patrick Devlin. He argued that the jury was the "best instrument" for determining the "primary facts" of a case because twelve laypersons were better at evaluating the credibility of witnesses than a single judge. However, Devlin admitted that in the actual operations of law, it was very difficult to separate issues of fact from those of law and justice ("the *aequum et bonum*"). Therefore, the real value of the jury trial was its ability to produce a just result without sacrificing the advantages of law. Contrary to Frank's claim that the jury eroded the rule of law, Devlin argued that juries were able to maintain the law even while they tempered it with justice. Finally, Devlin claimed that juries preserve "the independence and quality" of the judiciary and protect citizens from laws that are "harsh and oppressive." In sum,

---

[36]Alexis de Tocqueville, *Democracy in America*, ed. Phillips Bradley, trans. Henry Reeve, rev. Francis Bowen (New York: Knopf, 1966), p. 297.

[37]Sebille, "Trial by Jury: An Ineffectual Survival," *American Bar Association Journal* 10 (1924): 55. In the nineteenth century, Mark Twain's comments about the jury were almost as pejorative as those in the above quotation: "The jury system puts a ban upon intelligence and honesty, and a premium upon ignorance, stupidity, and perjury. It is a shame that we must continue to use a worthless system because it *was* good a thousand years ago." *Roughing It* (New York: Harper, 1913), vol. 2, p. 57.

BOX 1.3

JEROME FRANK ON THE JURY

. . . The first defense is that juries are better fact-finders than judges. . . .

Is that a correct appraisal? Would any sensible business organization reach a decision, as to the competence and honesty of a prospective executive, by seeking, on that question of fact, the judgment of twelve men or women gathered together at random—and after first weeding out all those men or women who might have any special qualifications for answering the questions? Would [a] historian thus decide a question of fact?

If juries are better than judges as fact-finders, then, were we sensible, we would allow no cases to be decided by a judge without a jury. But that is not our practice. . . .

I now come to the argument for the jury system most frequently advanced. It is contended that the legal rules (made by the legislatures or formulated by the judges) often work injustice, and that juries, through their general verdicts, wisely nullify those rules. . . .

[This argument] . . . has at least the virtue of honestly admitting the realities—of conceding that jurors often disregard what the trial judge tells the jurors about the [rules]. But as a rational defense of the jury system, it is surely curious. It asserts that, desirably, each jury is a twelve-man ephemeral legislature, not elected by the voters, but empowered to destroy what the elected legislators have enacted or authorized. Each jury is thus a legislative assembly, legislating independently of all others. . . .

I have one objection to such a description: I think it too sophisticated. It implies that the members of the ordinary jury say to themselves, "We don't like this legal rule of which the judge told us, and we won't apply it but will apply one of our own making." But when, as often happens, juries do not understand what the judge said to them about the applicable rule, it simply is not true that they refuse to follow it because they dislike it. Many juries in reaching their verdicts act on their emotional responses to the lawyers and witnesses; they like or dislike, not any legal rule, but they do like an artful lawyer for the plaintiff, the poor widow, the brunette with the soulful eyes, and they do dislike the big corporation, the Italian with a thick, foreign accent. We do not have uniform jury-nullification of harsh rules; we have juries avoiding—often in ignorance that they are so doing—excellent as well as bad rules, and in capricious fashion. . . .

You will find lawyers, legal philosophers and statesmen often using such phrases as "The supremacy of law," "The reign (or rule) of law," "A government of laws, and not of men.". . .

Now I submit that the jury is the worst possible enemy of this ideal of the "supremacy of law." For "jury-made law" is, par excellence, capricious and arbitrary, yielding the maximum in the way of lack of uniformity, of unknowability. It is acknowledged that jurors are governmental officials. Yet little, practically, is done to ensure that these officials, jurymen, "act upon principles and not according to arbitrary will," or to put effective restraints upon their worse prejudices. Indeed, through the general verdict, coupled with the refusal of the courts to inquire into the way the jurors have reached their decisions, everything is done to give the widest outlet to jurors' biases. If only a jury trial is properly conducted according to the procedural rules, the jurors' decision may be as arbitrary as they please; in such circumstances, their discretion becomes wholly unregulated and unreviewable.

The jury system, praised because, in its origins, it was apparently a bulwark against an arbitrary tyrannical executive, is today the quintessence of governmental arbitrariness. The jury system almost completely wipes out the principle of "equality before the law" which the "supremacy of law" and the "reign of law" symbolize—and does so, too, at the expense of justice, which requires fairness and competence in finding the facts in specific cases. If anywhere we have a "government of men," in the worst sense of that phrase, it is in the operations of the jury system. . . .

Source: Jerome Frank, *Courts on Trial: Myth and Reality in American Justice* (New York: Atheneum, 1949), pp. 126–132. Copyright 1949 (©) renewed 1976, by Princeton University Press. Reprinted by permission of Princeton University Press.

the jury is "a little parliament" that safeguards the democratic way of life—a "lamp that shows that freedom lives" (see Box 1.4).

Which of these two judges has a better understanding of the role of juries in the American criminal justice system? Are juries good fact finders? In your judgment, would a trained judge be better at evaluating the testimony of witnesses and determining who did what to whom than a jury of twelve persons randomly selected? And what about the possibility that a jury might nullify a law by acquitting a guilty defendant or convicting an innocent one? Does this sort of thing happen? Is it likely, for example, that a jury would ignore the instructions of the judge and acquit a defendant who was clearly guilty? If juries do nullify laws in this manner, do they do so intentionally? Should they have this power? Does this sort of power really contribute to a qualified and independent judiciary? Are there other, more effective ways to ensure that the judiciary is independent and of high quality? And finally, who is right, Frank or Devlin, about the impact that jury trials have on the rule of law?

The Frank-Devlin debate symbolizes how contentious the issue of the jury had become by the middle of the twentieth century. Of course, in *Palko* (1937), Justice Cardozo had already refused to acknowledge the right to a jury trial as fundamental, calling anyone who believed that a "fair and enlightened system of justice" would be impossible without it "narrow" and "provincial."[38] However, though Cardozo declined to impose this particular right on every state in the country, he never intimated that the jury was an unwise or pernicious institution.

---

[38]*Palko v. Connecticut,* 302 U.S. 319, 325 (1937).

BOX 1.4

SIR PATRICK DEVLIN ON THE JURY

. . . I am myself convinced that the jury is the best instrument for deciding upon the credibility or reliability of a witness and so for determining the primary facts. Whether a person is telling the truth, when it has to be judged, as so often it has, simply from the demeanor of the witness and his manner of telling it, is a matter about which it is easy for a single mind to be fallible. The impression that a witness makes depends upon reception as well as transmission and may be affected by the idiosyncrasies of the receiving mind; the impression made upon a mind of twelve is more reliable. Moreover, the judge, who naturally by his training regards so much as simple that to the ordinary man may be difficult, may fail to make enough allowance for the behavior of the stupid. The jury hear the witness as one who is as ignorant as they are of lawyers' ways of thought; that is the great advantage to a man of judgment by his peers.

❖   ❖   ❖

. . . [M]inisters of justice have to serve two mistresses—the law and the *aequum et bonum* or the equity of the case. Their constant endeavor is to please both. That is why the just decision fluctuates, as I say, between two points. In most systems the just decision is tied pretty closely to the law; the law may be made as flexible as possible, but the justice of the case cannot go beyond the furthest point to which the law can be stretched. Trial by jury is a unique institution . . . to enable justice to go beyond that point. . . .

The essential virtue then of trial by jury is that it is a mode of trial whereby the law, while remaining generally in control of the decision, loosens its grip on it so as to allow it to move nearer than it could otherwise do towards the *aequum et bonum*. Of course the jury cannot be allowed to stray too far from legal principles. Theoretically it is not recognized that they should stray at all: the system works by a practical acceptance of the fact that jurors will be jurors. . . .

. . . [The jury also] serves two other purposes of great importance in the constitution. The first and lesser of these is that the existence of trial by jury helps to ensure the independence and quality of the judges. Judges are appointed by the executive and I do not know of any better way of appointing them. But our history has shown that the executive has found it much easier to find judges who will do what it wants than it has to find amenable juries. . . .

I spoke of the quality of the judges as well as of their independence. . . . The malady that sooner or later affects most men of a profession is that they tend to construct a mystique that cuts them off from the common man. Judges, as much as any other professional, need constantly to remind themselves of that. For more than seven out of the eight centuries during which the judges of the common law have administered justice in this country, trial by jury ensured that Englishmen got the sort of justice they liked and not the sort of justice that the government or the lawyers or any body of experts thought was good for them. . . .

The second and by far the greater purpose that is served by trial by jury is that it gives protection against laws which the ordinary man may regard as harsh and oppressive. I do not mean by that no more than that it is a protection against tyranny. It is that: but it is also an insurance that the criminal law will conform to the ordinary man's idea of what is fair and just. If it does not, the jury will not be a party to its enforcement. They have in the past used their power of acquittal to defeat the full operation of laws which they thought to be too hard. . . .

         ✿   ✿   ✿

Each jury is a little parliament. The jury sense is the parliamentary sense. I cannot see the one dying and the other surviving. The first object of any tyrant in Whitehall would be to make Parliament utterly subservient to his will; and the next to overthrow or diminish trial by jury, for no tyrant could afford to leave a subject's freedom in the hands of twelve of his countrymen. So that trial by jury is more than an instrument of justice and more than one wheel of the constitution: it is the lamp that shows that freedom lives. . . .

Source: Sir Patrick Devlin, *Trial by Jury* (London: Methuen, 1966), pp. 140, 154–160, 164.

Frank, by contrast, implied exactly that. Neither the Constitution nor wisdom justified imposing the right to a jury trial on the states.

The wider debate on the jury's value forms a useful political backdrop to the constitutional litigation concerning the right to a jury trial that arose in the mid-1960s. In 1966, when Plaquemines Parish, Louisiana, was under a court order to integrate its schools, Gary Duncan, an African-American, allegedly struck a white student during a confrontation between four white students and Duncan's two cousins at the formerly all-white Boothville-Venice School. Duncan was convicted of simple battery by a Louisiana trial judge. The crime carried a possible two-year sentence, but the judge sentenced Duncan to serve only two months in jail and to pay a $150 fine.

In the brief that he filed for Duncan, Richard B. Sobel claimed that Duncan had been denied his federal constitutional right to a jury trial. He argued that the right to a jury trial for all nonpetty offenses should be incorporated into the due process clause of the Fourteenth Amendment, just as other provisions of the Sixth Amendment and the Bill of Rights had earlier been applied against the states. His justification for his position relied on the nature of the historical right to a jury trial and the actual role that juries play in contemporary criminal trials. The common-law right to a jury trial was old and sacred, one of the essential rights for which the colonists fought during the American Revolution. Thirty-eight states had granted a right to a jury trial that was equal in scope to the federal right. No great burden would therefore be placed on Louisiana if it were required to do the same. Moreover, the right to a jury trial "has become a vital balance wheel in the administration of American criminal justice." The fact that other systems, whether hypothetical or actual, did not use juries had no effect on the "essential" character of the right within the American system. The "necessity" of the right to a jury trial was especially clear in cases such as the present one—"where the personal and political leanings of the trial judge will often be antagonistic to the defendant." Such situations, "particularly in civil rights related prosecutions in the Deep South," were not uncommon. Not only could juries protect defendants from such "arbitrary official conduct," but also they could ensure that convictions were not tainted by judicial cognizance of inadmissible evidence.

Louisiana began its brief with the assertion that *Duncan* presented no constitutional issue because it was a petty case in which the defendant was not entitled to a jury trial even under federal law.[39] The bulk of Louisiana's brief, however, was directed against the idea that the right to a jury trial was a national right incorporated into the due process clause of the Fourteenth Amendment. Endorsing the older fundamental rights approach to due process, the brief argued that neither the Bill of Rights nor the Sixth Amendment had been applied against the states. Only the "right to a fair trial" had been incorporated into the Fourteenth Amendment. Earlier cases had applied certain provisions of the Sixth Amendment against the states only because the relevant provisions had been thought essential to the right to a fair trial, not because the Sixth Amendment had been incorporated. The common law, the nation's founders, and earlier Supreme Court decisions all concurred that a jury was not necessary for a fair trial. Though "it might be argued that compelled uniformity makes for convenience and efficiency in the administration of justice, it is fatal to liberty, and foreign to the principles which constitute the fabric of our society." The issue of when to use juries was therefore a policy matter for state legislatures. Louisiana, perhaps because of its distinctive history as a non-common-law state, has limited the use of juries to serious criminal cases. This result is not surprising in that juries, as many commentators have pointed out, are of questionable value. Finally, the defendant's attempt to "connect his arrest with 'opposition by parish officials to court-ordered desegregation'" and his "insinuation that the 'personal and political leanings of the trial judge' might have been antagonistic to him" have no support in the record of this case.

The briefs in *Duncan* provide an opportunity to consider whether the jury can usefully function as a check on "official arbitrary conduct." Is such a check needed? Is it possible that the jury was once a valuable check on the executive and the judiciary but that the rise of democratic government has made the institution superfluous and obsolete? Do you think it is likely that the judge in *Duncan* was biased against the defendant? Would you have the same concern if the case were completely unrelated to the civil rights struggle to integrate public schools in the South or if the trial were held in the North? Do you really think that during the 1960s, Duncan would have received better treatment at the hands of a southern jury? A northern one? Is a jury or a judge more likely to engage in "official arbi-

---

[39]Excerpts from this part of the brief are not included in our discussion.

trary conduct"? Is the right to a jury trial a "balance wheel" in the American criminal justice system or an "unbalanced" one? Is it an essential or a fundamental
right? What about the distinctive history of Louisiana's legal system? Should the
fact that French and Spanish law had an enormous impact on Louisiana until its
purchase by the United States in 1803 have any effect on whether the Supreme
Court should compel the state to recognize an old and sacred common-law right?

In a 7–2 decision, Justice Byron White delivered the opinion of the Court upholding Duncan's right to a jury trial. The key to White's justification for adding
this right to the set of national rights enforceable against the states was his judgment that it was "fundamental to the American scheme of justice." In a footnote
that explained in more detail how the Court came to its conclusion concerning the
fundamental character of the right to a jury trial, White admitted that the constitutional test had formerly been whether a "civilized system could be imagined that
would not accord the particular protection." This sort of theoretical and hypothetical test, however, was no longer appropriate. Now the proper standard was
whether the constitutional safeguard was "necessary to an Anglo-American regime
of ordered liberty." Therefore, though one could easily imagine a fair system without juries, the right to a jury trial was fundamental because the "structure and
style" of every state's criminal justice system "naturally complement jury trial, and
have developed in connection with and in reliance upon jury trial." White but-
tressed this argument with a "skeletal history" of the right to a jury trial, emphasiz-
ing how juries can function as an effective check against "corrupt" or "overzealous" prosecutors and "biased" judges. Not that a fair trial was impossible without a
jury. To the contrary, conceding that juries did have their flaws, White emphasized that states and the federal government could still use nonjury trials in petty
offenses and that defendants could waive the right to a jury trial. The right to a
jury trial was therefore somewhat anomalous. It was a fundamental right that was
not necessary for a fair trial.

Duncan v. Louisiana also included a sharp debate, second in importance only
to the one that had occurred earlier in *Adamson,* between two justices concerning
the meaning of due process and its relationship to the Bill of Rights. Coming at
the end of a process by which most of the provisions of the Bill of Rights, including those involving criminal procedure, had been applied against the states, the
second debate reflected the degree to which the Supreme Court had already created a national set of individual rights. On one side, in a concurring opinion, Justice Hugo Black reaffirmed his commitment to total incorporation but expressed
his willingness to support the policy of selective incorporation, if only because it
had in practice almost obtained his goal: full incorporation of the Bill of Rights. In
response to the criticism that the term "due process" was a "peculiar" way for the
framers of the Fourteenth Amendment to apply the Bill of Rights against the
states, Black said that total incorporation also rested on the privileges or immunities clause. Accordingly, he argued that it was peculiar for anyone to understand
the Fourteenth Amendment differently from the way he did. Finally, Black denied that total incorporation, whether achieved in one fell swoop or by a process
of selective incorporation, imposed a judicially created "straitjacket" on the states.
Repeating what he had said in 1947, Black insisted that it would be far more intru-

sive for the states if the Supreme Court used, on a case-by-case basis, the subjective standard of fundamental rights.

Justice John M. Harlan II wrote a dissent in *Duncan* that attacked both the majority opinion and Black's concurrence. Taking on the mantle of Felix Frankfurter and relying on the historical investigations of Charles Fairman, a prominent legal historian, Harlan rejected Black's doctrine of total incorporation. It was simply false to say that the framers of the Fourteenth Amendment intended to incorporate the Bill of Rights against the states. The historical basis for Black's doctrine of incorporation was simply untrue. However, Harlan did concede, interestingly enough, that total incorporation at least had the virtue of "internal consistency." It was wrong, but it did make sense. In contrast, Harlan characterized selective incorporation, the doctrine by which the Supreme Court had created national standards of criminal procedure, as "an uneasy and illogical compromise." The majority had denied that the Court could incorporate the Bill of Rights *in toto* but nonetheless imposed the full scope of the Sixth Amendment right to a jury trial on the states. No justification was given for this result. The "Court merely declares that the clause in question is 'in' rather than 'out.'" The majority's references to the fundamental character of the jury trial right cannot be taken seriously because "no real analysis of the role of the jury in making procedures fair is even attempted." As used in the Court's opinion, all that the word *fundamental* means is "'old,' 'much praised,' and 'found in the Bill of Rights.'" What the Court should have done, in Harlan's opinion, was return to Cardozo's *Palko* standard of fundamental fairness and a "gradual process of judicial inclusion and exclusion." Only then would the Court be giving "due recognition of constitutional tolerance for state experimentation and disparity."

Coming at the end of a process by which the Supreme Court had created through constitutional adjudication a national code of criminal procedure and a national set of substantive rights, Harlan's dissent echoed a form of federalism that had largely disappeared. At the time of the *Duncan* decision, not only had every important substantive right of the Bill of Rights been made applicable against the states, but the federal requirement of a grand jury indictment in criminal cases was the only significant criminal justice guarantee left outside the set of national individual rights (see Box 1.5). Hence it is indisputable that during the twentieth century, the Supreme Court has radically transformed American federalism.

Was the result justifiable? Has the creation of a "national bill of rights" made tyranny in the United States more likely by undermining the ability of states to function in a system of checks and balances? What about the values of democracy and experimentation that underlie the American commitment to federalism? Is it arguable that incorporation of the Bill of Rights has made it more difficult for states to solve the different sorts of criminal justice problems that they confront? Is it possible that liberty and democracy would be better served if the Supreme Court would allow states to experiment more than it does today with regard to criminal justice procedures? Or would such an alternative be intolerable because the United States is one country, not fifty states? Must all experimentation with criminal procedure take place at the national level, initiated by the Supreme

---

BOX 1.5

OUTLINE OF THE HISTORY OF INCORPORATION

1896: Fifth Amendment right to just compensation: *Missouri Pacific Railway Co. v. Nebraska*, 164 U.S. 403

1925: First Amendment right of free speech: *Gitlow v. New York*, 268 U.S. 652

1931: First Amendment right of a free press: *Near v. Minnesota*, 283 U.S. 697

1932: Sixth Amendment right to a fair trial: *Powell v. Alabama*, 287 U.S. 45

1937: First Amendment right of assembly: *De Jonge v. Oregon*, 299 U.S. 353

1940: First Amendment right to the free exercise of one's religion: *Cantwell v. Connecticut*, 310 U.S. 296.

1948: Sixth Amendment right to a public trial: *In re Oliver*, 333 U.S. 257

1949: Fourth Amendment right against unreasonable searches and seizures: *Wolf v. Colorado*, 338 U.S. 25

1958: First Amendment right of association: *NAACP v. Alabama*, 357 U.S. 449

1961: Fourth Amendment right to have illegally seized evidence excluded from the trial: *Mapp v. Ohio*, 367 U.S. 643

1962: Sixth Amendment right against cruel and unusual punishments: *Robinson v. California*, 370 U.S. 660

1963: Sixth Amendment right to counsel in all felony cases: *Gideon v. Wainright*, 372 U.S. 335

1964: Fifth Amendment right against self-incrimination: *Malloy v. Hogan*, 378 U.S. 1

1965: Sixth Amendment right to confront opposing witnesses: *Pointer v. Texas*, 380 U.S. 400

1965: First, Third, Fourth, Fifth, and Ninth Amendment right to privacy: *Griswold v. Connecticut*, 381 U.S. 479

1966: Sixth Amendment right to an impartial jury: *Parker v. Gladden*, 385 U.S. 363

1967: Sixth Amendment right to a speedy trial: *Klopfer v. North Carolina*, 386 U.S. 213

1968: Sixth Amendment right to a jury trial: *Duncan v. Louisiana*, 391 U.S. 145

1969: Fifth Amendment right against double jeopardy: *Benton v. Maryland*, 395 U.S. 784

1972: Sixth Amendment right to counsel in petty cases: *Argersinger v. Hamlin*, 407 U.S. 25

Court as it interprets the meaning of the Bill of Rights? The right to a jury trial is an excellent window into these more general questions that will constantly be found lurking in the pages of this volume. Did the Supreme Court make the right decision in *Duncan*? Does every defendant in a nonpetty case have a fundamental right to a jury trial? Why?

BIBLIOGRAPHY

Abraham, Henry. *Freedom and the Court.* 4th ed. New York: Oxford University Press, 1982.

Berger, Raoul. *The Fourteenth Amendment and the Bill of Rights.* Norman: University of Oklahoma Press, 1989.

Cortner, Richard. *The Supreme Court and the Second Bill of Rights: The Fourteenth Amendment and the Nationalization of Civil Liberties.* Madison: University of Wisconsin Press, 1981.

Curtis, Michael K. *No State Shall Abridge the Fourteenth Amendment and the Bill of Rights.* Durham, N.C.: Duke University Press, 1986.

Hickok, Eugene, ed. *The Bill of Rights: Original Meaning and Current Understanding.* Charlottesville: University Press of Virginia, 1991.

Israel, Jerold H. "Selective Incorporation: Revisited." *Georgetown Law Journal* 71 (1982): pp. 253–338.

Kalven, Harry, Jr., and Hans Zeisel. *The American Jury.* Boston: Little, Brown, 1966.

BRIEFS

DUNCAN'S BRIEF

[1. Introduction.] . . . The Sixth Amendment to the United States Constitution provides that "[i]n all criminal prosecutions, the accused shall enjoy the right to . . . trial, by an impartial jury. . . ." The Court has interpreted this guarantee to be applicable to the trial of all "crimes," but not to the trial of "petty offenses." It is perfectly clear that battery, punishable by two years' imprisonment, is a "crime" as defined by the decisions of this Court, and that, if the case had been tried in a federal court, appellant unquestionably would have been entitled to trial by jury under the Sixth Amendment. Thus, this appeal squarely raises the question of whether there is a comparable Fourteenth Amendment right to trial by jury in state criminal proceedings.

Sixty-seven years ago, in *Maxwell v. Dow,* the Court held that the Fourteenth Amendment does not make the jury trial guarantee of the Sixth Amendment applicable to state proceedings. Specifically, *Maxwell* sustained the use of an eight man jury in a state criminal trial, although two years earlier, in *Thompson v. Utah,* the Court held that the Sixth Amendment requires a jury of twelve in federal criminal trials. The result reached in *Maxwell* was based on the then prevailing view that the Fourteenth Amendment does not make any of the specific guarantees of the Sixth Amendment— or, indeed, of the Bill of Rights—applicable to the states, and that the mandate of due process of law is satisfied whenever a defendant is tried according to uniform procedures established by state law. . . .

More recent decisions of the Court have completely undermined the rationale of *Maxwell.* . . . Apart from the right to trial by jury, the court has held every guarantee of the Sixth Amendment applicable to state criminal proceedings. These decisions are part of a broader trend toward the application to state criminal trials of rights secured by the Bill of Rights. . . .

The decision to apply a particular guarantee of the Bill of Rights to state criminal proceedings has depended on the Court's determination as to whether the right is "so fundamental and essential to a fair trial that it is incorporated in the Due Process Clause of the Fourteenth Amendment." In *Pointer v. Texas,* the Court stated "[t]hat the fact that [a] right appears in the Sixth Amendment of our Bill of Rights reflects the belief of the Framers of those liberties and safeguards that [it is] a fundamental right essential to a fair trial in a criminal prosecution.". . .

. . . Under the conception of Fourteenth Amendment Due Process recently affirmed in *Gideon, Pointer* and *Washington v. Texas,* appellant submits that application of the Sixth Amendment jury trial guarantee to state criminal proceedings is required: (1) by historical and contemporary recognition of the fundamental nature of the jury trial right in our system of criminal law; and (2) by the essential role which the jury serves in assuring a defendant a fair trial in accordance with due process of law.

[2. Nature of the Right to a Jury Trial.] Trial by jury in criminal cases was considered to be a basic safeguard of individual liberties centuries before the adoption of the American Constitution. The right is traceable to the earliest Saxon colonies, and constituted one of the fundamental articles of the Magna Charta: "No freeman shall be taken or imprisoned, or be disseised of his freehold, or liberties . . . but by the lawful judgment of his peers. . . ." Soon after the thirteenth century trial by jury had become the principal institution for trial of criminal cases. Blackstone described the right to trial by jury in criminal cases as "the most transcendent privilege which any subject can enjoy, or wish for. . . . [T]he liberties of England cannot but subsist, so long as the *palladium* [of trial by jury] . . . remains sacred and inviolate."

The guarantee of trial by jury in criminal cases was further secured in England by its express inclusion in the English Bill of Rights of 1689. This document served as one of the basic sources for the Bill of Rights to the United States Constitution.

The right to trial by jury in criminal cases was fundamental to the American colonists. Indeed, Parliamentary infringement of this right in the colonies was one of the major grievances of the colonists against British rule. The Declaration of Rights issued in 1765 by the Stamp Act Congress, consisting of delegates from nine of the thirteen original colonies, stated: "Trial by jury is the inherent and invaluable right of every British subject of these colonies." The framers of the Declaration of Independence listed the denial "in many cases, of the benefit of Trial by Jury" as an example of the "repeated injuries and usurpations" of the King of England "all having in direct object the establishment of an absolute tyranny over these States."

Between the War of Independence and the formation of the American Union, constitutions were adopted by eleven of the former crown colonies. Without exception, these documents guaranteed trial by jury in criminal cases, after the pattern of English law. Trial by jury in criminal cases is one of the very few individual rights that the framers included in the body of the United States Constitution. It is the only such provision that is reiterated in the Bill of Rights. . . .

Over 100 years ago, in *Ex parte Milligan,* this Court described "the inestimable privilege of trial by jury . . . [as] a vital principle underlying the whole administration of criminal justice.". . .

In *Irwin v. Dowd,* the Court recognized the essential role of trial by jury in our legal heritage in the following terms:

England, from whom the Western world has largely taken its concepts of individual liberty and of the dignity and worth of every man, has bequeathed to us safeguards for their preservation, *the most priceless of which is trial by jury.* This right has become as much American as it was once the most English. Although this Court has said that the Fourteenth Amendment does not demand the use of jury trials in a state's criminal procedure, every state has constitutionally provided trial by jury. . . . *In the ultimate analysis, only the jury can strip a man of his liberty or his life. . . .*

The Court has shown its concern for the integrity of trial by jury in a long line of decisions, dating back to *Strauder v. West Virginia,* invalidating the systematic exclusion of Negroes from grand and petit juries. In recent years, this Court and the lower federal courts have further secured the common law mandate that no man be convicted other than by a "judgment of his peers" by insisting that juries in state and federal courts be selected in a manner that will ensure a representative cross section of the community on venire lists. . . .

It would be ironic indeed if a state were permitted to nullify this Court's carefully developed protections of the jury system by substituting for trial by jury trial by a single judge, who obviously does not represent a fair cross section of the community and who is frequently exposed to official and unofficial influences prejudicial to the defendant.

The practice of the American states with respect to trial by jury in criminal matters is a further measure of the essential nature of this guarantee. Every state makes some provision for trial by jury in criminal cases. More significantly, in thirty-eight states a right as broad as that given in federal courts by the Sixth Amendment is guaranteed by law; in each of these states a defendant in a criminal case subject to a maximum term of imprisonment in excess of six months cannot be convicted without the unanimous verdict of a twelve man jury. . . . With one narrow exception, Louisiana is the only jurisdiction in the United States where all right to trial by jury is denied in a class of cases in which the right is guaranteed at common law and under the Sixth Amendment. In Louisiana, all right to trial by jury—even a jury that does not meet common law requirements—is denied in a number of serious criminal cases, including at least one offense punishable by up to ten years' imprisonment. In most other cases, trial by a five man jury, or a twelve man jury, only nine of whom must concur in a verdict, is provided. A jury that conforms to the requirements of the common law and the Sixth Amendment is available in Louisiana only in capital cases. . . .

The general acceptance by the states of the right to trial by jury in criminal cases not only attests to the importance of this right; it precludes any argument that the result urged by the appellant would impose an intolerable burden on state procedure. The prevailing practice in the overwhelming majority of American states is incontrovertible evidence of the workability of a requirement that trial by jury be provided whenever a defendant may be imprisoned for a period in excess of six months.

In any event, considerations of burden are not an appropriate basis for limiting the application of constitutional rights.

> It is undoubtedly true that a judge can dispose of charges . . . faster and cheaper than a jury. But such trifling economies as may result have not generally been thought sufficient reason for abandoning our great constitutional safeguards aimed at protecting freedom and other basic human rights of incalculable value. Cheap, easy convictions were not the primary concern of those who adopted the Constitution and the Bill of Rights. Every procedural safeguard they established purposely made it more difficult for the government to convict those it accused of crimes. On their scale of values justice occupied at least as high a position as economy.

Blackstone warned against attacks on the jury trial in the name of convenience. "Let it be remembered, that delays and little inconveniences in the forms of justice, are the price that all free nations must pay for their liberty in more substantial matters; that these inroads upon this sacred bulwark of the nation are fundamentally opposite to the spirit of our constitution. . . ." The right to trial by jury "is not held by sufferance, and cannot be frittered away on any plea of state or political necessity."

[3. Role of the Jury.] The pervasive acceptance of the jury trial in our system of criminal law is largely attributable to the historic role of the jury in protecting accused persons against arbitrary official conduct. Blackstone warned against trial by a "justice . . . named by the Crown . . . who might . . . imprison any man that was obnoxious to the government, by an instant declaration that such is [his] will and pleasure." This court has recognized this important role of the petit jury:

> On many occasions, fully known to the Founders of this Country, jurors—plain people—have manfully stood up in defense of liberty against the importunities of judges and despite prevailing hysteria and prejudices. The acquittal of William Penn is an illustrious example.

The point was reiterated by Mr. Justice Black in his opinion in *Reid v. Covert:*

> Trial by jury in a court of law and in accordance with traditional modes of procedure . . . has served and remains one of our most vital barriers to governmental arbitrariness.

This case is an example of the continued vitality of these principles. Appellant is a Negro resident of Plaquemines Parish, Louisiana. He was arrested at the height of intense opposition by parish officials to court-ordered desegregation of the Plaquemines Parish public schools. The prosecution was initiated not by the indictment of a grand jury, but by a Bill of Information filed by the District Attorney, Leander H. Perez, Jr. The substance of the charge was that in attempting to break up a potentially violent confrontation near the Boothville-Venice School between four white boys and two Negro boys—both cousins of the appellant, who had recently transferred to the formerly all-white school—appellant slapped one of the white boys on the arm. At trial, appellant and the two Negro boys testified that appellant had not slapped the boy. The white boys, and a white onlooker some distance away, testified that he had. The trial judge resolved the factual dispute in favor of the state. . . .

It is plain that in cases such as this—where the personal and political leanings of the trial judge will often be antagonistic to the defendant—the potential for a factual determination that is influenced by considerations other than the evidence of record is very great. This situation, particularly in civil rights related prosecutions in the Deep South, is not uncommon. Because of the accepted limitation on federal review and state appellate review of factual determinations in state trial courts, the only effective remedy is to guarantee the accused the right to have the crucial factual determination of guilt or innocence made by a jury, rather than by a judge. Trial by twelve jurors representing a cross-section of the community not only dilutes the effect of any individual bias, it tends to make certain that persons not antagonistic to the accused will participate in the fact-finding process.

In our democratic society, trial by jury provides both symbolic expression and indispensable practical protection of the concept that the decision to adjudge a citizen a criminal and to deprive him of his liberty is too important to be committed to professional administrators alone—judges separated by class, by function, by experience and often by considerations of interest and political leaning from the people they judge. Community participation—in the form of trial by jury—has become a vital balance wheel in the administration of American criminal justice, protecting accused persons from judicial arbitrariness or discrimination. This historic role of the petit jury is an essential element of due process in our legal system.

The criminal jury has performed an important ameliorative function in the Anglo-American legal system. Because an accused may not be convicted, regardless of the strength of the case against him, without the concurrence of the jury, the jury is free to take what Chief Justice Cooley referred to as "the common sense view of a set of circumstances," and reject strict application of legal principles in favor of a result it considers just. . . . The essentially democratic role of the jury, "interposing 'the voice of the community' against the possible excessive zeal of prosecutors," has been consistently recognized by this Court and the lower federal courts.

In practical operation, the exercise of this ameliorative power by the jury has provided a valuable safeguard for the accused against wooden application of the criminal law. It has ensured that criminal convictions comport with the community's notions of fairness and equity. The right not to be convicted without the concurrence of the community, in the form of a unanimous jury verdict, is an essential ingredient of due process in our system of law.

Several related, intensely practical, virtues of jury trial are recognized by every experienced criminal practitioner and have contributed to the enduring faith which American justice places in the jury system. Although these endemic characteristics of jury trial serve principally to protect the defendant, it would be a mistake to regard them merely as the instrument of partisan tactical advantage. Rather, they have proved in day-to-day administration of our criminal law vital contributing factors, and often indispensable conditions, of a fair and rational trial process. In this connection the obvious point must be emphasized that the American jury cannot realistically be viewed out of the context of the entire complex of institutions and procedures which have evolved for the administration of criminal law in this country. Other institutions and procedures—involving differently qualified and selected judges, different methods of investigating and determining issues or different conceptions of evidence and proof—might develop methods of assuring trial fairness without the intervention of a jury. The American system, however, has been designed principally with the jury in view and for a number of reasons its fair administration requires maintenance of the right to jury trial. In the following subsections, the most significant of those reasons are identified. The concerns which they involve may not in isolation rise to the stature of independent federal constitutional rights. But in combination they compellingly support recognition of the right to trial by jury as a guarantor of the fair and regular criminal trial that due process of law requires.

This court has indicated that in a criminal case due process of law requires proof of guilt beyond a reasonable doubt. Of course, this standard was developed and defined in the context of trial by jury. Since it is plain that a prosecutor carries a far lesser burden in convincing one man rather than twelve of a defendant's guilt beyond a reasonable doubt, the constitutional standard is weakened when a defendant is tried to a judge.

In addition to the sheer weight of numbers, the diversity of a jury gives substance to the reasonable doubt standard, and insures that an accused will not be convicted unless jurors of varied backgrounds and outlook concur in the judgment. . . .

. . . The essential genius of the jury trial is its effect in neutralizing or diluting peculiar biases or predispositions that are held by all men "however pure, wise and eminent," and insuring that individual views will stand the test of confrontation and debate—that a judgment of conviction may emerge only if each juror becomes satisfied that guilt has been established beyond a reasonable doubt. Trial by judge denies the defendant these important protections. . . .

In a jury case, when the defense contends that evidence that the prosecution intends to offer is inadmissible under an exclusionary rule, a hearing is held by the trial judge, out of the presence of the jury, for the purpose of determining the validity of the constitutional claim. At this hearing, of course, the substance of the evidence in question is presented to the judge. The evidence can be submitted to the jury only if the trial judge determines, as a question of fact, that it has not been secured in violation of the constitutional rights of the defendant.

In *Jackson v. Denno,* the Court held that this separation of functions is mandatory under the Due Process Clause of the Fourteenth Amendment, and that the task of determining the admissibility of evidence—in *Jackson,* the voluntariness of a confession—cannot be delegated to the jury. The primary basis for the decision was the Court's recognition that jurors would be unable to exclude from their consideration a truthful, but involuntary, confession.

Appellant submits that the dangers perceived by the Court in *Jackson v. Denno* exist whenever a single body determines both the admissibility of evidence and the guilt or innocence of the accused. It is fictitious to assume that in a close case, the judgment of the trial judge will not be influenced by his certain knowledge of guilt, derived from his exposure to a truthful, but inadmissible, confession, or from his exposure to highly incriminating, but constitutionally inadmissible, physical evidence.

Proper operation of constitutional exclusionary rules and other rules relating to the exclusion of evidence, requires that the determination of admissibility not be made by the body determining guilt or innocence. Trial by jury permits the separation of these functions and guarantees the defendant's constitutional rights to have illegally obtained evidence and other inadmissible evidence "entirely disregarded.". . .

. . . Furthermore, the confusion of roles of the trial judge who also tries the facts tends to promote avoidance of clear cut rulings on evidentiary issues. "[I]n a bench case, some judges make it a practice to take defense objections to the admissibility of evidence under advisement, and then when it is clear that the prosecution has a sufficient case apart from the contested evidence, they will insulate themselves from reversal by announcing that they are not going to consider the evidence, but find the defendant guilty without it. This sort of evasion of tricky evidentiary issues cannot be worked in a jury trial."

In addition, the judge frequently comes to the determination of the guilt question against a background that makes impartial appraisal of the admissible evidence impossible. Informed by prior contacts with the case or with the defendant that he is unable to avoid, the judge who sits on the guilt issue almost invariably knows the defendant's prior record and other unfavorable personal facts. Moreover, he approaches determinations of credibility with attitudes hardened by observation of prior trials to which the defendant was not a party; and it is no accident, in particular, that he tends to believe police witnesses, since the judge has probably heard the same officer testify against a dozen, or a hundred, guilty defendants. The impact of these factors varies from case to case, but it is not the unusual situation in which one or all of them preclude a bench-tried defendant from having his guilt or innocence fairly heard on the admitted and admissible evidence and nothing else. . . .

[4. Conclusion.] In 1833, in his classic profile of "Democracy in America," de Tocqueville wrote that:

> The institution of trial by jury . . . places the real direction of society in the hands of the governed, or a portion of the governed. . . . He who punishes the criminal is therefore the real master of society. . . .

At this point in our history, when vast power over American life is exercised by an immense governmental structure in matters entirely unrelated to enforcement of the criminal law, it may be historical romanticism to adhere to the notion that the institution of the criminal jury "places the real direction of the society in the hands of the governed." But the role of dispensing criminal justice in a democracy is a particularly sensitive task and the right of the people to participate directly in this important function of government has been preserved in the form of the criminal jury. The increasing complexity and influence of modern government, where in most matters popular control is several times removed from the decision making process, underscores the urgency of preserving inviolate the direct voice of the community in the administration of the criminal law. . . .

Respectfully submitted,

RICHARD B. SOBOL

LOUISIANA'S BRIEF

[1. Right to a Jury Trial Not Incorporated.] On numerous occasions for well over a century, Appellant's theory that the due process clause of the Fourteenth Amendment incorporated the entire Bill of Rights has been presented to and rejected by this Court.

In 1833 this Court determined that the first eight amendments were directed at the Federal Government. Chief Justice Marshall, a staunch Federalist, stated "in almost every convention by which the Constitution was adopted, amendments to guard against the abuse of power were recommended. These amendments demanded security against the apprehended encroachments of the general government—not against those of the local governments. . . . These amendments contain no expression indicating an intention to apply them to the state governments. This Court cannot so apply them.". . .

. . . [T]he adoption of the Fourteenth Amendment, after the Civil War, gave new grist for the mills of those who would place all of the same limitations on local state government as are placed on the distant all powerful federal government by the Bill of Rights.

In 1873 [in the *Slaughterhouse Cases*] this Court again answered the argument in a manner favorable to maintaining state power unfettered by federal standards.

The Court held that the privileges and immunities of National citizenship are different from those of state citizenship and that the privileges and immunities clause of the Fourteenth Amendment does not make the privileges and immunities of national citizenship, as set forth in the Bill of Rights, applicable to state citizenship; nor does the due process clause of the Fourteenth Amendment incorporate the entire Bill of Rights as fundamental to life, liberty, or property. . . .

In 1883, in *Hurtado v. California*, this Court held that despite the Fifth Amendment, prosecutions by a State may be instituted by information at the instance of a public officer, rather than by the indictment of a grand jury. In the Hurtado case the accused maintained that the phrase "due process of law" was equivalent to "law of the land," as found in the 29th chapter of *Magna Carta;* and that by immemorial usage it had acquired a fixed and technical meaning and necessarily included the identical institutions which had crossed the Atlantic with the colonists and were transplanted from England and established in the fundamental laws of this country. In a thorough and scholarly opinion the Court discussed . . . that it was best not to go too far back into antiquity for the best securities of our liberties. Pointing out that it made more sense that liberty was preserved and developed by a progressive growth and wise adaptation to new circumstances of the forms and processes found fit to give, from time to time, new expression and greater effect to modern ideas of self-government, the Court [rejected the Hurtado's arguments]. . . .

In the year . . . 1899, this Court decided *Maxwell v. Dow,* which was a state prosecution by information for robbery. The accused launched a two-pronged attack under the Fourteenth Amendment, urging (1) that indictment by a grand jury and trial by a twelve-man unanimous jury was a right of national citizenship under the Fifth and Sixth Amendments and by virtue of the privileges and immunities clause of the Fourteenth and could not be abridged by the State, and (2) that indictment by a grand jury and trial by a twelve-man unanimous jury were essential to liberty under the due process clause of the Fourteenth. The Court disposed of the first contention on the authority of *The Slaughterhouse Cases,* holding that:

> the privileges and immunities of citizens of the United States do not *necessarily* include all the rights protected by the first eight amendments to the Federal Constitution against the powers of the Federal Government.

and that the provision for a grand or petit jury in a state criminal prosecution was neither included among the rights of national citizenship nor a fundamental right of state citizenship. In disposing of accused's second contention under the due process clause, the Court held that trial by jury was not a fundamental right, following the *Hurtado* case. "In our opinion," stated the court, "the right to be exempt from prosecution for an infamous crime, except upon a presentment by a grand jury, is of the same nature as the right to a trial by a petit jury of the number fixed by common law. . . . Trial by jury has never been affirmed to be a necessary requisite of due process of law. In not one of the cases cited and commented upon in the *Hurtado* case is a trial by jury mentioned as a necessary part of such process. . . ." Thus the majority opinion again rejected the theory that simply because a constitutional right exists limiting the federal government, it *necessarily* creates a limitation on the States. In order to be applicable to the states such a right must be determined to be essential to life, liberty, or property. The only dissent, by Mr. Justice Harlan, is pitched primarily on the privileges and immunities clause and is strikingly similar to the dissents in [the] later case of *Adamson v. California.* It was Mr. Justice Harlan's premise that the privileges and immunities clause of the Fourteenth Amendment encompassed all of the first ten amendments, that the Court could not pick and choose among them to determine which were fundamental and which were not under the due process clause, and that "there is no middle position."

Consequently, in *Maxwell v. Dow,* we find the identical arguments propounded and decided as are presented in the case at bar.

The rationale of the Court in *Maxwell v. Dow* is still valid today. The Court based its decision on a determination that a trial by a petit jury, like a presentment by a grand jury, is not such a fundamental right that a fair trial is impossible without it. This is the same test used by this Court in later cases in determining whether a right is so fundamental and essential that a fair trial cannot be had without it. . . .

In 1937 in *Palko v. Connecticut*, Mr. Justice Cardozo stated the following for this Court:

> We have said that in appellant's view the Fourteenth Amendment is to be taken as embodying the prohibitions of the Fifth. His thesis is even broader. Whatever would be a violation of the original bill of rights (Amendments I to VIII) if done by the federal government is now equally unlawful by force of the Fourteenth Amendment if done by a state. There is no such general rule.
>
> The Fifth Amendment provides, among other things, that no person shall be held to answer for a capital or otherwise infamous crime unless on presentment or indictment of a grand jury. This court has held that in prosecutions by a state, presentment or indictment by a grand jury may give way to informations at the instance of a public officer. . . . The Sixth Amendment calls for a jury trial in criminal cases and the Seventh for a jury trial in civil cases at common law where the value in controversy shall exceed twenty dollars. This court has ruled that consistently with those amendments trial by jury may be modified by a state or abolished altogether. . . .
>
> On the other hand, the due process clause of the Fourteenth Amendment may make it unlawful for a state to abridge by its statutes the freedom of speech which the First Amendment safeguards against encroachment by the Congress. . . .
>
> The line of division may seem to be wavering and broken if there is a hasty catalogue of the cases on the one side and the other. Reflection and analysis will induce a different view. There emerges the perception of a rationalizing principle which gives to discrete instances a proper order and coherence. *The right to trial by jury and the immunity from prosecution except as the result of an indictment may have value and importance. Even so, they are not of the very essence of a scheme of ordered liberty. To abolish them is not to violate a "principle of justice so rooted in the traditions and conscience of our people as to be ranked as fundamental." Few would be so narrow or provincial as to maintain that a fair and enlightened system of justice would be impossible without them. . . .*

From the above quotation . . . it is perfectly clear that the test used by this Court in the Palko decision for determining procedural due process is identical with that used by this Court in its most recent decisions: those privileges enunciated in the Bill of Rights which have been applied to the States are so applied only because neither liberty nor justice would exist if they were sacrificed and, with reference to a criminal prosecution, such rights were essential to a fair hearing. Therefore, the rationale of Justice Cardozo's Palko decision is very much alive today. . . .

The guarantees of the Sixth Amendment which have been applied to the States in this Court's more recent decisions have been applied not because they are found in the Sixth Amendment, but because they are essential to a fair trial, and a fair trial is protected by the due process clause of the Fourteenth. It is true that in some of this Court's more recent decisions, loose language was used which could be interpreted to mean that the Sixth Amendment applies directly and mechanically to the States through the Fourteenth, but such language is just a gloss through which the primary principle decided by the case shines: the right decreed to be binding on the States is implicit in due process because a fair trial would be impossible without it.

Thus, in *Gideon v. Wainwright*, this Court held that a fair trial, at least in a felony prosecution, necessarily includes the right to be represented by counsel, and that an indigent defendant must be afforded counsel by the state. . . .

In *Pointer v. State of Texas*, the use of a deposition taken at a preliminary hearing at which petitioner was not afforded the right of cross examination was held to be violative of due process because the opportunity of cross-examination of opposing witnesses is essential to a fair trial. . . .

In a recent decision, *Washington v. Texas*, this Court determined that the right of an accused to have compulsory process for obtaining witnesses in his favor is so fundamental and essential to a fair trial that it is incorporated in the Due Process Clause. . . .

It does not follow that because some provisions of the Bill of Rights have been found essential to liberty and justice, that all should be mechanically applied to the States. Although some individual justices have held such an opinion, a majority of this Court has never held that the Bill of Rights [applies] directly to the states through the Due Process Clause of the Fourteenth Amendment. This Court has never found a guarantee of the Bill of Rights applicable to the States without first determining that the particular guarantee is essential to liberty and justice. . . .

It might be argued that the wholesale application of the Bill of Rights provides certainty by standardizing this Court's protection of personal liberties, but the result, as has been pointed out by legal commentators, would stifle reform in the administration of justice, imposing overly rigid and burdensome restrictions on state criminal procedure, and thus invalidating a large number of current state practices, including instituting prosecutions by information instead of indictment, the modification of the twelve-man petit jury, and the practice of trying common law suits involving more than twenty dollars without a jury. . . .

Hopefully, the desire for uniformity throughout the nation in the administration of justice in spite of local differences that exist, and in spite of the long line of decisions denying the mechanical application of the entire Bill of Rights to the States, will not lead to the adoption of the extreme view repeatedly rejected since the Slaughterhouse Cases. . . .

It is most respectfully submitted that while it might be argued that compelled uniformity makes for convenience and efficiency in the administration of justice, it is fatal to liberty, and foreign to the principles which constitute the fabric of our society. . . .

[2. Jury Not Necessary for a Fair Trial.] There is little doubt that the right of trial by jury is of ancient origin. It must be noted, however, that the historical origin of the right is not at issue; and, although appellee in no way wishes to belittle the relevance of history or the importance of the right of jury trial, appellee is constrained to point out that the issue before this Honorable Court is the scope and extent of the right to jury trial. . . .

Appellant has proposed that trial by jury was recognized at common law and by the framers of the Constitution as an essential element of a fair trial. Since fundamental fairness is the very heart of due process, appellant has alleged history proves that where there is a trial without a jury, there is a trial without due process of law. This simply is not so. Indeed, history and the decisions of this Honorable Court clearly show that there may be fair trials without a jury.

Magna Carta truly was of monumental legal proportions. It set the framework for numerous rights of Englishmen and Americans. It is unfortunate, however, that some later writers have ascribed to Magna Carta all of our rights. More specifically, it is ridiculous to allege that Magna Carta proves the right of every Englishmen (and therefore every American) to have a trial by jury in any prosecution against him. Indeed, Magna Carta itself placed due process (or the law of the land) in juxtaposition with judgment of peers.

> No free man shall be taken or imprisoned or dispossessed, or outlawed, or banished, or in any way destroyed, nor will we go upon him, nor send upon him, *except by the legal judgment of his peers or by the law of the land.*

Thus, Magna Carta guaranteed the right to freedom unless such freedom was abridged by trial of peers *or* by due process. "The Great Charter did not guarantee 'trial by jury' to anyone."

From the year 1215 to the year of the adoption of the Constitution of the United States, there grew up side by side, in both England and the American colonies, the tradition of right to jury trial in most serious cases and non-jury trials or summary trials in numerous instances, including some serious offenses. . . .

It is indeed true that the right to jury trial was a burning issue in the minds of the colonists in the pre-revolutionary days. Thus, in the Declaration and Resolves of the First Continental Congress, dated October 14, 1774, there appears this resolution:

> Resolved, That the respective colonies are entitled to the common law of England, and more especially to the great and inestimable privilege of being tried by their peers of the vicinage according to the course of that law.

What underlay this declaration was not the extension of summary jurisdiction over minor offenses, such as battery, for which non-jury trial had long been the previous mode of trial. Rather, this declaration was motivated by certain Parliamentary acts which permitted the colonist, charged with treason, to be tried in England by a jury of Englishmen, rather than of fellow Americans. . . .

Similarly, the draftsmen of the Declaration of Independence complained of the deprivation ". . . in many cases of the benefits of trial by jury." However, it would be erroneous to conclude that this meant that they wanted trial by jury in every instance. . . . This, then, is the background against which the drafters of the United States Constitution authored the jury provisions of the Federal document. When the constitutional authors stated that there shall be a trial by jury for all *crimes* and in all *criminal prosecutions,* did they call for universal application of trial by jury in all penal actions against an individual?

This Honorable Court has answered that question in the negative as recently as in 1966. In *Cheff v. Schnackenberg*, the Court quoted with approval its holding in *District of Columbia v. Clawans:*

> It is settled by the decisions of this Court . . . that the right of trial by jury . . . does not extend to every criminal proceeding. At the time of the adoption of the Constitution there were numerous offenses, commonly described as 'petty,' which were tried summarily without a jury. . . .

Thus, history and the decisions of this Court concur in their findings that the right to jury trial does not extend to every prosecution in the name of the government against an individual. It should be noted, however, that this well recognized exception to jury trial does not entail an exception to the due process requirements of the Fifth or Fourteenth Amendments to the United States Constitution. . . .

Key concepts of due process prevail at every level. They apply to every prosecution, whether by States or by the Federal Government. They apply to trials of petty offenses by the Federal Government. The Fifth Amendment to the United States Constitution affords Federal petty offenders due process; it does not afford them a jury trial. Similarly, the Fourteenth Amendment affords State offenders due process; it does not afford them a jury trial.

[3. Louisiana's Distinctive History.] Appellee does not rest its case solely on the peculiarities of Louisiana history. However, it does feel that the history of Louisiana law clearly reflects the great trust that Louisiana has placed in its judiciary and the great emphasis it has placed on trial by judge without jury, both in criminal and civil matters. . . .

. . . [T]here was no jury trial under either the French or the Spanish administration. Upon Louisiana's becoming a possession of the United States, there was a broad authorization for non-jury trial, and a jury trial was granted in a case of simple battery only if demanded.

The case of *Natal v. State of Louisiana* establishes that at least since 1852, non-jury trials for violations of municipal ordinances were constitutionally authorized in Louisiana. . . .

Regarding State prosecutions for misdemeanors, since 1898 to date, almost seventy years, both the State's constitutions and legislative laws have precluded trial by jury.

For the most recent pronouncement of the Louisiana State Supreme Court upholding the constitutionality of non-jury trials of misdemeanors, see *State of Louisiana v. Reuben L. Jones*, decided December 11, 1967. Therein at p. 5, the court stated:

> It seems to be well established by the decisions of the United States Supreme Court that the constitutional right of trial by jury does not extend to every criminal proceeding, and that a jury is not demandable in trials for petty offenses. . . .

At pp. 6–7, the Court stated:

... [W]e are unable to perceive that an accused in a misdemeanor case is necessarily denied due process or a fair trial when he is tried by a judge instead of a
jury. A fair trial, as we understand the expression, means simply a trial that is just;
a trial in which the accused is given the benefit of all the safeguards provided by
the Constitution and laws and one in which evenhanded justice is dispensed. We
cannot conceive, in the absence of proof to the contrary, that there is any rational
basis for declaring that an unbiased judge cannot dispense justice in a misdemeanor case with the same quality of fairness and impartiality which could be expected of a jury which acts under the instructions of the judge. . . .

In summary, Louisiana has long entrusted its judiciary with broad powers in
the adjudication of personal and property rights. This Court paid due deference to
the propriety of maintaining such local legal institutions.

But beyond requiring conformity to standards of fundamental fairness that have
won legal recognition, this Court always has been careful not so to interpret this
Amendment (Fourteenth Amendment to U.S. Constitution) as to impose uniform procedures upon the several states whose legal systems stem from diverse
sources of law and reflect different historical influences.

[4. Other States.] Appellant's claim that in 38 states, a criminal defendant
subject to a maximum term of imprisonment in excess of six months cannot be
convicted without the unanimous verdict of a twelve-man jury is inaccurate and
misleading. . . .
     . . . [I]n Alabama, Delaware, Maine, New Hampshire, North Carolina, Rhode
Island, and Virginia, defendants must first submit to a trial before a judge without a
jury before they can appeal and receive a jury trial. The denial of the right to trial by
jury in the courts of primary jurisdiction, requiring the defendants to undergo the
expense and time loss inherent in an appeal in order to secure a jury trial, limiting
defendants to a short period within which to do so, and providing that their right is
waived unless exercised within the rigid rules prescribed, make it clear that those
states which provide such a system do not consider jury trial as fundamental or necessary to a fair trial. The discrepancy between the number of trials held without a
jury in New Hampshire (51,197) and the number of cases appealed for a trial de
novo before a jury (562) shows that there are many defendants who are unable or
unwilling to assume the risk and burden concomitant to an appeal. Only an unfettered right to a jury trial would meet due process requirements if jury trial [were]
essential to a fair trial. Those states requiring trial without a jury in inferior courts of
primary jurisdiction necessarily believe that such a trial is a fair one; otherwise such
trials would be void and empty proceedings.
     In Maryland, New Jersey, New York, Oregon, Puerto Rico, and the Virgin Is-
lands . . . misdemeanors carrying more than six months' penalty are tried without
juries and in Massachusetts . . . Defendants electing to be tried with a jury are
subjected to a chance of receiving heavier sentences. Such treatment by the states
is contrary to any attitude that jury trial is necessary for a fair trial. . . .
     [5. The Questionable Value of Juries.] Writing about juries in his work *The
Hunting of the Snark,* Lewis Carroll quipped:

The Jury had each formed a different view
   (Long before the indictment was read),
And they all spoke at once, so that none of them knew
   One word that the others had said.

Lewis Carroll, like many other critics of the jury, obviously did not consider them "sacred cows."

Louisiana, however, does not deny the merits of a trial by jury.

Nevertheless, that trial by jury is meritorious does not mean that it is essential to the fairness of the fact-finding process, or that it is the only fair means of determining facts in a trial. . . .

Appellant's attempt to connect his arrest with "opposition by parish officials to court-ordered desegregation" is totally unsupported by the record in this case. His insinuation that the "personal and political leanings of the trial judge" might have been antagonistic to him is also unsupported by even the minutest shred of evidence.

Had there been any substance to Appellant's insinuation that a fair trial was impossible because of the judge's bias, his remedy was to ask for a change of venue . . . or to ask the judge to recuse himself. . . .

The value of trial by jury has been debated for many years, and there are many arguments on both sides.

Trial by jury was criticized by Gunnar Myrdal in his work *An American Dilemma* as follows:

The jury for the most part, is more guilty of obvious partiality than the judge and the public prosecutor.

Complaints are frequently made as to the efficiency of the jury system as a fact-finding body. . . .

Wormser, in his work *The Law,* states that there is much to be said against the jury system, the most severe criticism being the caliber of the juries. He points out the anomaly of having a technical case decided by such an assortment of jurors as a plumber's helper, a cook, an unemployed actor, a window washer, two clerks, and six housewives who know nothing about business. . . .

McCart, in *Trial by Jury,* states that because of the right of defendants in state prosecutions to waive jury trials, only a minority of cases in the United States are tried by jury, and that this testifies to the public's confidence in the integrity of judges. . . .

Justice Story's opinion in *U.S. v. Battiste* is quoted by McCart on the question of juries following their emotions instead of the law:

In each they have the physical power to disregard the law as laid down to them by the Court. But I deny, that in any case, civil or criminal, they have the moral right to decide the law according to their own notions, or pleasure.

McCart points out that if the law of the case is left to the decision of a jury there can be no consistency in law, as jurors act in the field of emotions present in a trial.

Both Justice Story and McCart disagree with Appellant's eccentric theory that juries are of value because they can be inconsistent, can ignore the law, and can give popular rather than lawful verdicts. "When the jury appears in this somewhat lawless role, it is time to inquire whether the law does not need revision."

Some drawbacks of the jury system are presented in Kircheimer, *Political Justice*, wherein the author points out that at best the jury is a "cumbersome relic" having "the quality of an echo, throwing back the most forceful sounds it receives."...

The above criticisms are presented to show that the jury is not the model of perfection that Appellant's "glittering generalities" attempt to make it.

The jury system has drawbacks, as many authorities have stated. And it also has its salutary effects. This appellee does not deny, but affirms that the scope of jury trial is subject to modification by the States, and that the extent of modification existing in the Louisiana jury trial system is entirely consistent with the maintenance of liberty and a fair trial....

Respectfully submitted,
JACK P. F. GREMILLION,
Attorney General,
State of Louisiana.

THE OPINION

Mr. Justice White delivered the opinion of the Court....

The Fourteenth Amendment denies the States the power to "deprive any person of life, liberty, or property, without due process of law." In resolving conflicting claims concerning the meaning of this spacious language, the Court has looked increasingly to the Bill of Rights for guidance; many of the rights guaranteed by the first eight Amendments to the Constitution have been held to be protected against state action by the Due Process Clause of the Fourteenth Amendment. That clause now protects the right to compensation for property taken by the State; the rights of speech, press, and religion covered by the First Amendment; the Fourth Amendment rights to be free from unreasonable searches and seizures and to have excluded from criminal trials any evidence illegally seized; the right guaranteed by the Fifth Amendment to be free of compelled self-incrimination; and the Sixth Amendment rights to counsel, to a speedy and public trial, to confrontation of opposing witnesses, and to compulsory process for obtaining witnesses.

The text for determining whether a right extended by the Fifth and Sixth Amendments with respect to federal criminal proceedings is also protected against state action by the Fourteenth Amendment has been phrased in a variety of ways in the opinions of this Court. The question has been asked whether a right is among those "fundamental principles of liberty and justice which lie at the base of all our civil and political institutions"; whether it is "basic in our system of jurisprudence"; and whether it is "a fundamental right, essential to a fair trial." The claim before us is that the right to trial by jury guaranteed by the Sixth Amendment meets these tests. The position of Louisiana, on the other hand, is that the Constitution imposes upon the States no duty to give a jury trial in any criminal case, regardless of the seriousness of the crime or the size of the punishment which may be imposed. Because we believe that trial by jury in criminal cases is fundamental to the American scheme of justice, we hold that the Fourteenth Amendment guarantees a right of jury trial in all criminal cases which—were they to be tried in a federal court—would come within the Sixth Amendment's guarantee.[40] Since we consider the appeal before us to be such a case, we hold that the Constitution was violated when appellant's demand for jury trial was refused.

The history of trial by jury in criminal cases has been frequently told. It is sufficient for present purposes to say that by the time our Constitution was written, jury trial in criminal cases had been in existence in England for several centuries and carried impressive credentials traced by many to Magna Carta. . . .

Jury trial came to America with English colonists, and received strong support from them. Royal interference with the jury trial was deeply resented. . . . The First Continental Congress, in the resolve of October 14, 1774, objected to trials before judges dependent upon the Crown alone for their salaries and to trials in England for alleged crimes committed in the colonies. . . . The Declaration of In-

---

[40][Footnote by Justice White.] In one sense recent cases applying provisions of the first eight Amendments to the States represent a new approach to the "incorporation" debate. Earlier the Court can be seen as having asked, when inquiring into whether some particular procedural safeguard was required of a State, if a civilized system could be imagined that would not accord the particular protection. . . . The recent cases, on the other hand, have proceeded upon the valid assumption that state criminal processes are not imaginary and theoretical schemes but actual systems bearing virtually every characteristic of the common-law system that has been developing contemporaneously in England and in this country. The question thus is whether given this kind of system a particular procedure is fundamental—whether, that is, a procedure is necessary to an Anglo-American regime of ordered liberty. It is this sort of inquiry that can justify the conclusions that state courts must exclude evidence seized in violation of the Fourth Amendment; that state prosecutors may not comment on a defendant's failure to testify; and that criminal punishment may not be imposed for the status of narcotics addiction. Of immediate relevance for this case are the Court's holdings that the States must comply with certain provisions of the Sixth Amendment, specifically that the States may not refuse a speedy trial, confrontation of witnesses, and the assistance, at state expense if necessary, of counsel. Of each of these determinations that a constitutional provision originally written to bind the Federal Government should bind the States as well it might be said that the limitation in question is not necessarily fundamental to fairness in every criminal system that might be imagined but is fundamental in the context of the criminal processes maintained by the American States.

When the inquiry is approached in this way the question whether the States can impose criminal punishment without granting a jury trial appears quite different from the way it appeared in the older cases opining that States might abolish jury trial. A criminal process which was fair and equitable but used no juries is easy to imagine. It would make use of alternative guarantees and protections which would serve the purposes that the jury serves in the English and American systems. Yet no American State has undertaken to construct such a system. Instead, every American State, including Louisiana, uses the jury extensively, and imposes very serious punishments only after a trial at which the defendant has a right to a jury's verdict. In every State, including Louisiana, the structure and style of the criminal process—the supporting framework and the subsidiary procedures—are of the sort that naturally complement jury trial, and have developed in connection with and in reliance upon jury trial.

dependence stated solemn objections to the King's . . . "depriving us in many cases, of the benefits of Trial by Jury," and to his "transporting us beyond Seas to be tried for pretended offenses.". . .

Even such skeletal history is impressive support for considering the right to jury trial in criminal cases to be fundamental to our system of justice, an importance frequently recognized in the opinions of this Court. For example, the Court has said:

> Those who emigrated to this country from England brought with them this great privilege "as their birth-right and inheritance, as a part of that admirable common law which had fenced around and interposed barriers on every side against the approaches of arbitrary power."

Jury trial continues to receive strong support. The laws of every State guarantee a right to jury trial in serious criminal cases; no State has dispensed with it; nor are there significant movements underway to do so. . . .

The guarantees of jury trial in the Federal and State Constitutions reflect a profound judgment about the way in which law should be enforced and justice administered. A right to jury trial is granted to criminal defendants in order to prevent oppression by the Government. Those who wrote our constitutions knew from history and experience that it was necessary to protect against unfounded criminal charges brought to eliminate enemies and against judges too responsive to the voice of higher authority. The framers of the constitutions strove to create an independent judiciary but insisted upon further protection against arbitrary action. Providing an accused with the right to be tried by a jury of his peers gave him an inestimable safeguard against the corrupt or overzealous prosecutor and against the compliant, biased, or eccentric judge. If the defendant preferred the common-sense judgment of a jury to the more tutored but perhaps less sympathetic reaction of the single judge, he was to have it. Beyond this, the jury trial provisions in the Federal and State Constitutions reflect a fundamental decision about the exercise of official power—a reluctance to entrust plenary power over the life and liberty of the citizen to one judge or to a group of judges. Fear of unchecked power, so typical of our State and Federal Governments in other respects, found expression in the criminal law in this insistence upon community participation in the determination of guilt or innocence. The deep commitment of the Nation to the right of jury trial in serious criminal cases as a defense against arbitrary law enforcement qualifies for protection under the Due Process Clause of the Fourteenth Amendment, and must therefore be respected by the States.

Of course jury trial has "its weaknesses and the potential for misuse." We are aware of the long debate, especially in this century, among those who write about the administration of justice, as to the wisdom of permitting untrained laymen to determine the facts in civil and criminal proceedings. Although the debate has been intense, with powerful voices on either side, most of the controversy has centered on the jury in civil cases. Indeed, some of the severest critics of civil juries acknowledge that the arguments for criminal juries are much stronger. In addition, at the heart of the dispute have been express or implicit assertions that juries are incapable of adequately understanding evidence or determining issues of fact, and that they are unpredictable, quixotic, and little better than a roll of dice.

Yet, the most recent and exhaustive study of the jury in criminal cases concluded that juries do understand the evidence and come to sound conclusions in most of the cases presented to them and that when juries differ with the result at which the judge would have arrived, it is usually because they are serving some of the very purposes for which they were created and for which they are now employed.

The State of Louisiana urges that holding that the Fourteenth Amendment assures a right to jury trial will cast doubt on the integrity of every trial conducted without a jury. Plainly, this is not the import of our holding. Our conclusion is that in the American States, as in the federal judicial system, a general grant of jury trial for serious offenses is a fundamental right, essential for preventing miscarriages of justice and for assuring that fair trials are provided for all defendants. We would not assert, however, that every criminal trial—or any particular trial—held before a judge alone is unfair or that a defendant may never be as fairly treated by a judge as he would be by a jury. Thus we hold no constitutional doubts about the practices, common in both federal and state courts, of accepting waivers of jury trial and prosecuting petty crimes without extending a right to jury trial. However, the fact is that in most places more trials for serious crimes are to juries than to a court alone; a great many defendants prefer the judgment of a jury to that of a court. Even where defendants are satisfied with bench trials, the right to a jury trial very likely serves its intended purpose of making judicial or prosecutorial unfairness less likely.

Louisiana's final contention is that even if it must grant jury trials in serious criminal cases, the conviction before us is valid and constitutional because here the petitioner was tried for simple battery and was sentenced to only 60 days in the parish prison. We are not persuaded. It is doubtless true that there is a category of petty crimes or offenses which is not subject to the Sixth Amendment jury trial provision and should not be subject to the Fourteenth Amendment jury trial requirement here applied to the States. Crimes carrying possible penalties up to six months do not require a jury trial if they otherwise qualify as petty offenses. But the penalty authorized for a particular crime is of major relevance in determining whether it is serious or not and may in itself, if severe enough, subject the trial to the mandates of the Sixth Amendment. The penalty authorized by the law of the locality may be taken "as a gauge of its social and ethical judgments" of the crime in question. . . . In the case before us the Legislature of Louisiana has made simple battery a criminal offense punishable by imprisonment for up to two years and a fine. The question, then, is whether a crime carrying such a penalty is an offense which Louisiana may insist on trying without a jury.

We think not. So-called petty offenses were tried without juries both in England and in the Colonies and have always been held to be exempt from the otherwise comprehensive language of the Sixth Amendment's jury trial provisions. There is no substantial evidence that the Framers intended to depart from this established common-law practice, and the possible consequences to defendants from convictions for petty offenses have been thought insufficient to outweigh the benefits to efficient law enforcement and simplified judicial administration resulting from the availability of speedy and inexpensive non-jury adjudications. These same considerations compel the same result under the Fourteenth Amendment. . . .

In determining whether the length of the authorized prison term or the seriousness of other punishment is enough in itself to require a jury trial, we are counseled by *District of Columbia v. Clawans,* to refer to objective criteria, chiefly the existing laws and practices in the Nation. In the federal system, petty offenses are defined as those punishable by no more than six months in prison and a $500 fine. In 49 of the 50 States crimes subject to trial without a jury, which occasionally include simple battery, are punishable by no more than one year in jail. Moreover, in the late 18th century in America crimes triable without a jury were for the most part punishable by no more than a six-month prison term, although there appear to have been exceptions to this rule. We need not, however, settle in this case the exact location of the line between petty offenses and serious crimes. It is sufficient for our purposes to hold that a crime punishable by two years in prison is, based on past and contemporary standards in this country, a serious crime and not a petty offense. Consequently, appellant was entitled to a jury trial and it was error to deny it.

Mr. Justice Black, concurring . . .

. . . I am very happy to support this selective process through which our Court has since the Adamson case held most of the specific Bill of Rights protections applicable to the States to the same extent they are applicable to the Federal Government. Among these are the right to trial by jury decided today, the right against compelled self-incrimination, the right to counsel, the right to compulsory process for witnesses, the right to confront witnesses, the right to a speedy and public trial, and the right to be free from unreasonable searches and seizures.

All of these holdings making Bill of Rights' provisions applicable as such to the States mark, of course, a departure from the Twining doctrine holding that none of those provisions were enforceable as such against the States. The dissent in this case, however, makes a spirited and forceful defense of that now discredited doctrine. I do not believe that it is necessary for me to repeat the historical and logical reasons for my challenge to the Twining holding contained in my Adamson dissent and Appendix to it. What I wrote there in 1947 was the product of years of study and research. My appraisal of the legislative history followed 10 years of legislative experience as a Senator of the United States, not a bad way, I suspect, to learn the value of what is said in legislative debates, committee discussions, committee reports, and various other steps taken in the course of passage of bills, resolutions, and proposed constitutional amendments. My Brother Harlan's objections to my Adamson dissent history, like that of most of the objectors, relies most heavily on a criticism written by Professor Charles Fairman and published in the *Stanford Law Review.* I have read and studied this article extensively, including the historical references, but am compelled to add that in my view it has completely failed to refute the inferences and arguments that I suggested in my Adamson dissent. Professor Fairman's "history" relies very heavily on what was *not* said in the state legislatures that passed on the Fourteenth Amendment. Instead of relying on this kind of negative pregnant, my legislative experience has convinced me that it is far wiser to rely on what *was* said, and most [important], said by the men who actually sponsored the Amendment in the Congress. . . .

In addition to the adopting of Professor Fairman's "history," the dissent states that "the great words of the four clauses of the first section of the Fourteenth Amendment would have been an exceedingly peculiar way to say that 'The rights heretofore guaranteed against federal intrusion by the first eight Amendments are henceforth guaranteed against state intrusion as well.'" In response to this I can say only that the words "No State shall make or enforce any law which shall abridge the privileges or immunities of citizens of the United States" seem to me an eminently reasonable way of expressing the idea that henceforth the Bill of Rights shall apply to the States. What more precious "privilege" of American citizenship could there be than that privilege to claim the protections of our great Bill of Rights? I suggest that any reading of "privileges or immunities of citizens of the United States" which excludes the Bill of Rights' safeguards renders the words of this section of the Fourteenth Amendment meaningless. . . .

. . . I conclude, contrary to my Brother Harlan, that if anything, it is "exceedingly peculiar" to read the Fourteenth Amendment differently from the way I do.

While I do not wish at this time to discuss at length my disagreement with Brother Harlan's forthright and frank restatement of the now discredited Twining doctrine, I do want to point out what appears to me to be the basic difference between us. His view, as was indeed the view of Twining, is that "due process is an evolving concept" and therefore that it entails a "gradual process of judicial inclusion and exclusion" to ascertain those "immutable principles . . . of free government which no member of the Union may disregard." Thus the Due Process Clause is treated as prescribing no specific and clearly ascertainable constitutional command that judges must obey in interpreting the Constitution, but rather as leaving judges free to decide at any particular time whether a particular rule or judicial formulation embodies an "immutable principl[e] of free government" or is "implicit in the concept of ordered liberty," or whether certain conduct "shocks the judge's conscience" or runs counter to some other similar, undefined and undefinable standard. Thus due process, according to my Brother Harlan, is to be a phrase with no permanent meaning, but one which is found to shift from time to time in accordance with judges' predilections and understandings of what is best for the country. If due process means this, the Fourteenth Amendment, in my opinion, might as well have been written that "no person shall be deprived of life, liberty or property except by laws that the judges of the United States Supreme Court shall find to be consistent with the immutable principles of free government." It is impossible for me to believe that such unconfined power is given to judges in our Constitution . . . in order to limit governmental power. . . .

. . . There is not one word of legal history that justifies making the term "due process of law" mean a guarantee of a trial free from laws and conduct which the courts deem at the time to be "arbitrary," "unreasonable," "unfair," or "contrary to civilized standards." The due process of law standard for a trial is one in accordance with the Bill of Rights and laws passed pursuant to constitutional power, guaranteeing to all alike a trial under the general law of the land.

Finally I want to add that I am not bothered by the argument that applying the Bill of Rights to the States, "according to the same standards that protect those personal rights against federal encroachment," interferes with our concept of federalism in that it may prevent States from trying novel social and economic experiments. I have never believed that under the guise of federalism the States should be able to experiment with the protections afforded our citizens through the Bill of Rights. . . . It seems to me totally inconsistent to advocate, on the one hand, the power of this Court to strike down any state law or practice which it finds "unreasonable" or "unfair" and, on the other hand, urge that the States be given maximum power to develop their own laws and procedures. Yet the due process approach of my Brothers Harlan and Fortas does just that since in effect it restricts the States to practices which a majority of this Court is willing to approve on a case-by-case basis. No one is more concerned than I that the States be allowed to use the full scope of their powers as their citizens see fit. And that is why I have continually fought against the expansion of this Court's authority over the States through the use of a broad, general interpretation of due process that permits judges to strike down state laws they do not like.

In closing I want to emphasize that I believe as strongly as ever that the Fourteenth Amendment was intended to make the Bill of Rights applicable to the States. I have been willing to support the selective incorporation doctrine, however, as an alternative, although perhaps less historically supportable than complete incorporation. The selective incorporation process, if used properly, does limit the Supreme Court in the Fourteenth Amendment field to specific Bill of Rights protections only and keeps judges from roaming at will in their own notions of what policies outside the Bill of Rights are desirable and what are not. And, most [important] for me, the selective incorporation process has the virtue of having already worked to make most of the Bill of Rights' protections applicable to the States.

Mr. Justice Harlan, dissenting . . .

The Court's approach to this case is an uneasy and illogical compromise among the views of various Justices on how the Due Process Clause should be interpreted. The Court does not say that those who framed the Fourteenth Amendment intended to make the Sixth Amendment applicable to the States. And the Court concedes that it finds nothing unfair about the procedure by which the present appellant was tried. Nevertheless, the Court reverses his conviction: it holds, for some reason not apparent to me, that the Due Process Clause incorporates the particular clause of the Sixth Amendment that requires trial by jury in federal criminal cases—including, as I read its opinion, the sometimes trivial accompanying baggage of judicial interpretation in federal contexts. I have raised my voice many times before against the Court's continuing undiscriminating insistence upon fastening on the States federal notions of criminal justice, and I must do so again in this instance. With all respect, the Court's approach and its reading of history are altogether topsy-turvy. . . .

A few members of the Court have taken the position that the intention of those who drafted the first section of the Fourteenth Amendment was simply, and exclusively, to make the provisions of the first eight Amendments applicable to state action. This view has never been accepted by this Court. In my view, often expressed elsewhere, the first section of the Fourteenth Amendment was meant neither to incorporate nor to be limited to the specific guarantees of the first eight Amendments. The overwhelming historical evidence marshalled by Professor Fairman demonstrates, to me conclusively, that the Congressmen and state legislators who wrote, debated, and ratified the Fourteenth Amendment did not think they were "incorporating" the Bill of Rights and the very breadth and generality of the Amendment's provisions suggest that its authors did not suppose that the Nation would always be limited to mid-19th-century conceptions of "liberty" and "due process of law" but that the increasing experience and evolving conscience of the American people would add new "intermediate premises." In short, neither history nor sense supports using the Fourteenth Amendment to put the States in a constitutional strait-jacket with respect to their own development in the administration of criminal or civil law.

Although I therefore fundamentally disagree with the total incorporation view of the Fourteenth Amendment, it seems to me that such a position does at least have the virtue, lacking in the Court's selective incorporation approach, of internal consistency: we look to the Bill of Rights, word for word, clause for clause, precedent for precedent because, it is said, the men who wrote the Amendment wanted it that way. For those who do not accept this "history," a different source of "intermediate premises" must be found. The Bill of Rights is not necessarily irrelevant to the search for guidance in interpreting the Fourteenth Amendment, but the reason for and the nature of its relevance must be articulated.

Apart from the approach taken by the absolute incorporationists, I can see only one method of analysis that has any internal logic. That is to start with the words "liberty" and "due process of law" and attempt to define them in a way that accords with American traditions and our system of government. This approach, involving a much more discriminating process of adjudication than does "incorporation," is, albeit difficult, the one that was followed throughout the 19th and most of the present century. It entails a "gradual process of judicial inclusion and exclusion," seeking, with due recognition of constitutional tolerance for state experimentation and disparity, to ascertain those "immutable principles . . . of free government which no member of the Union may disregard." Due process was not restricted to rules fixed in the past, for that "would be to deny every quality of the law but its age, and to render it incapable of progress or improvement." Nor did it impose nationwide uniformity in details. . . .

Through this gradual process, this Court sought to define "liberty" by isolating freedoms that Americans of the past and of the present considered more important than any suggested countervailing public objective. The Court also, by interpretation of the phrase "due process of law," enforced the Constitution's guarantee that no State may imprison an individual except by fair and impartial procedures.

The relationship of the Bill of Rights to this "gradual process" seems to me to be twofold. In the first place it has long been clear that the Due Process Clause imposes some restrictions on state action that parallel Bill of Rights restrictions on federal action. Second, and more important than this accidental overlap, is the fact that the Bill of Rights is evidence, at various points, of the content Americans find in the term "liberty" and of American standards of fundamental fairness. . . .

In all . . . [past instances of incorporation], the right guaranteed against the States by the Fourteenth Amendment was one that had also been guaranteed

against the Federal Government by one of the first eight Amendments. The logically critical thing, however, was not that the rights had been found in the Bill of
Rights, but that they were deemed, in the context of American legal history, to be
fundamental. . . .

Today's court still remains unwilling to accept the total incorporationists' view
of the history of the Fourteenth Amendment. This, if accepted, would afford a co-
gent reason for applying the Sixth Amendment to the States. The Court is also, apparently, unwilling to face the task of determining whether denial of trial by jury
in the situation before us, or in other situations, is fundamentally unfair. Consequently, the Court has compromised on the ease of the incorporationist position,
without its internal logic. It has simply assumed that the question before us is
whether the Jury Trial Clause of the Sixth Amendment should be incorporated
into the Fourteenth, jot-for-jot and case-for-case, or ignored. Then the Court
merely declares that the clause in question is "in" rather than "out."

The Court has justified neither its starting place nor its conclusion. If the
problem is to discover and articulate the rules of fundamental fairness in criminal
proceedings, there is no reason to assume that the whole body of rules developed
in this Court constituting Sixth Amendment jury trial must be regarded as a unit.
The requirement of trial by jury in federal criminal cases has given rise to numerous subsidiary questions respecting the exact scope and content of the right. It
surely cannot be that every answer the Court has given, or will give, to such a
question is attributable to the Founders; or even that every rule announced carries equal conviction of this Court; still less can it be that every such subprinciple
is equally fundamental to ordered liberty.

Examples abound. I should suppose it obviously fundamental to fairness that
a "jury" means an "impartial jury." I should think it equally obvious that the rule,
imposed long ago in the federal courts, that "jury" means "jury of exactly twelve,"
is not fundamental to anything: there is no significance except to mystics in the
number 12. Again, trial by jury has been held to require a unanimous verdict of jurors in the federal courts, although unanimity has not been found essential to liberty in Britain, where the requirement has been abandoned. . . .

Even if I could agree that the question before us is whether Sixth Amendment jury trial is totally "in" or totally "out," I can find in the Court's opinion no
real reasons for concluding that it should be "in." The basis for differentiating
among clauses in the Bill of Rights cannot be that only some clauses are in the Bill
of Rights, or that only some are old and much praised, or that only some have
played an important role in the development of federal law. These things are true
of all. The Court says that some clauses are more "fundamental" than others, but
it turns out to be using this word in a sense that would have astonished Mr. Justice
Cardozo and which, in addition, is of no help. The word does not mean "analyti-
cally critical to procedural fairness" for no real analysis of the role of the jury in
making procedures fair is even attempted. Instead, the word turns out to mean
"old," "much praised," and "found in the Bill of Rights." The definition of "fundamental" thus turns out to be circular. . . .

The argument that jury trial is not a requisite of due process is quite simple.
The central proposition of *Palko*, a proposition to which I would adhere, is that
"due process of law" requires only that criminal trials be fundamentally fair. As

stated above, apart from the theory that it was historically intended as a mere shorthand for the Bill of Rights, I do not see what else "due process of law" can intelligibly be thought to mean. If due process of law requires only fundamental fairness, then the inquiry in each case must be whether a state trial process was a fair one. The Court has held, properly I think, that in an adversary process it is a requisite of fairness, for which there is no adequate substitute, that a criminal defendant be afforded a right to counsel and to cross-examine opposing witnesses. But it simply has not been demonstrated, nor, I think, can it be demonstrated, that trial by jury is the only fair means of resolving issues of fact.

The jury is of course not without virtues. It affords ordinary citizens a valuable opportunity to participate in a process of government, an experience fostering, one hopes, a respect for law. It eases the burden on judges by enabling them to share a part of their sometimes awesome responsibility. A jury may, at times, afford a higher justice by refusing to enforce harsh laws (although it necessarily does so haphazardly, raising the questions whether arbitrary enforcement of harsh laws is better than total enforcement, and whether the jury system is to be defended on the ground that jurors sometimes disobey their oaths). And the jury may, or may not, contribute desirably to the willingness of the general public to accept criminal judgments as just.

It can hardly be gainsaid, however, that the principal original virtue of the jury trial—the limitations a jury imposes on a tyrannous judiciary—has largely disappeared. We no longer live in a medieval or colonial society. Judges enforce laws enacted by democratic decision not by regal fiat. They are elected by the people or appointed by the people's elected officials, and are responsible not to a distant monarch alone but to reviewing courts, including this one.

The jury system can also be said to have some inherent defects, which are multiplied by the emergence of the criminal law from the relative simplicity that existed when the jury system was devised. It is a cumbersome process, not only imposing great cost in time and money on both the State and the jurors themselves, but also contributing to delay in the machinery of justice. Untrained jurors are presumably less adept at reaching accurate conclusions of fact than judges, particularly if the issues are many or complex. And it is argued by some that trial by jury, far from increasing public respect for law, impairs it: the average man, it is said, reacts favorably neither to the notion that matters he knows to be complex are being decided by other average men nor to the way the jury system distorts the process of adjudication.

That trial by jury is not the only fair way of adjudicating criminal guilt is well attested by the fact that it is not the prevailing way, either in England or in this country. . . .

. . . [In the United States, two] experts have estimated that, of all prosecutions for crimes triable to a jury, 75% are settled by guilty plea and 40% of the remainder are tried to the court. In one State, Maryland, which has always provided for waiver, the rate of court trial appears in some years to have reached 90%. The Court recognizes the force of these statistics in stating, "We would not assert, however, that every criminal trial—or any particular trial—held before a judge alone is unfair or that a defendant may never be as fairly treated by a judge as he would be by a jury." I agree. I therefore see no reason why this Court should reverse the conviction of appellant, absent any suggestion that his particular trial was in fact unfair, or compel the State of Louisiana to afford jury trial in an as yet unbounded category of cases that can, without unfairness, be tried to a court.

Indeed, even if I were persuaded that trial by jury is a fundamental right in some criminal cases, I could see nothing fundamental in the rule, not yet formulated by the Court, that places the prosecution of appellant for simple battery within the category of "jury crimes" rather than "petty crimes.". . .

The point is not that many offenses that English-speaking communities have, at one time or another, regarded as triable without a jury are more serious, and carry more serious penalties, than the one involved here. The point is rather that until today few people would have thought the exact location of the line mattered very much. There is no obvious reason why a jury trial is a requisite of fundamental fairness when the charge is robbery, and not a requisite of fairness when the same defendant, for the same actions, is charged with assault and petty theft. The reason for the historic exception for relatively minor crimes is the obvious one: the burden of jury trial was thought to outweigh its marginal advantages. Exactly why the States should not be allowed to make continuing adjustments, based on the state of their criminal dockets and the difficulty of summoning jurors, simply escapes me.

In sum, there is a wide range of views on the desirability of trial by jury, and on the ways to make it most effective when it is used; there is also considerable variation from State to State in local conditions such as the size of the criminal caseload, the ease or difficulty of summoning jurors, and other trial conditions bearing on fairness. We have before us, therefore, an almost perfect example of a situation in which the celebrated dictum of Mr. Justice Brandeis should be invoked. It is, he said, "one of the happy incidents of the federal system that a single courageous State may, if its citizens choose, serve as a laboratory. . . ." This Court, other courts, and the political process are available to correct any experiments in criminal procedure that prove fundamentally unfair to defendants. That is not what is being done today: instead, and quite without reason, the Court has chosen to impose upon every State one means of trying criminal cases; it is a good means, but it is not the only fair means, and it is not demonstrably better than the alternatives States might devise.

POSTSCRIPT

In a footnote in his dissent in *Duncan v. Louisiana*, Justice Harlan warned of "a major danger" of either total or selective incorporation. Federal rights might be weakened, he speculated, when the Supreme Court confronted the dilemma of whether to impose the "jot-for-jot" details of any particular federal right on the states. If the Court decided to incorporate the details, the Bill of Rights would become a judicially created "straitjacket" severely limiting how the states could experiment with criminal procedures. But if the Court declined to incorporate the details, the ideal of uniformity underlying incorporation would encourage the

Court to reexamine, and perhaps overturn, earlier Supreme Court precedents applying such details against the federal government. If the rights applicable against the states were to be exactly equivalent in scope to those applied against the federal government, there was a temptation to "water down" the federal right in what Harlan called "the needless pursuit of uniformity."[41]

Harlan's concern anticipated later developments of the constitutional right to a jury trial. The jot-for-jot features of the right to a jury trial that came before the Court after *Duncan* were the twelve-person rule and the requirement of unanimity. In the past, the Supreme Court had held that juries in the federal criminal system had to be composed of twelve persons and that their verdicts had to be unanimous, whether in favor of guilt or innocence.[42] A "hung jury" was grounds for a retrial. After *Duncan,* the question was whether these "specifics" of the federal right to a jury trial were to be imposed on the states, and if not, whether they should be abandoned at the federal level. Again, either option was troublesome. By applying these details of the federal right to a jury trial against the states, the Court seemed to be placing the states into a constitutional straitjacket of clearly nonfundamental rules of criminal procedure. By overturning the precedents supporting the specifics of the federal right to a jury trial, the Court seemed to be doing what Harlan had predicted—watering down federal rights.

In *William v. Florida* (1970), the Court upheld the constitutionality of a six-person jury in a state criminal trial.[43] Justice Byron White, who wrote the majority opinion, admitted that the common law had always followed the twelve-person rule and that the Court had heretofore interpreted the Sixth Amendment provision accordingly. Nevertheless, setting aside this history and any number of Supreme Court precedents, White argued that the relevant issue concerning the constitutionality of juries composed of less than twelve persons was whether they were compatible with the "purposes of the jury trial." Since the main purpose of the jury trial, as he had noted in his majority opinion in *Duncan,* was "to prevent oppression by the Government," White could see no reason why six-person juries could not fulfil this function as well as twelve-person juries. As long as their verdicts represented "the common sense judgment of a group of laymen," juries served as a safeguard against overreaching prosecutors and biased judges; it did not matter if they were composed of six or twelve persons.[44] Arguments that twelve-person juries favored the defendant and were more representative of the community failed to convince White. The inescapable conclusion was that the common-law requirement of twelve jurors was no more than a "historical accident."[45] Therefore, not only could states use juries composed of fewer than twelve

---

[41]*Duncan v. Louisiana*, 391 U.S. 145, 182, n. 20 (1968).

[42]The case upholding the twelve-person rule in the federal system was *Thompson v. Utah,* 170 U.S. 343 (1898).

[43]399 U.S. 78 (1970). The decision was 7–1. Justice Thurgood Marshall dissented, arguing that the Sixth Amendment required twelve-person juries and that this specific right should be applied against the states. See his dissent in idem, 116.

[44]Idem, 100.

[45]Idem, 102.

persons, but Congress could authorize the federal criminal justice system to do so as well.[46]

Justice Harlan concurred in the result, but he could accept neither the Court's reasoning nor the implication that the federal government could abandon the twelve-person requirement. First, he rejected the majority's policy-based claim that twelve-person juries were not necessary for the jury to fulfill its purpose. The fatal weakness of such an argument resided in its "uncertainty." "For if 12 jurors are not essential, why are six?"[47] Why are five? Indeed, why are three? Second, Harlan refused to "dilute" constitutional protections within the federal system to preserve the coherence of the doctrine of selective incorporation. Common law, the intent of the framers, and the principle of *stare decisis* all supported the retention of twelve-person juries at the federal level. Apart from the Court's unyielding commitment to the doctrine of selective incorporation, "it would have been unthinkable to suggest that the Sixth Amendment right to a trial by jury is satisfied by a jury of six."[48]

According to Harlan, selective incorporation was simply not worth its price: an inevitable dilution of federal rights. *Williams* placed into sharp contrast the difference between the traditional fundamental rights approach to due process and selective incorporation. The difference, in his view, was not merely "an abstract one whereby different verbal formulae achieve the same results. The internal logic of the selective incorporation doctrine cannot be respected if the Court is both committed to interpreting faithfully the meaning of the federal Bill of Rights and recognizing the governmental diversity that exists in this country.[49] For Harlan, the proper course was clear. The only way to interpret the Bill of Rights "faithfully" and recognize "governmental diversity" was to overturn *Duncan* and return to the traditional understanding of the relationship between the Bill of Rights and the states that was embodied in the fundamental rights approach to the due process clause of the Fourteenth Amendment.

Two years later, in *Apodaca v. Oregon* (1972), the Court declined to impose the federal rule requiring unanimous jury verdicts on the states.[50] The decision was close (5–4), divisive, and murky. Four justices said that unanimity was not constitutionally mandated by the Sixth Amendment, implying that the federal government could also abandon this particular rule. Four said that the unanimity rule was an essential part of the Sixth Amendment and that it should be incorporated into the Fourteenth Amendment, implying that both federal and state governments should be subject to it. The remaining justice, Lewis F. Powell, halved the difference. He concluded that the unanimity rule was included within the Sixth Amendment but not within the Fourteenth. The federal government had to respect the rule, but states did not.

---

[46]Idem, 103.

[47]Idem, 126.

[48]Idem, 122.

[49]Idem, 129.

[50]406 U.S. 404 (1972). Justice Harlan had retired in 1971, before the *Apodaca* decision.

In his plurality opinion, Justice White adhered to his *Duncan* analysis that only those aspects of the common-law right to a jury trial that were necessary for the jury's purpose of "preventing oppression" were constitutionally protected. The Sixth Amendment therefore included jury unanimity only if it was essential for this purpose. However, in regard to this specific function, White and three other justices perceived "no difference between juries required to act unanimously and those permitted to convict or acquit by votes of 10 to two or 11 to one."[51] Accordingly, both the states and the federal government could, if they wished, dispense with the need for jury unanimity. White had therefore once again indicated his willingness to modify a traditional understanding of a federal constitutional right for the sake of a uniform national right of criminal procedure and for the internal coherence of the doctrine of selective incorporation.

The four dissenters in the case—Justices Potter Stewart, William O. Douglas, Thurgood Marshall, and William Brennan—were also committed to preserving the logic of selective incorporation, but they were unwilling to water down federal rights for this purpose. Instead, they preferred to impose on the states the traditional jot-for-jot requirement of jury unanimity that had operated in the federal criminal justice system. Therefore, in *Apodaca,* eight justices accepted the assumptions of selective incorporation, though they disagreed about the specifics of what the Sixth Amendment demanded. Only Justice Powell distanced himself from selective incorporation, but he was the key fifth vote. How he balanced the conflicting issues of incorporation and jury unanimity has special relevance for the meaning of *Apodaca.*

In the end, Powell agreed with the dissenters that the Sixth Amendment necessitated unanimous juries but refused to incorporate this jot-for-jot rule into the Fourteenth Amendment's due process clause. First, Powell accepted White's *Duncan* analysis of the right to a jury trial. Despite the fact that a civilized criminal justice system could operate without juries, the right to a jury trial was fundamental in the context of the "basic Anglo-American jurisprudential system common to the states." It was therefore applicable against the states. However, Powell followed Harlan's reasoning that the incorporated right did not have to be exactly equivalent to the Sixth Amendment right enforced against the federal government. Which aspects of a federal right were to be applied against the states depended on the same standard: what was fundamental to the "Anglo-American jurisprudential system." This sort of approach, Powell averred, "readily accounts both for the conclusion that jury trial *is* fundamental and that unanimity *is not.*"[52] Powell therefore avoided both horns of the dilemma. He neither watered down federal rights nor applied them jot-for-jot against the states. He was able to chart this middle course only by abandoning the doctrine of selective incorporation in favor of a modified fundamental rights approach to due process reminiscent of Justices Harlan and Frankfurter.

---

[51]Idem, 411.

[52]Powell's concurrence in *Apodaca* is found in a companion case, *Johnson v. Louisiana,* 406 U.S. 356, 372, n. 9 (1972).

Powell clearly articulated the rationale for his understanding both of the due process clause of the Fourteenth Amendment and of the corresponding relationship of the Bill of Rights to the states. By "holding that the Fourteenth Amendment has incorporated 'jot-for-jot and case-for-case' every element of the Sixth Amendment," he said,

> the Court derogates principles of federalism that are basic to our system. In the name of uniform application of high standards of due process, the Court has embarked upon a course of constitutional interpretation that deprives the States of freedom to experiment with adjudicatory processes different from the federal model.[53]

Moreover, Powell added, "at a time when serious doubt exists as to the adequacy of our criminal justice system," imaginative local reform of criminal justice procedures "is of special importance."[54]

The clear implication of Powell's opinion was that states should be given more latitude in the area of criminal justice. Each state should have the option of becoming a "laboratory" for experimenting with a range of criminal procedures. What do you think of Justice Powell's argument? Is it sufficiently sensitive to the importance of unanimity in jury trials? Does the right to a jury trial mean much if the jury's verdict need not be unanimous? How far from the principle of unanimity should states be allowed to diverge? Would an 8–4 vote be permissible? What about a simple majority? Moreover, what if a state not requiring jury unanimity also reduced the size of its juries? Could a state convict a person of a nonpetty offense based on a 5–1 jury verdict? The Court addressed this specific question in *Burch v. Louisiana* (1979), ruling that such a criminal procedure deprived the accused of his constitutional right to a jury trial.[55] Was this a correct decision? Was it consistent with *Williams* and *Apodaca?* Did the Court properly balance the need for state experimentation against the value of national uniformity? At a minimum, *Burch* reveals the "close" character of current issues involving federalism and criminal procedure and the persistently troublesome nature of the relationship that the Bill of Rights has to the states.

---

[53]Idem, 375.

[54]Idem, 376.

[55]441 U.S. 130 (1979).

Police Confessions

MIRANDA V. ARIZONA
384 U.S. 436 (1966)

✦

Miranda v. Arizona was one of the Supreme Court's most controversial rulings. Even today, nearly three decades after it was handed down, it remains a political symbol of the era in which the Warren Court expanded the rights of criminal defendants and suspects. It is a decision that has divided Americans into two groups: those who think that the Court has coddled criminals and handcuffed law enforcement and those who think that it has properly protected vulnerable defendants from unfair treatment and abusive police tactics. The specific issue addressed in *Miranda* concerned the admissibility of confessions obtained during police interrogations. The Supreme Court ruled that all such confessions and incriminating remarks were inadmissible at trial unless the police, before the interrogation began, informed the defendant that he had the right to remain silent, that any statement that he did make may be used against him, and that he had the right to an attorney (either retained or appointed) before and during any questioning. Does this decision prove that the Court has become overly protective of the "rights" of suspects? Are dangerous criminals being let back on the street because the police cannot obtain enough evidence without a confession to convict them? Conversely, since our system of justice is an accusatorial one in which the state bears the burden of proving beyond a reasonable doubt that the defendant broke the law, is it "fair" for the police, relying on sophisticated "inquisitorial" techniques, to induce a defendant to incriminate himself? Is it constitutional for the state to "pressure" or "trick" the defendant into supplying the state with the proof it needs to meet the beyond-a-reasonable-doubt standard? By resolving such questions in *Miranda,* the Supreme Court was balancing the rights of the individual against the interests of the state. It is the perfect case to evaluate how the Court performs this function in the area of criminal justice.

Another interesting feature of *Miranda v. Arizona* also deserves notice. In this case, the American Civil Liberties Union (ACLU) filed an *amicus curiae* brief that had an overwhelming impact on the litigation; indeed, it changed the terms of the debate. Two years before *Miranda,* the Supreme Court had decided in *Escobedo v. Illinois* that the proper perspective to consider the constitutionality of police confessions was the Sixth Amendment right to counsel. However, in *Miranda,* the ACLU brief convinced the Court that the entire issue should be settled in terms of the Fifth Amendment privilege against self-incrimination. Not only is it rare for an *amicus* brief to have such an impact, but it is inherently interesting to ask why the Supreme Court switched horses in midstream. Was this sudden change simply an intellectual transformation? Were there practical problems with the Sixth Amendment approach? Did political perceptions have something to do with it? Questions such as these focus attention on the kinds of factors that can potentially influence the development of constitutional law. Of course, the underlying issue is whether any of these factors are appropriate influences on constitutional adjudication.

Despite the significance of these questions, they do not reveal the degree to which *Miranda* was a radical development of constitutional law. Before *Miranda,* the rule—inherited from the common law—was that a confession had only to be "voluntary" to be admissible. Moreover, prior to the twentieth century, this rule was a rule of evidence, not of constitutional law.[1] Involuntary confessions were unreliable, like hearsay, and were therefore not to be admitted into evidence. The privilege against self-incrimination had nothing to do with the exclusion of involuntary confessions. Historically, the law understood this particular privilege to pertain only to incriminating statements compelled by *legal* threats made by a magistrate. If a judge told a suspect to confess or be punished for perjury or contempt of court, the suspect could claim the right to remain silent. The privilege, however, did not extend to preliminary examinations before trial. A prisoner could not invoke it if executive officials used *illegal* threats and sanctions to coerce him into confessing. Such a confession was not legally admissible at trial, but it was inadmissible because it was unreliable evidence, not because it violated the defendant's right to remain silent.[2]

Because the federal rule excluding involuntary confessions was based on the law of evidence, the Supreme Court had no constitutional authority to compel states to respect the principle of voluntariness. Throughout the nineteenth century and during the first third of the twentieth, states were constitutionally free to introduce coerced confessions at criminal trials.[3] The "third degree" was therefore

---

[1]See *Hopt v. Utah,* 110 U.S. 574 (1884). One late-nineteenth- century Supreme Court decision, *Baum v. United States,* 168 U.S. 532 (1897), did base the rule excluding involuntary confessions on the Fifth Amendment privilege against self-incrimination; later decisions, however, followed the *Hopt* common-law approach rather than the constitutional one outlined in *Baum.* See *Ziang Sung Wan v. United States,* 266 U.S. 1 (1924); *Powers v. United States,* 223 U.S. 303 (1912); and *Perovich v. United States,* 205 U.S. 86 (1907).

[2]For a concise description of how common-law rules of evidence developed in regard to confessions, see Mark Berger, *Taking the Fifth* (Lexington, Mass.: Lexington Books, 1980), pp. 100–102.

[3]Of course, many state constitutions had provisions that restricted the admissibility of coerced confessions.

commonplace. Indeed, since the states were responsible for most of the criminal prosecutions across the country, it could be said that coerced confessions pervaded the American criminal justice system. It was not until the 1930s that public attention focused on this problem. In 1931, the National Commission on Law Observance and Enforcement reported:

> The third degree—that is, the use of physical brutality, or other forms of cruelty, to obtain involuntary confessions or admissions—is widespread. Protracted questioning of prisoners is commonly employed. Threats and methods of intimidation, adjusted to the age or mentality of the victim, are frequently used, either by themselves or in combination with some of the other practices mentioned. Physical brutality, illegal detention, and refusal to allow access of counsel to the prisoner [are] common.[4]

The commission's report, along with other exposés, revealed the degree to which state courts were not effectively controlling police abuses. The stage was set for the Supreme Court's groundbreaking decision in *Brown v. Mississippi* (1936).

On March 30, 1934, a white farmer was murdered in rural Mississippi. The sheriff picked up a black suspect and took him to the deceased's house, where a group of vigilantes hanged him from a tree twice without killing him and whipped him severely. Two days later, after a deputy sheriff beat him again, he confessed to the murder. Two other black suspects were beaten, and they also confessed to the crime. The Mississippi court convicted the three defendants despite the acknowledgment that the confessions were coerced. The Supreme Court overturned the conviction, but not on the grounds of the Fifth Amendment, which Chief Justice Charles E. Hughes said was "not here involved." Self-incrimination refers to "the processes of justice by which the accused may be called as a witness and required to testify. Compulsion by torture to extort a confession is a different matter."[5] Instead, the Court ruled that using a physically coerced confession to convict a defendant violated the due process clause of the Fourteenth Amendment:

> Because a State may dispense with a jury trial, it does not follow that it may substitute trial by ordeal. The rack and torture chamber may not be substituted for the witness stand. The State may not permit an accused to be hurried to conviction under mob domination—where the whole proceeding is but a mask—without supplying corrective process.[6]

The standard to be used in determining whether any police interrogation violated due process was "fundamental principles of justice." In regard to this case, the Court concluded, it "would be difficult to conceive of methods more revolting to the sense of justice than those taken to procure the confessions of these petitioners, and the use of the confessions thus obtained as the basis for conviction and sentence was a clear denial of due process."[7]

---

[4]*Report on Lawlessness in Law Enforcement* (Washington, D.C.: U.S. Government Printing Office, 1931), cited by Berger, *Taking the Fifth*, p. 105.

[5]*Brown v. Mississippi*, 297 U.S. 278, 285 (1936).

[6]Idem, 285–286.

[7]Idem, 286.

The most important aspect of the *Brown v. Mississippi* decision was that it extended the Constitution to police interrogations. The admissibility of confessions was no longer merely a matter of the law of evidence. Police confessions implicated due process even if they did not implicate the privilege against self-incrimination. The decision, however, hardly clarified what confessions were constitutionally inadmissible. It seemed that *Brown* made any confession triggered by violent brutality inadmissible, but it would be inaccurate to say that the decision constitutionalized the common-law rule of voluntariness. Nonetheless, a few years later, in *Lisenba v. California* (1941), the Court enshrined the voluntariness principle in the Fourteenth Amendment's due process clause. A defendant's confession was admissible unless it was "the result of the deprivation of his free choice to admit, to deny, or to refuse to answer."[8] Any police interrogation techniques that took away the defendant's "free choice," whether they violated "fundamental principles of justice" or not, were sufficient to invalidate the confession.

The voluntariness principle meant that confessions other than those that were physically coerced were inadmissible. For example, in *Ashcraft v. Tennessee* (1944), the Court described a thirty-six-hour interrogation in which the defendant was not allowed to sleep or rest as an "inherently coercive" situation, "irreconcilable with the possession of mental freedom."[9] Accordingly, the confession was thrown out on the ground of mental rather than physical compulsion. The Court came to a similar result in *Watts v. Indiana* (1949). Here the defendant was interrogated on and off by relays of officers for six days with inadequate food and rest. In his opinion in this case, Justice Felix Frankfurter said that there was "torture of mind as well as body; the will is as much affected by fear as by force."[10]

As noted earlier, the common-law rationale for excluding involuntary confessions emphasized their inherent unreliability. At first, this rationale aided judicial efforts to define an involuntary confession. Confessions were involuntary if police used tactics that undermined their reliability. However, as the Court began to exclude confessions that were psychologically coerced, a new rationale for excluding involuntary confessions arose. For instance, in *Watts v. Indiana,* a case that did not involve any physical coercion, Justice Frankfurter noted that the holding recognized the due process clause's "historic function of assuring appropriate procedure before liberty is curtailed or life is taken."[11] The implicit hint was that the Court was throwing out the confession not because of its unreliability but because exclusion would discourage abusive police tactics. Ten years later, Chief Justice Earl Warren explicitly endorsed this new rationale for excluding involuntary confessions:

> The abhorrence of society to the use of involuntary confessions does not turn alone on their inherent untrustworthiness. . . . It also turns on the deep-rooted

---

[8]*Lisenba v. California,* 314 U.S. 219, 241 (1941).

[9]*Ashcraft v. Tennessee,* 322 U.S. 143, 154 (1944).

[10]*Watts v. Indiana,* 338 U.S. 49, 52 (1949).

[11]Idem, 55. For further consideration of Justice Frankfurter's views of due process and its role of deterring abusive police tactics, see his majority opinions in *Rochin v. California,* 342 U.S. 165 (1952); and in *Rogers v. Richmond,* 365 U.S. 534 (1961).

feeling that the police must obey the law while enforcing the law; that in the end life and liberty can be as much endangered from illegal methods used to convict those thought to be criminals as from the actual criminals themselves.[12]

By 1959, use of abusive police tactics alone was enough to render even a reliable confession involuntary and therefore inadmissible.

From the 1930s until *Miranda,* judges measured the voluntariness of confessions by taking into account the "totality of circumstances." Apart from physically compelled confessions, which were inadmissible for this reason alone, all kinds of factors were considered: length and intensity of interrogation, denial of food and visitors, and the defendant's criminal background and personal characteristics (age, intelligence, and education). By the late 1950s, an increasingly important issue was the absence of counsel, especially if the defendant requested to see a lawyer. In *Crooker v. California* (1958), the Supreme Court rejected the argument that a confession was involuntary just because the police continued to interrogate the prisoner after he specifically asked to see his lawyer. However, four justices dissented, arguing that the due process clause requires "that the accused who wants a counsel should have one at any time after the moment of arrest."[13] One year later, in *Spano v. New York* (1959), the Court threw out a postindictment confession made after the defendant had requested to consult with his attorney. The Court came to this ruling by applying the traditional totality-of-circumstances approach, but in his concurring opinion, newly appointed Justice Potter Stewart said that "the absence of counsel when this confession was elicited was alone enough to render it inadmissible under the Fourteenth Amendment."[14] The meaning of this language was unclear at the time, but it suggested that the Supreme Court was on the verge of ruling that confessions, voluntary or not, were invalid if taken after a defendant requested an attorney. It was now possible that even if an indicted defendant voluntarily confessed to his crime, the confession would be inadmissible if it occurred after the defendant requested a lawyer.

In *Escobedo v. Illinois* (1964), the Supreme Court finally resolved some, but not all, of the unanswered questions concerning confessions that *Spano* had left dangling. By this time, the Court had applied the Sixth Amendment to the states in the landmark decision of *Gideon v. Wainwright* (1963). In all felony cases, states were obliged to supply indigent defendants with defense counsel at trial. Against this backdrop, in *Escobedo,* the Court considered whether the Sixth Amendment required the police to honor an *unindicted* suspect's request to consult with his lawyer during interrogation. In a 5–4 decision, the Court said yes. In his majority opinion, Justice Arthur Goldberg noted that twenty-two states, including Illinois, had supported the *Gideon* principle that an indigent defendant could not have a fair trial without a lawyer. But if the state could deny access to counsel during interrogation, Goldberg reasoned, the trial would be "no more than an appeal from the interrogation; and the 'right to use counsel at the formal trial [would be] a very hollow thing [if], for all practical purposes, the conviction is

---

[12]*Spano v. New York*, 360 U.S. 315, 320–321 (1959).

[13]*Crooker v. California*, 357 U.S. 433, 448 (1958).

[14]*Spano v. New York*, 360 U.S. 315, 326 (1959).

already assured by pretrial examination."[15]Accordingly, though Goldberg did occasionally refer in his opinion to the privilege of self-incrimination and to the defendant's "absolute right to remain silent," the thrust of his argument was that a suspect had to have the right to consult with his attorney during questioning if his right to counsel at trial was to have any meaning. The Sixth Amendment required that the right to counsel be extended to the police station in the preindictment period.[16] It did not matter if any particular confession was completely voluntary. According to Goldberg, if a suspect asked to see his lawyer, any later incriminating remarks, even if they were voluntary, were inadmissible.

The dissents in *Escobedo* objected to extending the Sixth Amendment to a time period prior to the formal initiation of criminal action by indictment, information, or arraignment. Police interrogations of nonindicted suspects were a part of criminal investigations; they were not a part of the formal adversarial process. The majority's ruling "imports into this investigation concepts historically applicable only after the onset of formal prosecutorial proceedings."[17] The fact that interrogations affect trials was obvious but irrelevant. If a suspect has a right to counsel during interrogation because what he says might affect the outcome of his trial, "one might just as well argue that a potential defendant is constitutionally entitled to a lawyer before, not after he commits a crime, since it is then that crucial incriminating evidence is put within the reach of the Government by the would-be accused."[18] Concluding that the Sixth Amendment was not applicable to the investigation stage, the dissents reaffirmed the principle that all confessions were admissible at trial if they were voluntary. The due process clause prohibited only confessions that were, based on the "totality of the circumstances," compelled. It did not require the police to inform the unindicted defendant of any constitutional right to remain silent or to give him access to his attorney before or during questioning.

The reaction to *Escobedo* was huge, intense, and divided. It covered the political spectrum and made itself felt in many institutional forums. Law journals provided extended analyses of the case and the topic of coerced confessions. *Time* magazine ran a cover story on Danny Escobedo.[19] Conferences were held at which law enforcement officials complained bitterly that the Court's criminal justice decisions, especially *Escobedo*, were making their job of protecting the public far more difficult. Lower federal judges who were dissatisfied with the direction

---

[15]*Escobedo v. Illinois*, 378 U.S. 478, 487 (1964).

[16]Goldberg described the holding of *Escobedo* in the following way "We hold, therefore, that where, as here, the investigation is no longer a general inquiry into an unsolved crime but has begun to focus on a particular suspect, the suspect has been taken into police custody, the police carry out a process of interrogations that lends itself to eliciting incriminating statements, the suspect has requested and been denied an opportunity to consult with his lawyer, and the police have not effectively warned him of his absolute constitutional right to remain silent, the accused has been denied 'the Assistance of Counsel' in violation of the Sixth Amendment to the Constitution as 'made obligatory upon the States by the Fourteenth Amendment,' and that no statement elicited by the police during the interrogation may be used against him at a criminal trial. Idem, 490–492.

[17]Idem, 494, Justice Stewart dissenting.

[18]Idem, 497, Justice White dissenting.

[19]*Time*, April, 29, 1966.

that the Warren Court was taking in the criminal justice area interpreted the *Escobedo* rule narrowly, while others, who supported the trend of the Warren Court's criminal justice decisions, extended and broadened the principles of the *Escobedo* decision[20] By June 1965, a year after the Court had handed down *Escobedo,* sixty-six petitions for certiorari containing police confession issues were once again before the Supreme Court.[21] Clearly, though *Escobedo*'s application of the Sixth Amendment to the problem of confessions had resolved some of the questions, many issues remained.

Later that summer, Chief Justice Earl Warren and Justice William Brennan, who had both supported the majority decision in *Escobedo,* attended the annual judicial conference of the Third Judicial Circuit. At this conference, four prominent speakers debated the merits of *Escobedo.* Former New York City Police Commissioner Michael J. Murphy and Fred Inbau, professor of law at Northwestern University Law School and author of a widely used police manual on interrogations, represented law enforcement and groups who felt that the Court's criminal justice decisions, especially *Escobedo,* had gone too far in the direction of protecting the rights of criminals. On the other side of the issue, Raymond J. Bradley, former director of the Philadelphia branch of the American Civil Liberties Union (ACLU), and Yale Kamisar, professor of law from the University of Michigan Law School, defended *Escobedo* and argued that its principles should be extended so that confessions would no longer play a prominent role in the American criminal justice system (see Box 2.1).

Which of these speakers articulates the proper balance between the right to remain silent and the interests of society? Murphy claims that "typical large city crimes" cannot be solved without confessions, whereas Kamisar implies that the police often seek confessions when they are unnecessary for conviction. In addition, Murphy says that the Warren Court is undermining public safety by making the job of law enforcement more difficult, while Kamisar suggests that those who attack the Warren Court are merely looking for scapegoats. How could these knowledgeable commentators contradict each other in this fashion? What is it about the criminal justice area? Why is there so little consensus about the basic facts? On a more theoretical level, Bradley argues that without an attorney present at questioning, all the important safeguards of our criminal justice system are in fact hollow. Is he right? What about Inbau's point that requiring the presence of a lawyer at questioning is an indirect way to abolish police confessions? Are police confessions necessary for law enforcement? Are they in any way improper?

After the conference, Chief Justice Warren said that the discussion had made him think "of the saying of the old hillbilly from Arkansas who said, 'You know, no

---

[20]Lower federal judges who were unhappy with *Escobedo* included Warren Burger, the future chief justice; J. Edward Lumbard, the chief judge of the U.S. Court of Appeals for the Second Circuit; and Judge Henry Friendly, who was also a member of the advisory committee of the American Law Institute that was, at the time *Escobedo* was decided, formulating a model code of prearraignment procedure that could be used by state legislatures to reform their procedures. One judge who favored a broad interpretation of *Escobedo* was David Bazelon, chief judge of the Court of Appeals for Washington, D.C. For the judicial and the broader public reaction to *Escobedo,* see Liva Baker, *Miranda: Crime, Law, and Politics* (New York: Atheneum, 1983), especially pp. 50–59, 86–89, 156–161.

[21]Ibid., p. 88.

BOX 2.1

JUDICIAL CONFERENCE ON *ESCOBEDO*

MICHAEL MURPHY, Former New York City Police Commissioner:
. . . I certainly am honored to have been selected to represent the police viewpoint on this vital issue. I say to you bluntly that law enforcement cries out in earnest for a reasonable application of the constitutional safeguards that we all cherish so that police officers can perform their sworn duty under law to deter crimes and to bring offenders to justice. To impose upon us unreasonable standards and at the same time extend the constitutional safeguards surrounding the individual is akin to requiring one boxer to observe the Marquis of Queensbury rules and to permit his opponent to gouge, strike foul blows and use every unfair advantage, as the referee turns his back. . . .

In my own experience, confessions are obtained from suspects as a result of careful, skillful and legal techniques, of which the police, and the community as well, can justly be proud.

. . . Let me describe to you as an illustration a fairly typical large city crime:

A woman living on the top floor of a tenement house in a row of similar structures with common rooftops is awakened at night by a noise; she sees in the darkness a dim figure standing over her with a masked face and a knife in hand. Raped and beaten, as she struggles futilely in terror, she regains full consciousness to find her valuables stolen and the intruder gone through an open window which leads to the fire escape and the roof. He has vanished into the night and the anonymity of the city. There are no fingerprints left at the scene, there is no match box or identification dropped in haste, there is nothing but a terrible moment of fear and violence which leaves behind no physical, tangible evidence. Some weeks later a confidential informant, whose identity must be preserved to protect his life and to insure his cooperation and the cooperation of his kind at a later date, indicates that a man named Joe in a semi-drunken state has made a cryptic reference to this incident. Joe is identified as an ex-convict with a record for similar incidents.

This is the police dilemma. It is clear that unless the suspect can be interrogated the investigation will not be furthered. It is also clear—and it is the unanimous opinion of our senior detective commanders—that advising a suspect of his right to remain silent and/or his right of counsel will probably have the practical effect of ending the interrogation before it has begun. . . .

RAYMOND J. BRADLEY, Philadelphia Branch of the ACLU:
. . . It seems to me that in this area of constitutional rights of an accused in criminal proceedings, we are suffering from a danger, namely, that we could have many of the forms of safeguards for the individual but that these forms could become empty phrases in the absence of any effective steps to implement them and to see to it that they were carried out by the people who were administering the laws and enforcing the laws. . . .

It seems to me to be somewhat incongruous to limit *Escobedo* to situations where the knowledgeable and the sophisticated and those who had been fortunate enough already to retain an attorney and therefore to ask for him, might find themselves protected in this situation, whereas one who was not told of that right, who may well be unsophisticated, unwary, not be completely knowledgeable about his rights, particularly in a situation where all of the pressures coming from those in whose custody he finds himself and from whose custody he is not going to be readily released, is that he ought to talk, and not only ought to but must, and that it would be better for him if he did, to say that that man, because he does not have the foresight or the education or the means to have already retained counsel, that he will be treated differently than the other individual would. . . .

We long ago decided that we did not want to make the job of the police an easy job because we were afraid of all of the dire consequences which could result from that kind of an approach. It was for this reason, I think, that we deliberately constructed an adversary system as against the inquisitorial system. It was for this reason that we adopted an Amendment such as the Fifth Amendment with its right against self-incrimination. And I would think it was for this reason that the states did the same thing.

I have not yet heard anyone who has attacked these decisions go the whole hog. I think the whole hog is what is really facing us here. And that is that we ought not to have a Fifth Amendment, because it seems to me that unless we are to go the whole hog we can have very little quarrel with what the court has done in the *Escobedo* decision. . . . But I don't hear anybody saying that is what we ought to do, although I think it is the unexpressed premise upon which they operate. . . .

FRED E. INBAU, *Northwestern University Law School:*
. . . I am not too concerned about the requirement that a person under arrest be warned of his right to remain silent. This is where I have a slight difference with Commissioner Murphy. I think you can still get confessions from people after having advised them of that. From a police standpoint it is a handicap, but it is one that I think we will just have to accept. I think we can go along with that and still be able to get confessions.

. . . [However, if] the United States Supreme Court comes along and says that all interrogations are outlawed, then we can't adjust to that. . . . Once we prohibit interrogations altogether, I think we have had it. . . .

The other thing that is of particular concern to me is the insistence—and Mr. Bradley suggested this, I think—that when the police arrest someone they cannot interrogate him unless he has an attorney present. Well, what is the attorney going to do? Gentlemen, let's be realistic. He is going to tell him to keep his mouth shut. If you are going to insist that counsel be there at the police level you might just as well start outlawing all confessions. . . .

Let me assure you gentlemen that there are ways of getting people to confess without beating them, without threatening them, without making promises of leniency. I have done it myself in hundreds and hundreds of instances. I wrote a little book on it advising the police how to do it. By using proper psychological techniques it can be done, and it is done in a vast majority of those cases. . . .

I want to close with little quote from Commissioner McCullough of the Royal Canadian Mounted Police, which expresses my own viewpoint, too. He said, "When the policeman exceeds his authority, bring him up short, but when he is doing, as most of them are doing, a tough, thankless and frequently dangerous job for you and for all you hold dear, for God's sake get off his back.". . .

YALE KAMISAR, University of Michigan Law School:
. . . Crime is a terribly complex problem. We all know that. It is baffling. It is frustrating. When people can't solve something readily, they look for scapegoats. . . .

Shortly after the landmark *Escobedo* case was handed down, one of the top assistants to Manhattan District Attorney Frank Hogan cited the *Whitmore* case as

> the perfect example of the importance of confessions in law enforcement. . . . Do you know that we had every top detective in town working on the Wylie-Hoffer murders and they couldn't find a clue. Not a clue! I tell you, if that kid hadn't confessed, we never would have caught the killer.

There is some uncertainty as to which way the *Whitmore* case cuts today. (Laughter) When Whitmore confessed, the chief of detectives assured the press: "We've got the right guy; no question about it." But Whitmore's confession has since been discredited and another man has since been indicted for the same murders.

I do not deny that it is a very common practice, a very familiar practice, to elicit confessions from defendants, especially in the "great" cases. How *essential* to conviction these confessions are is something else again. Professor Inbau pointed out that a murder suspect doesn't very often drop his hat—with his name in it—at the scene of the murder. What would happen if he *were* to do so?

This calls to mind the recent *Dorado* case. In *Dorado* the defendant did do just about this. On discovering the body of one Nevarez in a San Quentin prison yard, correctional officers made an immediate investigation. In nearby trashcans they found two sharpened knives with taped handles, one handle stained with blood (the chest wounds of the victim could have been inflicted by a small knife), and a bloodstained blue denim jacket with the name "Dorado" on the pocket—defendant was the only prisoner in San Quentin named "Dorado"—and a button missing. They found the button belonging to the blue denim jacket at the scene of the homicide.

When officers examined Dorado's cell, they found his bloodstained trousers and a roll of tape similar to that used to tape the knife handles. What did the officer do? They interrogated Dorado; they tried to get a confession out of him. What else? (Laughter) . . .

Undoubtedly the Court will continue to hand down decisions which will be violently attacked. There is much force in Judge Carl McGowan's comment that "were it otherwise, we might have a real, albeit a different, cause for concern about the current state of health of the judicial power."

It doesn't take great courage to attack the Courts violently. As I have tried to show, such attacks unfortunately do appeal to a great many people who are looking for easy, simplistic answers to very complex problems. . . .

Source: 39 *F. R. D* 375, 424–462 (1965).

matter how thin you make the pancake there are always two sides to it.'"[22] What did Warren mean? What are the "two sides?" What does the "thinness" of the pancake symbolize? Did Warren's comment obfuscate the issues, or did it contain real insight into the problem of how to balance the right to remain silent against society's interest in punishing criminals?

At the time that Warren quipped about the Arkansas hillbilly, Ernest Miranda had already filed his petition for certiorari at the Supreme Court. A few months later, on November 22, 1965, the Court agreed to consider Miranda's case along with three others involving confessions. The facts of the case were as follows. On March 13, 1963, Miranda had been arrested for robbery and rape, identified in a lineup, and then interrogated. There was no duress or brutality involved in the interrogation. The police claimed that they had told Miranda that he did not have to answer their questions, but they admitted that they had not informed Miranda that he had a right to consult with an attorney. During this interrogation, Miranda admitted that he had committed both crimes and then wrote and signed a written confession (see Box 2.2). At separate trials for robbery and rape, the confession and the testimony of the interrogating police officers led to his conviction for both crimes. He was sentenced to twenty to thirty years on the rape conviction and an additional twenty to twenty-five years for robbery.

Five briefs were filed in *Miranda*. The one filed on behalf of the defendant was written by John Frank and John J. Flynn, two prominent Phoenix attorneys who had been recruited by the local chapter of the ACLU. The state of Arizona, of course, also filed a brief. The other three *amici curiae* briefs were filed by the ACLU, the state of New York (joined by twenty-six other states), and the National District Attorneys Association. Taking their cue from the *Escobedo* decision, the Miranda and Arizona briefs argued the case in terms of the Sixth Amendment. Frank and Flynn cited the important Sixth Amendment cases of the twentieth century (*Powell v. Alabama, Betts v. Brady,* and *Gideon v. Wainwright*) to support the conclusion that the right to counsel "was a growing, not a static, constitutional right." As the right to counsel at trial has evolved, so the right has become more relevant to police interrogations. It is time, the brief argued, to extend the right to counsel to the police station. There is "a tide in the affairs of men, and it is

---

[22]Idem, 474, quoted by Baker, *Miranda*, p. 88.

A DESCRIPTION OF MIRANDA'S CONFESSION

A: He saw this girl walking on the street, he said, so he decided he would pull up ahead of her and stop. He stopped and got out of his car and opened the back door of his automobile. He said when the girl approached him he told her, he said, "Don't make any noise, and get into the car," and he said she got into the car, he said, in the back seat. After getting into the car, he said he took a small rope he had inside the car and he tied her hands and her ankles, then he got into the front seat behind the driver's wheel and he drove to a location several miles from there in the northeast direction to the area of a desert.

Q: Did he tell you what street this took place on?

A: He didn't know the street. . . . He said then when he got there he noticed that the girl was untied, and he got into the back seat and he asked her if she would, or he told her to take her clothes off and she said, "No, would you please take me home?" He said then he took her clothes off for her. After he had undressed her, she began to cry, and started begging him not to do this. She said she had never had any relations with a man before. He said he went ahead and performed the act of intercourse, and in so doing was only able to get about a half inch of his penis in and at which time he said he did reach a climax, but he didn't believe that he had reached a climax inside of her. He said after the act of intercourse, he then told her to get dressed and asked her where she lived and she told him in the area, she told him 10th or 12th Street. He couldn't remember where, so he said he drove her back to the area where he picked her up and dropped her off in that general area. . . .

Q: Was that the essence of the conversation you had with him at that time?

A: That was the essence of the conversation.

Q: Officer, was this conversation reduced, or was the defendant's conversation with you reduced to writing?

A: Yes, Sir, it was.

Q: Who wrote it down, Officer?

A: He wrote his own statement down. . . .

Q: Were you present, Officer, when he wrote this?

A: Yes, Sir, I was. . . .

Q: Is this the statement that you said the defendant reduced to writing?

A: Yes, Sir, it is. . . .

Miranda v. Arizona 67

[*DEFENSE ATTORNEY*]:   May I ask some questions on voir dire?

THE COURT: Yes, you may.

Q: Officer Cooley, in the taking of this statement, what did you say to the defendant to get him to make this statement?

A: I asked the defendant if he would tell us, write the same story that he had just told me, and he said that he would.

Q: Did you warn him of his rights?

A: Yes, Sir, at the heading of the statement is a paragraph typed out, and I read this paragraph to him out loud.

Q: Did you read that to him out loud?

A: Yes, Sir.

Q: But did you ever, before or during your conversation or before taking this statement, did you ever advise the defendant he was entitled to the services of an attorney?. . .

A: No, Sir.

Q: It is not in that statement?

A: It doesn't say anything about an attorney. . . .

The Signed Statement

I, Ernest A. Miranda, do hereby swear that I make this statement voluntarily and of my own free will, with no threats, coercion, or promises of immunity, and with full knowledge of my legal rights, understanding any statement I make may be used against me.

I, Ernest A. Miranda, am 23 years of age and have completed the 8th grade in school.

Seen a girl walking up the street stopped a little ahead of her got out of car walked towards her grabbed her by the arm and asked to get in the car. Got in car without force tied hands & ankles. Drove away for a few miles. Stopped asked to take clothes off. Did not, asked me to take her back home. I started to take clothes off her without any force, and with cooperation. Asked her to lay down and she did. Could not get penis into vagina got about 1/2 (half) inch in. Told her to get clothes back on. Drove her home. I couldn't say I was sorry for what I had done. But asked her to say a prayer for me.

I have read and understand the foregoing statement and hereby swear to its truthfulness.

ERNEST A. MIRANDA

Source: State v. Miranda, 98 Ariz. 18; 401 P.2d 721, 726–727 (1965), quoting from a transcript of the testimony that Detective Carroll Cooley gave at Miranda's trial.

this engulfing tide which is washing away the secret interrogation of the unprotected accused." The brief conceded that the effects of the rule that it was proposing were, though certainly costly, largely unknown. Nevertheless, since it made no sense to supply defendants at trial with counsel if they were not also provided with lawyers during interrogation, Miranda's lawyers concluded that the Court should extend the right to counsel to the police interrogation room.

Arizona's brief came to the opposite conclusion but also argued its case in terms of the Sixth Amendment. It noted that Miranda did not request to see his attorney and that the police had informed him of his right to remain silent. The idea that the police were nevertheless obliged to inform Miranda of his right to counsel and to provide him with counsel if he could not afford one ignores the "plain wording" of *Escobedo* and disregards "the factual and legal bases for the opinions cited in petitioner's historical analysis." Moreover, to extend the right to counsel to all interrogations would turn police officers into "part-time defense counsel" and would upset the adversarial system by giving guilty suspects "special chances for acquittal or other favorable result." But a criminal prosecution is not a "game of chance." It is a vital necessity for the security of the public. Consequently, the Sixth Amendment right to counsel should not be interpreted in such a way that the police are deprived of an "invaluable" tool in their efforts to prevent crime.

Two of the *amici* briefs, the one by the National District Attorneys Association and the other by the state of New York, dwelled on the practical problems of extending *Escobedo* to the facts of *Miranda.* The former listed eight problems that would arise if the police were required to inform suspects of their right to an attorney and six reasons why confessions played such an "essential" role in the American system. New York's brief assumed that the issues before the Court were ones of policy but argued that contemporary empirical knowledge was so meager that the Court should not rashly constitutionalize prearraignment procedure. Instead, the Court should wait and see how states responded to the American Bar Association's ongoing project on minimum standards of criminal justice and to the Model Code of Prearraignment Procedure that was soon to be published by the American Law Institute. Our federal system, the brief concluded, demanded no less. Relying on growing experience and empirical knowledge, state legislatures could formulate "workable rules in this area of strong conflicting values."

The ACLU brief, written primarily by Anthony Amsterdam, a professor of law at the University of Pennsylvania, unexpectedly focused on the Fifth Amendment privilege against self-incrimination. It claimed, first, that *Escobedo* was essentially a Fifth Amendment, not a Sixth Amendment, case. Escobedo had a right to counsel during his interrogation not because of some independent constitutional right to counsel, but because the presence of counsel was necessary to secure his constitutional privilege against self-incrimination. Indeed, even if there were no Sixth Amendment right to counsel, the result would of necessity have been the same in *Escobedo* because "the privilege against self-incrimination required the presence of counsel for its effectuation." The Fifth Amendment interpretation of *Escobedo* was preferable, the brief claimed, because the Sixth Amendment, by itself, gave no guidance as to when the right was activated in the prearraignment period. In contrast, the Fifth Amendment approach suggested that the right to counsel should "attach" whenever "the danger of compelled self-incrimination looms large." Since the Fifth Amendment self-incrimination clause had been applied against the states in *Malloy v. Hogan* (1964), the best approach to police confessions, according to the ACLU, was to evaluate them in terms of self-incrimination, not the right to counsel.

This conclusion had little bearing on the facts of *Miranda* unless it could be argued that all police custodial confessions were "inherently compelling—inherently violative of the subject's privilege against self-incrimination." To support this claim, Amsterdam adopted the brilliant tactic of taking long quotations from leading writers on police interrogation techniques. In effect, he ironically let the proponents of police confessions incriminate themselves. The quotations showed that interrogators "trapped" their "quarry" by "deceiving" them or by "overbearing" their will. The interrogators "dominated" their subjects by, for example, convincing them that their silence indicated guilt. Therefore, even if, as in *Miranda,* an interrogation included no explicit brutality or duress, it was still inherently coercive. "Protective devices" were needed to "to dispel" the "atmosphere" of compulsion. The privilege against self-incrimination required that the police not only inform the suspect of his rights, including his right to a lawyer, but also supply all indigent suspects with counsel before and during questioning. Any detrimental impact that such a rule would have on the crime rate and the rate of convictions had not been substantiated and was irrelevant in any case.

Oral argument in *Miranda* took place on February 28, 1966. It was an especially interesting example of oral constitutional argument for two reasons. First, the politically controversial character of the issues before the Court produced a very contentious session. Not only were the attorneys for both sides subject to vigorous questioning, but the justices themselves began to argue indirectly with one another. Throughout the argument, many of the justices' questions were in fact rejoinders to points made by other justices. Indeed, at one point, Justice Abe Fortas even admitted that his question was a response to comments made by Justice Potter Stewart and that it was perhaps "unfair" to discuss the issue through counsel. The session is therefore a good example of the sort of "shootout" that can occur at oral argument.

In such a predicament, what should the lawyers do? Should they keep their heads down, as the justices take intellectual potshots at one another, or should they join the fray by allying themselves with specific justices? Which is the better tactic? Does it depend on the circumstances? How did the lawyers in *Miranda* handle the situation?

The second interesting feature of the oral argument in *Miranda* is that it reveals that a substantial shift had occurred in the terms of constitutional argumentation. Most of the briefs had read *Escobedo* as primarily a Sixth Amendment case and assumed that *Miranda* would be decided accordingly. Only the ACLU brief had taken the position that *Miranda* was essentially a Fifth Amendment case and that the right to counsel at prearraignment proceedings was merely a means to secure the right to remain silent. The oral argument suggests that the ACLU brief had changed the character of the debate. Both the justices' questions and the lawyers' responses indicate the impact of the ACLU brief. The excerpts included here are taken from the parts of the oral argument that highlight the degree to which the privilege against self-incrimination had taken over the discussion of the facts and the probable decision. After oral argument, no one knew what the Court would decide, but the strong likelihood was that the decision would be framed in terms of the Fifth Amendment.

Chief Justice Earl Warren's majority opinion in *Miranda v. Arizona,* a 5–4 decision, represented a great victory for the ACLU. Anthony Amsterdam's efforts to reorient the Court's attention from the Sixth to the Fifth Amendment and his tactic of quoting from police interrogation manuals proved overwhelmingly successful. This result was not foreordained. Though *Malloy v. Hogan* (1964) had applied the Fifth Amendment against the states, the provision that no one "shall be compelled in any criminal case to be a witness against himself" was not obviously applicable to the context of police interrogation rooms. Historical precedent favored the view that investigations precede criminal cases and that the privilege only protected an individual when he was a witness in a formal criminal proceeding. Though the Supreme Court had earlier widened the scope of the privilege of self-incrimination, applying it to legislative hearings and grand jury proceedings, there was no assurance that the Supreme Court would accept the ACLU's central assumption that the privilege was applicable to police interrogations.

Moreover, even if the Supreme Court did accept the relevance of the Fifth Amendment to police confessions, the justices could have ruled that the privilege required only the old common-law rule that had already been enshrined in the Fourteenth Amendment's due process clause: based on the totality of the circumstances, legally admissible confessions had to be voluntary. The majority of the Court could sanctify the principle of voluntariness with the Fifth Amendment without concluding that Miranda's rights were violated or that police were obliged to inform suspects of their right to remain silent or their right to an attorney. As Warren admitted in his opinion, in the traditional sense, there was nothing involuntary about Miranda's confession. Hence, if its Fifth Amendment interpretation of *Escobedo* was to bear fruit, the ACLU had to convince the Supreme Court to narrow the concept of a voluntary confession.

Despite the uncertainties, the ACLU gamble paid off. Warren's opinion closely tracked the novel constitutional arguments contained in the ACLU brief. Warren included long excerpts from the same works on police interrogation techniques that had been quoted in the ACLU brief to substantiate the view that all custodial interrogations were "inherently compelling." The opinion endorsed the Fifth Amendment interpretation of *Escobedo,* reducing the right to counsel to a mere "protective device" for the Fifth Amendment right to remain silent. Warren's opinion departed from the ACLU brief in only one important respect: whereas the brief had implicitly argued that suspects could not voluntarily waive their right to counsel, the *Miranda* majority concluded that such waivers were possible. Though the state had the heavy burden of proving that the suspect waived his right to an attorney and his right to remain silent, voluntary confessions without an attorney present were still possible.

Does the Court's position make any sense? If police interrogations were as inherently coercive as the majority had said, how could a waiver of the suspect's right to consult an attorney ever be truly voluntary? If the police can prove that a waiver is voluntary, why should they not be permitted to prove that an uncounseled confession was voluntary? Is it possible that the Court could not accept the ACLU's position because it would be a *de facto* prohibition of all custodial interrogations? If the police cannot interrogate a suspect without a lawyer present, does this rule not in effect prohibit all interrogations? Would such a result be politically intolerable? Does the Court's position assume that all suspects informed of their rights will have enough sense not to talk to the police until after they have consulted with a lawyer? But what about the truly naive suspect who waives his right to consult with an attorney and then, without really knowing what is going on, quickly incriminates himself? If the whole point of the *Miranda* warnings is to ensure that suspects ignorant of their constitutional rights should not incriminate themselves in the coercive atmosphere of the police interrogation, why should the Court permit those who most need counsel to waive their right to it? Even if it is politically intolerable, does the ACLU approach make more sense?

It is interesting to speculate why the majority of Supreme Court justices followed the ACLU approach to police confessions. Perhaps one reason is that it avoided the whole problem of precisely identifying when and why the Sixth Amendment right to counsel attached before arraignment. The Fifth Amendment justification for the right to counsel implicitly suggested that the right should attach when the danger of self-incrimination became a significant likelihood. Accordingly, on this interpretation, the Court opted for the Fifth Amendment because it provided a good criterion as to *when* the police had to issue the familiar warnings.

Another possible explanation as to why the Court followed the ACLU approach to police confessions concerns the nature of the required warnings. By itself, the Sixth Amendment account did not seem to offer a good explanation of why the police had a constitutional obligation to inform suspects of their rights. People ignorant of the Constitution may have a constitutional right to counsel, but why did the state have to educate them as to their rights if they became suspects? In contrast, the Fifth Amendment privilege seemed capable of yielding an answer to this question. Given the compulsive atmosphere of custodial police interrogations, ignorant suspects had to be informed of their right to remain silent and their right to a lawyer or else any incriminating remarks would be involuntary.

The third option is that the Supreme Court turned to the Fifth Amendment to justify the *Miranda* ruling because the right to remain silent was a more widely cherished ideal in American legal and political culture than the right to counsel. Who would deny that a defendant had a right to remain silent and that the state had the burden of proving guilt beyond a reasonable doubt? In contrast, a right to a lawyer, especially one supplied by the state, was arguably less well grounded in American public opinion. Hence by deriving the right to an attorney at questioning from the privilege against self-incrimination, the Court exercised its rhetorical skills in a politically valuable way. Of course, given the controversial character of the *Miranda* ruling, the Court's majority needed every rhetorical advantage it could muster.

In your view, which of these accounts best explains why the Supreme Court switched horses in midstream? Why did the Court abandon the Sixth Amendment analysis of the problem of police confessions for the Fifth Amendment approach? Was it an intellectual transformation? Was it necessary to provide a coherent justification for specific warnings required by the decision? Did politics have something to do with it? Was it merely a rhetorical tactic? Which of these factors involve legitimate forms of judicial behavior? Which are appropriate? Which are not?

Three of the four dissenting justices wrote opinions in *Miranda*. Of the three, Justice Tom C. Clark was the least critical. He said that he was "unable to join the majority because its opinion goes too far on too little, while my dissenting brethren do not go quite far enough." The Court should not abandon the traditional approach that judged the voluntariness of a confession by the totality of the circumstances. Instead, one of the circumstances that should be considered is whether the police warned the suspect that he could have counsel present at the interrogation and that one would be appointed if he was indigent. "In the absence of warnings, the burden would be on the State to prove that counsel was knowingly and intelligently waived or that in the totality of the circumstances, including the failure to give the necessary warnings, the confession was clearly voluntary." In short, according to Clark, the defendant had to prove that his confession was involuntary unless the police failed to make the warnings. If no warnings were given, the burden of proof shifted, and the police had to prove that the confession was voluntary. Clark recommended this mid position lest the Court, lacking the necessary empirical knowledge, go "too far too fast."

Justices John M. Harlan II and Byron White issued strong dissents, calling the decision "poor constitutional law," motivated by "a deep-seated distrust of all confessions." Both of the dissents agreed that the main difficulty was not that the Court had extended the Fifth Amendment beyond formal judicial proceedings to informal police interrogations. Even though historically the Fifth Amendment had little to do with police confessions, the extension would have caused no concern if the Court had preserved the traditional due process test of what constituted a voluntary confession. But unfortunately, the Court used the Fifth Amendment extension as an opportunity to shift the criteria from simple voluntariness to "'voluntariness' in a utopian sense, or to view it from a different angle, voluntariness with a vengeance." Confessions that heretofore were properly understood as voluntary were now condemned as involuntary based on a "patently inadequate" factual claim that all police interrogations were inherently coercive. All the talk about the coercive atmosphere of police interrogations merely disguised that the Court was abandoning the traditional test of voluntariness and introducing a new rule excluding all confessions not preceded by *Miranda* warnings. The problem with this result was not just that the Court was making policy but that it was making poor policy that ignored society's interest in "general security." By excluding all non-Mirandized confessions, the Court was depriving the police of a valuable tool of law enforcement. Criminals who would have been convicted on "the most satisfactory evidence" will be released or acquitted at trial because, without confessions, the state will not be able prove guilt beyond a reasonable doubt. Only state legislatures were entitled to initiate a reform of criminal procedure that had such potentially dangerous consequences.

The law enforcement community reacted vehemently against *Miranda*. The decision had outlawed, not some deviant or peripheral aspect of police procedure, but what police took to be an essential tool of their trade: confessions. Since they felt somewhat underappreciated, police compliance with the decision was minimal and grudging. The decision hardly dispelled the "adversarial" or, perhaps better, "inquisitorial" character of police interrogations. Indeed, to many in the law enforcement profession, *Miranda* was "a slap in the face."[23] The Court was saying that the public could not trust the police not to "trick" or "pressure" a defendant into confessing. Is this what *Miranda* meant? Was it really a decision about trust? Can the American people trust the police?

At the time of the decision, the public's reaction to *Miranda* tended to side with the police, though the Supreme Court did have its defenders. President Lyndon B. Johnson's Commission on Law Enforcement and the Administration of Justice published a report, *The Challenge of Crime in a Free Society,* in February 1967, eight months after *Miranda* was decided. The report sanctioned Johnson's view that the best way to fight crime was through a "war on poverty," not by fighting to overturn the Warren Court decisions that had recently extended the rights of criminal defendants and suspects. However, seven members of the commission wrote an addendum to the report that specifically attacked the Supreme Court's recent decisions, especially *Miranda.* They urged Congress that "whatever can be done to right the present imbalance through legislation . . . should have high priority." In regard to confessions, they specifically recommended a return to the principle of voluntariness.[24]

Congress soon thereafter considered ways to rectify the perceived imbalance between the *Miranda* rights of the accused and the needs of the community. Senator John L. McClellan, a Democrat from Arkansas who opposed the Warren Court decisions in the criminal justice field, chaired the subcommittee of the Senate's Judiciary Committee that conducted hearings on crime-related topics from March to July 1967. Four options were under review: a statutory reinstatement of the principle of voluntariness (McClellan's preference), a statute limiting the Court's appellate jurisdiction in criminal cases, a constitutional amendment overturning *Miranda,* or acceptance of the status quo by doing nothing. The hearings were overwhelmingly critical of *Miranda.* Witness after witness, especially those from the law enforcement community, lamented what the Court had done. Newspaper editorials from around the country condemning *Miranda* were collected and inserted in the record (two examples appear in Box 2.3). However, two ACLU attorneys, Vincent L. Broderick and Lawrence Speiser, were given the opportunity to testify. McClellan's conversation with these two defenders of civil lib-

---

[23]Quoted by Baker, *Miranda,* p. 177.
[24]Ibid., pp. 201–204.

BOX 2.3

EDITORIALS ON *MIRANDA*

When the Police are Handcuffed
(*Philadelphia Inquirer*)

Persons accused of committing crimes are entitled to full protection of their Constitutional rights. There should be no question about that. However, when these rights are interpreted in such a way that they are magnified beyond the bounds of reason and common sense, then the inevitable result is a mockery of the law and a shameful degrading of law-enforcement officers.

The public has rights, too. One of those rights is to be protected against criminal activity and to be assured that police are unhindered in carrying out legitimate investigative work to prevent crimes and to apprehend perpetrators of crimes.

There are increasing instances of suspects in criminal cases arrogantly assuming attitudes of defiance when taken into custody and harassing law officers with outrageous demands and insults. . . .

The woes of law-enforcement officers begin long before the defendant gets to jail, if he ever does. In Philadelphia the other day a suspect in a morals case was found hiding in a clothes closet—hardly a place for a law-abiding citizen to be, when the police come calling—but he naturally had no explanations to offer after being informed of his inalienable right to say nothing.

In another arrest, pertaining to investigation of the loan shark racket, police found the suspect well prepared with a handy slip of paper setting forth his rights under the Fifth Amendment—a convenient item to fall back on, until the lawyer gets there.

To give defendants their full rights is one thing. To mollycoddle them, to fawn over them, to deliberately give them the upper hand and to place the police in a subservient position—that is unjustifiable nonsense.

It's time to take the handcuffs off the policeman doing his duty and put them where they belong.

Rhode Island Versus the Supreme Court
(*Chicago Tribune*, June 24, 1967)

The Rhode Island state police have been ordered to disregard the recent "do-gooder" rulings of the Supreme Court in their effort to stem a rising tide of crime. In issuing the order, Col. Walter E. Stone, the superintendent, said that "hoodlums have turned the streets into a jungle." The latest incident was a shooting fray Wednesday in Providence.

"I've ordered my men to grab these guys on sight," Col. Stone said, "and frisk them and make sure they're not armed. This situation requires firm, tough policemen. . . . We're not going to be guided by do-gooder decisions of the last year or two which have been protecting these guys and putting halos around their heads."

He said he had told his men to "forget Miranda and Escobedo," the two Supreme court decisions which have done most to restrict the actions of police. . . .

Col. Stone is obviously taking a risk, but up to a reasonable point it is a risk that needs to be taken. The risk, of course, is that the courts may throw out any charges he brings, thus setting the defendants free again. The reason it needs to be taken is that the existing rulings have hampered police all over the country in gathering evidence. . . .

These rulings will stand until the Supreme Court itself reverses, modifies, or "clarifies" them. The only way this is likely to come about is for a police department to do what Col. Stone has ordered his to do, and for the prosecution and the lower courts to risk rejection or reversal themselves by seeing that the matter is once again appealed to the Supreme Court.

True, there is little immediate hope that the Supreme Court, with its reinforced "liberal" majority, is likely to reverse itself. But . . . the court will probably not ignore public opinion. If crime and disrespect for the rights of the public continue to mount, the popular clamor for change will soon be deafening.

Source: Hearings before the Subcommittee on Criminal Laws and Procedures of the Committee on the Judiciary, United States Senate, 90th Cong., 1st Sess., 1967, pp. 1144–1146, 1191.

erties is quite revealing. It obliquely shows how the issues that sharply divided Americans during the late 1960s—the Vietnam War, the counterculture, the civil rights movement, the crime wave—were entangled with one another, producing sharply different reactions to the Warren Court's criminal justice decisions (see Box 2.4). Therefore, at the time, *Miranda* was quite divisive. It underlined divisions within American society that even today have not been completely overcome.

In the following year, Senator McClellan and his colleagues in Congress, reflecting the growing public concern about crime, enacted the Omnibus Crime Control and Safe Streets Act. Title II of this legislation proclaimed that all voluntary confessions were to be admissible in federal trials. Whether warnings were given and whether the suspect had assistance of counsel were factors to be considered, but the law specifically said that neither was conclusive on the issue of voluntariness. However, because the Justice Department continued to give the warnings required by *Miranda* even after the omnibus crime bill was enacted into law, the Supreme Court never had the opportunity to consider the constitutionality of Title II. The statute's value was therefore largely symbolic. It symbolized the degree to which the American public rejected the balance that the Supreme Court had struck in *Miranda* between individual rights and the interests of the public.

Of course, *Miranda* too is a symbol. But whereas the symbolic value of Title II has long since died out, that of *Miranda* survives to this day. Though there is little agreement about the impact *Miranda* had on confessions and the crime rate, there is little doubt that it has had an important impact on American politics. "Law and order" was an important issue in the elections of 1968. In a position paper issued in May of that year, Richard M. Nixon, who won the presidential election in November, summed up his views on the crime problem by saying that

BOX 2.4

SENATOR McCLELLAN VERSUS THE ACLU

❋   ❋   ❋

SENATOR McCLELLAN:
The American Civil Liberties Union, are they interested in people keeping their obligations of citizenship?

MR. BRODERICK:
It certainly is.

McCLELLAN:
You never place any emphasis on it; you always place the emphasis on rights, and nobody says what I ought to do to help my country. That is the thing that has gotten us off on the wrong track in this country. It used to be patriotic for those who thought there was a central obligation to preserve their country and to sacrifice for it. And today, all we hear is: "Rights. Rights. Rights." And never an obligation.

MR. SPEISER:
They are not mutually exclusive. The protection of rights of citizens is a way of protecting our country. They are not inconsistent.

McCLELLAN:
That is not the only thing.

SPEISER:
That is quite true.

McCLELLAN:
We put all the emphasis on that today. You see the beatniks going around, and all these bozos, saying "I am a human being." That is all they can boast of, "I am a human being." Nothing that they ever did, nothing they ever contributed, no ambition or anything; nothing to sustain or support a wholesome society. All they say is "I am a human being." I tell you, unless we decide in America that we are going to fight this war on crime, we are sunk. I say that to you.

I know you are good citizens; I know we have honest differences of opinion, but I feel it very deeply. . . .

BRODERICK:
In my judgment, we will do ourselves a still greater disservice if we emphasize law and order to the exclusion of other considerations such as individual liberties. It would be relatively simple——

McCLELLAN:
You put that ahead of law and order, and you say you could not have civil liberties without law and order.

BRODERICK:

I say that . . . it will be relatively easy to establish an atmosphere of law and order in the United States.

It was easy to do it in Nazi Germany; it was easy to do in Communist Russia. We have a problem, because in establishing and maintaining an atmosphere of law and social order, we also have a tradition of respecting individual rights and individual liberties. One of the previous speakers said there was no incompatibility between law and social order on the one hand, and civil liberties and individual rights on the other hand. I go further than that. Without law and social order and without the effect of law enforcement to maintain the climate of law and social order, there will be no such thing as individual liberties, because the liberty of the strong will be a license that runs over the liberties of everyone else. . . .

❖   ❖   ❖

SENATOR MCCLELLAN:

Let us get back to my question: On the issue, on the direct issue, raised by the action of the Supreme Court in the *Miranda* case, I assume . . . you would favor doing nothing?

MR. SPEISER:

You are right, Mr. Chairman, and the reason for that choice is that we do not feel that the confession problem has any effect or much effect, if any, on the question of crime in the United States. . . .

MCCLELLAN:

But the point is, the point that I am making is: If harm is going to come to this country by reason of the law of the land as now decreed by the Supreme Court, I think every citizen who loves his country and wants to preserve liberty would want to try to do something about it. We may have different ideas about what we want to do; we may have different ideas as to the consequences of these decisions. Those of us who have an abiding conviction that they have done great harm and will obstruct and hinder and hamper law enforcement and diminish law and order, think we should try to do something about it.

You are satisfied with it, with the status quo . . . and see no evil consequences of it. You have a perfect right to say: "Let us do nothing; this is all right; let us live with it." That is what you are talking about when you talk about the democratic processes. I believe in democracy. You have the perfect right to disagree with me, and I have the right to disagree with you. I happen to be in a position where I can vote on an issue here. It is a vote you cannot control, but you have representatives here and the people have different viewpoints and the people are represented, and we, the Congress, can by inaction make a serious mistake if this condition needs remedying, and we ignore it.

Speiser:
I think this is a thoroughly useful debate, and I think that it is one of the good things in our democracy that we are here debating this kind of problem. . . .

McClellan:
You heard what I said this morning. I think time is beginning to run out on this crime situation. I may be wrong. I hope I am.

Speiser:
The difficulty with that, Mr. Chairman, is that we have countervailing interests, countervailing values, in our society. . . .

Source: Hearings before the Subcommittee on Criminal Laws and Procedures of the Committee on the Judiciary, United States Senate, 90th Cong., 1st Sess., 1967, pp. 1167–1168, 1173, 1174–1175.

Miranda was "hamstringing the peace forces in our society and strengthening the criminal forces."[25] Clearly, appearing in such a political context, the case had become a symbol of all of the protections that the Warren Court had recently granted to criminal defendants. Over the years, *Miranda* has not completely lost this symbolic character. The warnings have become a part of popular culture, appearing in movies, TV shows, novels, and magazine articles. It is therefore the perfect case to consider the way in which the Supreme Court has balanced the individual rights of criminal suspects and defendants against the needs of the community. Does *Miranda* prove that the Supreme Court coddles criminals, or does it show the Court functioning at its best, protecting the rights of alleged criminals from the abusive and coercive tactics of the police?

BIBLIOGRAPHY

Baker, Liva. *Miranda: Crime, Law, and Politics.* New York: Atheneum, 1983.

Berger, Mark. *Taking the Fifth.* Lexington, Mass.: Lexington Books, 1980.

Kamisar, Yale. *Police Interrogation and Confessions.* Ann Arbor: University of Michigan Press, 1980.

Levy, Leonard W. *Origins of the Fifth Amendment.* New York: Oxford University Press, 1968.

Packer, Herbert L. *The Limits of the Criminal Sanction.* Stanford, Calif.: Stanford University Press, 1968.

---

[25]Ibid., p. 211.

B R I E F S

Miranda's Brief

[1. Right to Counsel.] . . . When Miranda walked out of Interrogation Room 2 on March 13, 1963, his life for all practical purposes was over. Whatever happened later was inevitable; the die had been cast in that room at that time. There was no duress, no brutality. Yet when Miranda finished his conversation with Officers Cooley and Young, only the ceremonies of the law remained; in any realistic sense, his case was done. We have here the clearest possible example of Justice Douglas' observation, "What takes place in the secret confines of the police station may be more critical than what takes place at the trial."

The question presented is whether a defendant in such circumstances is entitled to be told of his right to counsel and to have a meaningful opportunity to consult counsel before the law disposes of him. For "what use is a defendant's right to effective counsel at every stage of a criminal case if, while he is held awaiting trial, he can be questioned in the absence of counsel until he confesses?"

We deal here with growing law, and look to where we are going by considering where we have been. . . .

While English statutes did not provide for counsel in felony cases before 1836, in practice counsel did participate in English criminal trials before the American Revolution. This is of consequence in understanding early American constitutional and statutory provisions of substantially the same vintage as the Bill of Rights. Many of these expressly or in practice asserted a right to counsel . . . and some of them even at that early time required that appointed counsel be made available. . . . Speaking broadly, therefore, the Sixth Amendment was in general accord with the English and American practice of its time: "In all criminal prosecutions, the accused shall enjoy the right . . . to have the assistance of counsel for his defense."

Sixth Amendment problems came to the Court surprisingly late, both as to federal and state procedure.

The leading case is *Johnson v. Zerbst.* In that case, petitioner, without counsel, had been convicted of counterfeiting. There was a conflict as to whether or not he had asked for counsel. The decision decisively established as an "obvious truth that the average defendant does not have the professional legal skill to protect himself when brought before a tribunal with power to take his life or liberty. . . . " The opinion, quoting from *Powell v. Alabama,* repeats that a defendant "'requires the guiding hand of counsel at every step in the proceedings against him.'" Hence in *Johnson v. Zerbst,* the Court declared that "the Sixth Amendment withholds from Federal Court, in all criminal proceedings, the power and authority to deprive an accused of his life and liberty unless he has or waives the assistance of counsel.". . .

The development of a constitutional doctrine as applied to state proceedings can be grouped around three key decisions, *Powell v. Alabama; Betts v. Brady;* and *Gideon v. Wainwright.*

Powell is too familiar to warrant restatement. In this famous rape case, counsel was appointed but exercised only a nominal function, permitting defendants to be hustled to trial. The function of counsel was described as "pro forma." The Court held that:

> defendants were not accorded the right of counsel in any substantial sense. To decide otherwise would simply be to ignore actualities. . . . The prompt disposition of criminal cases is to be commended and encouraged. But in reaching that result the defendant, charged with a serious crime, must not be stripped of his right to have sufficient time to advise with counsel and prepare his defense.

This Court in *Powell* recognized that the right to counsel was a growing, not a static, constitutional right. It refused to be guided by the standards of England at the time the Constitution was adopted, following instead the more liberal practice of the various colonies. The right to counsel was held to be one of those "'fundamental principles of liberty and justice which lie at the base of all our civil and political institutions.'". . . This, said the Court, was true for men of intelligence and even more true for "the ignorant and illiterate, or those of feeble intellect." The trial court therefore must first give the defendant the right to employ counsel, and second, if need be, must appoint counsel. The Court made no decision as to non-capital cases, but as to capital cases it held that:

> where the defendant was unable to employ counsel, and is incapable adequately of making his own defense because of ignorance, feeble-mindedness, illiteracy, or the like, it is the duty of the court, whether requested or not, to assign counsel for him as a necessary requisite of due process of law; and that duty is not discharged by an assignment at such a time or under such circumstances as to preclude the giving of effective aid in the preparation and trial of the case. . . .

Immediately after *Powell*, the right to counsel cases began to relate directly to the forced confession cases. . . . Thus in *Brown v. Mississippi*, the leading confession by torture case, the Court mentioned *Powell* as illustrative of the principles of basic justice, observing that "the state may not deny to the accused the aid of counsel." In *Brown*, trial counsel failed to make proper objections to confessions obtained by violent beating. In *Chambers v. Florida*, a long additional step was taken. In *Brown*, it was indisputable that physical violence had been applied to the defendants. In *Chambers* there was a factual dispute as to whether or not there had been physical compulsion. This Court nonetheless held that the protracted questioning, in all of the circumstances, banned the confession under the Fourteenth Amendment, noting that the defendants had been held and interrogated "without friends, advisers, or counselors.". . .

Betts, like *Powell*, is too familiar to need restatement. The case held, in its chief conclusions, that while counsel was required in capital cases and in some undefined other cases, it was not required in all cases. . . .

During the reign of *Betts*, the confession cases turned on "special circumstances.". . . This same specialized notion of the circumstances applied also to the right to counsel as it related to the interrogation. An example is *Haley v. Ohio*. In this case a fifteen year old boy was interrogated for five hours before he confessed to murder. The judgment of the Court reversing the conviction was announced by Justice Douglas, and joining with him in an opinion were Justices Black, Murphy and Rutledge. This opinion particularly stressed that "at no time was this boy advised of his right to counsel.". . .

It was asserted that the petitioner had signed a confession, and that the signed confession asserted that he knew fully of his rights. Said these four Justices: "That assumes, however, that a boy of fifteen, without aid of counsel, would have a full appreciation of that advice and that on the facts of this record he had a freedom of choice. We cannot indulge those assumptions." The four Justices made [it] clear that they were not announcing a principle simply for boys in custody, but one which applied equally to any defendant: "The Fourteenth Amendment prohibits the police from using the private, secret custody of either man or child as a device for wringing confessions from them.". . .

In overruling *Betts,* Justice Black for the Court closed the circle by applying the principle of his own 1938 opinion of *Johnson v. Zerbst* to state proceedings. This Court in *Gideon* thus erased the fundamental distinction between the state and federal cases by holding that the Sixth Amendment guarantee of counsel was of such character that it applied to the states in full. The Court . . . declared that "The right of one charged with crime to counsel may not be deemed fundamental and essential to fair trials in some countries, but it is in ours." Justice Douglas, concurring, noted that this did not mean that some kind of a watered-down version of the Sixth Amendment was made applicable to the states—its totality applied to both.

It follows that so far as the Sixth Amendment is concerned, after March 18, 1963, there is no difference between the right to counsel as provided in that Amendment in the two court systems. *Gideon* was followed shortly by *Haynes v. Washington,* holding that the failure to tell a defendant under interrogation that he is entitled to be represented by counsel is one of the factors relevant to determining whether his confession was voluntary. . . .

The issue is whether, under the Sixth Amendment to the Federal Constitution as made applicable to the states by the Fourteenth, there is the same right to counsel at interrogation of an arrested suspect as there is at arraignment or at trial.

The right does exist. It is the same. This is not the result of a single case, *Escobedo* or any other. Rather, there is a tide in the affairs of men, and it is this engulfing tide which is washing away the secret interrogation of the unprotected accused. . . . Once the Sixth Amendment is clearly applicable to the states, then the constitutional standards are the same. *Escobedo,* although all that was involved there was a fact situation in which a request [for counsel] had been made and denied, necessarily transcends its facts because it recognizes the interrogation as one of the sequence of proceedings covered by the Sixth Amendment. . . .

We have in this galaxy of cases not a series of isolated phenomena, but reflections of basic belief. . . . [T]he "principle is that any accused—whether rich or poor—has the right to consult a lawyer before talking with the police."

This case is not to be decided by the color-matching technique of determining whether one case looks just like another case. We deal with fundamentals of liberty, and so, in consequence, with basic belief. The suggestion that the defendant must ask for counsel is to make a great matter depend upon a formal distinction. . . .

[2. Practical Concerns.] With so many members of this Court concerned with the constitutional rule from the practical standpoint of law enforcement, that matter requires independent consideration. The principal practical concerns are two: first, that the system established will be expensive; and second, that it will prevent the detection and punishment of the guilty. At a time when American society is deeply and justly concerned both with rising crime rates and with the menacing existence of organized crime, these are genuinely serious problems.

We begin by observing that the principles here advocated will have exactly zero effect on organized crime. This case involves an important constitutional principle, but it must not be made more important than it is. This case is not a grand caucus on whether sin or virtue should be the order of the day; we are dealing with the precise problem of whether a person charged with crime is to be made effectively aware of his right to counsel at the interrogation stage, and whether he is to be supplied counsel if he needs it at that point. None of this has any application to organized crime at all. The criminal gangs know perfectly well what tools, both physical and legal, they may use in their battle with society. The confession and right to counsel cases which have been before this Court so constantly since *Powell v. Alabama* have almost never involved gang-type criminals. The crimes from *Powell* (rape) to *Miranda* (rape) have almost always been rapes and murders, involving defendants poor, poorly educated, and very frequently, as here, of very limited mental abilities. The rich, the wellborn, and the able are adequately protected under existing constitutional standards, and the sophisticates of crime do not need this protection. We are talking here about precisely what was involved in *Chambers v. Florida* twenty-five years ago, the "helpless, weak, outnumbered."

Public defender systems cost money. Many defendants are indigents, and extending the right to counsel into the interrogation stage will increase personnel, paperwork, costs of all kinds. It will make some kind of public defender system virtually obligatory. But the cost increase will by no means be limited to defense costs. As Mr. J. Edgar Hoover observed in 1952, full use of proper scientific methods should make it unnecessary for officers to use dishonorable methods of detection; this inescapably means increased prosecution costs. A laboratory costs more than a strap, and so does the training of those who wield a microscope rather than a whip.

There are undoubtedly cheaper methods of law enforcement than those contemplated by the American Constitution. While some critics have contested the right to counsel in cost terms, no member of this Court has ever attempted to put a price tag on constitutional rights. Pepper in the eyes is cheaper than a fair trial and respect for constitutional rights in law enforcement will inescapably cost money.

Let it.

Some members of this Court have had severe doubts about the effect of the application of these principles in the operation of the criminal law, and some outside criticisms have been uninhibited. Professor Inbau regards *Escobedo* as "the hardest body blow the Court has struck yet against enforcement of law in this nation." More temperate criticism of *Escobedo* develops the view that it "creates unnecessary and undesirable impediments to police investigation.". . .

There are other conflicting views. The New York City Police Commissioner in September of 1965 estimated that confessions were essential to conviction in 50 per cent of the homicides committed in New York in 1964 and, on the other hand, State Supreme Court Justice Nathan R. Sobel describes the view that confessions are the backbone of law enforcement as "carelessly nurtured nonsense." New York District Attorney Frank S. Hogan says that the police are heavily dependent on confessions to get convictions in many cases and that "the whole purpose of a police investigation is frustrated if a suspect is entitled to have a lawyer during preliminary questioning, for any lawyer worth his fee will tell him to keep his mouth shut." On the other hand, Brooklyn District Attorney Aaron E. Koota believes that a person should have a lawyer "at the moment he comes into contact with the law." While some law enforcement officials claim that 75 to 85 per cent of all convictions are based on confessions, Judge Sobel's study, based on 1,000 Brooklyn indictments from February to April, 1965, showed that fewer than 10 per cent involved confessions. . . .

As a practical matter, we cannot know with assurance whether the amplification of the right to counsel in the interrogation period will severely handicap the police; we end by trading opinions. . . . But assuming that there may be some unpredictable decline in the efficiency of the conviction machinery, there are some distinctly practical pluses to be balanced against this. As Justice Douglas said in *United States v. Carignan*, when a person is detained without arraignment,

> the accused is under the exclusive control of the police, subject to their mercy, and beyond the reach of counsel or of friends. What happens behind doors that are opened and closed at the sole discretion of the police is a black chapter in every country—the free as well as the despotic, the modern as well as the ancient.

We are not talking with some learned historicity about the *lettre de cachet* of pre-Revolutionary France or the secret prisons of a distant Russia. We are talking about conditions in the United States, in the Twentieth Century, and now.

Moreover, some of the cost and efficiency comes from giving American citizens exactly what they are entitled to under the Constitution. It is, after all, the man's privilege to be silent, and it does smack of denial of equal protection to say that this is a right only for those well educated enough to know about it. But one need not reach to constitutional principle; there are, practically, equally important workaday considerations. . . .

The day is here to recognize the full meaning of the Sixth Amendment. As a matter of constitutional theory and of criminal procedure, if a defendant cannot waive counsel unwittingly in one part of the conviction procedure, he should not be able to waive it at another. As a matter of practicality in law enforcement, we cannot know the precise effects of giving counsel at the beginning as the law does at the end; but we can know that there is not the faintest sense in deliberately establishing an elaborate and costly system of counsel—to take effect just after it is too late to matter. Yet that is precisely the *Miranda* case.

We invoke the basic principles of *Powell v. Alabama:* "He requires the guiding hand of counsel at every step in the proceedings against him." When Miranda stepped into Interrogation Room 2, he had only the guiding hand of Officers Cooley and Young.

We respectfully submit that the decision of the court below should be reversed.

Respectfully submitted,
JOHN P. FRANK
JOHN J. FLYNN

ARIZONA'S BRIEF

[1. Miranda Treated Fairly.] . . . Petitioner states that his life for all practical purposes was over when he walked out of Interrogation Room #2 on March 13, 1963. The real fact is that Miranda's life was unalterably destined ten days earlier during the late evening hours of March 2 and the early morning hours of March 3, when he kidnapped and raped his victim, Patricia Wier. What followed must not be described in cynical terms as "the ceremonies of the law"; they were, and are, the carefully ordained processes of our judicial system, designed, at the optimum, to discover the truth, mete out justice to all, insure the guilty their just and proper recompense and vindicate the innocent. To be sure, thoroughly interwoven into these processes at all stages and levels is the implementation and zealous protection of those cherished rights and privileges guaranteed to all by the Constitutions of the United States and the several states; no police officer, prosecutor or judge dedicated to the basic precepts of our system of government advocates that it should be any different.

Unfortunately, or perhaps fortunately, so long as human beings rather than computers administer the processes of justice, mistakes and error will occur and injustices will be done. The courts of our land, including this Court with its highest and most final jurisdiction, are daily exposing and correcting these mistakes to the best of their ability. The question here before the Court is whether there was such a mistake or error in this case of a dimension to result in the denial of petitioner's right to counsel as set down in the Constitution of the United States, and as proclaimed by this Court in its decisions thereunder.

The very description of the petitioner . . . subtly introduces a factual issue into this case which is of the gravest importance in resolving the ultimate legal question.

The words so carefully used were "poorly educated, mentally abnormal." No doubt other descriptive words and phrases could have been added—poor, motherless, unloved, downtrodden, culturally deprived, misguided, unguided, harassed, *ad infinitum.*

It is practically impossible to pick up a national magazine [or] professional journal, or listen to an address without some dramatic usage of these descriptive adjectives to characterize some greater or lesser portion of the American population. And in the proper perspective, such attention, whether it be by this Court, the Congress, the executive, or state and local governments, is long overdue and, hopefully, will do something about the root-source of our most perplexing problems—not the least of which is the rising crime rate.

However, to use these heart-rending descriptions in an attempt to justify or excuse the knowing and deliberate violation of our criminal statutes and the imposition of violence and suffering and depravation upon some individuals of our society by others is misleading to say the least. Of this ilk, Miranda is a clear example.

Perhaps an eighth grade education, under a literal definition of the term and in the context of our affluent society, is a "poor education." Under no stretch of the imagination, however, can Miranda be deemed to be uneducated or illiterate. In addition to his formal schooling, petitioner had considerable and varied experiences which broadened his knowledge, particularly in the area which is of primary importance to us now. . . .

Miranda is also labeled as "mentally abnormal." The basis for this is the psychiatric report. While Miranda had an "emotional illness," it is questionable that this even made him "abnormal." Clearly the diagnosis of the psychiatrist was to the effect that the illness was not disabling and that Miranda was able to understand the predicament he was in and knew the conduct society demanded of him at the time he chose to ignore those demands.

Admittedly there is no possible element of police brutality or coercion in this case, whether direct or subtle. Yet petitioner, nevertheless, paints a picture of police disregard for rights guaranteed by our Constitution. The picture is inaccurate—but proving it so is almost a practical impossibility.

The articles, the studies, and the cases, dealing, as they almost unanimously do, with the negative aspect of the problem, make it difficult to see the rule because of the emphasis on the exception. It is true that all police officers are not interested in protecting the rights of the accused; it is true that there are convictions obtained by use of trumped-up evidence and wrongfully elicited incriminating statements and confessions; but these are the very few exceptions to the general rule. For every case of police insensitivity to individual rights, there are literally thousands of unreported incidents of the unstinting efforts of police and prosecutors which result in the extrication of an otherwise helpless and innocent victim, hopelessly intertwined in a web of circumstantial evidence of guilt. . . .

This Court, together with all the courts of our land, should and will continue to firmly and courageously deal with the exceptions to this rule. We must be careful, however, not to foreclose, limit or unduly hamper investigative techniques which, in their legitimate use, are not barred by any Constitutional mandate, solely because a few use the techniques to effect an unconstitutional result. The promulgation of such a rule of constitutional dimension in any given case would be as necessary as "Dr." Jerry Colonna's recently suggested solution to Bob Hope's medical problem of a sore and infected big toe—to cut off Hope's head to relieve the excess weight on the toe. While it goes without saying that the problem of the big toe would most certainly be forever solved, it is questionable whether the patient would be at all happy with the ancillary side effects of the treatment. . . .

[2. Criminal Justice Not a Game.] Petitioner, it seems, would have us interpret our adversary system of criminal justice as giving the accused a right to "win" the contest. While it may be inherent in the very nature of our system, with its vital and essential safeguards to individual freedom, that a person who actually commits a criminal act may have extra opportunities to escape punishment for his crime, it must be clear without comment or citation that the intent of the

Constitutional safeguards were to insure, as much as humanly possible, that the innocent and unpopular would not be wrongfully harassed, intimidated or convicted—not that the guilty should have any special chances for acquittal or other favorable result.

If the prosecuting authorities have gained an overwhelming advantage over a particular defendant, assuming they have done so by proper methods, and not by violating any of his constitutional rights, this is to be highly commended, not condemned. It is a vital attribute of our society that the law enforcement machinery apprehend, convict and punish and/or rehabilitate those who would break the laws and endanger, if not destroy, our domestic tranquility. Law enforcement is not a game of chance. There is no "gamesmanship" or "sportsmanship" involved here, at least insofar as the criminal is concerned. He follows no code of conduct or canons of ethics. The death, suffering and deprivation caused by crime [are] as real to those who are touched by its sting as [are the horrors] of any war ever fought. Certainly the criminal gives no quarter; and none should be given in return except as is required to insure the integrity and continuation of the system which we all cherish.

Criminals, like the rest of us, are inherently unequal. Some are skilled, some not; some intelligent, some not; some trained, some not; some blabber-mouths, some not; some strong, some not; some cruel, some not, etc. It certainly would not be urged that if a criminal is foolish enough to leave physical clues, the police should not be allowed to use them because X, who committed the same crime, was more careful. Or if Y was callous enough, or "intelligent" enough, to kill his rape victim to prevent identification, certainly Z, who also raped, should not be given the same opportunity to kill so as to have an equal chance at the trial to "win." So, too, there are differences between what happened to Ernesto A. Miranda as contrasted with what happened to Danny Escobedo which militate in favor of a different resolution of their problem by this Court.

[3. The *Escobedo* Decision.] The decision in this case must rest upon the scope and effect to be attributed to this Court's [*Escobedo*] decision concerning right to counsel at the interrogation stage. . . .

Petitioner prefers to dwell on the implicit in *Escobedo*. The explicit facts of the case are considered by respondent to be highly relevant and very crucial to the indicated result in *Miranda*.

Danny Escobedo had retained counsel and repeatedly requested to consult with him. The requests were all denied. Escobedo was even told at one time that his lawyer didn't want to see him. On the contrary, Escobedo's lawyer was trying desperately to see his client, and was thwarted at every turn by the police, in spite of a specific Illinois statute requiring the police to admit the lawyer. Escobedo had no record of previous experience with the police. He was interrogated not only by police officers, but by a skilled and experienced lawyer. Escobedo was told that another suspect had pointed the finger at him as the guilty one. At no time was he ever advised of his constitutional rights by either the police or the prosecutor.

Ernesto A. Miranda was not represented by counsel at the time of the questioning here involved. He had not requested that counsel be provided, or that he be given an opportunity to consult with counsel prior to talking to the police. The officers did not deny him an opportunity to consult with counsel, nor did they in any way use chicanery in their questioning of Miranda. Petitioner had had considerable and varied experience with the police on previous occasions. Petitioner was advised of his constitutional rights, specifically including his right to remain silent, the fact that his statement had to be voluntary, and that anything he did say could be used against him.

In setting forth the holding of the case, this Court very carefully enumerated the factors which resulted in the denial of counsel to *Escobedo:*

> We hold, therefore, that where, as here, the investigation is no longer a general inquiry into an unsolved crime but has begun to focus on a particular suspect, the suspect has been taken into police custody, the police carry out a process of interrogations that lends itself to eliciting incriminating statements, the suspect has requested and been denied counsel, and the police have not effectively warned him of his absolute constitutional right to remain silent, the accused has been denied "the assistance of counsel" in violation of the Sixth Amendment to the Constitution as "made obligatory upon the states by the Fourteenth Amendment," and that no statement elicited by the police during the interrogation may be used against him at a criminal trial.

Of the five specific elements, which might be set forth as: (1) Accusatory Stage; (2) Police Custody; (3) Interrogation to elicit incriminating statements; (4) Request and Denial of an opportunity to consult counsel; and (5) Effective Warning of his absolute right to remain silent, petitioner contends that only (4) is absent here and that its absence is not crucial. . . .

. . . [To] discount item (4) concerning the request is to completely ignore not only the plain wording of the opinion in *Escobedo,* but to completely disregard the factual and legal bases for the opinions cited in petitioner's historical analysis as demanding the ultimate ruling sought herein. . . .

The decision in *Escobedo* announces an exclusionary rule directed against the affirmative conduct of police and prosecutors calculated to deny to an accused his right to counsel. Any incriminating statements received thereafter, regardless of the fact that they are clearly the product of the free and uncoerced will of the accused, are inadmissible. . . .

A contrary application would result in attempting to make police officers part-time defense counsel and part-time magistrates, or deprive them completely of an investigative technique which, in its proper use and application, is as [valuable] as any modern, scientific tool for the detection and prevention of crime. . . .

If the rule sought by petitioner is forthcoming, we can only re-echo the ominous warnings and misgivings of the dissenters in *Massiah* and *Escobedo.* Miranda and Escobedo are not equal and there is no Constitutional reason for this Court to equate them in the manner sought by petitioner, any more than there would be for this Court to balance their skill in committing and concealing their crime. No amount of scientific advancements in crime detection will produce evidence which a clever criminal has not been foolish enough to provide for discovery. If a criminal has been clever in the commission of his crime, but is foolish or careless in his handling of the police interrogation of him concerning that crime, the evidence obtained as a result of the only honest investigative avenue left open to the law enforcement agency should not be suppressed unless that evidence is determined not to be the product of the free and uncoerced will of the accused, or if it is obtained after the police have undertaken a course of conduct calculated to deny the accused his right to counsel. Certainly nothing less will be tolerated, but the United States Constitution requires no more.

Respectfully submitted,
DARREl F. SMITH,
Attorney General of Arizona.

NATIONAL DISTRICT ATTORNEYS ASSOCIATION'S *AMICUS* BRIEF

[1. Detrimental Effects of Required Warnings.] . . . Will warning an individual of his right to remain silent and of his right to counsel preclude the needed confession? Frankly, no one knows and an empirical study is not possible. But, if the admonishment is without this effect, then, either it is being administered improperly or there is simply no reason for such a rule existing.

By assuming the posture of one accused (acknowledging the obvious limitations of this premise), namely his concern with discovery of the misdeed (if not other misdeeds) and his natural instinct for preserving freedom and life, it is possible to derive a valid answer. . . . Subjectively we know that misdeeds are not readily admitted. Some of the effects of a required admonishment include [the following]:

1. Problems in the use of acceptable interrogation techniques already exist and to overcome the admonishment adds to that burden.

2. Every confession will be tainted with the issue of waiver of counsel.

3. The question then becomes: is waiver possible? If, in reply to an admonishment, the accused asks, "Should I get a lawyer? Why do I need a lawyer? What will a lawyer do for me? etc." Having reached this impasse, must the interrogator simply advise the accused to retain counsel and thereafter stop his attempt to learn the truth, or, is it permissible for him now to proceed to convince the accused that he does not need an attorney? Can an accused ever effectively waive his right to counsel once he has mentioned, in response to a warning, that maybe he should have one? Thus, another issue to plague the courts is created.

4. Admittedly, in the pretrial investigatory period which includes time for interrogation, the defendant is at a disadvantage. But in our system of justice this imbalance is adjusted by the rights of the defendant at trial: (a) that he need not be witness against himself; (b) that he is entitled to a unanimous verdict of his peers; (c) that he cannot be again brought to answer, once acquitted; (d) that he must be found guilty beyond a reasonable doubt. Furthermore, there is no right in the state to appeal and there is no discovery procedure to obtain from the defendant himself the names of witnesses, etc. No one would suggest that these trial protections be altered, but if the pretrial investigation, which must involve interrogation of suspects and witnesses (both of whom could or could not be culprits in the crime), is eliminated, then our system of justice must fail but for a concomi-

tant revision in our form of trial. If the foundation of our system of justice is rocked, something must give way; the consequences may not be what this Court, any lawyer, or any citizen would want.

5. The "fear" of admonishment is that it will benefit only the recidivist and the professional. The first offender and the Culombes, Fikeses, Haleys, Paynes or Recks will not be the beneficiaries. The innocent will take offense to the caution.

6. Many of the restrictions upon law enforcement, albeit for the good of the individual, must of necessity greatly burden these men who are charged with the protection of the public. That the police officer is the subject of distrust is evidenced by (a) the detailed information required in affidavits to obtain warrants, (b) the required corroboration of informer information, and (c) the trend to accept the suspect's word over that of the police officer. And so, by establishing unworkable requirements do we not further undermine and demoralize the police officer, forcing him to "stretch the truth"?. . .

7. Exculpatory statements also will not be easy to obtain, thereby inviting defendants to change their minds and perjure themselves on the stand.

8. Will impossibility of performance force not only the police to uncover loopholes but the prosecutor and the trial courts as well to pursue this path—objective looking to one side? Trial judges, both state and federal, as well as most appellate courts, in their sympathy with the law enforcement officers' plight, are inclined to encourage law enforcement officers to "avoid" the stringent requirements of the rules. . . .

[2. Importance of Confessions.] The fact that confessions are used extensively . . . may not necessarily demonstrate justification for their presence. . . . [A]n outline of a few of the reasons, without great detail as to "why" or "reason" for the "why," may be of assistance to the Court:

1. Basically, crimes are covert by nature, and, zealous assertions to the contrary, many crimes are impossible to solve without a confession.

2. Confessions are the prime source of other evidence. Even if it is possible to solve crimes in the "scientific police laboratory" (a misconception often perpetuated by the police themselves), the evidence that is analyzed often must come from admissions: the existence of the gun and the location thereof, the location of an automobile (e.g., in an assault), etc. The doctrine of the fruit of the poisonous tree will make an inadmissible confession of even greater consequence.

3. Critics claim the urgent need is for more and better police officers. Reality dictates that although there be the need, there never will be sufficient police officers to prevent incipient crime and to investigate the millions of crimes committed in the United States. The selection of crimes to be investigated merely will be reduced. Assuming the existence of the required unlimited financing, nevertheless there are not enough FBI-caliber men, with college, law school or other advanced training, available or attainable for the cop's beat. Even on that dark hypothesis, which has some remedy by way of actual training, a "college degree per se does not a good police officer make."

4. There is a direct corollary between pleas of guilty and confessions. . . . This is even more obvious when a distinction is made of the term "confessions": by

eliminating therefrom the "exculpatory statement." It has been said that if all defendants pleaded not guilty and demanded trial by jury, justice in the United States would come to an abrupt halt. Can there be any doubt that an increased call upon court and prosecution personnel and facilities, already overtaxed, would adversely affect the administration of justice in the United States? Although all of us advocate justice, whatever the pecuniary cost, idealism must give way to the reality of an overburdening demand that cannot be (or will not be) absorbed by the economy.

If cases are to be disposed of, heavy reliance will be given to bargaining. Is it the purpose of our system of law to encourage perjury upon the part of the defendant? Is it to allow the natural desire of self-preservation to be expressed by refusal to plead guilty because the confession is determined inadmissible and thus guilt cannot be proved beyond a reasonable doubt? Does such an inducement discourage rehabilitation? Is the purpose of our administration of criminal laws to limit convictions of the guilty?

5. Typically, Borchard and the Frank studies are cited as authority for the proposition that innocent persons are convicted. To say that innocent persons are not convicted is to defy reality.

While every innocent person convicted is a haunting reminder, unfortunately human beings are involved so that no matter what the rule such tragedies will occur. However, the dates of those cases, the number thereof and the infrequent correlation between confession and the wrongful conviction must be taken into consideration. In 29 of the 65 cases reported by Borchard, the innocent person was convicted by eyewitness testimony, all the others being laid to causes other than confessions except in two "notable" instances. In virtually all of the very few cases involving any form of statement, it is unlikely that a . . . warning would have been of assistance because of the mental deficiency of the defendant. There may well be in the converse more innocent persons convicted because of lack of a confession.

6. Juries are reluctant to convict one who has admitted no wrongdoing. A direct correlation between trial and conviction is evident. . . . [A] plea of not guilty, lacking an admissible confession, often is subject to being dismissed at the discretion of the prosecuting attorney as difficult or impossible to convict. . . .

Respectfully submitted,
DUANE R. NEDRUD,
Executive Director, National District Attorneys Association.

NEW YORK'S *AMICUS* BRIEF

. . . [S]ome of the constitutional issues presented by these petitioners appear to be [the following]:

(a) At what point after the initial contact between a police officer and an individual in which the individual's knowledge of or connection with an actual or suspected crime is discussed does the individual have a constitutional right to the assistance of counsel?

(b) When the right described in (a) arises does the individual have a simultaneous or subsequent constitutional right to be effectively informed of a right to counsel?

(c) When the rights described in (a) and (b) have arisen and if the individual is unable, for financial or other reasons, to obtain counsel for himself, are the arresting authorities, either then or subsequently, constitutionally obligated to provide him with counsel?

(d) Are statements made by an individual, at a time when his rights under (a), (b) or (c) have been violated, constitutionally inadmissible?. . .

[1. Need for Empirical Knowledge.] In approaching these issues the State of New York and the other *amici curiae* wish to emphasize their strong support for measures effectively designed to reduce the legal disadvantages which commonly afflict the poor and unsophisticated. There is deep and widespread need for better public education in the structure and detail of individual rights and for the provision of counsel for the indigent.

The question remains how far and in what ways the law in general and Federal Constitutional Law in particular can best contribute to those ends, in the setting of a society in which other values, including the speedy apprehension of criminals and safety of the citizenry, also have an important place. . . .

. . . [T]he Court cannot resolve these issues by seeking the original intention of those who framed the Bill of Rights or by verbal exegesis of the "Assistance of Counsel" clause, and must therefore find the primary material for decision in its appreciation of contemporary standards and circumstances. . . .

. . . Since the Court is not here bound by history or verbal logic, the constitutional standard may be applied with great flexibility, giving full weight to the bearing of contemporary empirical evidence of the need for and probable effect of the changes here sought.

These changes are not uniformly outlined, but in all these cases the defendants seek the establishment of a rule, to become effective at some point during pre-arraignment interrogation, at which the arrestee must either waive, obtain, or be provided with counsel, on pain of exclusion from evidence of any statement made in the absence of counsel.

Under any of these proposals, it seems clear that the consequences would be:

(a) great reduction or virtual elimination of pre-arraignment interrogation of arrestees; or

(b) provision of counsel on a vast scale for arrestees, most of whom are indigent; or

(c) both (a) and (b) in varying degrees and unpredictable ratios.

We do not suggest that the statement of these consequences establishes them as undesirable. But we do suggest that they are of such a nature that further empirical investigation and analysis are necessary as a basis for general rule-making whether judicial or legislative. . . .

Since in these cases, therefore, empirical evidence of the consequences of the proposed rules based on experience from their actual operation is altogether lacking, it would seem especially important to seek evidence from other sources. One would want to know, if only in part, the answer to questions such as the following:

(a) How important is pre-arraignment questioning in the identification and apprehension of those subsequently convicted of crime?

(b) How important are pre-arraignment statements as evidence for the conviction of those accused?

(c) What would be the effect on the interrogation process of (1) previous warning of the right to remain silent; (2) previous informing of the right to assistance of counsel; (3) a requirement that counsel either be waived or be present?

(d) How, in practice, would counsel be made available at the pre-arraignment stage?

This kind of empirical data can, in fact, be obtained, and would be of great value, particularly if studied in relation to available evidence on the effectiveness of alternative means of achieving the same goals. . . .

We recognize, of course, that the utility of police interrogation in law enforcement is not the only factor bearing on the issues presented by these cases. But if competing values must be considered, then it is necessary to have as accurate a gauge of their weight as is possible.

On that score, it must be recognized that our present knowledge is far from complete. . . . Nevertheless, it is clear that there is a widespread belief among judges, prosecutors, and police officials that interrogation is of *great* importance to law enforcement. . . .

Assuming (as one must in the present state of knowledge) that police questioning is an essential part of law enforcement, the next question generated by these cases goes to the effect on the interrogation process of the warning admonitions with respect to constitutional rights and, more important, of the actual presence of counsel during the course of interrogation.

Lack of knowledge on this point is openly acknowledged in the petitioner's brief in No. 759 (*Miranda*) wherein it is stated that: "As a practical matter, we cannot know with assurance whether amplification of the right to counsel in the interrogation period will severely handicap the police; we end by trading opinions." We earnestly suggest that some knowledge of this matter is vital for enlightened decision-making, particularly of constitutional dimension. . . .

In this brief, we have urged that the scope of the right to the assistance of counsel prior to arraignment presents problems which are not ripe for constitutional disposition. In support of this viewpoint, we have sought to draw the Court's attention to a number of aspects of the problem, where, we believe, empirical evidence is insufficient for definitive rule-making, and to the uncertainties still surrounding the specific proposals that have been made to extend the right to counsel into the pre-arraignment stage.

[2. Role of the Legislature.] We would like to close this portion of the brief on an affirmative note, by pointing out that the Constitution is by no means the only tool for the solution of problems of criminal procedure and that legislatures, state courts and professional organizations are currently concerned and actively engaged with pre-arraignment questions including the right to counsel. Nor is the field devoid of ideas and proposals alternative to those urged by petitioners in the present cases. . . .

Large-scale scholarly efforts—most significantly the American Bar Association's project on minimum standards of criminal justice and the drafting of a Model Code of Pre-Arraignment Procedure by the American Law Institute—are underway, and may be expected to provide a basis for constructive action by state legislatures and courts. Even if the states did not all promptly adopt new statutory rules in light of the ALI Model Code, the Code—and its offshoots in the states that used it as a model—would provide valuable guidelines for courts faced with recurring problems in this area. . . .

If some . . . states have not yet had occasion to pursue the questions, or have reaffirmed more limited concepts of the right to counsel, that is still an insufficient reason for this Court to enlarge the constitutional requirements. The opportunity for constructive and varied development is one of the great values of the federal system. To let pass an opportunity such as presently exists for the development by the states of workable rules in this area of strong conflicting values would do great disservice to the principles of federalism and, we suggest, to the healthy development of criminal procedure in the United States. . . .

Respectfully submitted,
Louis J. Lefkowitz,
Attorney General of the State of New York.

ACLU's *AMICUS* BRIEF

[1. Privilege Against Self-incrimination.] . . . [T]his Court held that during his interrogation Escobedo had been denied "the Assistance of Counsel" in violation of the Sixth Amendment of the Constitution as made obligatory upon the States by the Fourteenth Amendment, and thus the incriminatory statement elicited during this interrogation could not be used against him at his criminal trial.

In holding that *Escobedo* had been denied his Sixth Amendment right to counsel the Court relied on the facts that he had been extensively interrogated where the "purpose of the interrogation was to 'get him' to confess his guilt despite his constitutional right not to do so. At the time of his arrest and throughout the course of the interrogation, the police told [Escobedo] that they had convincing evidence that he had fired the fatal shots. Without informing him of his absolute right to remain silent in the face of this accusation, the police urged him to make a statement.". . .

It . . . seems clear that the Court held that Escobedo had been denied his right to the Assistance of Counsel because, under the circumstances of that case, providing counsel to Escobedo was necessary to protect effectively his basic right not to be compelled to incriminate himself. The fundamental quality of the privilege against self-incrimination is emphasized by considering the independent significance of the two rights. The privilege against self-incrimination is so central to our system of justice, that it is hard to conceive of our society without it; yet, it would seem fair to say that if there were no such privilege, *Escobedo* might well have come to a different result. On the other hand, it seems clear that the absence of a right to counsel should have had no effect on the result; in the circumstances of *Escobedo,* the privilege against self-incrimination required the presence of counsel for its effectuation.

Such a marriage of the Fifth Amendment privilege and Sixth Amendment right to counsel (as made applicable by the Fourteenth Amendment) is not unique to *Escobedo.* The Court has often recognized the fact that the Assistance of Counsel is necessary to protect effectively other constitutional rights. . . .

The difference between this approach to *Escobedo* and one that concentrates solely on an isolated right to counsel is not only of academic interest; it vitally concerns the proper application of the decision. The view that concentrates on the right to counsel necessarily is directed to an inquiry as to when such [a] right attaches. One way of approaching this is to attempt to discover a point in time or stage in the process for such attachment. Before that point is reached, *Escobedo* has no application; after it is reached, *Escobedo* requires counsel. It is submitted that such an all-or-nothing approach may go both too far and not far enough. A rigid requirement of providing counsel under any and all circumstances after the crucial point in time is reached may require the provision of counsel under circumstances where counsel is not necessary to the effectuation of a person's right not to be compelled to incriminate himself. Moreover, it might stifle desirable reform in State law or police practices aimed at the possibility of effectuating this right through means other than providing counsel. On the other hand the counsel-or-nothing approach may result in not providing adequate protection when it is found that the point in time at which the right to counsel attaches has not been reached, although the danger of compelled self-incrimination looms large. . . .

If, therefore, *Escobedo* rests upon effectuation of a person's right not to be compelled to incriminate himself, resolution of the issues here presented concerning its application require an analysis of this right and how it must be effectuated in the context of police investigation. We, therefore, turn to these issues.

As this Court has only recently stated:

> [The privilege against self-incrimination] reflects many of our fundamental values and most noble aspirations:. . . our preference for an accusatorial rather than an inquisitorial system of criminal justice; our fear that self-incriminating statements will be elicited by inhumane treatment and abuses; our sense of fair play which dictates "a fair state-individual balance by requiring the government to leave the individual alone until good cause is shown for disturbing him and by requiring the government in its contest with the individual to shoulder the entire load". . . ; our respect for the inviolability of the human personality and of the right of each individual "to a private enclave where he may lead a private life". . . ; our distrust of self-deprecatory statements; and our realization that the privilege, while sometimes "a shelter to the guilty," is often "a protection to the innocent."

This Court has recognized "that the American system of criminal prosecution is accusatorial, not inquisitorial, and that the Fifth Amendment privilege is its essential mainstay. . . . Governments, state and federal, are thus constitutionally compelled to establish guilt by evidence independently and freely secured. . . . The Fourteenth Amendment secures against State invasion the same privilege that the Fifth Amendment guarantees against federal infringement—*the right of a person to remain silent unless he chooses to speak in the unfettered exercise of his own will. . . .*"

Although it was not until two years ago in *Malloy v. Hogan* that the Court held that the Fifth Amendment as such applied to the States, the Court in *Malloy* recognized and relied upon the fact that, even prior to this decision, there had been a "marked shift" to the Fifth Amendment federal standard in State "involuntary" confession cases. "The shift reflects recognition that the American system of criminal prosecution is accusatorial, not inquisitorial, and that the Fifth Amendment privilege is its essential mainstay.". . .

[2. Coercive Character of Police Interrogations.] It seems hardly necessary to argue at length that typical police custodial interrogation designed to elicit a confession is inherently compelling—inherently violative of the subject's privilege against self-incrimination. The subject is arrested and held incommunicado by the police until they are finished interrogating him. He is completely within their control, surrounded by hostile forces, and cut off—except at the whim of the police—from any contact with the outside world that might give him support. Indeed, such a situation may well have been created for the explicit purpose of making the subject confess against his will.

This purpose and the effectiveness of incommunicado interrogation in achieving the purpose have been recognized by the leading writers on police interrogation techniques. Inbau & Reid, *Criminal Interrogation and Confessions* (1962) (hereinafter cited as *INBAU & REID*), states that "[t]he principal psychological factor contributing to a successful interrogation is *privacy*—being alone with the person under interrogation" (emphasis in the original). O'Hara, *Fundamentals of Criminal Investigation* (1959) (hereinafter cited as *O'HARA*), emphasizes this point and explains the reasons:

> If at all practicable, the interrogation should take place in the investigator's office or at least in a room of his own choice. The subject should be deprived of every psychological advantage. In his own home he may be confident, indignant, or recalcitrant. He is more keenly aware of his rights and more reluctant to tell of his indiscretions of criminal behavior within the walls of his home. Moreover his family and other friends are nearby, their presence lending moral support. In his own office, the investigator possesses all the advantages. The atmosphere suggests the invincibility of the forces of the law.

Both of these books as well as numerous other police manuals present varied and sophisticated methods to be used by police interrogators in extracting confessions through incommunicado custodial interrogation. The basic theme of these works is well summed up in the following language of Inbau & Reid, *Lie Detection and Criminal Interrogation*:

[T]he interrogator's task is somewhat akin to that of a hunter stalking his game. Each must patiently maneuver himself or his quarry into a position from which the desired object [obtaining a confession] may be obtained. . . .

Their basic attitude is one of getting the subject [quarry] to confess despite himself—by trapping him into it, by deceiving him, or by more direct means of overbearing his will. . . .

A key element in police interrogation, as demonstrated by *Escobedo* and numerous other cases, is the manifestation by the police interrogator that he expects to obtain a confession from the suspect and that he is prepared to interrogate, under incommunicado circumstances, until he does. . . . Both of these are recognized and recommended interrogation techniques. The first interrogation tactic recommended by *INBAU & REID* is: "Display an Air of Confidence in the Suspect's Guilt." This "air of confidence" is to be used along with patience and persistence. "Not only must the interrogator have patience, but he must also display it. It is well, therefore, to get the idea across, in most case situations, that the interrogator has 'all the time in the world.'"

O'HARA, after setting forth various "stratagems" to compel incriminating statements makes the following recommendation of "perseverance":

> In the preceding paragraphs emphasis has been placed on kindness and stratagems. The investigator will, however, encounter many situations where the sheer weight of his personality will be the deciding factor. Where emotional appeals and tricks are employed to no avail, he must rely on an oppressive atmosphere of dogged persistence. He must interrogate steadily and without relent, leaving the subject no prospect of surcease. He must dominate his subject and overwhelm him with his inexorable will to obtain the truth. He should interrogate for a spell of several hours pausing only for the subject's necessities in acknowledgment of the need to avoid a charge of duress that can be technically substantiated. In a serious case, the interrogation may continue for days, with the required intervals for food and sleep, but with no respite from the atmosphere of domination. It is possible in this way to induce the subject to talk without resorting to duress or coercion. This method should be used only when the guilt of the subject appears highly probable.

Can there be any doubt that under such circumstances many "subjects" of police interrogation will assume that the police have a right to an answer, and, indeed, to what the police regard as the "correct" answer—a confession of guilt? "It is probable that even today, when there is much less ignorance about these matters than formerly, there is still a general belief that you must answer all questions put to you by a policeman, *or at least that it will be the worse for you if you do not*" (emphasis added). The whole purpose of such interrogation is to produce in the subject "the fear that if he remained silent it would be considered an admission of guilt," or indeed, that it might otherwise be "worse" for him.

INBAU & REID recommend an "effective way to deal with a subject" who, despite all other pressures, has the knowledge of and the gall to insist upon his right not to be compelled to incriminate himself or asks to see a relative, friend or attorney:

IF A SUBJECT REFUSES TO DISCUSS THE MATTER UNDER INVESTI-
GATION, CONCEDE HIM THE RIGHT TO REMAIN SILENT, AND
THEN PROCEED TO POINT OUT THE INCRIMINATING SIGNIFI-
CANCE OF HIS REFUSAL.

The most effective way to deal with a subject who refuses to discuss the matter under investigation is to concede to him the right to remain silent. This usually has a very undermining effect. First of all, he is disappointed in his expectation of an unfavorable reaction on the part of the interrogator. Secondly, a
concession of this right to remain silent impresses the subject with the apparent
fairness of his interrogator.

After this psychological conditioning, the interrogator should then proceed to
point out to the subject the incriminating significance of his refusal to talk. The
following comments have been found to be very effective: "Joe, you have a right
to remain silent. That's your privilege and I'm the last person in the world who'll
try to take it away from you. If that's the way you want to leave this, O.K. But let
me ask you this. Suppose you were in my shoes and I were in yours and you called
me in to ask me about this and I told you, 'I don't want to answer any of your
questions.' You'd think I had something to hide, and you'd probably be right in
thinking that. That's exactly what I'll have to think about you and so will everybody else. So let's sit here and talk this whole thing over."

After the subject has been talked to in this manner, the interrogator should
then immediately ask the subject some innocuous questions that have no bearing
whatsoever on the matter under investigation. For instance, the interrogator may
inquire of the subject, "How long have you lived in this city?"; "Where are you
working?"; "How long have you worked there?" As a rule the subject will answer
such questions, and then gradually the examiner may start in with questions pertaining to the offense under investigation. Except for the career criminal, there
are very few persons who will persist in their initial refusal to talk after the interrogator has handled the situation in this suggested manner.

If a subject expresses a desire to talk to a relative, or to an employer, or to any
other person, the interrogator should respond by suggesting that the subject first
tell the truth to the interrogator himself rather than get anyone else involved in
the matter. If the request is for an attorney, the interrogator may suggest that the
subject save himself or his family the expense of any such professional service,
particularly if he is innocent of the offense under investigation. The interrogator
may also add, "Joe, I'm only looking for the truth, and if you're telling the truth,
that's it. You can handle this by yourself."

Is there any doubt that a statement produced under such circumstances results
from undermining the "subject's" right "to remain silent unless he chooses to speak
in the unfettered exercise of his own will"?

Can it be seriously asserted that the extracting of confessions under such circumstances conforms to our accusatorial system under which "society carries the
burden of proving its charge against the accused not out of his own mouth . . .
[and] must establish its case, not by interrogation of the accused even under judicial safeguards, but by evidence independently secured through skillful investigation"[?] Where there has been a confession elicited through misapprehension, fear,
trick or stratagem, has there not been a violation of the basis of our system that

"[t]he law will not suffer a prisoner to be made the deluded instrument of his own conviction"[?] Indeed, such police interrogation has been aptly characterized as the worst of both worlds: "It is the inquisitorial system without its safeguards.". . .

[3. Right to Counsel as a Protective Device.] The issue now is what protective devices need be added to this police custodial interrogation to make the process conform to Fifth Amendment requirements, i.e., to dispel the government-established compelling atmosphere. . . .

Obviously an effective warning of the privilege is a keystone of its effective enforcement. It is equally clear that there is a need to provide the presence of someone at interrogation in whom the subject can confide and who will bolster his confidence. As discussed above, it is a prime function of police custodial incommunicado interrogation to tear a subject away from all things in which he can rely for support and place him in complete subservience to the interrogator. The aim is to have him dominated by the interrogator. In order to dispel such circumstances, therefore, it is manifestly necessary that the incommunicado environment be eliminated. The presence of counsel will tend to accomplish this aim. Not only is counsel a person outside the police force, he is one who can meet the accomplished police interrogator on a level of at least partial equality. By training and experience he should not be afraid to stand up to unrestrained governmental power. He is someone in whom the subject can freely confide. It is his job to be a wholehearted advocate for the subject with no conflicting interests in this regard. . . .

The Court in *Escobedo* quite clearly recognized [the value of counsel at interrogations] . . . when it found that even a prior warning of the right to remain silent given to Escobedo by his attorney was not effective in dispelling the compelling circumstances presented by new police stratagems. Despite these prior warnings, Escobedo was compelled to incriminate himself when presented with the classic interrogation technique of an accomplice's accusation—a technique clearly designed to overcome the subject's desire not to speak. . . .

The above-stated facts of *Escobedo* indicate also that prior access to counsel rather than the presence of counsel at interrogation is not sufficient to protect the subject's Fifth Amendment right not to be compelled to incriminate himself; the effectuation of that right necessitated that Escobedo have counsel present when he was confronted with the new police stratagem of the accomplice's accusation. As the Court stated: "The 'guiding hand of counsel' was essential to advise petitioner of his rights in this delicate situation.". . .

It is true that in *Escobedo*, the subject of custodial police interrogation had retained counsel and requested to see him. The relevance of these facts, however, depends upon the proper analysis of the rights protected by that decision; the analysis contained in this brief clearly shows . . . [that the fact that Escobedo asked to see his counsel is] not at all significant. The issue always remains a determination of what is necessary to dispel the compelling atmosphere of the interrogation. It is true that when Escobedo asked for and was denied the right to consult his attorney this clearly reinforced the compelling nature of the interrogation. The refusal told him in no uncertain terms that the police were in charge, that they were determined to get him to confess and that they would not let him see his attorney until they chose to do so—after he confessed.

Yet, as the above discussion has shown, even absent this aggravating element of *Escobedo,* such interrogation was inherently compelling and only the presence of counsel could dispel that atmosphere. Indeed, it might be argued that Escobedo's expressed request to consult with counsel indicated that the usual compelling nature of the interrogation would not work as effectively on him as on others. Escobedo obviously had a sense that he had some rights and was not completely subject to the will of the interrogator. A requirement that there must be a request would only result in placing the ignorant and inexperienced—those who most need the services of an attorney to dispel the compelling nature of the interrogation—at a distinct disadvantage in the enforcement of their constitutional rights. "The defendant who does not ask for counsel is the very defendant who most needs counsel; we cannot penalize a defendant, who, not understanding his constitutional rights, does not make the formal request and by such failure demonstrates his helplessness. To require the request would be to favor the defendant whose sophistication or status had fortuitously prompted him to make it."

The same analysis leads clearly to the result that it is irrelevant that a subject of police custodial interrogation cannot afford retained counsel. It cannot seriously be maintained that an indigent subject's Fifth Amendment rights are less deserving than those of an affluent one. Since the presence of counsel is as necessary to effectuate an indigent subject's Fifth Amendment right as those of a more affluent interrogation subject, counsel must be equally available to both. . . .

[4. Decision's Impact on Crime and Confessions.] It is argued to this Court that restrictions on the powers of the police freely to interrogate suspects as here advocated will prevent effective police work and thus contribute to what is asserted to be a mounting crime rate and that, therefore, the balance in this area must and should be struck, not on the side of the protection of individual liberties, but on the side of this asserted police need.

It is submitted that even if these claims of police need were substantiated, the Constitution requires that the balance here be struck on the side of effectively enforcing an accused's Fifth Amendment right not to be compelled to incriminate himself. . . .

This ultimate balancing issue, however, need not be reached as the case for the asserted police "need" has not been made out.

The first point in the police-necessity thesis is the postulate that there is a clear link between court decisions protecting the rights of the accused and an alleged upward advance in the rate of criminal behavior. Even if it is assumed that there has been a rise in criminal behavior in the last few years, an issue not at all free from doubt, it is clear that there has been no showing of a link between such a rise and court decisions securing individual liberties.

Assuming *arguendo* that interrogation opportunity is necessary to solve crimes and convict criminals, is it clearly a matter of "simple logic" that there is a causal connection between restricting this opportunity and an increased incidence of criminal behavior? It hardly needs to be stated that the roots of crime are planted in a number of complex social factors such as: discrimination, environment, drug addiction and unemployment, as well as individual psychological and psychiatric variants. We are only now beginning to gain the necessary knowledge in order to cope with and treat causes rather than symptoms. It is just too simplistic a form of logic to ascribe criminal behavior to court decisions. . . .

More significantly, there is no substantiation for the claim that confessions are necessary to the conviction of the guilty. Attempts to obtain confessions may be used as "easier" substitutes for proper, independent police investigatorial processes. Moreover, confessions are sometimes sought even when ample other evidence is already in hand. Police have attempted to elicit confessions when the crime has been committed in front of a dozen witnesses, indeed when it has been committed in the presence of the police themselves. . . .

In summation on this point, it seems quite evident that while not clearly refuting the claim, neither simple logic nor the available statistical evidence supports the argument that opportunities for secret, unrestrained and unhampered police and prosecutorial interrogation are essential to controlling or reducing the incidence of criminal behavior.

If there is more data in this area that should or can be produced, the burden of production clearly rests on government and not on an individual accused. An individual accused has neither the motivation nor [the] resources to produce data relevant to a determination of the "need" for allowing the unrestrained police interrogation desired by those who assert the existence of such a need. On the other hand, government has both the continuing interest and the resources to produce such data if, in fact, it can be done. Thus far, nothing has been produced that could by any stretch be deemed to justify overriding a suspect's constitutional rights because of overwhelming societal necessity. . . .

It seems clear that in a scale composed of the unsupported necessity assertions of police and prosecutors on one side and the effectuation and protection of a person's constitutional right not to be compelled to incriminate himself on the other, the balance must be struck on the side of the Constitutional right.

Respectfully submitted,
ANTHONY G. AMSTERDAM
PAUL J. MISHKIN,
Attorneys for *Amicus Curiae*.

ORAL ARGUMENT

MR. FLYNN [Miranda's Attorney]:   . . . We have the Third Circuit decision in *Russo*, which would indicate that principle and logic are being applied to the decision, and in the words of Mr. Justice Goldberg, that when the process shifts from the investigation to one of accusation, and when the purpose is to elicit a confession from the defendant, then the adversary process comes into being. . . .

JUSTICE STEWART: What do you think is the result of the adversary process coming into being when this focusing takes place? What follows from that? Is there, then, a right to a lawyer?

FLYNN: I think that the man at that time has the right to exercise, if he knows, and under the present state of the law in Arizona, if he is rich enough, and if he's educated enough to assert his Fifth Amendment right, and if he recognizes that he has a Fifth Amendment right to request counsel. But I simply say that at that stage of the proceeding, under the facts and circumstances in *Miranda* of a man of limited education, of a man who certainly is mentally abnormal, who is certainly an indigent, that when that adversary process came into being that the police, at the very least, had an obligation to extend to this man not only his clear Fifth Amendment right, but to accord to him the right of counsel. . . .

STEWART: What is it that confers the right to a lawyer's advice at that point and not an earlier point? The Sixth Amendment?

FLYNN: No. The attempt to erode, or to take away from him, the Fifth Amendment right that already existed—and that was the right not to convict himself, and be convicted out of his own mouth.

STEWART: Didn't he have that right earlier?

FLYNN: If he knew about it.

STEWART: Before this became a so-called "adversary proceeding"?

FLYNN: Yes, Your Honor, if he knew about it and if he was aware—if he was knowledgeable.

STEWART: Then did he have the right to a lawyer's advice earlier?

FLYNN: If he could afford it, yes; and if he was intelligent enough and strong enough to stand up against police interrogation and request it, yes.

STEWART: What I'm getting at is, I don't understand the magic in this phrase of "focusing," and then all of a sudden it becomes an adversary proceeding. And then I suppose if you literally mean that it becomes an adversary proceeding, then you're entitled to all the rights that a defendant is given under the Constitution that would be given in a criminal trial. If you mean less than that, then you don't really mean it has now become the equivalent of a trial.

FLYNN: Well, I simply mean that when it becomes an adversary proceeding, at the very least, a person in Ernest Miranda's position needs the benefit of counsel, and unless he is afforded that right to counsel he simply has, in essence, no Fifth or Sixth Amendment right, and there is no due process of law being afforded to a man in Ernest Miranda's position.

JUSTICE FORTAS: Is it possible that prior to this so-called "focusing," or let's say prior to arrest—if those don't mean the same thing—that a citizen has an obligation to cooperate with the state, give the state information that he may have relevant to the crime; and that upon arrest, or upon this "focusing," that the state and the individual then assume the position of adversaries, and there is, at the very least, a change in that relationship between the individual and the state; and, therefore, in their mutual rights and responsibilities? I don't know whether that's what my Brother Stewart is getting at, and perhaps it is unfair to discuss this through you—

[Laughter.]

FORTAS: —but if you have a comment on it, I'd like to hear it.

FLYNN: I think the only comment that I could make is that, without getting ourselves into the area of precisely when focusing begins, that I must in this instance limit it to the fact situation and the circumstances of Ernest Miranda, because for every practical purpose, after the two-hour interrogation, the mere formality of supplying counsel to Ernest Miranda at the time of trial, is what I would submit would really be nothing more than a mockery of his Sixth Amendment right to be represented in court, to go through the formality, and a conviction takes place.

❖   ❖   ❖

JUSTICE STEWART: Is there any claim in this case that this confession was compelled—was involuntary?

MR. FLYNN: No, Your Honor.

STEWART: None at all?

FLYNN: None at all.

JUSTICE WHITE: Do you mean that there is no question that he was not compelled to give evidence against himself?

FLYNN: We have raised no question that he was compelled to give this statement, in the sense that anyone forced him to do it by coercion, by threats, by promises, or compulsion of that kind.

WHITE: "Of that kind"? Was it voluntary, or wasn't it?

FLYNN: Voluntary in the sense that the man, at a time without knowledge of his rights—

WHITE: Do you claim that his Fifth Amendment rights were violated?

FLYNN: I would say his Fifth Amendment right was violated, to the extent—

WHITE: Because he was compelled to do it?

FLYNN: Because he was compelled to do it?

WHITE: That's what the Amendment says.

FLYNN: Yes, to the extent that he was, number one, too poor to exercise it, and number two, mentally abnormal.

WHITE: Whatever the Fifth is, you say he was compelled to do it?

FLYNN: I say it was taken from him at a point in time when he absolutely should have been afforded the Sixth Amendment—

WHITE: I'm talking about violating the Amendment, namely the provision that he was—to violate the Fifth Amendment right, he has to be compelled to do it, doesn't he?

FLYNN: In the sense that Your Honor is presenting to me the word "compelled," you're correct.

WHITE: I was talking about what the Constitution says.

JUSTICE BLACK: He doesn't have to have a gun pointed at his head, does he?

WHITE: Of course he doesn't. So he was compelled to do it, wasn't he, according to your theory?

FLYNN: Not by gunpoint, as Mr. Justice Black has indicated. He was called upon to surrender a right that he didn't fully realize and appreciate that he had. It was taken from him.

✧   ✧   ✧

MR. NELSON [Arizona's Attorney]:   . . . As I understand it, there is no right not to incriminate himself. The right is for him not to be compelled, whether it's subtle compulsion or direct, but it is still a right not to be compelled to incriminate yourself. At least this is my understanding, and he doesn't have a right not to incriminate himself. He has a right not to be compelled to incriminate himself by some means, either direct or devious. Now I think if the extreme position is adopted that says he has to either have counsel at this stage or intellectually waive counsel, that a serious problem in the enforcement of our criminal law will occur.

   First of all, let us make one thing certain. We need no empirical data as to one factor: what counsel will do if he is actually introduced. I am talking now about counsel for defendant. At least among lawyers there can be no doubt as to what counsel for the defendant is to do. He is to represent him 100 percent, win, lose, or draw—guilty or innocent. That's our system. When counsel is introduced at interrogation, interrogation ceases immediately.

JUSTICE BLACK: Why?

NELSON: . . . Let's assume the client said, "Yes, I am guilty. I did it." He had all the requisite intents. He makes a statement to his lawyer in confidence that he did it, and asks his lawyer what he should do. . . .

   Let's further assume that he advises his client, "Well, I think you ought to confess. I think there's a possibility for a light sentence. You did it. They have other evidence; or maybe they don't have any other evidence"—let's say they don't have any other evidence—"and you can confess."

The fellow says, "Well, I don't want to confess. I don't want to go to the gas chamber if I don't have to. Is there anything else that you, as my lawyer, can do for me?" Well, what has he got to tell him? Under our system, he has got to tell him, "Yes, you don't have to say anything. And the fact that you don't say anything can't in any way hurt you, inferred or otherwise, and we can put the State to its burden of proof."

BLACK: Why does our system compel his lawyer to do that?

NELSON: He is compelled by the system to do this.

BLACK: Well, why does it do it? For what purpose? What's the object on the part of the lawyer?

NELSON: Because we believe that it's right, and proper, that the criminal defendant not be deprived of his life, liberty, or property, without due process of law.

BLACK: And something about giving testimony against himself.

NELSON: Right. I mean this is just one issue. The lawyer has to guard all these rights. But I'm saying that the practical effect of introducing counsel at the interrogation stage is going to stop the interrogation for any and all purposes, except what counsel decides will be in the best interest of his defendant. Otherwise, counsel will not be doing his job.

BLACK: Isn't that about the same thing as the practical effect and object of the Amendment, which says he shall not be compelled to give testimony against himself? Is there any difference between the objects there, and purposes of the two—what the lawyer tells him, and what the Fifth Amendment tells him?

NELSON: Well, certainly that's the object of what his lawyer tells him.

BLACK: Isn't that the object of the Amendment?

NELSON: Well, that is the question, of course. . . .

BLACK: Is there anything fantastic in the idea that the Fifth Amendment—that the protection against being compelled to testify against oneself—might be read reasonably as meaning there should be no pre-trial proceedings when he was there in the possession of the state?

NELSON: Of course to me, I think there is. I think there is a valid interest—

BLACK: There is a valid interest, of course, if they can convict him—and that's their business, to try to convict him.

NELSON: Right. . . .

THE OPINION

Mr. Chief Justice Warren delivered the opinion of the Court. . . .

. . . We have undertaken a thorough re-examination of the *Escobedo* decision and the principles it announced, and we reaffirm it. That case was but an explication of basic rights that are enshrined in our Constitution—that "no person . . . shall be compelled in any criminal case to be a witness against himself," and that "the accused shall . . . have the Assistance of Counsel"—rights which were put in jeopardy in that case through official overbearing. . . .

[1. Coercive Character of Police Interrogations.] An understanding of the nature and setting of this in-custody interrogation is essential to our decisions today. The difficulty in depicting what transpires at such interrogations stems from the fact that in this country they have largely taken place incommunicado. . . .

. . . Interrogation still takes place in privacy. Privacy results in secrecy and this in turn results in a gap in our knowledge as to what in fact goes on in the interrogation rooms. A valuable source of information about present police practices, however, may be found in various police manuals and texts which document procedures employed with success in the past, and which recommend various other effective tactics. These texts are used by law enforcement agencies themselves as guides. It should be noted that these texts professedly present the most enlightened and effective means presently used to obtain statements through custodial interrogation. By considering these texts and other data, it is possible to describe procedures observed and noted around the country.[26]

The officers are told by the manuals that the "principal psychological factor contributing to a successful interrogation is *privacy*—being alone with the person under interrogation.". . .

To highlight the isolation and unfamiliar surroundings, the manuals instruct the police to display an air of confidence in the suspect's guilt and from outward appearance to maintain only an interest in confirming certain details. The guilt of the subject is to be posited as a fact. The interrogator should direct his comments toward the reasons why the subject committed the act, rather than court failure by asking the subject whether he did it. Like other men, perhaps the subject has had a bad family life, had an unhappy childhood, had too much to drink, had an unrequited desire for women. The officers are instructed to minimize the moral seriousness of the offense, to cast blame on the victim or on society. These tactics are designed to put the subject in a psychological state where his story is but an elaboration of what the police purport to know already—that he is guilty. Explanations to the contrary are dismissed and discouraged.

The texts thus stress that the major qualities an interrogator should possess are patience and perseverance. . . .

---

[26]Passages from the police interrogation manuals that were quoted in the ACLU brief have been omitted from the excerpts taken from the Supreme Court's opinion.

The manuals suggest that the suspect be offered legal excuses for his actions in order to obtain an initial admission of guilt. Where there is a suspected revenge-killing, for example, the interrogator may say:

Joe, you probably didn't go out looking for this fellow with the purpose of shooting him. My guess is, however, that you expected something from him and that's why you carried a gun—for your own protection. You knew him for what he was, no good. Then when you met him he probably started using foul, abusive language and he gave some indication that he was about to pull a gun on you, and that's when you had to act to save your own life. That's about it, isn't it, Joe?

Having then obtained the admission of shooting, the interrogator is advised to refer to circumstantial evidence which negates the self-defense explanation. This should enable him to secure the entire story. One text notes that "Even if he fails to do so, the inconsistency between the subject's original denial of the shooting and his present admission of at least doing the shooting will serve to deprive him of a self-defense 'out' at the time of trial."

When the techniques described above prove unavailing, the texts recommend they be alternated with a show of some hostility. One ploy often used has been termed the "friendly-unfriendly" or the "Mutt and Jeff" act:

. . . In this technique, two agents are employed. Mutt, the relentless investigator, who knows the subject is guilty and is not going to waste any time. He's sent a dozen men away for this crime and he's going to send the subject away for the full term. Jeff, on the other hand, is obviously a kindhearted man. He has a family himself. He has a brother who was involved in a little scrape like this. He disapproves of Mutt and his tactics and will arrange to get him off the case if the subject will cooperate. He can't hold Mutt off for very long. The subject would be wise to make a quick decision. The technique is applied by having both investigators present while Mutt acts out his role. Jeff may stand by quietly and demur at some of Mutt's tactics. When Jeff makes his plea for cooperation, Mutt is not present in the room.

The interrogators sometimes are instructed to induce a confession out of trickery. The technique here is quite effective in crimes which require identification or which run in series. In the identification situation, the interrogator may take a break in his questioning to place the subject among a group of men in a line-up. "The witness or complainant (previously coached, if necessary) studies the line-up and confidently points out the subject as the guilty party." Then the questioning resumes "as though there were now no doubt about the guilt of the subject." A variation on this technique is called the "reverse line-up":

The accused is placed in a line-up, but this time he is identified by several fictitious witnesses or victims who associated him with different offenses. It is expected that the subject will become desperate and confess to the offense under investigation in order to escape from the false accusations.

The manuals also contain instructions for police on how to handle the individual who refuses to discuss the matter entirely, or who asks for an attorney or relatives. The examiner is to concede him the right to remain silent. "This usually has a very undermining effect. First of all, he is disappointed in his expectation of an unfavorable reaction on the part of the interrogator. Secondly, a concession of this right to remain silent impresses the subject with the apparent fairness of his interrogator." After this psychological conditioning, however, the officer is told to point out the incriminating significance of the suspect's refusal to talk. . . .

From these representative samples of interrogation techniques, the setting prescribed by the manuals and observed in practice becomes clear. In essence, it is this: To be alone with the subject is essential to prevent distraction and to deprive him of any outside support. The aura of confidence in his guilt undermines his will to resist. He merely confirms the preconceived story the police seek to have him describe. Patience and persistence, [and] at times relentless questioning, are employed. To obtain a confession, the interrogator must "patiently maneuver himself or his quarry into a position from which the desired objective may be attained." When normal procedures fail to produce the needed result, the police may resort to deceptive stratagems such as giving false legal advice. It is important to keep the subject off balance, for example, by trading on his insecurity about himself or his surroundings. The police then persuade, trick, or cajole him out of exercising his constitutional rights.

Even without employing brutality, the "third degree," or the specific stratagems described above, the very fact of custodial interrogation exacts a heavy toll on individual liberty and trades on the weakness of individuals. . . .

[2. Privilege Against Self-incrimination.] In these cases, we might not find the defendant's statement to have been involuntary in traditional terms. Our concern for adequate safeguards to protect precious Fifth Amendment rights is, of course, not lessened in the slightest. In each of the cases, the defendant was thrust into an unfamiliar atmosphere and run through menacing police interrogation procedures. The potentiality for compulsion is forcefully apparent, for example, in *Miranda,* where the indigent Mexican defendant was a seriously disturbed individual with pronounced sexual fantasies. . . . To be sure, the records do not evince overt physical coercion or patent psychological ploys. The fact remains that in none of these cases did the officers undertake to afford appropriate safeguards at the outset of the interrogation to insure that the statements were truly the product of free choice.

It is obvious that such an interrogation environment is created for no purpose other than to subjugate the individual to the will of his examiner. This atmosphere carries its own badge of intimidation. To be sure, this is not physical intimidation, but it is equally destructive of human dignity. The current practice of incommunicado interrogation is at odds with one of our Nation's most cherished principles—that the individual may not be compelled to incriminate himself. Unless adequate protective devices are employed to dispel the compulsion inherent in custodial surroundings, no statement obtained from the defendant can truly be the product of his free choice. . . .

We sometimes forget how long it has taken to establish the privilege against self-incrimination, the sources from which it came and the fervor with which it was defended. Its roots go back into ancient times. . . .

. . . The privilege was elevated to constitutional status and has always been "as broad as the mischief against which it seeks to guard." We cannot depart from this noble heritage. . . .

. . . We have recently noted that the privilege against self-incrimination—the essential mainstay of our adversary system—is founded on a complex of values. All these policies point to one overriding thought: the constitutional foundation underlying the privilege is the respect a government—state or federal—must accord to the dignity and integrity of its citizens. To maintain a "fair state-individual balance," to require the government "to shoulder the entire load," to respect the inviolability of the human personality, our accusatory system of criminal justice demands that the government seeking to punish an individual produce the evidence against him by its own independent labors, rather than by the cruel, simple expedient of compelling it from his own mouth. In sum, the privilege is fulfilled only when the person is guaranteed the right "to remain silent unless he chooses to speak in the unfettered exercise of his own will.". . .

. . . In *Malloy*, we squarely held the privilege applicable to the States, and held that the substantive standards underlying the privilege applied with full force to state court proceedings. . . . Aside from the holding itself, the reasoning in *Malloy* made clear what had already become apparent—that the substantive and procedural safeguards surrounding admissibility of confessions in state cases had become exceedingly exacting, reflecting all the policies embedded in the privilege. The voluntariness doctrine in the state cases, as *Malloy* indicates, encompasses all interrogation practices which are likely to exert such pressure upon an individual as to disable him from making a free and rational choice. The implications of this proposition were elaborated in our decision in *Escobedo v. Illinois*, decided one week after *Malloy* applied the privilege to the States.

Our holding there stressed the fact that the police had not advised the defendant of his constitutional privilege to remain silent at the outset of the interrogation, and we drew attention to that fact at several points in the decision. This was no isolated factor, but an essential ingredient in our decision. The entire thrust of police interrogation there, as in all the cases today, was to put the defendant in such an emotional state as to impair his capacity for rational judgment. The abdication of the constitutional privilege—the choice on his part to speak to the police—was not made knowingly or competently because of the failure to apprise him of his rights; the compelling atmosphere of the in-custody interrogation, and not an independent decision on his part, caused the defendant to speak.

A different phase of the *Escobedo* decision was significant in its attention to the absence of counsel during the questioning. There, as in the cases today, we sought a protective device to dispel the compelling atmosphere of the interrogation. In *Escobedo*, however, the police did not relieve the defendant of the anxieties which they had created in the interrogation rooms. Rather, they denied his request for the assistance of counsel. This heightened his dilemma, and made his later statements the product of this compulsion. The denial of the defendant's request for his attorney thus undermined his ability to exercise the privilege—to remain silent if he chose or to speak without any intimidation, blatant or subtle. The presence of counsel, in all the cases before us today, would be the adequate protective device necessary to make the process of police interrogation conform to the dictates of the privilege. His presence would insure that statements made in the government-established atmosphere are not the product of compulsion. . . .

Today, then, there can be no doubt that the Fifth Amendment privilege is available outside of criminal court proceedings and serves to protect persons in all settings in which their freedom of action is curtailed in any significant way from being compelled to incriminate themselves. We have concluded that without proper safeguards the process of in-custody interrogation of persons suspected or accused of crime contains inherently compelling pressures which work to undermine the individual's will to resist and to compel him to speak where he would not otherwise do so freely. In order to combat these pressures and to permit a full opportunity to exercise the privilege against self-incrimination, the accused must be adequately and effectively apprised of his rights and the exercise of those rights must be fully honored. . . .

At the outset, if a person in custody is to be subjected to interrogation, he must first be informed in clear and unequivocal terms that he has the right to remain silent. For those unaware of the privilege, the warning is needed simply to make them aware of it—the threshold requirement for an intelligent decision as to its exercise. More important, such a warning is an absolute prerequisite in overcoming the inherent pressures of the interrogation atmosphere. It is not just the subnormal or woefully ignorant who succumb to an interrogator's imprecations, whether implied or expressly stated, that the interrogation will continue until a confession is obtained or that silence in the face of accusation is itself damning and will bode ill when presented to a jury. Further, the warning will show the individual that his interrogators are prepared to recognize his privilege should he choose to exercise it. . . .

The warning of the right to remain silent must be accompanied by the explanation that anything said can and will be used against the individual in court. This warning is needed in order to make him aware not only of the privilege, but also of the consequences of forgoing it. It is only through an awareness of these consequences that there can be any assurance of real understanding and intelligent exercise of the privilege. Moreover, this warning may serve to make the individual more acutely aware that he is faced with a phase of the adversary system—that he is not in the presence of persons acting solely in his interest.

The circumstances surrounding in-custody interrogation can operate very quickly to overbear the will of one merely made aware of his privilege by his interrogators. Therefore, the right to have counsel present at the interrogation is indispensable to the protection of the Fifth Amendment privilege under the system we delineate today. Our aim is to assure that the individual's right to choose between silence and speech remains unfettered throughout the interrogation process. A once-stated warning, delivered by those who will conduct the interrogation, cannot itself suffice to that end among those who most require knowledge of their rights. A mere warning given by the interrogators is not alone sufficient to accomplish that end. Prosecutors themselves claim that the admonishment of the right to remain silent without more "will benefit only the recidivist and the professional." Even preliminary advice given to the accused by his own attorney can be swiftly overcome by the secret interrogation process. Thus, the need for counsel to protect the Fifth Amendment privilege comprehends not merely a right to consult with counsel prior to questioning, but also to have counsel present during any questioning if the defendant so desires. . . .

If an individual indicates that he wishes the assistance of counsel before any interrogation occurs, the authorities cannot rationally ignore or deny his request on the basis that the individual does not have or cannot afford a retained attorney. The financial ability of the individual has no relationship to the scope of the rights involved here. The privilege against self-incrimination secured by the Constitution applies to all individuals. The need for counsel in order to protect the privilege exists for the indigent as well as the affluent. . . .

Once warnings have been given, the subsequent procedure is clear. If the individual indicates in any manner, at any time prior to or during questioning, that he wishes to remain silent, the interrogation must cease. At this point he has shown that he intends to exercise his Fifth Amendment privilege; any statement taken after the person invokes his privilege cannot be other than the product of compulsion, subtle or otherwise. Without the right to cut off questioning, the setting of in-custody interrogation operates on the individual to overcome free choice in producing a statement after the privilege has been once invoked. If the individual states that he wants an attorney, the interrogation must cease until an attorney is present. At that time, the individual must have an opportunity to confer with the attorney and to have him present during any subsequent questioning. If the individual cannot obtain an attorney and he indicates that he wants one before speaking to police, they must respect his decision to remain silent. . . .

If the interrogation continues without the presence of an attorney and a statement is taken, a heavy burden rests on the government to demonstrate that the defendant knowingly and intelligently waived his privilege against self-incrimination and his right to retained or appointed counsel. This Court has always set high standards of proof for the waiver of constitutional rights, and we re-assert these standards as applied to in-custody interrogation. Since the State is responsible for establishing the isolated circumstances under which the interrogation takes place and has the only means of making available corroborated evidence of warnings given during incommunicado interrogation, the burden is rightly on its shoulders. . . .

Whatever the testimony of the authorities as to waiver of rights by an accused, the fact of lengthy interrogation or incommunicado incarceration before a statement is made is strong evidence that the accused did not validly waive his rights. In these circumstances the fact that the individual eventually made a statement is consistent with the conclusion that the compelling influence of the interrogation finally forced him to do so. It is inconsistent with any notion of a voluntary relinquishment of the privilege. Moreover, any evidence that the accused was threatened, tricked, or cajoled into a waiver will, of course, show that the defendant did not voluntarily waive his privilege. The requirement of warnings and waiver of rights is fundamental with respect to the Fifth Amendment privilege and not simply a preliminary ritual to existing methods of interrogation. . . .

In dealing with statements obtained through interrogation, we do not purport to find all confessions inadmissible. Confessions remain a proper element in law enforcement. Any statement given freely and voluntarily without any compelling influences is, of course, admissible in evidence. The fundamental import of the privilege while an individual is in custody is not whether he is allowed to talk to the police without the benefit of warnings and counsel, but whether he can be interrogated. There is no requirement that police stop a person who enters a police station and states that he wishes to confess to a crime, or a person who calls the police to offer a confession or any other statement he desires to make. Volunteered statements of any kind are not barred by the Fifth Amendment and their admissibility is not affected by our holding today. . . .

[3. Effect on Law Enforcement.] In announcing these principles, we are not unmindful of the burdens which law enforcement officials must bear, often under trying circumstances. We also fully recognize the obligation of all citizens to aid in enforcing the criminal laws. This Court, while protecting individual rights, has always given ample latitude to law enforcement agencies in the legitimate exercise of their duties. The limits we have placed on the interrogation process should not constitute an undue interference with a proper system of law enforcement. As we have noted, our decision does not in any way preclude police from carrying out their traditional investigatory functions. Although confessions may play an important role in some convictions, the cases before us present graphic examples of the overstatement of the "need" for confessions. In each case authorities conducted interrogations ranging up to five days in duration despite the presence, through standard investigating practices, of considerable evidence against each defendant. . . .

. . . From the testimony of the officers and by the admission of respondent, it is clear that Miranda was not in any way apprised of his right to consult with an attorney and to have one present during the interrogation, nor was his right not to be compelled to incriminate himself effectively protected in any other manner. Without these warnings the statements were inadmissible. The mere fact that he signed a statement which contained a typed-in clause stating that he had "full knowledge" of his "legal rights" does not approach the knowing and intelligent waiver required to relinquish constitutional rights. . . .

Mr. Justice Clark, dissenting [in Miranda*] . . .*

It is with regret that I find it necessary to write in these cases. However, I am unable to join the majority because its opinion goes too far on too little, while my dissenting brethren do not go quite far enough. . . .

The *ipse dixit* of the majority has no support in our cases. Indeed, the Court admits that "we might not find the defendants' statements [here] to have been involuntary in traditional terms." In short, the Court has added more to the requirements that the accused is entitled to consult with his lawyer and that he must be given the traditional warning that he may remain silent and that anything that he says may be used against him. Now, the Court fashions a constitutional rule that the police may engage in no custodial interrogation without additionally advising the accused that he has a right under the Fifth Amendment to the presence of counsel during interrogation and that, if he is without funds, counsel will be furnished him. When at any point during an interrogation the accused seeks affirmatively or impliedly to invoke his rights to silence or counsel, interrogation must be forgone or postponed. The Court further holds that failure to follow the new procedures requires inexorably the exclusion of any statement by the accused, as well as the fruits thereof. Such a strict constitutional specific inserted at the nerve center of crime detection may well kill the patient. Since there is at this time a paucity of information and an almost total lack of empirical knowledge on the practical operation of requirements truly comparable to those announced by the majority, I would be more restrained lest we go too far too fast. . . .

The rule prior to today—as Mr. Justice Goldberg, the author of the Court's opinion in *Escobedo*, stated it in *Haynes v. Washington*—depended upon "a totality of circumstances evidencing an involuntary . . . admission of guilt.". . .

I would continue to follow that rule. Under the "totality of circumstances" rule of which my Brother Goldberg spoke in *Haynes,* I would consider in each case whether the police officer prior to custodial interrogation added the warning that the suspect might have counsel present at the interrogation and, further, that a court would appoint one at his request if he was too poor to employ counsel. In the absence of warnings, the burden would be on the State to prove that counsel was knowingly and intelligently waived or that in the totality of the circumstances, including the failure to give the necessary warnings, the confession was clearly voluntary. . . .

. . . In this way we would not be acting in the dark nor in one full sweep changing the traditional rules of custodial interrogation which this Court has for so long recognized as a justifiable and proper tool in balancing individual rights against the rights of society. It will be soon enough to go further when we are able to appraise with somewhat better accuracy the effect of such a holding. . . .

Mr. Justice Harlan, dissenting . . .

I believe the decision of the Court represents poor constitutional law and entails harmful consequences for the country at large. How serious these consequences may prove to be only time can tell. But the basic flaws in the Court's justification seem to me readily apparent now once all sides of the problem are considered. . . .

[1. Poor Constitutional Law.] The new rules are not designed to guard against police brutality or other unmistakably banned forms of coercion. Those who use third-degree tactics and deny them in court are equally able and destined to lie as skillfully about warnings and waivers. Rather, the thrust of the new rules is to negate all pressures, to reinforce the nervous or ignorant suspect, and ultimately to discourage any confession at all. The aim in short is toward "voluntariness" in a utopian sense, or to view it from a different angle, voluntariness with a vengeance.

To incorporate this notion into the Constitution requires a strained reading of history and precedent and a disregard of the very pragmatic concerns that alone may on occasion justify such strains. I believe that reasoned examination will show that the Due Process Clauses provide an adequate tool for coping with confessions and that, even if the Fifth Amendment privilege against self-incrimination be invoked, its precedents taken as a whole do not sustain the present rules. Viewed as a choice based on pure policy, these new rules prove to be a highly debatable, if not one-sided, appraisal of the competing interests, imposed over widespread objection, at the very time when judicial restraint is most called for by the circumstances. . . .

Having decided that the Fifth Amendment privilege does apply in the police station, the Court reveals that the privilege imposes more exacting restrictions than does the Fourteenth Amendment's voluntariness test. It then emerges from a discussion of *Escobedo* that the Fifth Amendment requires for an admissible confession that it be given by one distinctly aware of his right not to speak and shielded from "the compelling atmosphere" of interrogation. From these key premises, the Court finally develops the safeguards of warning, counsel, and so forth. I do not believe these premises are sustained by precedents under the Fifth Amendment.

The more important premise is that pressure on the suspect must be eliminated though it be only the subtle influence of the atmosphere and surroundings. The Fifth Amendment, however, has never been thought to forbid *all* pressure to incriminate [oneself] in the situations covered by it. . . .

The Court appears similarly wrong in thinking that precise knowledge of one's rights is a settled prerequisite under the Fifth Amendment to the loss of its protections. A number of lower federal court cases have held that grand jury witnesses need not always be warned of their privilege, and Wigmore states this to be the better rule for trial witnesses. No Fifth Amendment precedent is cited for the Court's contrary view. There might of course be reasons apart from Fifth Amendment precedent for requiring warning or any other safeguard on questioning but that is a different matter entirely. . . .

[2. Effect on Law Enforcement.] Examined as an expression of public policy, the Court's new regime proves so dubious that there can be no due compensation for its weakness in constitutional law. . . . [P]recedent reveals that the Fourteenth Amendment in practice has been construed to strike a different balance, that the Fifth Amendment gives the Court little solid support in this context, and that the Sixth Amendment should have no bearing at all. Legal history has been stretched before to satisfy deep needs of society. In this instance, however, the Court has not and cannot make the powerful showing that its new rules are plainly desirable in the context of our society, something which is surely demanded before those rules are engrafted onto the Constitution and imposed on every State and county in the land. . . .

What the Court largely ignores is that its rules impair, if they will not eventually serve wholly to frustrate, an instrument of law enforcement that has long and quite reasonably been thought worth the price paid for it. There can be little doubt that the Court's new code would markedly decrease the number of confessions. To warn the suspect that he may remain silent and remind him that his confession may be used in court are minor obstructions. To require also an express waiver by the suspect and an end to questioning whenever he demurs must heavily handicap questioning. And to suggest or provide counsel for the suspect simply invites the end of the interrogation.

How much harm this decision will inflict on law enforcement cannot fairly be predicted with accuracy. . . . We do know that some crimes cannot be solved without confessions, that ample expert testimony attests to their importance in crime control, and that the Court is taking a real risk with society's welfare in imposing its new regime on the country. The social costs of crime are too great to call the new rules anything but a hazardous experimentation.

While passing over the costs and risks of its experiment, the Court portrays the evils of normal police questioning in terms which I think are exaggerated. Albeit stringently confined by the due process standards interrogation is no doubt often inconvenient and unpleasant for the suspect. However, it is no less so for a man to be arrested and jailed, to have his house searched, or to stand trial in court, yet all this may properly happen to the most innocent given probable cause, a warrant, or an indictment. Society has always paid a stiff price for law and order, and peaceful interrogation is not one of the dark moments of the law.

This brief statement of the competing considerations seems to me ample proof that the court's preference is highly debatable at best and therefore not to be read into the Constitution. However, it may make the analysis more graphic to consider the actual facts of one of the four cases reversed by the Court. *Miranda v. Arizona* serves best, being neither the hardest nor easiest of the four under the Court's standards.

On March 3, 1963, an 18-year-old girl was kidnapped and forcibly raped near Phoenix, Arizona. Ten days later, on the morning of March 13, petitioner Miranda was arrested and taken to the police station. At this time Miranda was 23 years old, indigent, and educated to the extent of completing half the ninth grade. He had "an emotional illness" of the schizophrenic type, according to the doctor who eventually examined him; the doctor's report also stated that Miranda was "alert and oriented as to time, place, and person," intelligent within normal limits, competent to stand trial, and sane within the legal definition. At the police station, the victim picked Miranda out of a lineup, and two officers then took him into a separate room to interrogate him, starting about 11:30 a.m. Though at first denying his guilt, within a short time Miranda gave a detailed oral confession and then wrote out in his own hand and signed a brief statement admitting and describing the crime. All this was accomplished in two hours or less without any force, threats or promises and—I will assume this though the record is uncertain—without any effective warnings at all.

Miranda's oral and written confessions are now held inadmissible under the Court's new rules. One is entitled to feel astonished that the Constitution can be read to produce this result. These confessions were obtained during brief, daytime questioning conducted by two officers and unmarked by any of the traditional indicia of coercion. They assured a conviction for a brutal and unsettling crime, for which the police had and quite possibly could obtain little evidence other than the victim's identifications, evidence which is frequently unreliable. There [were], in sum, a legitimate purpose, no perceptible unfairness, and certainly little risk of injustice in the interrogation. Yet the resulting confessions and the responsible course of police practice they represent are to be sacrificed to the Court's own finespun conception of fairness which I seriously doubt is shared by many thinking citizens in this country. . . .

In closing this necessarily truncated discussion of policy considerations attending the new confession rules, some reference must be made to their ironic untimeliness. There is now in progress in this country a massive re-examination of criminal law enforcement procedures on a scale never before witnessed. Participants in this undertaking include a Special Committee of the American Bar Association, under the chairmanship of Chief Judge Lumbard of the Court of Appeals for the Second Circuit; a distinguished study group of the American Law Institute, headed by Professors Vorenberg and Bator of the Harvard Law School; and the President's Commission on Law Enforcement and the Administration of Justice, under the leadership of the Attorney General of the United States. Studies are also being conducted by the District of Columbia Crime Commission, [by] the Georgetown Law Center, and by others equipped to do practical research. There are also signs that legislatures in some of the States may be preparing to re-examine the problem before us.

It is no secret that concern has been expressed lest long-range and lasting reforms be frustrated by this Court's too rapid departure from existing constitutional standards. Despite the Court's disclaimer, the practical effect of the decision made today must inevitably be to handicap seriously sound efforts at reform, not least by removing options necessary to a just compromise of competing interests. Of course legislative reform is rarely speedy or unanimous, though this Court has been more patient in the past. But the legislative reforms when they come would have the vast advantage of empirical data and comprehensive study, they would allow experimentation and use of solutions not open to the courts, and they would restore the initiative in criminal law reform to those forums where it truly belongs. . . .

Mr. Justice White, dissenting . . .

That the Court's holding today is neither compelled nor even strongly suggested by the language of the Fifth Amendment, is at odds with American and English legal history, and involves a departure from a long line of precedent does not prove either that the Court has exceeded its powers or that the Court is wrong or unwise in its present reinterpretation of the Fifth Amendment. It does, however, underscore the obvious—that the Court has not discovered or found the law in making today's decision, nor has it derived it from some irrefutable sources; what it has done is to make new law and new public policy in much the same way that it has in the course of interpreting other great clauses of the Constitution. This is what the Court historically has done. Indeed, it is what it must do and will continue to do until and unless there is some fundamental change in the constitutional distribution of governmental powers.

But if the Court is here and now to announce new and fundamental policy to govern certain aspects of our affairs, it is wholly legitimate to examine the mode of this or any other constitutional decision in this Court and to inquire into the advisability of its end product in terms of the long-range interest of the country. At the very least the Court's text and reasoning should withstand analysis and be a fair exposition of the constitutional provision which its opinion interprets. Decisions like these cannot rest alone on syllogism, metaphysics or some ill-defined notions of natural justice, although each will perhaps play its part. In proceeding to such constructions as it now announces, the Court should also duly consider all the factors and interests bearing upon the cases, at least insofar as the relevant materials are available; and if the necessary considerations are not treated in the record or obtainable from some other reliable source, the Court should not proceed to formulate fundamental policies based on speculation alone.

[1. Unsubstantiated Facts.] First, we may inquire what are the textual and factual bases of this new fundamental rule. To reach the result announced on the grounds it does, the Court must stay within the confines of the Fifth Amendment, which forbids self-incrimination only if *compelled*. Hence the core of the Court's opinion is that because of the "compulsion inherent in custodial surroundings, no statement obtained from [a] defendant [in custody] can truly be the product of his free choice," absent the use of adequate protective devices as described by the Court. However, the Court does not point to any sudden inrush of new knowledge requiring the rejection of 70 years' experience. . . . Rather than asserting new knowledge, the Court concedes that it cannot truly know what occurs during custodial questioning, because of the innate secrecy of such proceedings. It extrapolates a picture of what it conceives to be the norm from police investigatorial manuals, published in 1959 and 1962 or earlier, without any attempt to allow for adjustments in police practices that may have occurred in the wake of more recent decisions of state appellate tribunals or this Court. But even if the relentless application of the described procedures could lead to involuntary confessions, it most assuredly does not follow that each and every case will disclose this kind of interrogation or this kind of consequence. Insofar as appears from the Court's opinion, it has not examined a single transcript of any police interrogation, let alone the interrogation that took place in any one of these cases which it decides today. Judged by any of the standards for empirical investigation utilized in the social sciences the factual basis for the Court's premise is patently inadequate.

Although in the Court's view in-custody interrogation is inherently coercive, the Court says that the spontaneous product of the coercion of arrest and detention is still to be deemed voluntary. An accused, arrested on probable cause, may blurt out a confession which will be admissible despite the fact that he is alone and in custody, without any showing that he had any notion of his right to remain silent or of the consequences of his admission. Yet, under the Court's rule, if the police ask him a single question such as "Do you have anything to say?" or "Did you kill your wife?" his response, if there is one, has somehow been compelled, even if the accused has been clearly warned of his right to remain silent. Common sense informs us to the contrary. . . .

On the other hand, even if one assumed that there was an adequate factual basis for the conclusion that all confessions obtained during in-custody interrogation are the product of compulsion, the rule propounded by the Court would still be irrational, for, apparently, it is only if the accused is also warned of his right to counsel and waives both that right and the right against self-incrimination that the inherent compulsiveness of interrogation disappears. But if the defendant may not answer without a warning a question such as "Where were you last night?" without having his answer be a compelled one, how can the Court ever accept his negative answer to the question of whether he wants to consult his retained counsel or counsel whom the court will appoint?. . .

[2. Consequences of the Decision.] Criticism of the Court's opinion, however, cannot stop with a demonstration that the factual and textual bases for the rule it propounds are, at best, less than compelling. Equally relevant is an assessment of the rule's consequences measured against community values. The Court's duty to assess the consequences of its action is not satisfied by the utterance of the truth that a value of our system of criminal justice is "to respect the inviolability of the human personality" and to require government to produce the evidence against the accused by its own independent labors. More than the human dignity of the accused is involved; the human personality of others in the society must also be preserved. Thus the values reflected by the privilege are not the sole desideratum; society's interest in the general security is of equal weight.

The obvious underpinning of the Court's decision is a deep-seated distrust of all confessions. As the Court declares that the accused may not be interrogated without counsel present, absent a waiver of the right to counsel, and as the Court all but admonishes the lawyer to advise the accused to remain silent, the result adds up to a judicial judgment that evidence from the accused should not be used against him in any way, whether compelled or not. This is the not so subtle overtone of the opinion—that it is inherently wrong for the police to gather evidence from the accused himself. And this is precisely the nub of this dissent. I see nothing wrong or immoral, and certainly nothing unconstitutional, in the police's asking a suspect whom they have reasonable cause to arrest whether or not he killed his wife or in confronting him with the evidence on which the arrest was based, at least where he has been plainly advised that he may remain completely silent. . . .

This is not to say that the value of respect for the inviolability of the accused's individual personality should be accorded no weight or that all confessions should be indiscriminately admitted. This Court has long read the Constitution to proscribe compelled confessions, a salutary rule from which there should be no retreat. But I see no sound basis, factual or otherwise, and the Court gives none, for concluding that the present rule against the receipt of coerced confessions is inadequate for the task of sorting out inadmissible evidence and must be replaced by the *per se* rule which is now imposed. Even if the new concept can be said to have advantages of some sort over the present law, they are far outweighed by its likely undesirable impact on other very relevant and important interests.

The most basic function of any government is to provide for the security of the individual and of his property. These ends of society are served by the criminal laws which for the most part are aimed at the prevention of crime. Without the reasonably effective performance of the task of preventing private violence and retaliation, it is idle to talk about human dignity and civilized values. . . .

. . . There is, in my view, every reason to believe that a good many criminal defendants who otherwise would have been convicted on what this Court has previously thought to be the most satisfactory kind of evidence will now, under this new version of the Fifth Amendment, either not be tried at all or will be acquitted if the State's evidence, minus the confession, is put to the test of litigation.

I have no desire whatsoever to share the responsibility for any such impact on the present criminal process.

In some unknown number of cases the Court's rule will return a killer, a rapist or other criminal to the streets and to the environment which produced him, to repeat his crime whenever it pleases him. As a consequence, there will not be a gain, but a loss, in human dignity. The real concern is not the unfortunate consequences of this new decision on the criminal law as an abstract, disembodied series of authoritative proscriptions, but the impact on those who rely on the public authority for protection and who without it can only engage in violent self-help with guns, knives and the help of their neighbors similarly inclined. There is, of course, a saving factor: the next victims are uncertain, unnamed and unrepresented in this case. . . .

POSTSCRIPT

The Supreme Court appointments that followed Richard Nixon's victory in the presidential election of 1968 signaled a retreat from the Warren Court's approach to the rights of criminal defendants and suspects. In 1969, following Earl Warren's retirement, Nixon appointed to the chief justiceship Warren Burger, an acknowledged opponent of *Miranda*. Three additional Nixon appointees, all of whom were perceived to be opposed to the trend of the Warren Court's criminal justice decisions, followed: Harry A. Blackmun (1970), Lewis F. Powell, Jr. (1972), and William H. Rehnquist (1972). Blackmun had been a close friend of Warren Burger's; Powell, one of the members of President Johnson's Commission on Law Enforcement and the Administration of Justice, had been critical of *Escobedo* and *Miranda;* and Rehnquist served as head of the Justice Department's Office of Legal Counsel during the first term of the Nixon administration. The predictable result was a slow but steady erosion of *Miranda*'s scope and status. This decision has always been a controversial political symbol, but after the rulings since, the question is whether *Miranda* is anything more than a symbol.

In *Harris v. New York* (1971), Chief Justice Burger and newly appointed Justice Blackmun joined the three dissenters from *Miranda* to form a majority that narrowed the scope of that landmark precedent.[27] In this case, the police had gained a confession from a suspect who had been given a defective set of warnings. Under *Miranda,* the confession was inadmissible to prove the defendant's guilt, but it was less clear whether the state could use the confession to impeach the defendant's credibility if he took the stand. In a majority opinion written by Burger, the Supreme Court ruled that the state could use the confession for impeachment purposes. Though some of the language of the *Miranda* opinion could "be read as indicating a bar to the use of any uncounseled statement for any purpose,"[28] it did not require that result. "The shield provided by *Miranda* cannot be perverted into a license to use perjury by way of a defense, free from the risk of confrontation with prior inconsistent utterances."[29] If the prosecution could establish that a suspect was lying on the stand by using his own earlier incriminating

---

[27]401 U.S. 222 (1971).

[28]Idem, 224.

[29]Idem, 226.

remarks, it could do so whether or not the remarks were properly preceded by the *Miranda* warnings. Justices Hugo Black, William O. Douglas, William Brennan, and Thurgood Marshall dissented from the Court's decision.

In *Oregon v. Haas* (1975), the Court returned to the issue of whether the prosecution could use incriminating remarks obtained in violation of *Miranda* to impeach the credibility of a defendant who chose to testify. In this case, the suspect demanded to see a lawyer but then incriminated himself after the police refused to honor the request. If the prosecution could use these statements at trial to impeach the defendant's credibility, the police would have little incentive to grant a defendant's request to see a lawyer. After all, if the police honored such a request, the interrogation would in the great majority of cases end because the lawyer would instruct the defendant not to answer any questions. Hence from a police perspective, it might be better to continue the interrogation. Though any resulting incriminating statements could not be introduced as evidence of the defendant's guilt, they could at least be used for impeachment purposes. The police would have less incentive to comply with *Miranda,* and the defendant would be less likely to take the stand in his own defense, with the probable consequence that the jury would tend to view the defendant less favorably.

In a majority opinion written by Blackmun, the Court extended the *Harris* rule. The prosecution could impeach Haas's credibility with statements obtained from him after he asked to see a lawyer. The Court could see no significant difference between *Harris* and *Haas.* The reasons that "sufficed for the result in *Harris*" demanded "a like result in Haas's case."[30] As to the concern that after a suspect had asked for a lawyer "the officer may have little to lose and perhaps something to gain by way of possibly uncovering impeachment material," Blackmun described this possibility as "speculative." It was more likely, he continued, that the police would continue to engage in unlawful interrogations because they were simply unaware that the warnings that they had given the defendant were defective. "In any event, the balance was struck in *Harris,* and we are not disposed to change it now."[31] As long as the police did not engage in coercive or abusive tactics, they could, for the purpose of obtaining evidence for impeachment, continue to interrogate a prisoner after he had asked to see a lawyer. Justices Brennan and Marshall dissented from the Court's decision.[32]

It was, of course, possible for the state to use information obtained in violation of *Miranda* for purposes other than to impeach the credibility of a defendant who takes the stand in his own defense. For example, the state could use such information to gather additional evidence against the defendant. The Court evalu-

---

[30]*Oregon v. Haas*, 420 U.S. 714, 722 (1975).

[31]Idem, 723.

[32]In 1990, the Supreme Court refused to broaden the "impeachment exception" by permitting the state to impeach *all* defense witnesses with statements obtained in violation of *Miranda;* see *James v. Illinois,* 493 U.S. 307 (1990). The current rule is that only the defendant's credibility can be constitutionally attacked in this fashion. However, *James* was a 5–4 decision, and two of the justices in the majority—Brennan and Marshall—have since retired from the Court. They were replaced by David Souter and Clarence Thomas.

ated the constitutionality of this practice in *Michigan v. Tucker* (1974).[33] In this case, the police obtained from a rape suspect the name of a witness without informing him that he had a right to court-appointed counsel if he was indigent. The Court ruled that it was permissible for the state to use the testimony of this witness to convict the defendant. In an opinion written by Justice Rehnquist, the Court reasoned that excluding such testimony served no purpose. It would neither measurably deter police misconduct nor aid the truth-finding function of courts. Citing *Harris v. New York*, the Court concluded that the Fifth Amendment did not prohibit the police from *all* use of incriminating statements that were, though voluntarily given, obtained in violation of the *Miranda* rules. The prosecution could not convict a defendant on the basis of such statements, but it could to some extent convict a defendant on the basis of evidence gained from such statements.[34]

Rehnquist's *Tucker* opinion not only narrowed the scope of *Miranda* but also reduced its constitutional status. Rehnquist claimed that the Court in *Miranda* had "recognized that these procedural safeguards were not themselves rights protected by the Constitution but were instead measures to insure that the right against compulsory self-incrimination was protected."[35] The actual constitutional right was to be free from compelled self-incrimination as defined by the principle of voluntariness. The *Miranda* rules were merely means of "practical reinforcement." They were judicially created "prophylactic standards" that were to be applied only when they were necessary to preserve our adversary system, to deter police misconduct, or to ensure the reliability of evidence admitted at trials.[36]

After *Tucker*, the Court continued to decrease the practical import of the warnings by reducing the legal significance of an assertion of *Miranda* rights. For example, in *Michigan v. Mosley* (1975), the Court ruled that the police may "try again" to obtain incriminating information from a defendant who had claimed his right to remain silent.[37] A "significant" period of time must separate the two interrogations, and the second interrogation must be preceded by the *Miranda* warnings, but if these two conditions were met, any incriminating remarks gained by

---

[33]417 U.S. 433 (1974).

[34]The significance of *Tucker* was unclear because the police interrogation in this case occurred prior to the *Miranda* decision (therefore, the police did not know that they had to inform the suspect of his right to a court-appointed attorney), though the trial was held afterward. Hence the majority opinion avoided the broad question of whether *all* "fruits" of statements obtained in violation of *Miranda* were to be excluded.

[35]*Michigan v. Tucker*, 417 U.S. 444 (1974).

[36]In his dissent, Justice Douglas objected to the majority's reading of *Miranda* and to the characterization of the *Miranda* rules as mere "prophylactic standards." He noted that the Court would have been powerless to overturn Miranda's conviction unless there was a constitutional basis for the warnings. True, the Court in *Miranda* had said that the warnings were necessary "'unless other fully effective means are adopted to notify the person' of his rights." But there was no evidence in *Tucker* that the state had utilized other means to protect the defendant's right against self-incrimination. Hence the defendant's incriminating remarks did not meet "*constitutional* standards," and all evidence obtained from the incriminating remarks should therefore have been excluded from the trial. Idem, 463.

[37]423 U.S. 96 (1975).

the second interrogation could be used to convict the defendant. *Miranda* did not require exclusion if the defendant, after first invoking his right to remain silent, changed his mind and confessed.[38]

Another means by which the Supreme Court eroded *Miranda* was with a relatively tight definition of what constituted "custodial interrogation." The police had to give the warnings only if the questioning qualified as a custodial interrogation. In *Berkemer v. McCarty* (1984), the Court ruled that roadside questioning of a motorist was not custodial questioning even though the police officer had already decided to make an arrest.[39] Such questioning did not have the inherently coercive character of a stationhouse interrogation, and therefore the warnings were not required and any incriminating remarks made by the motorist were admissible. Even questioning that occurs in a police station may not rise to the level of a custodial interrogation. The Supreme Court has ruled that if a suspect "voluntarily" accompanies the police to the stationhouse, any incriminating remarks would be admissible. This was the rule even if the questioning was designed to elicit such incriminating information.[40]

In *Illinois v. Perkins* (1990), the Court considered the admissibility of incriminating remarks made by a jailed suspect in "casual conversation" with an undercover agent. The Court ruled that such conversation, even if it was reasonably likely to elicit an incriminating response, was not a custodial interrogation. The situation lacked the "police-dominated atmosphere" and the "compulsion" inherent to custodial interrogations. "There is no empirical basis for the assumption that a suspect speaking to those whom he assumes are not officers will feel compelled to speak by the fear of reprisal for remaining silent or in the hope of more lenient treatment should he confess."[41] Hence incriminating remarks gained by this technique were fully admissible. "*Miranda* was not meant to protect suspects from boasting about their criminal activities in front of persons whom they believe to be their cellmates."[42]

In this fashion, the Supreme Court whittled away at the edges of *Miranda*. However, the Court did not make its first explicit exception until *New York v.*

---

[38]For a later case with a result similar to the one in *Mosley*, see *Oregon v. Elstad*, 470 U.S. 298 (1985). In contrast to *Mosley*, the Supreme Court ruled in *Edwards v. Arizona*, 451 U.S. 477 (1981), that the police could not "try again" if the suspect asserted his right to counsel rather than his right to remain silent. Once a suspect requests counsel, the police cannot interrogate him until counsel has been made available unless the suspect himself "initiates further communication, exchanges, or conversations with the police." Idem, 485. See also *Minnick v. Mississippi*, 498 U.S. 146, 111 S.Ct. 486 (1990).

[39]468 U.S. 420 (1984).

[40]See *Oregon v. Mathiason*, 429 U.S. 492 (1977); and *California v. Beheler*, 463 U.S. 1121 (1983).

[41]*Illinois v. Perkins*, 496 U.S. 292, 296–297 (1990).

[42]Idem, 298. An earlier case had ruled that *Miranda* applied to "any words or actions on the part of the police . . . that the police should know are reasonably likely to elicit an incriminating response from the suspect. . . . A practice that the police should know is reasonably likely to evoke an incriminating response from a suspect thus amounts to interrogation." *Rhode Island v. Innis*, 446 U.S. 291, 301 (1980). Rather than focusing on the likelihood of incrimination, *Perkins* defined interrogation based on the existence of compulsion.

Quarles (1984).[43] In an opinion written by Justice Rehnquist, the Court created a "public safety" exception to the rule requiring *Miranda* warnings. Answers to police questions that were "reasonably prompted by a concern for the public safety" were admissible despite the fact that they were not preceded by *Miranda* warnings. In this case, one of four police officers surrounding a rape suspect handcuffed him and then asked him where his gun was. Only after the suspect told the officer where it was did the officer formally arrest the suspect and advise him of his rights. The Court said that the warnings were properly delayed until after the gun was found because they might have encouraged the suspect to keep silent. If the suspect had asserted his right to remain silent, the hidden gun might not have been found. The safety of the public justified making an exception to the *Miranda* rules because the warnings were not themselves constitutional rights. The rules were only "prophylactic" guidelines. Hence the police officer could testify at the trial that the suspect told him where the gun was and the gun itself could be offered as evidence of the suspect's guilt. It did not matter, Rehnquist reasoned, that the actual motive of the police officer's question about the location of the gun was unrelated to public safety. The exception applied if the question was "reasonably prompted by a concern for the public safety." If a police officer would be acting reasonably by asking a question for the sake of public safety, the suspect's answer was admissible regardless if no *Miranda* warnings had been given.

Four dissenting justices—Sandra Day O'Connor, John Paul Stevens, Marshall, and Brennan—objected to the way that the majority in *Quarles* balanced the value of public safety against the suspect's right against compulsory self-incrimination. The principle of *Miranda* was that incriminating remarks obtained without the specified warnings violated the Fifth Amendment and were therefore inadmissible. If public safety required the police to question suspects without the warnings, that did not mean that evidence gained thereby became admissible:

> The majority does not argue that police questioning about issues of public safety is any less coercive than custodial interrogations into other matters. The majority's only contention is that police officers could more easily protect the public if *Miranda* did not apply to custodial interrogations concerning the public's safety. But *Miranda* was not a decision about public safety; it was a decision about coerced confessions.[44]

In fact, the dissent noted, the majority assumed that the exception would enable the police to gain information from suspects that they would have refused to provide if properly warned. The decision was therefore a license for the police to violate the Fifth Amendment rights of suspects if and when they reasonably thought that the public safety required it. The dissenters concluded that although the police could violate the *Miranda* rules whenever they thought it was necessary for public safety, the Fifth Amendment prohibited the use of such coerced statements at trial.

---

[43]467 U.S. 649 (1984).

[44]Idem, 684.

Following *Quarles,* a divided Court has repeatedly endorsed Chief Justice Rehnquist's assumption that the *Miranda* warnings can be balanced against other values because they are not themselves rights but merely "prophylactic" rules. In *Oregon v. Elstad* (1985), a decision that permitted evidence to be introduced at trial even though the police had initially failed to inform the suspect of his rights, the Court reasoned that if "errors are made by law enforcement officers in administering the prophylactic *Miranda* procedures, they should not breed the same irremediable consequences as police infringement of the Fifth Amendment itself."[45] Police can, by properly informing the suspect of his rights, rectify an initial failure to Mirandize the suspect. Once the suspect was properly Mirandized, all subsequent incriminating remarks would be admissible.

In 1986, in a majority opinion written by Chief Justice Rehnquist, the Court upheld the admissibility of a confession of a mentally ill person who confessed because "God's voice" had ordered him to confess or commit suicide. Speaking for a five-justice majority, Rehnquist argued that the "sole concern of the Fifth Amendment, on which *Miranda* was based, is governmental coercion."[46] Accordingly, since the police had not coerced the confession, it did not matter that the suspect was mentally ill and had not "freely" chosen to incriminate himself. *Miranda* did not stand for the principle that only confessions that were completely voluntary should be introduced at trial but rather that only confessions coerced by the state should be excluded. "The purpose of excluding evidence seized in violation of the Constitution is to substantially deter future violations of the Constitution."[47] Since the state had not coerced the mentally ill suspect, there was nothing to deter. His confession therefore fell outside *Miranda* and the Fifth Amendment.

In the same year, the Court also ruled that a confession was admissible even though the police had failed to inform the suspect that his sister had retained a lawyer for him and even though the police had told the lawyer that they would not be interrogating the suspect. In coming to this conclusion, the Court said it was "now well established" that the *Miranda* warnings were "'not themselves rights protected by the Constitution'"; they were only "prophylactic" guidelines that the Court applied when it thought they were necessary to protect a suspect's right against self-incrimination.[48] In this case, even though the police had acted unethically by lying to the attorney and by keeping vital information from the suspect, they had given the suspect the warnings and had done nothing unlawful. Society's "legitimate law enforcement interests" therefore justified admitting the defendant's confession as evidence.

In 1989, in another opinion written by Chief Justice Rehnquist, the Court ruled that the warnings did not have to be given in the exact form described in *Miranda.* In this case, *Duckworth v. Eagan,* the suspect was initially told that if he could not afford a lawyer, one would be appointed for him "if and when you go to

---

[45]*Oregon v. Elstad,* 470 U.S. 298, 309 (1985).

[46]*Colorado v. Connelly,* 479 U.S. 157, 170 (1986).

[47]Idem, 166.

[48]*Moran v. Burbine,* 475 U.S. 412, 424 (1986).

court." The defense argued that this form of the warnings was constitutionally flawed because it gave the impression that unless the defendant could afford counsel, he would not have the benefit of state-supplied counsel until after questioning. Nevertheless, despite this possible interpretation of the warnings that the police gave to Eagan, the Court ruled his confession admissible. Based on his view that the Miranda warnings were not constitutional rights themselves but prophylactic measures, Rehnquist argued that the warnings given in this case "touched all of the bases required by *Miranda*."[49]

The line of cases that characterized the *Miranda* warnings as prophylactic rules rather than as constitutional rights persuaded the Reagan administration that perhaps *Miranda* itself could be overruled. After all, if the warnings were not constitutional rights, what authority did the Supreme Court have to impose them on the states? In 1986, the Department of Justice published a report that advocated overruling *Miranda*.[50] Attorney General Edwin Meese told Solicitor General Charles Fried to find a test case to bring to the Supreme Court.[51] However, nothing came of these efforts to reverse *Miranda*, perhaps because there was no consensus that a change was necessary, not even within the law enforcement community. In 1987, the executive director of the International Association of Chiefs of Police observed that the police were divided about *Miranda* and noted that a generation of officers had been abiding by the decision throughout their entire careers.[52] By this time, though debate concerning the status of *Miranda* still raged in the law journals,[53] a large part of the American law enforcement community had not only reconciled itself to *Miranda* but also thought that the decision had probably helped professionalize the police force. Of course, it may well be that the police accepted *Miranda* in 1987 only because the Supreme Court, over the previous twenty years, had significantly narrowed its scope. The ultimate question is whether the Supreme Court has cut too much out of *Miranda*, undermining its substantive principles and leaving it an empty symbol of the American commitment to the rights of criminal defendants and suspects. Has the Court gone too far? What is the proper balance between the rights of individuals, especially the right to remain silent, and the legitimate law enforcement needs of society?

---

[49]*Duckworth v. Eagan*, 492 U.S. 195, 109 S.Ct. 2875, 2880 (1989).

[50]U.S. Department of Justice, Office of Legal Policy, *Report to the Attorney General on the Law of Pretrial Interrogation* (Washington, D.C.: U.S. Government Printing Office, 1986).

[51]Jonathan I. Z. Agronsky, "*Meese v. Miranda*: The Final Countdown," *American Bar Association Journal*, Nov. 1, 1987, cited by Mark Berger, "Compromise and Continuity: *Miranda* Waivers, Confession Admissibility, and the Retention of Interrogation Protections," *University of Pittsburgh Law Review* 49 (1988): 1008, n. 7.

[52]Berger, "Compromise and Continuity," 1009, n. 8; see also 1011, n. 16.

[53]See Stephen J. Schulhofer, "Reconsidering *Miranda*," *University of Chicago Law Review* 54 (1987): 435–461; Joseph D. Grano, "*Miranda*'s Constitutional Difficulties: A Reply to Professor Schulhofer," *University of Chicago Law Review* 55 (1988): 174–189; Gerald M. Caplan, "Questioning *Miranda*," *Vanderbilt Law Review* 38 (1985): 1417–1476; and Welsh S. White, "Defending *Miranda*: A Reply to Professor Caplan," *Vanderbilt Law Review* 39 (1986): 1–22.

Plea Bargaining

NORTH CAROLINA V. ALFORD
400 U.S. 25 (1970)

✦

The incorporation of the Bill of Rights into the Fourteenth Amendment—the subject of Chapter 1—is one of the Supreme Court's most impressive accomplishments. It fundamentally changed American federalism, in part by erecting national standards of criminal justice. A similar achievement, one that *Miranda v. Arizona*, the subject Chapter 2, symbolizes best, was the Warren Court's extension of the criminal justice guarantees that were nationalized. The general result was a criminal justice system that remains unparalleled in the contemporary world. No other country has granted criminal defendants the kinds and scope of rights that are now so often taken for granted in the United States: the right to a jury trial, the right to remain silent, the right to confront one's accusers, the right to a speedy trial, the right to an appeal, the right to counsel on appeal. Of course, because these rights favor the defendant, they have made the state's task of proving guilt "beyond a reasonable doubt" more difficult. When a state takes away a person's life, liberty, or property, it must follow an elaborate procedure governing arrest, pretrial motions, the trial, and postconviction proceedings. However, it is arguable that the practice of plea bargaining, in which the defendant waives the aforementioned rights and pleads guilty in exchange for a reduction of charges or sentence, seriously undermines the value of these procedural guarantees. Considering that approximately 90 percent of all criminal convictions are currently obtained by guilty pleas, the claim is that the "real" system of criminal justice in the United States is not the "formal" procedural one but rather the "informal" one of negotiation between prosecutors and defense attorneys in which the crucial decisions are made outside the courtroom. After the defense counsel and the prosecutor "strike a deal," all that is usually left is mere "form." A judge "formally" accepts the defendant's guilty plea and sentences the defendant according to the terms of the plea bargain.

Some critics of plea bargaining insist that it is unconstitutional because it penalizes defendants who insist on exercising their formal criminal justice rights, for example, their right to a (jury) trial. The argument is that if those who plead guilty receive more lenient sentences than those who go to trial and are convicted, plea bargaining necessarily involves placing "unconstitutional conditions" on the rights of criminal defendants.[1] The potential constitutional problem inherent in plea bargaining is highlighted if a defendant pleads guilty to a reduced charge of murder yet nonetheless proclaims his innocence, explaining that he pleaded guilty (waiving his constitutional rights) only because he feared that a jury trial would end in a death sentence. Can a state impose the death penalty only on those who exercise their right to a (jury) trial, or does such a rule, at its worst, unconstitutionally allow the prosecutor to coerce "innocent" defendants into pleading guilty to reduced charges? The Supreme Court considered these kinds of questions in *North Carolina v. Alford* (1970). It is good case to reflect on the constitutionality of plea bargaining, both in general and in the specific context in which a capital defendant pleaded guilty but refused to admit his guilt.

The contrasts between the formal adversarial system and the informal one of bargaining are quite evident. The former is an open system designed to see if the state can, without violating the defendant's rights, prove beyond a reasonable doubt that the defendant committed a specific criminal act deserving a certain amount of punishment. The latter is a relatively closed system in which factors that should have no role in the formal process—for example, the size of the prosecutor's caseload, the defendant's previous record, and the existence of any inadmissible evidence—often have a decisive impact. The two systems are therefore quite different in their operation and, presumably, in their results.

Many critics object to plea bargaining on grounds other than its unconstitutionality. Some claim that it is inefficient, others that it is immoral and unjust.[2] Kenneth Kipniss makes the latter point by drawing an interesting analogy. He suggests that plea bargaining is no different in principle from bargaining for grades in an academic setting (see Box 3.1). In both cases, the criminal and the student, as well as the state and the teacher, are satisfied with the outcome. Everyone is better off. However, according to Kipniss, what makes grade negotiation "laughable" is "what makes plea bargaining outrageous." The criminal justice system is not a context for negotiation but for retribution. Just as students should receive the grades that they deserve, so criminals should receive the punishment that they deserve. What do you think of Kipniss's analogy? Is plea bargaining similar to grade negotiation? Does the analogy convince you that plea bargaining is "outrageous," or is it possible that an overburdened educational system could jus-

---

[1]The doctrine of unconstitutional conditions holds that the government "may not condition the receipt of its benefits upon the nonassertion of constitutional rights." "Academic Freedom and Federal Regulation of University Hiring," *Harvard Law Review* 92 (1979): 891–892. See also Howard E. Abrams, "Systemic Coercion: Unconstitutional Conditions in the Criminal Law," *Journal of Criminal Law and Criminology* 72 (1981): 128–164.

[2]For a recent discussion of the wisdom of plea bargaining, see the three articles on this topic published in the *Yale Law Journal* 101 (1992): 1909–2009.

GRADE BARGAINING

. . . Generally speaking, prosecutors and defendants are pleased with the advantages they gain by negotiating a plea. And courts, which gain as well, are reluctant to vacate negotiated pleas where only "proper" inducements have been applied and where promises have been understood and kept. Such judicial neutrality may be commendable where entitlements are being exchanged. But the criminal justice system is not such a context. Rather it is one in which persons are justly given, not what they have bargained for, but what they deserve, irrespective of their bargaining position.

To appreciate this, let us consider another context in which desert plays a familiar role: the assignment of grades in an academic setting. Imagine a "grade bargain" negotiated between a grade-conscious student and a harried instructor. A term paper has been submitted and, after glancing at the first page, the instructor says that if he were to read the paper carefully, applying his usually rigid standards, he would probably decide to give the paper a grade of D. But if the student were to waive his right to a careful reading and conscientious critique, the instructor would agree to a grade of B. The grade-point average being more important to him than either education or justice in grading, the student happily accepts the B, and the instructor enjoys a reduced workload.

One strains to imagine legislators and administrators commending the practice of grade bargaining because it permits more students to be processed by fewer instructors. Teachers can be freed from the burden of having to read and to criticize every paper. One struggles to envision academicians arguing for grade bargaining in the way that jurists have defended plea bargaining, suggesting that a quick assignment of a grade is a more effective influence on the behavior of students, urging that grade bargaining is necessary to the efficient functioning of the schools. There can be no doubt that students who have negotiated a grade are more likely to accept and to understand the verdict of the instructor. Moreover, in recognition of a student's help to the school (by waiving both the reading and the critique), it is proper for the instructor to be lenient. Finally, a quickly assigned grade enables the guidance personnel and the registrar to respond rapidly and appropriately to the student's situation.

What makes all of this laughable is what makes plea bargaining outrageous. For grades, like punishments, should be deserved. Justice in retribution, like justice in grading, does not require that the end result be acceptable to the parties. To reason that because the parties are satisfied the bargain should stand is to be seriously confused. For bargains are out of place in contexts where persons are to receive what they deserve. And the American courtroom, like the American classroom, should be such a context. . . .

Source: Kenneth Kipniss, "Criminal Justice and the Negotiated Plea," *Ethics* 86 (1976): 104–105.

tifiably pursue a policy of grade negotiation? What if a set of graded but un-recorded exams were destroyed in a fire and a significant number of the students did not want to retake the exam? Could an overworked teacher and these students come to a "reasonable accommodation"? What would you do as a student? As an overworked teacher?

Despite the interesting character of such questions, the key issue for our pur-poses remains whether the informal process of plea bargaining is constitutional. Even if plea bargaining is unjust and inefficient—itself a debatable issue—that does not *necessarily* make it unconstitutional. It might merely complement the formal system of trial without violating the Constitution. Hence the issue ad-dressed in this chapter is whether the practice of plea bargaining unconstitution-ally penalizes defendants who want to exercise their constitutional rights. The *Al-ford* litigation will put this issue into sharp focus.

Alford is also worthy of our attention because it insightfully shows that consti-tutional law is often a "moving target" for the lawyers involved in constitutional lit-igation. Not only must constitutional lawyers cite the most recent relevant Supreme Court decisions, but they must also be willing and able to adapt and modify their arguments if this becomes necessary in the course of litigation. The interests of their clients come first. If it will serve their clients' interests, appellate lawyers must abandon positions to which they are personally committed. The lawyers in *Alford* confronted such a situation because the Supreme Court had ini-tially considered *Alford* along with three other cases involving the constitutionality of plea bargaining: *Parker v. North Carolina, Brady v. United States,* and *Mc-Mann v. Richardson.*[3] However, perhaps because *Alford* presented more difficult issues than the other three cases, the Supreme Court decided *Parker, Brady,* and *McMann* in May 1970 but rescheduled *Alford* for reargument later that year. Therefore, during the summer the parties in *Alford* had the opportunity to file supplemental briefs that took into account what the Court had said in May. In the fall, they had to reargue the case with the recent decisions firmly in mind. Conse-quently, comparing the supplemental briefs and the 1970 oral arguments to the main briefs that were filed the year before is quite revealing. It shows how lawyers for both sides adapted their positions to the new legal situation. *Alford* is therefore a good example of how lawyers tactically reorient their arguments as they try to serve their clients in the ever-changing process of constitutional adjudication.

Plea bargaining today is a pervasive feature of the American criminal justice system and is widely accepted by appellate courts. Though it has been around for a long time, it was at one time neither practiced nor tolerated. Only in the second half of the nineteenth century did the practice of trading leniency for guilty pleas emerge.[4] One major factor explaining this trend in the direction of plea bargain-ing, especially in large urban areas, was the expanding caseload brought on by the rising crime rate and the increasing scope of the criminal law. The American crim-inal justice system, itself becoming more bureaucratic and professionalized, strug-gled to find some means to "process" the vast number of criminal defendants. Plea

---

[3]397 U.S. 790 (1970); 397 U.S. 743 (1970); 297 U.S. 759 (1970).

[4]See Albert W. Alschuler, "Plea Bargaining and Its History," *Columbia Law Review* 79 (1979): 16–26.

bargaining was the result. Participants in the system—prosecutors, defense counsel, and judges—adapted to this informal, less adversarial way of settling cases. It was easier, took less time, and avoided all the irritants of the formal adversarial system.[5] Everyone seemed to benefit, including the defendant, who in most cases (as is true of today's defendants) was factually guilty. Hence the increasing caseload was not the only reason why this efficient method of disposing of cases spread quickly.

The American public was largely ignorant of plea bargaining until the 1920s, when a series of public crime commissions and surveys revealed how widespread the practice had become.[6] An editorial in the *Chicago Tribune* in 1928 reflected to some extent the public's attitude toward this new "informal" method of criminal procedure: the editors called plea bargaining an "incompetent, inefficient, and lazy method of administering justice."[7]

Early appellate reaction to plea bargaining was also negative. In a nineteenth-century case, the Wisconsin Supreme Court described plea bargaining as "hardly, if at all, distinguishable in principle from a direct sale of justice." No court could respect such deals without abdicating "its proper functions." The Wisconsin court also argued that the profession of law conducted its business in the open, not in secret negotiations. "Professional weapons are wielded only in open contest" because public "litigation is . . . the safest test of justice."[8] In a 1904 case, the Louisiana Supreme Court underlined the problem of plea bargaining and the innocent defendant. "In the instant case the accused accepted the certainty of conviction of what he took to be a minor offense. . . . Not only was there room for error, but the thing was, what an innocent man might do who found that appearances were against him, and that he might be convicted notwithstanding his innocence."[9] The Georgia Court of Appeals emphasized that it was improper to offer any inducement for a guilty plea: "The law . . . does not encourage confessions of guilt, either in or out of court. . . . The affirmative plea of guilty is received because the prisoner is willing, voluntarily, without inducement of any sort, to confess his guilt and expiate his offense."[10]

Despite these early rejections of plea bargaining by appellate courts, throughout the twentieth century the practice of exchanging leniency for guilty pleas grew in trial courts across the country. The Bureau of the Census reported that guilty pleas in felony cases grew from 77 percent in 1936 to 86 percent in 1940.[11] During the 1960s, the Warren Court's nationalization and expansion of the criminal justice guarantees of the Bill of Rights paradoxically contributed to an increase in

---

[5]See Milton Heumann, *Plea Bargaining* (Chicago: University of Chicago Press, 1977).

[6]Ibid., 26–32.

[7]*Chicago Tribune*, April 27, 1928, p. 1, cited by Alschuler, "Plea Bargaining and Its History," 31.

[8]*Wight v. Rindskopf*, 43 Wis. 344, 354–357 (1877).

[9]*State v. Coston*, 113 La. 718, 720, 37 So. 619, 620 (1904).

[10]*Griffin v. State*, 12 Ga. App. 615, 622–623 (1913). The three cases referred to in this paragraph are discussed in Alschuler, "Plea Bargaining and Its History," 21–23.

[11]U.S. Department of Commerce, Bureau of the Census, *Judicial Criminal Statistics,* published annually, 1933–1945.

plea bargaining. Though plea bargaining was already pervasive by this time, these decisions not only gave defendants more rights to bargain with but also strained the resources of prosecutors and judges. The number of pretrial motions and postconviction proceedings went up radically, monopolizing the time of criminal justice officials. Longer trials and the increasing amount of criminal appellate litigation exacerbated the problem, especially after the crime rate jumped during the 1960s. The public's anxiety about the crime rate and the "crisis" in the criminal justice system grew enormously throughout the latter half of the 1960s. In March 1969, *U.S. News & World Report* published an article titled "Breakdown of Courts in America" (see Box 3.2). It shows the sort of "news" the American public was reading as the Supreme Court turned to the issue of the constitutionality of plea bargaining.

Even before the Warren Court nationalized and expanded the rights of defendants and suspects, plea bargaining functioned as the criminal justice system's safety valve. Recognizing its importance, prominent public commissions and legal organizations came to its defense during the 1960s. In 1967, the President's Commission on Law Enforcement and the Administration of Justice argued that plea bargaining was no longer a necessary evil:

> It would be a serious mistake, however, to assume that the guilty plea is no more than a means of disposing of criminal cases at minimal cost. It relieves both the defendant and the prosecution of the inevitable risks and uncertainties of trial. It imports a degree of certainty and flexibility into a rigid, yet frequently erratic system.[12]

In this passage, the commission implied that the informal system of exchanging leniency for guilty pleas was at least in some respects preferable to the formal system of trial. Clearly, the general attitude toward plea bargaining among legal experts had changed considerably since the 1920s.

In 1968, the American Bar Association (ABA) Project on Minimum Standards for Criminal Justice explained why defendants who pleaded guilty should be treated more leniently than those who insisted on their right to a jury trial. Expediency and cost were not, the ABA argued, the reasons why plea bargaining was justified. Instead, plea bargaining was justified because it was a good institution; it served a number of values. In addition, the ABA admitted that punishing defendants more severely if they chose to go to trial was unethical and unconstitutional but then argued that plea bargaining did no such thing. In the ABA's view, a defendant's waiver of constitutional rights can be "rewarded" with a lenient sentence without "penalizing" the exercise of the defendant's constitutional rights. A defendant convicted at trial is not punished more harshly than the law allows; he is merely punished without leniency. Hence plea bargaining "rewarded" defendants who waived their rights but did not penalize those who exercised them (see Box 3.3).

The distinction that the ABA drew between rewarding those who pleaded guilty and penalizing those who did not and its justification of plea bargaining did

---

[12]*The Challenge of Crime in a Free Society* (Washington, D.C.: U.S. Government Printing Office, 1967), p. 135.

BOX 3.2

BREAKDOWN OF COURTS IN AMERICA

The crime crisis is causing a breakdown of criminal justice in the U.S.

Courts are clogged by criminal cases. The backlog has grown to mountainous proportions. Meantime, although jails are jammed, crime keeps increasing, nationwide, year after year.

All of this is bringing calls from leaders of the bar and experts in law enforcement for a vast restructuring and upbuilding of the system of justice to end the upsurge of crime.

The Federal Bureau of Investigation's latest compilation of reports from state and local police agencies found the rise in violent crime last year running at a national rate of 21 percent above the figure for 1967.

Crime was up in every part of the country—in the suburbs and rural areas as well as in the cities.

Statistics tell a story of worsening terror in the streets. Armed robbery increased 37 percent. Other rises registered included murder, up 15 percent; forcible rape, up 17 percent; aggravated assault, up 13 percent. . . .

. . . A report issued by the Administrative Office of the U.S. Courts shows that nationally the backlog of criminal cases has more than doubled in the last decade, although the number of cases filed "remained relatively stable." Main reason: The new emphasis on rights of defendants, flowing from Supreme Court decisions, has lengthened the time needed to handle the average case. . . .

. . . Speaking to the National Emergency Conference of the National Council on Crime and Delinquency, William T. Gossett, president of the American Bar Association, made these points:

1. Between 1960 and 1967, the overall rate of violent crime in the U.S. rose by 57 percent.
2. During that period, the robbery rate increased 70 percent; aggravated assault, 51 percent; forcible rape, 45 percent; murder, 22 percent.
3. As a result, the courts, especially in some large cities, now have a case backlog of "staggering proportions.". . .

. . . Chief Inspector Sanford D. Garelik of the New York City police department recently declared that "demonstration of legal guilt in our society is becoming ludicrously difficult." He added:

"It is self-defeating, to say the least, to have to arrest the same people over and over again.

"It seems as if our system of criminal justice is being perverted into a system of criminal injustice—injustice to a repeatedly victimized public."

A law-enforcement official in Washington cited these elements of the intensifying breakdown:

"In the new 'era of protection' for the accused, attorneys have been quick to seize upon the tactic of delay and to take advantage of the ease of release on bail, even though chronic violent offenders may be involved.". . .

. . . From an official who has spent more than 20 years fighting crime:

"There is no easy way to solve our crime troubles. These troubles are going to get worse and many millions of people will live in fear until public opinion is aroused to the point where courts are forced to be tougher, swifter and much more efficient.

"In short, what is needed is a massive overhaul of the whole system of criminal justice in this country."

Source: U.S. News & World Report, March 10, 1969, pp. 58–60.

not convince the critics of plea bargaining. The most formidable critic who explicitly responded to the ABA's endorsement of plea bargaining was Albert W. Alschuler, a professor then at the University of Colorado Law School. In a law journal article, he denigrated the distinction between justifiable reward and improper penalty. He argued that those who defended the distinction were on either horn of a dilemma: they must either inflict "undeserved" punishment on a defendant who exercised the right to a jury trial or give a sentence "that will fail to accomplish the legitimate purposes of the criminal law" to a defendant who pleaded guilty. In addition, Alschuler criticized ABA's defense of plea bargaining. His conclusion was that the ABA's rationale was no more than "an elaborately dressed version of the cost-saving utilitarian argument" that the ABA had explicitly rejected. According to Alschuler, plea bargaining was an indefensible institution that unconstitutionally burdened the defendant's right to trial (see Box 3.4).

What do you think of the ABA's and Alschuler's arguments? Can one "reward" a defendant who pleads guilty without "penalizing" one who goes to trial? If one defendant who commits the same offense as another and is as equally culpable pleads guilty and receives a five-year sentence, has this defendant been rewarded, or has the other defendant, who went to trial and was given a significantly longer sentence, been penalized for exercising his constitutional rights? And what of the ABA's defense of plea bargaining? Is the ABA right that prompt resolution of some cases through plea bargains allows the courts to concentrate on contested cases in which guilt is not as clear-cut? What about the purported link that the ABA draws between plea bargaining and the defendant's responsibility? What do you make of Alschuler's specific criticisms of the ABA's rationale? Do you think he was right that the ABA's defense of plea bargaining was nothing but an "elaborately dressed" utilitarian argument? But what if he was right? Perhaps plea bargaining saves enough money to justify itself. How many more judges, prosecutors, and defense counselors would the system need if plea bargaining were prohibited? Can money justify plea bargaining if it burdens a defendant's constitutional rights? How much are constitutional rights worth? Are there other reasons that the ABA did not mention that would justify plea bargaining? If so, what are they?

BOX 3.3

THE ABA ON PLEA BARGAINING

. . . The plea of guilty is probably the most frequent method of conviction in all jurisdictions; in some localities as many as 95 percent of the criminal cases are disposed of in this way. The assumption underlying these standards is that conviction without trial will and should continue to be a most frequent means for the disposition of criminal cases. This assumption is not based upon notions of expediency, but rather upon the conclusion that a number of values are served by the disposition of many criminal cases without trial. By his plea, the defendant aids in ensuring the prompt and certain application of correctional measures to him. He also aids in avoiding delay in the disposition of other cases, thereby increasing the probability of prompt and certain application of correctional measures to other offenders.

In addition, the plea provides a means by which the defendant may acknowledge his guilt and manifest a willingness to assume responsibility for his conduct. Also, in some cases the plea will make it possible to avoid a public trial when the consequences of such publicity outweigh any legitimate need for a public trial. Pleas to lesser offenses make possible alternative correctional measures better adapted to achieving the purposes of correctional treatment, and often prevent undue harm to the defendant from the form of conviction. Such pleas also make it possible to grant concessions to a defendant who has given or offered cooperation in the prosecution of other offenders.

Conviction on a plea of guilty or *nolo contendere*, then, is not merely a matter of administrative convenience. Even if more prosecutors, judges, and defense counsel were available and trial of all cases were possible, conviction without trial would continue to be a necessary and proper part of the administration of criminal justice. It may be noted, however, that a high proportion of pleas of guilty and *nolo contendere* does benefit the system. Such pleas tend to limit the trial process to deciding real disputes and, consequently, to reduce the need for funds and personnel. If the number of judges, courtrooms, court personnel, and counsel for prosecution and defense were to be increased substantially, the funds necessary for such increases might be diverted from elsewhere in the criminal justice process. Moreover, the limited use of the trial process for those cases in which the defendant has grounds for contesting the matter of guilt aids in preserving the meaningfulness of the presumption of innocence.

It may thus be concluded that the frequency of conviction without trial not only permits the achievement of legitimate objectives in cases where pleas of guilty and *nolo contendere* are entered, but also enhances the quality of justice in other cases as well.

❈   ❈   ❈

[D]isparity in treatment is not to be accomplished by the imposition of excessive penalties on those who stand trial. The defendant who goes to trial should not be punished for putting the state to its proof, and the defendant should receive only that sentence which properly serves the deterrent, protective, and other objectives of the criminal justice system.

It has been contended, of course, that if any disparity exists between the defendant who stands trial and other defendants, the former is receiving excessive punishment. That view is rejected here. There is an essential difference between system A, in which defendants who go to trial receive the greatest punishment justifiable under accepted principles of penology and some defendants who plead guilty or *nolo contendere* receive something less because of the circumstances surrounding their plea, and system B, in which disparity results from giving defendants who stand trial greater punishment than can be justified. Numerous appellate cases support the position that a policy of leniency following a plea is proper but that its converse, "extra" severity following trial, is not.

Source: American Bar Association, Project on Minimum Standards for Criminal Justice, *Standards Relating to Pleas of Guilty*, February 1967, pp. 1–3, 14.

The Supreme Court, it would seem, avoided the question of the constitutionality of plea bargaining for as long as it could.[13] It was not until *United States v. Jackson* (1968) that the country's highest court finally said something that had a bearing on the issue.[14] The case concerned the Federal Kidnapping Act, which punished kidnapping with prison sentences unless a jury recommended death. In other words, the statute imposed the death penalty only on defendants who sought to win acquittals before juries. The Supreme Court ruled that the death penalty provisions of the statute violated the Fifth Amendment privilege against self-incrimination and the Sixth Amendment right to a jury trial.

Though the Supreme Court's ruling in *Jackson* pertained only to the death penalty provisions of a federal statute, Justice Potter Stewart's majority opinion contained language that had a bearing on the constitutionality of plea bargaining. According to Stewart, the statute was unconstitutional even though it did not "coerce" defendants into waiving their Fifth and Sixth Amendment rights. "A procedure need not be inherently coercive in order that it be held to impose an impermissible burden upon the assertion of a constitutional right."[15] A statute that merely "encouraged" a waiver of rights could also be unconstitutional. The test was whether the law "needlessly chill[ed] the exercise of basic constitutional rights." Even if the chilling effect was incidental, it was an "unconstitutional condition" on the exercise of a constitutional right if it was "unnecessary and there-

---

[13]For a list of plea bargaining cases in which the Supreme Court denied certiorari during the 1960s, see Alschuler, "Plea Bargaining and Its History," 37, n. 208.

[14]390 U.S. 570 (1968).

[15]Idem, 583.

BOX 3.4

ALBERT W. ALSCHULER CRITICIZES THE ABA

... [A]bout a decade ago, some prominent advocates of plea bargaining articulated a series of penological rationales for extending special consideration to defendants who plead guilty. These rationales usually were designed to show that, although it is improper to penalize a defendant for exercising the right to trial, it is appropriate to reward a defendant for pleading guilty. The American Bar Association and the American Law Institute were among the prestigious authorities who endorsed this perceived distinction between rewarding the waiver of a right and penalizing its exercise. . . . Of course, even defenders of the distinction would concede that it is largely theoretical; it is usually impossible for an observer (other than perhaps the sentencing authority itself) to determine whether a particular defendant has been "penalized" for standing trial or has failed to receive a "reward" for pleading guilty. More seriously, the ABA-ALI position raises an epistimological issue. If the concepts of reward and penalty are relative—if these concepts derive their meaning only from each other—the assertion that some defendants are rewarded and none penalized is simply schizophrenic. . . .

An apparent escape from this conclusion, however, lies in hypothesizing a "proper" sentence for each criminal offender. A "proper" sentence might be defined as one that is adequate to accomplish whatever objectives of the criminal law one accepts as persuasive. In retributive terms, the "proper" sentence is simply the sentence that the offender "deserves"; if one accepts more utilitarian justifications for punishment, it may be the sentence necessary to accomplish deterrent, incapacitative, or rehabilitative goals. . . .

If it is possible to envision a "proper" sentence for each offender, at least as an abstract matter, an increase in this sentence when the offender has exercised his right to trial can be seen as an inappropriate penalty, and a reduction in the sentence when the offender has pleaded guilty can be seen as a reward. The concept of a "proper" sentence thus gives meaning to the distinction between reward and penalty, but this concept merely refines the dilemma. As most defenders of plea bargaining concede, an offender should not be subjected to "undeserved" or "gratuitous" suffering because he has exercised the right to trial; but a reward to the offender who pleads guilty, although desirable from his perspective, may be equally inappropriate. It inevitably seems to require the imposition of a sentence that will fail to accomplish the legitimate purposes of the criminal law.

As a theoretical matter, any system of plea negotiation that turns an offender's punishment partly on his choice of plea would seem to find itself on one horn or the other of this dilemma. . . .

❀   ❀   ❀

In support of its earlier position [that plea bargaining was justified because it permitted the "prompt and certain application of correctional measures"] the ABA relied upon Jeremy Bentham's classic analysis of the importance of prompt and certain punishment as a deterrent to crime. It said, "It has long been recognized that punishment need not be as severe if it is certain and prompt in application."...

... Of course ... [the] potential offender might also know about plea bargaining, but it seems doubtful that this awareness would add to the *in terrorem* effect of the criminal law. To the contrary, a potential offender would recognize that a defendant ordinarily enters a bargained guilty plea only when this alternative seems even less threatening than our very un-Benthamite long-form procedure. It would plainly be a perversion of Bentham's position to suggest that a potential offender might refrain from crime, not out of fear that the criminal justice system would punish him promptly, but out of fear that he might promptly punish himself because prosecutorial offers are too generous to refuse.

The ABA also argued that concessions to defendants who plead guilty might be appropriate when "the concessions will make possible alternative correctional measures which are better adapted to achieving rehabilitative, protective, deterrent, or other purposes of correctional treatment, or will prevent undue harm to the defendant from the form of conviction. . . ." What the ABA meant by this elaborate language was that it did not like the mandatory sentences attached to some offenses and the stigmatizing labels and collateral civil disabilities attached to others. . . .

In the absence of legislative reform, the ABA apparently believed that plea bargaining could be defended as a form of guerrilla warfare against unjust laws. Its commentary did not discuss the obvious problems of democratic theory and of separation of powers that arise when prosecutors and trial judges substitute their personal concepts of justice for those that legislative bodies, acting within their constitutional authority, have enacted into law. All in all, the ABA's position seemed an odd one for a group that purports to revere the rule of law to adopt.

... The ABA next maintained that concessions to a guilty-plea defendant might be justified because "the defendant has made public trial unnecessary when there are good reasons for not having the case dealt with in a public trial. . . ." The victim of a crime, especially a sex crime and especially a very young victim, may be seriously embarrassed and emotionally upset when required to testify about the crime at a public trial. The victim's powerful interests, however, are not the only ones at stake. Not only is the defendant's interest in obtaining a public trial protected by the Constitution, but the Supreme Court recently held that the interest of the public in attending criminal trials is so compelling that even the desire of both the defendant and the prosecutor for privacy cannot justify the public's exclusion.

. . . Moreover, to say that some kinds of evidence should not be heard in public is not to say that they should not be heard at all. The ABA's reasoning at most suggests that prosecutors should be allowed to bargain for a waiver of the defendant's right to the presence of the public at his trial, not that they should be allowed to bargain for a waiver of the right to trial itself.

. . . The ABA's final argument was that charge and sentence concessions could be appropriate when "the defendant by his plea has aided in avoiding delay (including delay due to crowded dockets) in the disposition of other cases and thereby has increased the probability of prompt and certain application of correctional measures to other offenders."

It seems doubtful that any defendant, when asked his reason for pleading guilty, would respond, "I want to be out of the way so that other defendants can get what is coming to them." The ABA's argument did not suggest any magnanimity or strength of character on the part of a guilty-plea defendant; it was instead an elaborately dressed version of the cost-saving utilitarian argument [that the ABA had explicitly renounced]. . . .

Source: Albert W. Alschuler, "The Changing Plea-Bargaining Debate," *California Law Review* 69 (1981): 658–660, 718–21.

fore excessive."[16] Based on these criteria, Stewart concluded that the provisions of the federal kidnapping law that gave only juries the power to impose the death penalty were "unnecessary." They constituted an "unconstitutional condition" on the constitutional right to a jury trial.[17]

Stewart's analysis implicitly raised the question as to whether plea bargaining constituted an unconstitutional condition. Certainly prosecutorial promises of leniency encouraged guilty pleas. If a statute was unconstitutional because it encouraged waivers of rights, why was a prosecutorial promise of leniency not similarly unconstitutional? Was it because plea bargaining was "necessary," whereas confining death sentences to jury trials was not? But in what way was plea bargaining "necessary"? Was plea bargaining a "logical" necessity? A practical one?

Stewart also said in his *Jackson* opinion that if a practice "had no other purpose or effect than to chill the assertion of constitutional rights by penalizing them, then it would be patently unconstitutional."[18] What is the purpose of plea bargaining? Is it to chill the defendant's right to trial? In what sense? What if a

---

[16]Idem, 582.

[17]Stewart's conclusion that the federal law was unconstitutional did not mean that Stewart rejected all guilty pleas, not even all those made under the kidnapping law. He said that just because this law impermissibly encouraged guilty pleas "hardly implies that every defendant who enters a guilty plea to a charge under the Act does so involuntarily." Idem, 583. According to Stewart, the key to the validity of any guilty plea was that it had to be completely voluntary.

[18]Idem, 581.

prosecutor merely wanted to reduce his caseload? Would that make plea bargaining permissible, or would it nonetheless chill the defendant's right to a jury trial? Why should it matter why the prosecutor engages in plea bargaining? As a practical matter, does plea bargaining chill constitutional rights regardless of the prosecutor's ultimate objective?

In late 1969, the Court became familiar with the facts and issues of *North Carolina v. Alford* (1970) as it also heard arguments in *Brady v. United States, Parker v. North Carolina,* and *McMann v. Richardson.*[19] On December 2, 1963, Forsyth County had indicted Henry C. Alford for first-degree murder, a crime that under the laws of North Carolina could result in the death penalty if a jury convicted him and did not recommend leniency. However, Alford could avoid any chance of incurring the death penalty by pleading guilty, an option that would result in a mandatory life sentence. The death penalty provisions of the North Carolina law were therefore similar to those of the Federal Kidnapping Act that had been invalidated in *Jackson.* There were, however, two differences. The North Carolina statute mandated the death penalty upon conviction, unless the jury recommended mercy, whereas the earlier federal law had left the death penalty to the discretion of the jury. In addition, the North Carolina statute, unlike the federal one, did not give the defendant the option of a bench trial. If the defendant wanted a trial, it had to be a jury trial; if the defendant wanted to avoid any chance of the death penalty, he had to give up not only his right to a jury trial but also his right to a trial before a judge. Therefore, one general issue in *Alford* was whether these differences in the statutes were significant. Did the North Carolina statute fall within the *Jackson* ruling?

The other major issue of *Alford* was plea bargaining. Apart from the constitutionality of the statute, the state offered Alford the following deal: he could avoid the first-degree murder charge and the possible death sentence by pleading guilty to second-degree murder punishable by a mandatory thirty-year sentence. Here, unlike in *Jackson,* was a classic plea bargain. Jackson could only claim that the death penalty provision of the federal kidnapping law had coerced him into waiving his constitutional rights. Alford confronted a similar threat, but also an additional encouragement to plead guilty. If he pleaded guilty to the second-degree murder charge, he would avoid both the death penalty and life imprisonment. He would receive only the thirty-year sentence.

With these options before him, Alford took the unusual course of accepting the plea bargain while claiming that he was innocent of the crime charged: "I just pleaded guilty because they said if I didn't they would gas me for it, and that is all." The issue before the Court was whether the death penalty provisions of the North Carolina law or the plea bargain, or both together, unconstitutionally imposed conditions on Alford's Fifth and Sixth Amendment rights.

---

[19]In *McMann v. Richardson,* 297 U.S. 759 (1970), the Court upheld guilty pleas in three separate cases notwithstanding the fact that the defendants claimed that their guilty pleas were induced by coerced confessions. In *Parker v. North Carolina,* 397 U.S. 790 (1970), the Court upheld a guilty plea despite the similarity of the North Carolina statute to the one invalidated in *Jackson.* The particular statute at issue is discussed at length in *Alford.*

In its brief to the Supreme Court, the state of North Carolina tried to distinguish *Jackson* from *Alford* on the ground that the federal death penalty provisions invalidated in *Jackson* gave the jury the power to impose death sentences, whereas the North Carolina statute mandated the death penalty upon conviction unless the jury recommended leniency. However, the state's main contention was that even if its statute had a "*Jackson*-type defect," not all pleas of guilty under the statute were necessarily invalid. The Court "should not hold void all pleas entered in a procedure so firmly entrenched in the history of the judicial system," especially since Alford had pleaded guilty to a lesser offense. Relying heavily on the dissent that Chief Judge Clement Haynesworth issued at the circuit court level, the state emphasized that Alford had plea-bargained. Just as any other defendant who pleads guilty to a lesser offense is not coerced, neither is a defendant who avoids any possibility of the death penalty or life imprisonment by pleading guilty to second-degree murder. It would, the state concluded, be "tragic indeed" if *Jackson* were held to outlaw plea bargaining—a "time honored method of determining guilt without trial."

Attorney Doris R. Bray, appointed by the Supreme Court, wrote the brief for Henry Alford. She contended, first, that there was no meaningful distinction between the federal provisions invalidated in *Jackson* and those under which Alford had pleaded guilty. In both cases, the defendant faced "the awesome decision of whether to risk the possibility of the death penalty or to waive his right to have his guilt determined by a jury." Second, the fact that Alford had pleaded guilty to a lesser offense made no difference because the state never gave him the option of pleading not guilty to the lesser offense. Even if Alford was bargaining, "such bargaining is impermissible under the reasoning of this Court in *Jackson*." Obviously, plea bargaining "encourages a defendant to plead guilty and waive his right to a jury trial, and, thus, accomplishes the very result which was condemned as unconstitutional in *Jackson*." In any event, the brief concluded, even if not every plea bargain should be made illegal, certainly those in which the defendant either refuses to admit guilt or "involuntarily" pleads guilty to avoid the death penalty should not be accepted. Since both criteria were true of Alford, his plea of guilty should be set aside.

Also in *Alford*, a number of prominent lawyers affiliated with the effort by the Legal Defense Fund of the National Association for the Advancement of Colored People (NAACP) to abolish the death penalty wrote an *amici curiae* brief on behalf of Albert Bobby Childs, Marie Hill, and Robert Lewis Roseboro, all of whom were North Carolina prisoners sentenced to death under the same statute that Alford was challenging. Whereas Alford claimed that his guilty plea was "coerced," the three prisoners on death row claimed that their death sentences unconstitutionally "penalized" them for exercising their right to a jury trial. Since the purpose of the *amici curiae* brief was to win relief for inmates on North Carolina's death row, it could not rely on the specific facts of Alford's guilty plea, especially his repeated claims of innocence. Instead, the *amici* made a broader argument without attacking plea bargaining in general. Most guilty pleas and plea bargains were fine, but not those "coerced" by an unconstitutional death penalty statute. "All that need be determined here is that no defendant may be compelled to gamble with his life to secure his constitutional right to a trial." *Jackson* had ruled that a statute that imposed such a "gamble" on a defendant was unconstitutional. Therefore, at a minimum, prisoners on death row who had pleaded guilty under laws similar to North Carolina's must be given a hearing at which the state would have the burden of proving that the plea was voluntary.

In May 1970, the Supreme Court decided the three other plea-bargaining cases but rescheduled *Alford* for reargument later that year. The lawyers involved in the *Alford* litigation studied the newly released opinions. They had to respond to what the Court had said. If it was feasible to do so, they incorporated the court's new decisions into their arguments. If not, they either abandoned positions that the Court had rejected or formulated criticisms of what the Court had said. All sides had to adapt to the new legal situation.

Of the opinions delivered in May, the one most directly relevant to the issues raised in *Alford* was the *Brady* opinion. In this case, the Supreme Court had considered the appeal of a man who had pleaded guilty and been sentenced to life imprisonment under the Federal Kidnapping Act before *Jackson* had been decided. Given what the Court had said in *Jackson,* it might seem that the Court would accept Brady's claim that his plea had been unconstitutionally encouraged, if not by prosecutorial promises of leniency, then by the fear of the death penalty. However, in an opinion written by Justice Byron White, who had dissented in *Jackson,* the Court rejected Brady's arguments, narrowed the scope of *Jackson,* and generally endorsed the practice of plea bargaining.

Jackson, White said, "ruled neither that all pleas of guilty encouraged by the fear of a possible death sentence are involuntary nor that such encouraged pleas are invalid whether involuntary or not." A state could constitutionally encourage defendants to waive their constitutional rights, even if it did so by way of the defendant's fear of death, as long as the decision to plead guilty was both "voluntary" and "intelligent."[20] White was therefore perfectly willing to concede that but for the death penalty provision of the law, Brady would not have pleaded guilty. Even if "the statute caused the plea in this sense," it did "not necessarily prove that the plea was coerced and invalid as an involuntary act." Of course, a state could "not produce a plea by actual or threatened physical harm or by mental coercion overbearing the will of the defendant." But since there was no "evidence that Brady was so gripped by fear of the death penalty or hope of leniency that he did not or could not, with the help of counsel, rationally weigh the advantages of going to trial against the advantages of pleading guilty," his plea of guilty was voluntary and valid.[21]

Rather than showing that the state had, in an overbearing way, overwhelmed his will and his ability to choose rationally, Brady was claiming that a guilty plea was "coerced and invalid if influenced by the fear of a possibly higher penalty for the crime charged if a conviction is obtained after the State is put to its proof."[22]

---

[20]Idem, 747.

[21]Idem, 750.

[22]Idem, 750–751.

This claim, White insisted, had no merit. After all, the state "to some degree encourages pleas of guilty at every important step in the criminal process," from arrest until trial. Such pleas "are no more improperly compelled than is the decision by a defendant at the close of the State's evidence at trial that he must take the stand or face certain conviction."[23] Moreover, White added, exchanging leniency for guilty pleas is not unconstitutional merely

> because both the State and the defendant often find it advantageous to preclude the possibility of the maximum penalty authorized by law. For a defendant who sees slight possibility of acquittal, the advantages of pleading guilty and limiting the probable penalty are obvious—his exposure is reduced, the correctional processes can begin immediately, and the practical burdens of a trial are eliminated. For the State there are also advantages—the more promptly imposed punishment after an admission of guilt may more effectively attain the objectives of punishment; and with the avoidance of trial, scarce judicial and prosecutorial resources are conserved for those cases in which there is a substantial issue of the defendant's guilt or in which there is substantial doubt that the State can sustain its burden of proof.[24]

Consequently, bargained pleas of guilty are not only compatible with the constitutional requirement of voluntariness but also quite rational, for both the defendant and the state. This conclusion would be insupportable if "offers of leniency substantially increased the likelihood that defendants, advised by competent counsel, would falsely condemn themselves."[25] However, White refused to believe that trial judges would often accept the pleas of those who were not guilty of the offenses with which they were charged.

Justice William Brennan concurred in the result in *Brady* but rejected the majority's interpretation of *Jackson* and its analysis of the requirements of a voluntary plea. To make a plea invalid, it was not necessary, Brennan urged, that the state render the defendant "incapable of rational choice."[26] Instead, if "a particular defendant can demonstrate that the death penalty scheme exercised a significant influence upon his decision to plead guilty, then, under *Jackson,* he is entitled to reversal of the conviction based upon his illicitly produced plea."[27] Hence, according to Brennan, not all plea bargains were unconstitutional. If a defendant could show that an unconstitutional capital punishment scheme—for example, one in which only the jury could impose the death penalty—had a "significant" impact on his decision not to exercise his right to a jury trial, his guilty plea should be set aside.[28] But in *Brady* the trial judge had determined that the defendant had pleaded guilty because he had found out that his accomplice intended to plead

---

[23] Idem, 750.

[24] Idem, 752.

[25] Idem, 758.

[26] *Parker v. North Carolina,* 397 U.S. 790, 802 (1970). Brennan's dissent in this case included his concurrence in *Brady.*

[27] Idem, 808.

[28] Idem, 813.

guilty and testify against him. Consequently, "Brady's plea was triggered by the confession and plea decision of his codefendant and not by any substantial fear of the death penalty."[29] The plea was therefore a valid one.

The *Brady* decision clearly favored North Carolina's position in *Alford.* The state's lawyers immediately took advantage of the situation by filing a supplemental brief. In it, the state stressed the Court's assertion in *Brady* that competent assistance of counsel could establish the "voluntary" and "intelligent" character of guilty pleas. Certainly in *Alford,* the state insisted, lower state court findings showed that the defendant's court-appointed trial counsel, Fred G. Crumpler, did everything in his power to ensure that Alford's plea met these criteria. Moreover, the state added to its brief an appendix of the full transcript of the hearing at which Alford had pleaded guilty. This transcript showed clearly, in the state's judgment, that "an adequate basis in fact was established to support petitioner's plea." Though selected passages of the transcript showed that Alford had maintained his innocence throughout, a full reading would explain why Alford's plea bargain was "both voluntary and intelligent." In the state's view, it had a very strong case against Alford.

During the summer of 1970, Bray also filed a supplemental brief. She could not, however, as North Carolina had done, build her case on *Brady.* Because the Court in *Brady* had generally endorsed plea bargaining and held that a plea of guilty, even if motivated by the possibility of a death sentence, could be "voluntary" and "intelligent," Bray abandoned any notion that plea bargaining *per se* was unconstitutional. Calculating her client's interest, she narrowed her argument to the particular facts of Alford's plea. Alford was an uneducated African-American, in a southern city, who was accused of killing another black man, Nathaniel Young, in an argument over a white woman. The advice he received from his lawyer concerning the "aggravating" circumstances of his case pressured Alford to plead guilty because he greatly feared the death penalty. Moreover, Alford never admitted his guilt, not even to his lawyer, who was himself unclear as to whether Alford was pleading innocent or guilty. In such circumstances, the plea should be ruled involuntary and invalid.[30]

What is your view of the particular facts of the *Alford* case? Even if plea bargaining is, in your view, constitutional because it is necessary or because it only rewards defendants who plead guilty and does not penalize those who exercise their right to a (jury) trial, do you think Alford's plea was voluntary? What do you think of the transcripts of the original proceedings that are included in both supplemental briefs? Do you agree with North Carolina that the presence of Fred Crumpler ensured that Alford's plea was voluntary? Do these records tell you enough about the facts of the case to make an informed judgment concerning the voluntary character of Alford's plea? Do they show that the state had a strong case against

---

[29]Idem, 815.

[30]The Legal Defense Fund lawyers who wrote the *amici* brief in *Alford* had no reason to submit a supplemental brief because the Court had completely rejected their contention that the mere existence of an unconstitutional death penalty statute was enough to invalidate all pleas made under it or to require states to prove that these pleas were voluntary.

Alford? Why did the trial judge ask so many questions concerning Alford's previous criminal activities? Were these proper questions? Does it concern you that appellate courts often make decisions based on such transcripts?

Jacob L. Safron, who represented North Carolina, and Doris Bray, who continued her court-appointed work on behalf of Henry Alford, had different experiences when the case was reargued before the Supreme Court on October 14, 1970. Safron recited the events of the night of the murder of Nathaniel Young, described the hearing at which Alford had pleaded guilty, recounted the history of the case, and cited the cases that supported the state's position that the plea should not be reversed. As the Court's questions were few and friendly, Safron's part of the oral argument became something of a monologue.

In contrast, though Bray handled the situation well, she rarely said anything with which a justice did not take issue. She had the difficult task of arguing that certain plea bargains (those involving defendants who refused to admit their guilt or who greatly feared the death penalty) were involuntary without implying that all plea bargains were therefore unconstitutional. The tactic that Bray followed was to deny that *Alford* involved plea bargaining. Because the state had given Alford the option of pleading guilty to a lesser offense, she had reason to fear, from what the Court had said in *Brady*, that the Court might conclude that the plea had to be considered voluntary for that very reason. A plea bargain had to be voluntary because it was a "bargain." Bray therefore tried to convince the Court that *Alford* was a special type of invalid plea bargain: one in which a defendant proclaiming his innocence had pleaded "legally" guilty because of his fear of the death penalty. Though Bray had some difficulty defining the exact line at which judges should refuse guilty pleas, she argued that Alford's plea was clearly beyond it.

During August 1970, while the Court was considering *Alford*, an article on the crisis of New York City's criminal-justice system appeared in the popular *Life* magazine (see Box 3.5). The author, Dale Wittner, discussed the rising crime rate and its inevitable impact on the criminal justice system. In New York City, justice had become "an endless assembly line" in which the prosecutor arranged the deals that were then "rubber-stamped" by judges. For those caught up in this process, the prosecutor, not the judge, symbolized the law. The power that the prosecutor exercised was "incredible." The article implicitly asked whether one man should be making these decisions, especially since the prosecutor's main concern was not justice but rather "the disposition of cases."

In your judgment, does this article capture the kind of ambivalence that the American public continues to feel about the practice of plea bargaining? Of what significance is the fact that public commissions and organized legal groups, such as the American Bar Association, endorsed plea bargaining during the 1960s, and a popular magazine published the kind of article excerpted here? Is it possible that the American people are more committed to the formal constitutional process of trial than legal experts and the organized bar? Or is it more likely that the experts and the bar are just more knowledgeable about the efficiency of plea bargaining and the valuable role it plays in the American criminal justice system?

In its consideration of *Alford*, the Supreme Court ultimately had to decide whether to follow the reasoning of *Brady* or *Jackson*. In a majority opinion written

---

BOX 3.5

LOGJAM IN OUR COURTS

... In every major city the symptoms are the same. Crime increases at an average rate of 14% a year, more than doubling every six years. Court backlogs of pending cases, which 10 years ago were measured in weeks, now add up to months and years. Harried judges, prosecutors and public defenders are forced to treat each case like a piece of unimportant manufacture on an endless assembly line. Prosecutions are haphazard. Justice is the subject of bargaining. The possibility of punishment diminishes—and with it, respect for the law. . . .

. . . An assistant district attorney, inheriting a case weakened by long delay, must weigh the chances of conviction. When they favor the defendant, he either dismisses the charge altogether to save the state the expense of a futile trial, or he tries to strike a bargain in which the severity of the charge is reduced in return for a plea of guilty. In legal jargon this practice is known as "plea bargaining." It has become such a flagrant part of New York City justice that another metaphor has evolved: "giving the courthouse away.". . .

With the calendars of many courts regularly listing 70 or 80 cases a day, the average judge is buried under tons of paperwork. He no longer has enough time for listening to testimony and for deciding guilt or innocence. Instead, judges have been relegated by the system to the function of clerks. They are paid $30,000 a year, privileged to wear judicial robes and occupy elevated seats under the words "In God We Trust." But for most of them, a court day consists of overseeing a roll call of cases, adjourning most of them to new dates in other court sections, waiting for defendants, attorneys and witnesses to appear, and occasionally rubber-stamping a bartered guilty plea and sentencing the defendant.

Much of the power once held by the judge has fallen to the prosecutor. Frank Silverstein, 29, graduated from Brooklyn Law School only a year ago. Now, at a salary of $11,000, he is a criminal court assistant to the Bronx District Attorney. To the hundreds of people who each day cross the obscenely scribbled threshold of the Bronx Criminal Courthouse, young Frank Silverstein is the fulcrum of justice; he is the law. . . .

"The power of this job is incredible," says Silverstein. "It's more than any one man should have. Do you know what it's like to face a defendant in court and know that if he is convicted, or even if he is held in jail for trial because he can't make bail, he is going to lose his job and his family will have to go on welfare?. . ."

Of his negotiating power, Silverstein rationalizes that in a case weakened by delay "it's better that a guilty defendant be convicted of *something* without a trial than turned loose by a jury because the evidence has become too weak to get a conviction. Even when you drop charges entirely, you figure that at least you've disposed of a case." And disposition of cases, far more than careful justice, has become the benchmark by which the city's criminal courts are measured. . . .

Along with the presumption of guilt, which has replaced the presumption of innocence in New York City courts, goes the presumption that a defendant is entitled to bargain. Every day there are cases in which the first conversation between a defendant and his lawyer is not over the facts of the case but over what kind of deal can be made.

In a Manhattan courtroom recently a young man charged with burglary was offered the opportunity of pleading guilty to the less serious charge of possession of stolen property. His Legal Aid lawyer was all smiles as he turned away from a huddle with the prosecutor to tell the defendant what he assumed would be good news. "But," the defendant blurted, "I didn't do it!". . .

Source: Dale Wittner, "Logjam in Our Courts," *Life,* August 7, 1970, pp. 18ff.

by Justice Byron White, the Court upheld Alford's guilty plea and thereby, to a degree, abandoned the substantive reasoning of *Jackson*. First, the Court reaffirmed the notion that a guilty plea motivated by a desire to avoid the death penalty was not, for that reason alone, involuntary. Second, in regard to Alford's repeated statements that he was innocent of the act to which he had pleaded guilty, the Court noted that the state had a strong case against the defendant. Moreover, other courts had concluded that it would be inappropriate to force any defendant to go to trial, "particularly when advancement of the defense might 'end in disaster.'" Though the Supreme Court had never granted a defendant "an absolute right to have his guilty plea accepted," it had ruled that no constitutional error occurred if a guilty plea was accepted "even though evidence before the judge indicated that there was a valid defense." In support of this principle, White noted an interesting case in which a defendant preferred to plead guilty rather than rely on an insanity defense that might subject him to indefinite commitment to a mental institution. The Court's conclusion was that judges do not violate the rights of defendants who, though legally innocent of the charge, pleaded guilty because of the risks of going to trial. Therefore, whether Alford "realized or disbelieved his guilt," he "quite reasonably" pleaded guilty given the strength of the state's case and the likelihood of conviction. Such a bargain was in the interest of the defendant. And because such constitutional guarantees as the privilege against self-incrimination and the right to a jury trial were designed for the sake of criminal defendants, they should not be interpreted in an "arid" way that would jeopardize "the very human values they were meant to preserve."

What do you think of White's arguments? Should a legally innocent defendant be allowed to plead guilty? What if the defendant pleaded guilty to avoid indefinite commitment to a mental institution? Does plea bargaining always or usually work to the advantage of defendants? If it does, can one claim that plea bargaining unconstitutionally penalizes the rights of defendants? Would any such conclusion be based, as White argues, on an "arid" interpretation of criminal justice rights, one that would jeopardize "the very human values they were meant to preserve"? What are the "human values" to which White refers? Is the right to remain silent or the right to a jury trial meant to function as a means by which a guilty defendant receives less punishment than he deserves? Or are these rights meant to increase the likelihood that innocent people are not unjustly convicted? In short, in what way are the human values underlying criminal justice rights related to plea bargaining?

William Brennan, joined by two other justices, wrote a short dissent that echoed what he had said earlier in *Brady*. Once again he made it clear that not all plea bargains were unconstitutional. Indeed, he too was unwilling to say that a plea bargain "accompanied by a contemporaneous denial of acts constituting the crime" was necessarily invalid. However, he urged that such a denial was relevant to an assessment of whether a guilty plea "was voluntarily and intelligently made." In addition, he added, the effect that the unconstitutional death penalty provisions of the North Carolina statute had on the defendant must also be "given weight in determining the voluntariness of a plea." When these two factors were applied to the record of the present case, Brennan thought the proper conclusion obvious. Alford was "so gripped by fear of the death penalty" that his decision to plead guilty was not voluntary but "the product of duress as much so as choice reflecting physical constraint." Alford's guilty plea should therefore be set aside.

Does Brennan's position have merit? Are most plea bargains acceptable, but Alford's not because he had been "gripped by fear of the death penalty"? And what about North Carolina's apparently unconstitutional death penalty law? Does the nature of this law have a bearing on whether Alford's plea was valid or not? Of what significance are Alford's repeated claims of innocence? How do you balance these claims against the purported strength of the state's case and the fact that Alford was represented by a seemingly competent attorney? In such cases as these, is White correct that plea bargains are, from the defendant's point of view, "quite reasonable"? Should a judge accept a plea of guilty from a defendant whose factual guilt is unclear? How much doubt must a judge have before refusing to accept a guilty plea?

If Alford's plea were overturned, could North Carolina prosecute Alford for first-degree murder? Is that what Brennan wants? What if he were then convicted and sentenced to death? Does this possibility have any bearing on how *Alford* should have been decided? Was it likely that Alford would have won an acquittal at his retrial because the state would have a difficult time, seven years after his initial plea, proving Alford guilty "beyond a reasonable doubt"? Would witnesses be difficult to find? Would they remember? Do you think that these projected problems explain why Alford sought to have his guilty plea reversed? Are such issues relevant to whether Alford's plea bargain was constitutional or not? If you were on the Supreme Court, would they have had a bearing on how you would have decided *Alford*?

For practical purposes, *Brady* and *Alford* settled the constitutionality of plea bargaining. These two cases upheld the constitutionality of the informal procedure by which 90 percent of the criminal cases are resolved in this country. Hence the unavoidable question is whether the extent of plea bargaining has undermined the practical significance of the formal criminal procedures and rights that the Supreme Court nationalized and extended during the Warren Court era. In the great majority of cases, criminal defendants do not exercise their formal rights, but instead bargain them away through an informal negotiation between the prosecutor and the defense attorney. Of course, functioning in this manner, the rights incorporated into the Fourteenth Amendment are still very important. Not only have the decisions applying the Bill of Rights against the states produced a uniform constitutional code of procedure that is actually used in 10 percent of the criminal cases, but they have also substantially improved the negotiating power of criminal defendants in the rest of the cases that end in guilty pleas. Where do you think the real significance of the decisions incorporating the criminal procedure provisions of the Bill of Rights against the states lies, in their impact on the formal procedure or on plea bargaining? If, in your opinion, the latter impact is more important, does this undermine the legitimacy of the decisions themselves? Given the extent of plea bargaining, is there any reason to call what the Supreme Court accomplished in the criminal justice field a Pyrrhic victory? If so, in what way?

BIBLIOGRAPHY

Alschuler, Albert W. "The Changing Plea-Bargaining Debate." *California Law Review* 69 (1981): 652–730.

———. "The Supreme Court, the Defense Attorney, and the Guilty Plea." *University of Colorado Law Review* 47 (1975): 1–71.

Heumann, Milton. *Plea Bargaining.* Chicago: University of Chicago Press, 1977.

Law and Society Review 13, no. 2 (1979).

Rosett, Arthur, and Donald R. Cressey. *Justice by Consent.* Philadelphia: Lippincott, 1976.

Schulhofer, Stephen. "Plea Bargaining as Disaster." *Yale Law Journal* 101 (1992): 1979–2015.

BRIEFS

ALFORD'S BRIEF

[1. Analysis of North Carolina Statute.] In *United States v. Jackson,* this Court held that the death penalty clause in the Federal Kidnaping Act constitutes an "impermissible burden upon the assertion of a constitutional right." Under the Act, the punishment for kidnaping, if the kidnaped person has not been liberated unharmed, is imprisonment for a term of years or for life, or death if the jury shall so recommend. Thus, under the Act only the jury could impose the death penalty, and a defendant charged under the Act could avoid the possibility of capital punishment, by pleading guilty or by pleading not guilty and waiving his right to a jury trial. This Court held in *Jackson* that a death penalty which is applicable only to those defendants who assert the right to contest their guilt before a jury discourages a defendant's assertion of his Fifth Amendment right not to plead guilty and deters his exercise of his Sixth Amendment right to demand a jury trial.

Under the North Carolina statutory scheme for imposition of the death penalty, the penalty for each capital crime is death unless the jury recommends that the punishment be imprisonment for life. If the defendant pleads guilty and his plea is accepted by the Court, the mandatory punishment is life imprisonment. The United States Court of Appeals for the Fourth Circuit correctly held in *Alford v. North Carolina* that in all material respects the North Carolina statutory scheme is identical to that declared unconstitutional in *United States v. Jackson*, and is, therefore, in violation of the Fourteenth Amendment right of due process, which includes the right to plead not guilty and the right of trial by jury. . . .

The constitutional infirmity of the penalty provisions of the Federal Kidnaping Act existed because of the effect which those provisions have upon a person charged under the Act. The effect of the North Carolina statutory scheme for imposition of the death penalty upon one accused of a capital crime is identical. In each instance, the defendant faces the awesome decision of whether to risk the possibility of the death penalty or to waive his right to have his guilt determined by a jury. Indeed, the North Carolina scheme is even more objectionable than that prescribed by the Federal Kidnaping Act, for in North Carolina the defendant in a capital case must risk the death penalty in order to assert his innocence at all since in North Carolina a defendant who pleads not guilty cannot waive his right to a jury trial and be tried by a judge. Thus, the North Carolina defendant, in order to avoid the possibility of capital punishment, must waive not only his right to a trial by jury, but also his right to a trial to determine his guilt and consequently his right to confront and cross-examine witnesses against him as established in *Pointer v. Texas*.

In his dissent in the case of *State v. Spence,* Justice Bobbitt of the North Carolina Supreme Court, in comparing the North Carolina statutory scheme for imposition of the death penalty with that of the Federal Kidnaping Act, noted: "If there be any real difference, it would seem that the pressure upon a defendant to enter a plea that will avoid "the risk of death" would be greater under our statutes.". . .

Nor is the semantic distinction which the State has attempted to make with regard to whether the jury's authority is to mitigate the penalty or to impose a more severe penalty significant. What is relevant and significant is that the statutory scheme for imposing the death penalty in North Carolina has a "chilling effect" upon the assertion by the accused on his rights not to plead guilty and to demand a jury trial under the Fourteenth Amendment and "needlessly encourages" him to plead guilty. That such a scheme of punishment has the effect which this Court surmised that it has in its opinion in *Jackson* is vividly established by the record in the case now before this Court, which effectively demonstrates that the only reason for Alford's guilty plea was his fear that he might receive the death penalty if he allowed his guilt or innocence to be determined by a jury.

[2. Plea Bargaining.] The State has argued that the *Jackson* decision is not applicable to the case now before the Court because Alford pleaded guilty to second degree murder rather than to first degree murder, the capital crime for which he was indicted. Alford was never given the option of pleading not guilty to a lesser offense. His choice was either to plead not guilty to a capital offense or to plead guilty and avoid risking the death penalty. It is obvious from the record that the paramount factor in this decision was Alford's desire not to risk the possibility of capital punishment, not the prospect of being permitted to plead guilty to a lesser offense. Whether his sentence was life imprisonment, as it would have been had he pleaded guilty to first degree murder, or thirty years' imprisonment, which he received for pleading guilty to second degree murder, could not have been significant to his decision. In rejecting this argument, the Fourth Circuit said:

> It is immaterial in our view that petitioner pleaded guilty to murder in the second degree rather than to murder in the first degree under which he was charged. For all that appears in the record, the state had not surrendered its right to prosecute petitioner for first degree murder until the time when he agreed to plead guilty to second degree murder. Of course, if the state had determined that it would only prosecute for second degree murder, *and this fact had been known to the petitioner before his plea was entered,* then it could hardly be maintained that his guilty plea was a product of a fear of the death penalty. To us the *Jackson* defect in the North Carolina statutes potentially infects the validity of the acceptance of a plea of guilty to any lesser included offense. . . .

Chief Judge Haynesworth's primary concern in his dissent in *Alford v. North Carolina* was that the majority seemed to disapprove plea bargaining, which Judge Haynesworth considers "both useful and desirable in the administration of justice.". . . However, even if Alford was plea bargaining, it is submitted that such bargaining is impermissible under the reasoning of this Court in *Jackson*. What *Jackson* requires is for the penalty for a single offense to be uniform, whether the defendant pleads guilty or not guilty and whether or not he waives his right to a jury trial. It is apparent that plea bargaining encourages a defendant to plead guilty and waive his right to a jury trial, and, thus, accomplishes the very result which was condemned as unconstitutional in *Jackson*.

In any event, plea bargaining should never be permitted where a defendant consistently proclaims his innocence and declares that he is submitting his guilty plea only to avoid a more severe penalty. "Plea bargaining that induces an innocent person to plead guilty cannot be sanctioned. Negotiation must be limited to the quantum of punishment for an admittedly guilty defendant." Alford has never been "admittedly guilty." In fact, he has consistently asserted his innocence and, indeed, at the trial itself denied any guilt. In the face of such denial, the trial judge made no real inquiry into the matter and did not attempt to ascertain from the defendant whether he was guilty. Alford's plea cannot be upheld on the ground that it was the result of plea bargaining. . . .

. . . The decision of the United States Court of Appeals for the Fourth Circuit should be affirmed because Alford's plea of guilty was involuntary. It is well settled that a plea of guilty which is not entirely voluntary is void. . . .

A reading of the record in the case now before this Court leads to the inescapable conclusion that Alford's plea of guilty was in fact involuntary. The United States Court of Appeals for the Fourth Circuit so found:

> ... *Jackson* ... must be read, however, to hold that a prisoner is entitled to relief if he can demonstrate that ... his principal motivation to plead guilty or to forego a trial by jury was to avoid the death penalty. *Jackson* thus defined a new factor to be given weight in determining the voluntariness of a plea—a factor present in full measure in the instant case because of the North Carolina statutory scheme. As we read *Jackson,* we must determine the extent to which, if at all, petitioner was moved to plead guilty because of the incentive which the North Carolina statutory scheme supplied to achieve that result.
>
> In light of the principles we distill from *Jackson,* we have no hesitancy in concluding from our examination of the record that petitioner's plea of guilty was made involuntarily, and that petitioner is entitled to relief by habeas corpus.

The record in the present case overwhelmingly establishes that Alford's only reason for pleading guilty was to avoid risking the possibility of the death penalty. At the trial itself, Alford took the stand at his own request and, after relating his version of what had happened on the night of the murder, said:

> ... I pleaded guilty on second degree murder because they said there is too much evidence, but I ain't shot no man, but I take the fault for the other man. We never had an argument in our life and I just pleaded guilty because they said if I didn't they would gas me for it, and that is all.

After Alford testified, in response to questioning by his attorney, that he had authorized the plea, he reiterated:

> Well, I'm still pleading that you all got me to plead guilty. I plead the other way, circumstantial evidence; that the jury will prosecute me on—on the second. You told me to plead guilty, right. I don't—I'm not guilty but I plead guilty.

And when the court asked Alford if it was still his desire to plead guilty, he replied:

> Yes sir, I plead guilty on—from the circumstances that he told me.

According to the testimony presented at the state post-conviction hearing, Alford consistently asserted his innocence prior to his trial and agreed to plead guilty with great hesitancy and only after his attorney had informed him that in his (the attorney's) opinion Alford would receive the death penalty if he pleaded not guilty and was tried before a jury, and only after his sister and other friends urged him to plead guilty because pleading guilty would be better than risking the death penalty.

Furthermore, as the Fourth Circuit noted, "No court has ever found that he [Alford] pleaded guilty other than to avoid possible imposition of the death penalty." Judge Haynesworth in his 1966 memorandum decision dismissing an earlier petition filed by Alford, said:

> The state judge found that Alford decided to plead guilty because he had no defense to the State's case against him for first degree murder and because the guilty plea allowed him to escape the possibility of the death sentence. There is ample evidence to support this finding of fact and I see no reason to disagree with it.

Nothing in the record suggests that Alford has ever deviated from his repeated assertions of his innocence or from his contention that his only reason for pleading guilty was to avoid the possibility of the capital punishment.

> Respectfully submitted,
> DORIS R. BRAY,
> Counsel for Appellee.

NORTH CAROLINA'S BRIEF

[1. Analysis of North Carolina Statute.] In *United States v. Jackson,* this Court held the selective death penalty provision of the Federal Kidnaping Act imposes an "impermissible burden upon the assertion of a Constitutional right". We submit the decision in *Jackson* is limited to the statutory scheme established by the Federal Kidnaping Act, does not have wider applicability, and is not applicable to this situation where Alford pled guilty to a lesser offense, punishable only by a term of years, and not by death.

The Federal Rules of Criminal Procedure permit a defendant to plead guilty, or plead not guilty and be tried by a jury, or plead not guilty and waive a jury trial. Thus the defendant charged with kidnaping who asserts his right to a jury trial faces "the risk of death" as the price of his "free exercise" of that Constitutional right. . . .

The North Carolina Constitution prohibits a trial upon a plea of not guilty "but by the unanimous verdict of a jury of good and lawful persons in open court. . . ." This right cannot be waived. The defendant cannot plead not guilty and waive a jury trial. The determinative facts must be found by a jury.

A defendant charged with a capital crime (first degree murder, first degree burglary, arson and rape) may plead not guilty and be tried by a jury, or he may plead guilty, and if the court accepts the plea, the defendant must be sentenced to life imprisonment. If the defendant pleads not guilty and if the jury finds him guilty, the penalty is death unless the jury recommends mercy.

The death sentence is imposed by statute upon the jury's finding the defendant guilty of a capital crime. The jury is not, as in the *Jackson* case, usurping the province of the judge in sentencing the defendant, but serving as the trier of the facts. However, the jury is given the discretion in each of the capital crimes to recommend life imprisonment. . . .

The ability of the jury to mitigate the statutory punishment is contra to the unconstitutional burden imposed upon the defendant in the Federal Kidnaping Act. The North Carolina capital jury is given the ability to recommend mercy upon a capital conviction. The federal jury, and only the jury, upon a conviction for kidnaping had the ability to impose the death penalty, rather than permit the court to impose a sentence for any term of years or for life.

In reviewing the differences between the Federal Kidnaping Act and the North Carolina Statutes, the Supreme Court of North Carolina in *State of North Carolina v. Otis Eugene Peele,* stated:

We think there are certain material differences in the Federal Kidnaping Act and in North Carolina Statutes 14-21 and 15-162.1, and that *Jackson* is not authority for holding the death penalty in North Carolina may not be imposed under any circumstances for the crime of rape. In the kidnaping act the law fixes imprisonment in the penitentiary, but provides that the jury may impose the death penalty. The North Carolina rape statute provides that the death penalty shall be ordered unless the jury, at the time it renders its verdict of guilty, as a part thereof fixes the punishment at life imprisonment. True, G.S. 15-162.1 provides that a defendant charged with rape, if represented by counsel, may tender a plea of guilty, which, if accepted by the State with the Approval of the Court, shall have the effect of a verdict of guilty by the jury with a recommendation the punishment be life imprisonment. The State, acting through its solicitor, may refuse to accept the plea, or the judge may decline to approve it. In either event, there must be a jury trial, although the facts are not in serious dispute. Except as provided in G.S. 15-162.1, the North Carolina practice will not permit a defendant to plead guilty to a capital felony. G.S. 15-187 provides the death sentence shall be executed ". . . against any person in the state of North Carolina *convicted* of a crime punishable by death. . . ."

G.S. 15-162.1 is primarily for the benefit of a defendant. Its provisions may be invoked only on his written application. It provides that the State and the defendant, under rigid court supervision, may, without the ordeal of a trial, agree on a result which will vindicate the law and save the defendant's life. As stated in the *Jackson* case, there are "defendants who would greatly prefer not to contest their guilt." Practical experience indicates only in extreme cases does the jury fail to recommend life imprisonment rather than the death penalty. The possibility of a death penalty, however, has deterring effect—how much, no one knows. . . .

[2. Plea Bargaining.] "Are all pleas of guilty in a statute containing a *Jackson* type defect invalid?" We submit not. *Jackson* is not authority for a conclusion of such broad constitutional impact and should not be applied to void every conviction where a defendant has entered a guilty plea. This Court stated in *Jackson* that the Kidnaping Act "needlessly" penalized a defendant who stood on his right to plead not guilty before a jury—and Mr. Justice Stewart stated that defendants who acknowledged their guilt and wish to avoid the ignominy of public trial have traditionally been allowed to plead guilty, and, in addition, that a flexible and efficient judicial system requires the use of guilty pleas. . . .

Not having previously spoken directly on the issue of defendants who plead guilty to capital offenses, and in light of the various safeguards imposed prior to the acceptance of such pleas, this Court should not hold void all pleas entered in a procedure so firmly entrenched in the history of the judicial system. . . .

Although the State of North Carolina is appealing from the holding of the Fourth Circuit in its application of *Jackson*, we emphasize yet another defect in *Alford* arising from the factual basis of this case, by quoting at length from Chief Judge Haynesworth of the Fourth Circuit in his dissent as he aptly describes the non-applicability of *Jackson* to lesser plea situations, and Alford's plea in particular:

. . . I think a critical difference lies in the fact that Alford did not enter a plea of guilty to the charge of murder in the first degree. His plea of guilty was to the lesser offense of murder in the second degree, the maximum statutory punishment for which is imprisonment for not more than thirty years. . . .

The plea of guilty to murder in the second degree, however, was not the product of the constitutional infirmity in the statute. Had the infirmity not been present, the risk of capital punishment on a conviction of murder in the first degree would have constituted precisely the same pressure for a plea of guilty to a lesser included offense. Had North Carolina's statute provided that upon a conviction of murder in the first degree, whether after a trial on a plea of not guilty or after acceptance of a plea of guilty, the judge in his discretion could impose the death sentence, or imprisonment for life or for a term of years, there would have been no constitutional defect in the statute. Yet, in those circumstances, the pressure upon Alford to enter a plea to murder in the second degree would not have differed in the slightest from the pressure he actually experienced.

. . . [If Alford's guilty plea is rejected and if] he is well advised, he will again tender a plea of murder in the second degree. He will have gained nothing, and needless time and money will have been expended because of an infirmity in the statute which bears no causal relationship to the entry of the plea which the majority strikes.

Whenever a defendant bargains for a plea to a lesser, included offense, he is substantially motivated by fear of exposure to the greater punishment authorized upon conviction of the crime as charged. If the maximum punishment for the greater offense is death, there are emotional overtones which are not present if the maximum punishment is imprisonment for life or for a term of years, but the presence of a risk of capital punishment creates no conceptual distinction in a determination of the validity of bargaining for a plea to a lesser, included offense. The death penalty is no longer imposed with frequency, and a defendant may have a greater fear of the risk of a more likely sentence of life imprisonment than of the risk of less likely capital punishment. A difference in the prospect of imprisonment of one year rather than ten, of five years rather than twenty, of twenty years rather than life can weigh momentously with a defendant.

Such plea bargaining, when the defendant is properly represented, is both useful and desirable in the administration of justice. It greatly conserves judicial time and energy, leaving the courts available for the trial of cases in which there is no basis for accommodation between the parties. It is a very humane avenue of protection for a person charged with crime who recognizes his exposure to the risk of heavy punishment.

There is nothing in *Jackson* which intimates disapproval of that kind of plea bargaining. Its absence, or the absence of agreement, is the thing that produced the *Jackson* dilemma. Yet, that is all that happened here. Alford successfully bargained for a plea to a lesser included offense, which made him immune to life imprisonment as well as to capital punishment. He would have done the same thing had the capital punishment provision of the statute not been constitutionally defective. He may be expected to do the same thing again at his retrial. In *Jackson* the statutory defect created the issue; here it has no causal connection with it.

We submit that a defendant, charged with a capital felony, who is represented by counsel, does not act under coercion when, on the strength or weight of the evidence establishing his guilt, he pleads guilty to murder in the second degree or manslaughter, voluntary or involuntary. Neither does a defendant charged with rape act under coercion when he pleads guilty to an assault with intent to commit rape or an assault on a female by a male person over the age of eighteen (18) years. Nor under like circumstances does a defendant charged with burglary in the first degree, arson, or any other felony act under coercion when he pleads guilty to a lesser degree of the same crime, or an attempt to commit the crime so charged, or an attempt to commit a lesser degree of the crime so charged. Similarly, we submit that a defendant charged with a felony is not acting under coercion when he pleads guilty to an included misdemeanor.

There can be no doubt that when a defendant pleads guilty to an included crime of a lesser degree, both he and his counsel take into consideration the evidence of the State, the evidence available to the defendant, and all other factors pertinent to the advisability of tendering such plea, including the possibility of conviction by the jury of the crime as charged, or of a more serious lesser degree of the crime as charged, and the possibility of greater punishment as a result of the conviction of the original charge or a higher included degree of a lesser charge. . . .

We submit [that] in *Jackson* this Court recognized the utility of the guilty plea and it would be tragic indeed if *Jackson* denies this time honored method of determining guilt without trial, with the attendant burden that will be placed on all courts. . . .

ROBERT MORGAN,
Attorney General of the State of North Carolina.

AMICI BRIEF

Amici Albert Bobby Childs, Marie Hill, and Robert Lewis Roseboro are North Carolina prisoners under sentences of death. When charged with a capital crime, each was given by North Carolina statutory practice the choice of pleading guilty, thereby assuring a sentence of life imprisonment, or of risking the death penalty after jury trial upon a plea of not guilty. Each pleaded not guilty and, upon conviction, was sentenced to die. . . .

The defendants in each of these cases rely heavily on *United States v. Jackson* and *Pope v. United States* in which this Court invalidated the death penalty provisions of the Federal Kidnaping Act and the Federal Bank Robbery Act respectively. Those statutes were invalidated because, by allowing a defendant who pleaded guilty (or waived jury trial) to escape the risk of the death penalty, they "needlessly encourage[d]" waiver of the constitutional rights to plead not guilty and have a jury trial. The Court of Appeals in *Alford* began its constitutional analysis with a determination that North Carolina's death penalty statutes—which like the federal statutes in *Jackson* allowed avoidance of any risk of the death penalty by a plea of guilty—were unconstitutional. . . .

Having concluded that the North Carolina death penalty statutes are unconstitutional, we are nevertheless impelled to acknowledge, as did the Court of Appeals in *Alford,* that the presence of an unconstitutional sentencing system such as North Carolina's does not, of itself, resolve these cases. As the Court of Appeals said in *Alford,* "a defendant who has pleaded guilty when charged with a capital offense in North Carolina is not necessarily entitled to post-conviction relief as a matter of law." The court recognized that this Court refrained in *Jackson* from holding that every plea of guilty to a Federal Kidnaping Act charge was involuntary. The question of the validity of such guilty pleas is, we submit, one of fact; it cannot be resolved other than by a full and fair evidentiary hearing, at which a sensitive and probing analysis of the motivations of the plea is made within the framework of the applicable presumptions and rules assigning the burden of proof. . . .

This Court has long been concerned to insure that guilty pleas be not made involuntarily. The question of voluntariness of a plea is a federal one, as is any question of the waiver of federally secured rights. Special caution regarding the guilty plea is entirely fitting, for a guilty plea constitutes a waiver of *all* constitutionally secured procedural guarantees; thus this Court recently observed that a guilty plea "demands utmost solicitude of which courts are capable" to ensure that the waiver is truly voluntary.

The cases prohibiting involuntary pleas do not confine themselves to coercion by physical force or threats of violence; the inducement deemed so great to vitiate a plea "can be 'mental as well as physical'; 'the blood of the accused is not the only hallmark of an unconstitutional inquisition.' . . . Subtle pressures may be as telling as coarse and vulgar ones."

Some pressures are deemed too great to permit their intrusion into the process by which the defendant determines whether to exercise his constitutional right to deny and contest guilt or to enter a plea of guilty. The prospect of an apparently unavoidable deprivation of constitutional rights at trial, for example, may be sufficient to destroy the voluntariness of the plea, as where a defendant pleads guilty in the face of a trial wherein he is threatened by an unconstitutionally obtained confession. Misrepresentations by the prosecutor (for example, as to his ability to insure the defendant a particular sentence) are another example of circumstances which will warrant setting aside a plea of guilty. The same is true of unkept judicial promises of leniency.

Equally impermissible are prosecutorial threats to prosecute the spouse or a close friend of the defendant unless he pleads guilty. Indeed, statements of the trial judge to the effect that if the defendant elects to stand trial and is convicted, he will be given the maximum sentence have been found to invalidate a guilty plea as a matter of law.

Of course guilty pleas, properly interposed, are an essential ingredient of the efficient administration of justice. What these cases teach, however, is that certain kinds of inducements are too pressureful, too insensitive of the right of defendants to elect freely whether or not to stand trial. Those inducements, for that reason, do not pass constitutional muster. It is in this context that the role of the death penalty must be assessed.

Much of the analysis has already been performed by this Court in *United States v. Jackson.* This Court there found that statutes such as North Carolina's "needlessly encourage" guilty pleas and . . . are unconstitutional. Identification of the potentially coercive force of the death penalty in *Jackson* was in accordance with an increasing recognition that the risks of standing trial are "made particularly perilous in the context of [a] . . . charge with a possible death penalty."

It bears emphasis that the constitutionality of a fairly administered system of plea bargaining is not implicated by a recognition of the coercive quality of the threatened imposition of the death penalty. All that need be determined here is that no defendant may be compelled to gamble with his life to secure his constitutional right to a trial; the state may not use the death penalty as the basis for inducing guilty pleas. . . .

At the least, a defendant who has entered a plea within a statutory framework such as North Carolina's is entitled to an evidentiary hearing at which the voluntariness of his plea is determined. Conceivably, it might be shown at such a hearing that the plea was the product of wholly proper considerations. It will not do, however, simply to allow the defendant the opportunity to demand such a hearing and impose upon him the customary burden of proof imposed upon one seeking to set aside a conviction. Here the burden must be shifted, for the plea was entered in suspicious circumstances that render it presumptively bad. The likelihood that it was motivated by improper pressures is so great that the burden of showing that it was not must fasten upon the State. This approach recognizes the constitutional values implicit in *Boykin,* while leaving it open to the State to show that, notwithstanding the inevitable suspicion that the plea was the improper product of the unconstitutional differential sentencing system, it was in fact motivated by different, and permissible, considerations.

Respectfully submitted,

JACK GREENBERG   JAMES M. NABRIT, III   MICHAEL MELTSNER
NORMAN AMAKER   JACK HIMMELSTEIN   CHARLES S. RALSTON
ANTHONY AMSTERDAM   JEROME B. FALK, JR.   JAMES E. LANNING
J. LE VONNE CHAMBERS   JAMES E. FERGUSON, II

ALFORD'S SUPPLEMENTAL BRIEF

[1. Voluntariness of Plea.] This Court has long enunciated the principle that a guilty plea not voluntarily and intelligently entered is constitutionally invalid. The record must affirmatively disclose that such a plea was both "voluntary" and "intelligent." It is submitted that the record in the present case establishes beyond question that the determination of the appellee, Henry C. Alford, to plead guilty was neither voluntary nor intelligent and that this Court should affirm the decision of the United States Court of Appeals for the Fourth Circuit. . . .

The circumstances surrounding Alford's guilty plea were significantly different from those surrounding the pleas of Brady or Parker. The record clearly shows that Alford's will was overborne by the circumstances in which he found himself and that he was "so gripped by fear of the death penalty . . . that he did not and could not, with the help of counsel, rationally weigh the advantages of going to trial against the advantages of pleading guilty."

Alford is a Negro with virtually no formal education. He was accused of murdering another Negro because of an argument arising over a white woman who was in the company of Alford at the time. Because of these facts—that the accused, a Negro, was in the company of a white woman in a Southern city—Alford was told by his attorney that the circumstances were "aggravated" and that he could be affected by "any prejudiced persons" who might be on the jury. [31] At the post-conviction hearing, Alford's attorney denied actually having told Alford that if he did not plead guilty, he would surely get the death penalty, although the attorney did testify that he told Alford in his opinion he could not win the case and that the facts were aggravated. It is clear that Alford in fact believed that under the circumstances he would receive the death penalty unless he pleaded guilty. At the trial itself, Alford took the stand at his own request and stated that he was innocent and that he "just pleaded guilty because they said if I didn't they would gas me for it, and that is all." He repeated this assertion several times in response to questioning by his own attorney and by the court. . . .

The record in the present case demonstrates that Alford has never admitted his guilt to the crime with which he was charged, either to the court or to his own attorney. . . .

A reading of the record reveals that Alford was torn between his desire to plead not guilty and the awesome alternative of risking the death penalty, a penalty he was convinced he would receive if he were tried by a jury. He continually wavered between the two alternatives until finally, after having become convinced from statements of his attorney and of his sister of the inevitability of the death penalty, he consented to plead guilty. And even at his trial, he felt compelled not to allow the guilty plea to go unqualified. The record portrays a man so caught up in this dilemma that it was virtually impossible for him voluntarily and intelligently to enter a plea of guilty. Even at the trial, his attorney stated to the

---

[31][Footnote from brief, citing the record of a postconviction hearing in the *Alford* litigation.]

Q. Now, Mr. Crumpler, did you ever discuss with the defendant or tell the defendant that things would go bad for him because the woman involved was a white woman?

A. No, sir, I don't recall using the word, white. I explained to him that the facts were aggravated and that for that reason—the way the killing occurred, that in my opinion I didn't think the jury would look upon it favorably.

By the Court:

Q. You gave him all of the information that you thought he ought to have in your opinion by representing him?

A. Yes, sir.

A. Your Honor, I might add that in reference to that question that I discussed this matter with him. I explained to him that there were aggravated circumstances and that the jury would render a fair determination and that I had no way to predict their verdict. However, that with the statements given me by the State's witnesses and also the place that it had occurred, which wasn't one of the most commendable places in the county, and concerning if there was any prejudiced persons, that I could not tell who was prejudiced, and that that might affect him, and I brought out every fact that I thought the jury might determine, and I explained to him that I was not prejudiced, I had no feeling about it, and I was as truthful as I could be in representing him.

court: "I don't know what to do with the man."[32] And yet, in the face of Alford's vacillation and obvious quandary, the court accepted the plea with very little comment or inquiry.

It is well established that determination of whether a guilty plea is the voluntary and intelligent act of the accused requires a consideration of the state of mind of the defendant at the time the plea was made. This determination is often difficult, perhaps sometimes impossible. However, in the present case, the state of mind of Alford is vividly demonstrated by the record as being so overpowered by the circumstances in which he found himself that it was virtually impossible for him intelligently to enter a voluntary guilty plea. There can be little doubt that Alford's plea was in fact coerced by the existence of the North Carolina statutory scheme of imposing the death penalty under the circumstances of this case.

Respectfully submitted,

DORIS R. BRAY,

Counsel for Appellee.

NORTH CAROLINA'S SUPPLEMENTAL BRIEF

[1. Role of Counsel.] In *Brady* the Court laid great stress on competent assistance of counsel in assuring that guilty pleas would be "otherwise valid." Counsel was relied on to serve two critical purposes: first, to act as a shield against coercive influences which would rob the plea of its voluntariness, and second, as a guide to insure as nearly as possible that the defendant knows the consequences likely to result from his decision on the plea.

In the present case petitioner's representation by court-assigned counsel has been found adequate twice in the Federal Courts and once in the State Courts. . . .

The State Court findings adopted by the Federal District Court in *Henry C. Alford v. State of North Carolina* make it plain that counsel did all that was possible in assuring that his client's plea was both voluntary and intelligent:

---

[32][Footnote from the brief, citing the same record as above.] . . . At the post-conviction hearing, Alford's attorney testified as follows:

Q. Now, at any time did you make a statement to the Court that you didn't know what to do with the man?

A. I certainly did.

Q. And in that statement, Mr. Crumpler, did you mean at that time that you were not sure what plea you should enter for the man?

A. I meant simply this: that I had advised and consulted with him as far as I thought it best to, and in my opinion as much as I could, that under the circumstances I wasn't sure what the proper course was and I left it up to the Court to make that decision.

Q. And then, Mr. Crumpler, you were in doubt as to what position you were in as to what plea you were to enter if you left it up to the Court?

A. Would you repeat that?

Q. You didn't know what position you were in as to his plea, did you?

A. I had no doubt of my position as to what his plea was at that time. I was doubtful of his position and for that reason I left it up to the Court to determine what his plea was.

That before the plea was entered, Fred G. Crumpler, Jr., who is an able trial lawyer, with extensive experience in the trial of criminal cases, *made a thorough investigation of the case, including the questioning of the investigating officers, all other witnesses for the State, and other persons who appeared to have some information.* That the said attorney contacted all witnesses named to him by the defendant, except a person designated as 'Jap,' who could not be located; that the said attorney found that none of the witnesses could give testimony helpful to the defendant, but that all of their testimony was detrimental to the defendant. That the said attorney further found that the evidence against the defendant was overwhelming and that the petitioner was confronted with a very serious case of murder. *That the said attorney discussed the matter with the petitioner on several occasions, and advised him of the testimony that the witnesses would give against him, and also advised him of the possible verdicts that a jury could render in the case.*

It thus appears from the State Court findings that through counsel's diligent investigation petitioner was effectively shielded from any "coercive impact of a promise of leniency." And it further appears that counsel's advice as to possible verdicts and as to the strength of the State's case acted to assure that petitioner's plea was made intelligently. Just as in *Brady* there is no evidence here that petitioner "did not or could not, *with the help of counsel,* rationally weigh the advantages of going to trial against the advantages of pleading guilty."

[2. Strength of State's Case.] There is a factual difference between the present case, on [the] one hand, and *Parker* and *Brady,* on the other. The petitioners, Parker and Brady, both admitted that they had in fact committed the crimes charged before their guilty pleas were accepted. In the case now before the Court, the petitioner maintained his innocence in the trial court while continuing to restate his desire to plead guilty. It could be urged that petitioner's failure to admit his guilt removes the present case from the holding of *Parker* and *Brady.* . . .

. . . [H]owever, as noted above, lower courts have already determined that petitioner's plea was entered voluntarily and knowingly. Whatever the reasons for petitioner's reluctance to admit his guilt, these judicial determinations that petitioner's plea was constitutionally valid should be afforded due consideration.

Furthermore, in light of the overwhelming evidence presented against him at trial, a full transcript of which is attached as an appendix to this supplemental brief, there can be no doubt that an adequate basis in fact was established to support petitioner's plea. Surely, this Court's expectations expressed in *Brady* that "courts will satisfy themselves that pleas of guilty are voluntarily and intelligently made by competent defendants with adequate advice of counsel . . . " have been met in this case. The fact that petitioner refused to admit his guilt should not be made a point of distinction in the face of clear findings that petitioner's plea was both voluntary and intelligent.

Respectfully submitted,
ROBERT MORGAN,
Attorney General of the State of North Carolina.

Appendix

NORTH CAROLINA)   IN THE SUPERIOR COURT

)

FORSYTH   )   DECEMBER 2, 1963 TERM

)

)

STATE OF NORTH CAROLINA   )

)   TRANSCRIPT

-vs-   )   OF

)   PROCEEDINGS

HENRY C. ALFORD   )

)

)

. . . MR. LUPTON [For the State]:   Your Honor, in this case Henry C. Alford is charged with the murder of Nathaniel Young on or about the 22nd day of November, 1963. Henry C. Alford, what is your plea?

MR. CRUMPLER [For the Defendant]:   We tender a plea of guilty to second degree murder.

THE COURT [The Honorable Walter E. Johnson, Jr.]:   Let the record show that when the case was called for trial the defendant, through his attorney, tendered to the State a plea of guilty to second degree murder, which plea is accepted by the State.

CRUMPLER: Thank you, Your Honor.

LUPTON: Your Honor, I believe, if it's satisfactory with you, I'll put the detective on the stand first.

THE COURT: All right.

E. I. Weatherman, being first sworn to state the truth, the whole truth and nothing but the truth, testified on his oath as follows:

DIRECT EXAMINATION

By Mr. Lupton:

Q. You are E. I. Weatherman, Detective in the Police Department?

A. Yes sir, that's correct.

Q. Now, go ahead and tell us what you learned in your investigation and tell us what each one of the witnesses told you, sir.

A. About 9:08 P.M., 11-22-63, Gilmore's Funeral Home notified the station that they had a request to pick up a person at a shooting on Claremont Avenue. As a consequence of this, Detective Pinkston went to the Kate Bitting Hospital and there learned that Nathaniel Young, male, colored, age forty, 1409 East 7½ Street was dead on arrival and that Dr. Vreeland had ruled that death was due to a gunshot wound which had entered the lower part of the heart on the left side of his chest. We then contacted James Teams, Eliza Toney, and others, who stated that they were at the home of Nathaniel Young at 1409 East 7½ Street around 8:00 o'clock on the 22nd, and that Henry C. Alford came in the house with a white girl, Georgia Lee Holder; that Alford and Georgia Lee went to the kitchen and that they got a drink of whiskey apiece; that they hugged and kissed back there and bought maybe two drinks of liquor; that the jukebox was playing and that Georgia Lee danced with Alford and one or two other colored males, and that Alford then came back in the front room and gave Nathaniel a dollar, stating that he wanted to use the bedroom. James Teams stated that he was in a chair near the bedroom and that Alford called Georgia Lee and they went into the bedroom and that Alford said that that was the last dollar that he had, and that Georgia Lee stated that he would have to have more than that and that he would—that they would have to come out of the room; that they stayed there about four or five minutes after that.

Q. She was a white girl?

A. That's right. They stayed there about four or five minutes and Alford said to Georgia Lee, said, "Let's go," and Georgia Lee said, "No, I'm not going. I'm going to stay here." Alford stated, "Well, you came here with me and you're going to leave with me," and he got ahold of her and attempted to pull her out of the chair and James stood up and said, "She don't have to go with you if she don't want to, she can stay here," and that Alford stated then that she came with him and that she was going to leave with him, and that Nathaniel said that he wasn't going to have anything in his house, that she could stay there if she wanted to. Alford then grabbed the coat of Georgia Lee and went out the door. Nathaniel and Rudolph Harris ran out the door after him and they returned in just a short time and stated that they were unable to catch Alford and get the coat back. They were standing around in the room, the rest of them, and in about ten or fifteen minutes there was a knock on the door and Nathaniel asked who was at the door and said somebody mumbled something that they couldn't understand and that Nathaniel opened the door and when he had it opened some short distance, some eight to twelve inches, there was a blast and Nathaniel fell to the floor. James Teams said that he ran out the door shortly but he was unable to see anyone around. We then contacted Ruby McGill, 1112 East 10½ Street, where Alford had been living, and Ruby—as a consequence of an interview with her—stated that she and Henry had been living together for some three years; that they were at this address about five months; that Henry left around dark, stating that he would be back in a few minutes; that about two and a half to three hours later he came back in and stated that he was breathing hard; appeared to have been running, and stated that, "God-damn son-of-a-bitches been running me and I'm going back and kill him." She stated that at that time he said Nathaniel Young, and that he repeated it a couple or three times, that he was going back and kill the son-of-a-bitch and the other fellow with him also. She stated that he got his shotgun out of the wardrobe and four shells; that she and Shirley asked him not to, told him there was no use in that, and said that he kept repeating that he was going back and that he went out the door. We talked to Betty Jean Robinson, who stated that she was on the porch of a store at 1202 10½ Street, which is a little better—about a half a block from the home—in the direction of Nathaniel Young's home, and she stated that she and Paul Hill was standing on the porch and Henry C. Alford came by them with a gun. In her statement to us, Ruby McGill stated that after he left with the gun, that he came back in approximately thirty to thirty-five minutes and stated that—said, "Honey, I done killed that Nathaniel and I'm going to leave you with the furniture." She said, "You don't have no business killing any man," and he said, "Yes, I killed that god-damn son-of-a-bitch. I'm not going to have anyone to kill me. I went to the door and when I shot him he just turned his head around and fell on the floor."

Q. He said he shot him?

A. Then we talked with Shirley. She stated that she was there; that she asked him not to go down there and he told her to mind her own business. While we was attempting to pick up Alford in regard to this we went to the home of Sidney Lackey, who lives down a couple houses across the street, and we first went to his home around 11:00 o'clock and asked him if Henry had been there. He said, after waking him, said that he had come in there and told him if the officers come looking for me tell them that I haven't been here. And I talked with Sidney later and he stated that after we left he went out and found Alford and asked him why we was looking for him and he told him he shot a man. Betty Robinson, in talking with her, she stated that she went to Alford's home after we were there—and we carried Ruby McGill to the station—that she went there around 12:00 o'clock and that Henry C. Alford was there and he gave her a coat—and the coat has been identified as the one that Georgia Lee Holder had—and that they went out and he bought her two drinks of whiskey which he paid a dollar and a half for; that he asked her for her address and her full name; stated that he had shot a man and that he would be gone a long time. We arrested Henry C. Alford about 1:00 o'clock at 11th and Cleveland Avenue the same night. He stated to us that he went to the home of Nathaniel Young with Georgia Lee Holder and that the statements of the other witnesses was true up to the time he went home; that when he went home that he did not return.

Q. Well then, he admitted what had taken place with reference to Georgia Lee Holder; is that right?

A. That's right. And Georgia Lee Holder, we talked with her and she stated that was true.

Q. He paid $1 for the room to Nathaniel?

A. That's right, got Georgia Lee Holder in the room.

Q. And something was said about him not having any more money and she would not have anything more to do with him?

A. That's correct.

Q. And then the argument ensued and Nathaniel told him to get out?

A. Well, he didn't tell him that he had to get out.

Mr. Lupton: Take the witness.

Cross-examination

By Mr. Crumpler:

Q. Mr. Weatherman, I believe when you found Henry, did he have a gun with him at that time?

A. No sir, he did not.

Q. Where did you locate the gun?

A. In the wardrobe at his home, the home of he and Ruby McGill.

Q. Were there—did he have any shells with him or in—

A. There was two shells turned over that Ruby stated was in the home.

Q. And as far as you can determine, no witnesses stated there was more than one shot fired?

A. One shot was fired.

Q. The examination of the gun showed that if the gun had been fired it had been cleaned; is that correct?

A. That's correct. When I talked to Henry he said, "My gun is clean."

Q. Right. Now, I believe also that Henry told you that at some time during the night that he had ridden in a cab?

A. Yes sir, that is true. We were looking for him in a cab.

Q. It was cab number 2?

A. I don't know.

Q. But in any event, the information was that he had in fact ridden in the cab but it was after the time—

A. That is correct.

Q. Do you know what kind of a shot was in the man's body?

A. No sir, I do not.

Q. What kind of a shot did the shells have themselves?

A. One of them didn't have any markings on it. It looked like maybe it was marked off, and the other was a number four, long-range shell.

Q. They were different—the two shells were different?

A. Yes sir, in my opinion they were. There was no markings on one of them that I could find.

MR. CRUMPLER: No further questions.

A. He stated that he had bought these shells from a man at the store and that he just got them out of a large box where he had twelve gauge shells. And the gun, in my opinion, smelled as if it had been recently fired.

THE COURT: All right. Step down.

MR. LUPTON: Your Honor, the State will tender the other witnesses.

THE COURT: Do you care to examine any of these witnesses, Mr. Crumpler?

MR. CRUMPLER: Your Honor, if the Court would allow me I would like to examine Sidney Lackey and possibly one more, and I'll be as brief as I can.

THE COURT: All right.

Sidney Lackey, being first sworn to state the truth, the whole truth and nothing but the truth, testified on his oath as follows:

DIRECT EXAMINATION

By Mr. Crumpler:

Q. Your name is Sidney Lackey?

A. Yes.

Q. I believe you were at the home of Ruby McGill on the afternoon or night some time or another?

A. Yes, I was.

Q. And, Sidney, I'll explain to you why I'm asking you this question. There is some doubt in Henry's mind as to which statement you made. Did Henry come there and get a gun at any time while you were there?

A. No, sir.

Q. And you don't have any knowledge about his having or his not having a gun?

A. No, sir.

Q. And the fact is, you never saw him leave with his gun and never heard him in an argument?

A. No.

Q. And the only knowledge that you have is the knowledge of the statement that he made to you that he had shot a man?

A. That's right.

Q. What time do you say the statement was made?

A. I'll say between 10:30 and 11:00.

Q. And where was the statement made, in his house or yours?

A. Mine.

Q. Sidney, did Ruby at any time run you away from the house for drinking?

A. Yes, she told me to get out.

Q. I believe there was a dispute over $3 that she said you owed her for some time?

A. No, sir.

Q. What was the dispute? Why did she ask you to leave?

A. I got into a fight with a fellow who walked in, wanted to know who I was and what I was doing there.

MR. CRUMPLER: No further questions, Your Honor.

MR. LUPTON: Come down.

THE COURT: Which other witness do you want to examine?

MR. CRUMPLER: This girl here, Your Honor.

Shirley Wright, being first sworn to state the truth, the whole truth and nothing but the truth, testified on her oath as follows:

DIRECT EXAMINATION

By Mr. Crumpler:

Q. Shirley, what is your full name?

A. Shirley Wright.

Q. Were you in the house of Ruby McGill during the night or any time during the night?

A. I wasn't there too long.

Q. What other people were there during the time that you were there?

A. I don't know.

Q. Well, was Ruby McGill there?

A. Yes.

Q. Was Sidney Lackey there?

A. I don't know. I didn't see him.

Q. Was William Jackson there?

A. I don't know.

Q. Now, what time of the night was it that—I believe you stated that Henry came there and got a gun?

A. Yes. I don't know what time it was. I guess about 9:00, something like that. It wasn't too late.

Q. How long was it before you saw Ruby again—I mean Henry—after that time?

A. I didn't see him any more. See, I left.

Q. You left after that?

A. After he came in and got his gun I left.

Q. Well, describe exactly what happened when he came to get the gun.

A. Well, when he come and got the gun I had went to the back room and I come out and he had got the gun, you know, and he said, "I'm going to kill that nigger." So—he didn't say who, and I didn't ask him. I just told him no, you know, don't do it, and that's all he said to me.

Q. Did you see him get any shells at that time?

A. No, I didn't.

Q. What kind of gun, did you see?

A. No, I didn't. It was a long one.

Mr. Crumpler: No further questions.

The Court: Well, is there anything else?

Mr. Crumpler: Your Honor, if you'll give me just a second. Your Honor, the defendant wishes to take the stand.

The Court: All right. Let him be sworn.

Henry C. Alford, being first duly sworn to state the truth, the whole truth and nothing but the truth, testified on his oath as follows:

DIRECT EXAMINATION

By Mr. Crumpler:

Q. Henry, you have asked to take the stand in order that you can make whatever statement you want. Go ahead and tell His Honor what you would like to say.

A. Yes, sir. Well, the night—well, on that night I was walking down to Nathaniel's house and met Georgia, and she said she wanted a little drink of whiskey and couldn't find any, and I said that we'll go to a friend's house on $7^1/_2$, and when we got there the radio was playing, or records somewhere, and we danced, and nobody was arguing in the house, and so—and I talked to Georgia and—I didn't have but $1 because I bought a half a pint of whiskey, and she wanted me to have more money. I got my check but I didn't have it with me. It was left in my wardrobe when I changed my work clothes. And I went to Claremont—I carried her coat—they got after me for the coat and then—they didn't get the coat. I went up to 7th Street and come back to Greenwood, and I come back down Greenwood and I went home, and I seen the check was in the billfold. I wanted to know—and I came back out and said—Ruby told me to go across the street, and so I collected her $3, and she had tried to collect it and he wouldn't give it to her, and there was no admission about no gun or shooting over there, and his girl friend he lives with came to the door and said, "The law is around over there at your house," and I said, "What are they over there for?" and she said she didn't know, and I said, "Well, let me go out the back door," and I went out the back door and said, "I'm going to cash my check," and I got a cab and went to cash my check, and so when I come back I met Betty. Betty said the law had been to my house and got Ruby and the shotgun, and I said, "What was they doing with the shotgun?" and she said she didn't know, but that they had got Ruby and the shotgun. And so I give Betty a dime to call to the police headquarters and ask why Ruby was up there and see how much bond was she under. I thought she was going to jail for whiskey, but they didn't have no bond, and they asked her where is Henry C. Alford at, asked Betty on the phone, and we started up the street and—she said she didn't know—and we went up the street, going up Cleveland, and went to my house, and there wasn't no whiskey in the house but the gun was gone like she said, and so we went back across Cleveland and bought a drink of whiskey to her cousin's house and we came back, and I said, "Well, what are they going to do with her?" first, and I says, "You go down the street," and so I was walking down Cleveland and Betty went down towards the officers' car—she lives down that way about three doors from me—from where I live, and so I walked down there, and the officer came up by himself and he—and he called me—I walked on the left-hand side of Cleveland and he said, "Hey fellow, what is your name?" and I told him, and he wanted to know where I was going, and I told him to Ruby McGill's, and I was walking on Cleveland and he drove up behind me and stopped me again and said for me to come here a minute in the car, and at that time he was by himself, and he walked around to the door and I got in the car, and he said, "What is your name?" and I told him, and he said, "Where do you live?" and I told him 1112 East 10½, and by that time I heard one of the officers talking on the two-way radio about Ruby saying I had on a black cap and black coat on the two-way radio, and some more officers come up, and right behind them come some more, and they stopped and—Joe Mc-Fadden and another one—that was four officers' cars at one time there, and Joe McFadden come over there and says, "That's Henry Alford," and they arrested me, and I pleaded guilty on second degree murder because they said there is too much evidence, but I ain't shot no man, but I take the fault for the other man. We never had an argument in our life and I just pleaded guilty because they said if I didn't they would gas me for it, and that is all.

MR. CRUMPLER: Your Honor, it is going to be necessary—I have, as best as I could, set these facts out in this affidavit, but I want to ask him a few questions.

Q. Now, you have consulted with me on several occasions before we came to court?

A. Yes, sir.

Q. And that is two or three times for the last two or three terms?

A. Yes, sir.

Q. And during that time you have had the privilege of being—seeing me and also seeing your sister and the other friends that have been around—the right to visit you and help prepare your case?

A. Yes, sir.

Q. And, also, I have advised you, as your attorney, of the various degrees of murder and the difference between second and first degree and your rights of appeal and the Court's power and discretion in each of those cases?

A. Yes, sir.

Q. And including the right of a jury to find you not guilty, and to the right to plead before the Governor of the State of North Carolina?

A. Yes, sir.

Q. And you authorized me to tender a plea of guilty to second degree murder before the Court?

A. Yes, sir.

Q. And in doing that, you have again affirmed your decision on that point?

A. Well, I'm still pleading that you all got me to plead guilty. I plead the other way, circumstantial evidence; that the jury will prosecute me on—on the second. You told me to plead guilty, right. I don't—I'm not guilty but I plead guilty.

THE COURT: Well, he says that you plead guilty to second degree murder.

A. Yes, sir.

By the Court:

Q. Is that your desire now?

A. Yes, sir. I plead guilty on—from the circumstances that he told me.

MR. CRUMPLER: I don't know what to do with the man.

THE COURT: You are court-appointed?

MR. CRUMPLER: Yes, sir. Your Honor, if the Court would allow me I—

THE COURT: I want to ask him some questions myself up here.

By the Court:

Q. You were born down in Rocky Mount on May 18, 1918, weren't you?

A. Yes, sir.

Q. June 18, 1918?

A. Yes.

Q. Now, how many times have you served penitentiary sentences in your life?

A. About three times.

Q. How many people have you been charged with murdering in your life?

A. One accident.

Q. Where was that?

A. In Virginia.

Q. Well, you killed that person? You served a sentence for that?

A. Yes, sir.

Q. How long did you serve for killing that man?

A. Six years.

Q. What was your sentence?

A. Ten.

Q. And you got out in six years?

A. Yes, sir.

Q. Well now, how many times have you been convicted of armed robbery?

A. Nine times. (*Note:* Nine times, or no times)

Q. What else have you been convicted of?

A. Whiskey and stuff like that.

Q. What did you serve on those?

A. I pulled time for hauling stolen goods in Robeson County.

Q. How much time did you make in that case?

A. Four years altogether.

Q. What else have you been convicted of?

A. I don't know.

Q. Well, you said you served three sentences.

A. Well, one was for forgery. I wrote some checks.

Q. How much time did you serve for forgery?

A. Two years.

Q. Well, you didn't come to Winston-Salem till 1960, did you?

A. No, sir.

Q. And since you came to Winston-Salem you have been convicted of carrying a concealed weapon here?

A. Here?

Q. Yes, on August 19, 1960.

A. Nothing but a pocket knife.

Q. Just a pocket knife?

A. Yes.

Q. Well, you were convicted of assault, charged in two cases of assault with a deadly weapon in 1960 when you came here, weren't you?

A. No, sir. I don't know anything about that.

Q. Well, you were up before Judge Sams on October 2, 1963, for cursing and abusing an officer?

A. Yes sir, I was up for that.

Q. And you were found guilty of it.

A. Yes, I pleaded guilty.

Q. And you were up for disorderly conduct in October; is that right?

A. Yes.

Q. And you were up for assault on some woman in September, is that right?

A. Yes.

Q. And you have been convicted of driving an automobile intoxicated and driving after your license was revoked and violation of the prohibition law all since you came here in 1960?

A. Yes.

THE COURT: All right. Stand down.

MR. CRUMPLER: That is all of the evidence that I have on his behalf, Your Honor.

THE COURT: Well, let the defendant stand up. It is the judgment of the Court that he be confined in the State's Prison for a term of thirty years.

ORAL ARGUMENT

❋   ❋   ❋

MR. SAFRON [North Carolina's Attorney]: . . . On the evening of November 22, 1963, Nathaniel Young, a Negro, operated an establishment in the city of Winston-Salem, Forsyth County, North Carolina, which can best be described as a "party house."

There was a knock at the door and Nathaniel Young partially opened that door and he was cut down by a shotgun blast.

Earlier that evening, Henry C. Alford had come to that house. Henry Alford also is Negro. Alford had been accompanied to that house by a young white lady. They had purchased several drinks of liquor by the drink, sold in that house, which is illegal under the North Carolina Prohibition law, and then Henry Alford gave Nathaniel Young, the proprietor, his last dollar in order to rent a room for several hours that evening in the house.

Alford was accompanied into that room by his girlfriend. But several minutes later they left, because Henry Alford no longer had any money.

He wanted this young lady to leave this house with him. She didn't want to go. Nathaniel Young, the proprietor, advised Alford that she [could] stay here.

An argument followed. Henry Alford grabbed the young lady's coat and, while being chased by Nathaniel Young and someone else, he took her coat, ran out the door, and these two followed him.

THE COURT: Where do all these facts come from?

SAFRON: These facts, your honor, are represented to the Superior Court of Forsyth County upon the tender of Henry C. Alford's plea; prior to the acceptance of the plea by the Court.

A complete transcript of the testimony presented by the State is included as an appendix to the State's supplemental brief filed in this case. This brief was a part of the record in the Fourth Circuit Court of Appeals.

THE COURT: Yes, now, that is the testimony of Mr. Weatherman, detective in the Police Department?

SAFRON: The testimony of Detective Weatherman and the testimony of several other witnesses, a young lady who was a girlfriend of the young lady with whom Henry Alford lived testified as to his obtaining the weapon, testimony of the young lady who saw Henry Alford walk down the street with his weapon, the testimony of a gentleman to whom Henry Alford had admitted killing the deceased that night and whom he had originally asked not to reveal his having seen him if the police come looking for him.

THE COURT: Is that the standard operating procedure in your State—guilty pleas to have a full case put in against the man?

SAFRON: I wouldn't use the word full case, your honor, but I would say this. In each and every instance, upon the entry of a plea of guilty, there is a presentation of the State's evidence.

THE COURT: Is this only in capital cases?

SAFRON: No, your honor, this is in all cases.

THE COURT: All felony cases?

SAFRON: Yes, your honor. The Court wants to be assured that the State does have a case against the defendant and, of course, at the same time, the Court wants to hear evidence, so that the Court would be in a better position to determine the sentence to impose upon the conviction.

This is a general operating procedure. . . .

❋   ❋   ❋

MR. SAFRON: . . . Now, both the *Brady* and *Parker* cases cited by this Court this last spring involved the question of the validity of pleas of guilty entered to capital offenses under which circumstances the plea guaranteed that the accused would escape the possible imposition of the sentence of death.

The issue presented, as stated by this Court in *Brady*, was whether it violates the Fifth Amendment to influence or encourage a guilty plea by the opportunity or promise of leniency, and whether a guilty plea is coerced and invalid if influenced by fear of a possibly higher penalty to the crime charged, if a conviction is obtained after the State has been put to its proof.

In both *Brady* and *Parker*, this Court denied relief, holding that an otherwise valid plea is not involuntary because induced by defendant's desire to limit the possible maximum penalty to less than that authorized if there is a jury trial.

In so holding, this Court rejected the contention that *United States vs. Jackson*, which had previously held invalid a provision in the federal Kidnaping Act, . . . rendered invalid the defendant's tender of a plea of guilty to the offense.

As this Court stated in *Brady*, a plea of guilty entered by the expectations of a completely counseled defendant that the State will have a strong case against him, is not subject to later attack because the defendant's lawyer correctly advised him with respect to then existing law as to possible penalties.

✿   ✿   ✿

MRS. BRAY [Alford's Attorney]:   . . . [W]hat is important in determining whether or not a guilty plea is voluntary is not what we think he should have done and whether we think he made the privy decision, but what was his state of mind at the time he entered that plea.

THE COURT: Mrs. Bray, you want us to set up the rule that in a case where the plea is made of this type and the petitioner in Habeas Corpus says that I did this because of the fear of capital punishment, that that [the plea] has to be upset without more. What do you have more than his word?

BRAY: Well, we have more than that in this case.

THE COURT: What?

BRAY: What we have is the man's continuing pronouncements of his innocence at the very trial at which he pleaded guilty, and his continuing compulsion never to let that guilty plea enter unqualified.

THE COURT: But what do we have other than his word that the only reason for his pleading guilty to second-degree was threat of the death penalty? You have nothing other than his word.

BRAY: Perhaps not. But we have nothing to indicate that there was any other reason.

THE COURT: What about the affidavit of the lawyer?

BRAY: Sir?

THE COURT: What about the affidavit of his lawyer?. . .

BRAY: I am sure that the lawyer advised him of the consequences of his plea. That seems to be well-established by the record.

However, just the advice of the lawyer, it seems to me, doesn't insulate the coercive effect of this statutory scheme on this defendant.

All the advice in the world is no good if the defendant is incapable, because of the overwhelming fear of the death penalty, of making any sort of a rational evaluation of advice he has received.

THE COURT: You keep saying the overwhelming fear of the death penalty. There was also an overwhelming fear of this evidence against him, wasn't that present, too?

BRAY: Well, I suppose that is necessarily present, because there could be no fear of the death penalty without the State having substantial evidence, which would substantiate a conviction.

THE COURT: That is my problem. I don't see how he can separate in his own mind which was the overwhelming influence, as between the threat of the death penalty and the amount of evidence against him, and the fact that he didn't have anything to defend himself with.

BRAY: Well, I doubt if he did separate it in his own mind. But they are so intertwined that I don't think the Court can separate them either.

If those two elements are separated, then I can't see how *Jackson* or the statutory scheme could ever have a coercive effect, as *Jackson* stated it did, because there would never be a real fear of the death penalty if the State did not have a substantial case against the defendant.

If there was no substantial case, then the chances are there would have been no indictment for first-degree murder. So it seems to me that it is impossible to separate the two and that the overwhelming evidence doesn't in any way dissipate the coercive effect of the fear of the death penalty.

THE COURT: Suppose he had been sentenced to life imprisonment and that he had been afraid of life imprisonment. Would that be enough to set aside the judgment?

BRAY: Well, your honor, it seems to me that the death penalty is such a different sort of thing.

THE COURT: It is death, of course, but a life sentence to some people is more threatening than the death sentence. Are we to draw a distinction between the fear that is generated in the human mind, the fear of being executed, and of the life term? That is what we have to do, isn't it?

BRAY: Yes, sir, I think that is what you have to do.

✿   ✿   ✿

THE COURT: Do you think it was a plea bargain?

MRS. BRAY: Do I think it was a plea bargain? No, sir, I don't think it was a plea bargain. I think that the record shows that the facts of the second-degree murder guilty plea just have nothing to do with this case, and I don't think it made any difference in his mind whether he got life imprisonment . . . or thirty years.

✿   ✿   ✿

THE COURT: Mrs. Bray, following up my question, that there is no trial of this case after he said I didn't do it, and I'm not guilty of it, etc., etc., suppose the judge had said all right, I will not accept your plea of second-degree murder and we will go to trial on second-degree murder, I would assume the same judge would give him the same thirty years?

MRS. BRAY: Well, he never, however, had that choice.

THE COURT: He never had the chance to go to the jury, is that your point?

BRAY: Yes, sir. He never had a chance to have a trial at all.

THE COURT: For second-degree murder. He has had an opportunity to have a trial for first-degree murder.

BRAY: Yes, sir, correct. But there never was any indication that the State would permit him to plead not guilty to second-degree murder. For that reason, I don't think that plea bargaining is a real issue at all in this case.

THE COURT: If the prosecutor was faced with a rule such as you suggest, I doubt if he would ever have accepted a plea of second-degree murder in this case. He had a strong case, he had strong evidence. . . .

BRAY: Well, that may very well be, but I question whether that has much to do with whether the plea was . . . voluntary or not.

　　The other essential fact is that the defendant has never admitted his guilt either to the Court or to the attorney. This is clear from the record, from the post-conviction hearing. He has just never admitted his guilt to anyone. . . .

THE COURT: Well, what would you have the trial judge do when the accused insists I am innocent, but nevertheless I will plead guilty to this lesser offense? What do you think the trial judge ought to do?

BRAY: I think that if that is the final word of the defendant, he ought not to accept the plea.

THE COURT: Just tell him he has to go to trial?

BRAY: Yes, sir. . . .

❖　　　❖　　　❖

THE COURT: Do I understand you, though, Mrs. Bray, that in any instance of a guilty plea, that in the absence of some admission by the accused of conduct of the nature charged . . . the judge ought to refuse to accept, whatever the circumstances, a plea of guilty to any offense? Is that what you are telling us?

MRS. BRAY: I don't know whether I would go that far. I think—

THE COURT: Would you say where, perhaps, he denies it, expressly denies it?

BRAY: I would certainly go that far. I think that any defendant who feels in Court compelled to deny it ought not to be permitted to plead guilty.

THE COURT: When he says "I ain't shot no man," that is denial, isn't it?

BRAY: I think in this case, under these facts, there should never have been a guilty plea accepted.

THE COURT: Suppose we didn't have that in this case, in this record, "I ain't shot no man, some other fellow did," we didn't have that statement at all, but we had everything else, would you be here?

BRAY: If we had this serious a crime, I think I may. But I think there must be a line somewhere, I am not sure where it is—for example, I think a man ought to be able to plead guilty to a traffic offense, pay his money in Court even if he thinks he wasn't speeding.

THE COURT: What if a man just pleads guilty, says I plead guilty, and nothing more, and the record does not show that he expressly admitted shooting the man, just said I am guilty, and then later seeks to upset his guilty plea on the grounds that the record does not show an admission of the act?

BRAY: Well, no, I don't think that is enough to upset it in itself.

THE COURT: You think that, unless otherwise qualified, saying I am guilty implicitly admits the act?

BRAY: As long as it was otherwise voluntary, as long as he had full knowledge of all the consequences.

THE COURT: Well, then, you do draw the line at the point where, in this record at least, the accuse[d] denies the–act?

BRAY: Yes. . . .

THE OPINION

Mr. Justice White delivered the opinion of the Court. . . .

Alford sought post-conviction relief in the state court. Among the claims raised was the claim that his plea of guilty was invalid because it was the product of fear and coercion. After a hearing, the state court in 1965 found that the plea was "willingly, knowingly, and understandingly" made on the advice of competent counsel and in the face of a strong prosecution case. Subsequently, Alford petitioned for a writ of habeas corpus, first in the United States District Court for the Middle District of North Carolina, and then in the Court of Appeals for the Fourth Circuit. Both courts denied the writ on the basis of the state court's findings that Alford voluntarily and knowingly agreed to plead guilty. In 1967, Alford again petitioned for a writ of habeas corpus in the District Court for the Middle District of North Carolina. That court, without an evidentiary hearing, again denied relief on the grounds that the guilty plea was voluntary and waived all defenses and nonjurisdictional defects in any prior stage of the proceedings, and that the findings of the state court in 1965 clearly required rejection of Alford's claim that he was denied effective assistance of counsel prior to pleading guilty. On appeal, a divided panel of the Court of Appeals for the Fourth Circuit reversed on the ground that Alford's guilty plea was made involuntarily. In reaching its conclusion, the Court of Appeals relied heavily on *United States v. Jackson,* which the court read to require invalidation of the North Carolina statutory framework for the imposition of the death penalty because North Carolina statutes encouraged defendants to waive constitutional rights by the promise of no more than life imprisonment if a guilty plea was offered and accepted. Conceding that Jackson did not require the automatic invalidation of pleas of guilty entered under the North Carolina statutes, the Court of Appeals ruled that Alford's guilty plea was involuntary because its principal motivation was fear of the death penalty. By this standard, even if both the judge and the jury had possessed the power to impose the death penalty for first-degree murder or if guilty pleas to capital charges had not been permitted, Alford's plea of guilty to second-degree murder should still have been rejected because impermissibly induced by his desire to eliminate the possibility of a death sentence. We noted probable jurisdiction. We vacate the judgment of the Court of Appeals and remand the case for further proceedings.

We held in *Brady v. United States* that a plea of guilty which would not have been entered except for the defendant's desire to avoid a possible death penalty and to limit the maximum penalty to life imprisonment or a term of years was not for that reason compelled within the meaning of the Fifth Amendment. Jackson established no new test for determining the validity of guilty pleas. The standard was and remains whether the plea represents a voluntary and intelligent choice among the alternative courses of action open to the defendant. That he would not have pleaded except for the opportunity to limit the possible penalty does not necessarily demonstrate that the plea of guilty was not the product of a free and rational choice, especially where the defendant was represented by competent counsel whose advice was that the plea would be to the defendant's advantage. The standard fashioned and applied by the Court of Appeals was therefore erroneous and we would, without more, vacate and remand the case for further proceedings with respect to any other claims of Alford which are properly before that court, if it were not for other circumstances appearing in the record which might seem to warrant an affirmance of the Court of Appeals.

As previously recounted, after Alford's plea of guilty was offered and the State's case was placed before the judge, Alford denied that he had committed the murder but reaffirmed his desire to plead guilty to avoid a possible death sentence and to limit the penalty to the 30-year maximum provided for second-degree murder. Ordinarily, a judgment of conviction resting on a plea of guilty is justified by the defendant's admission that he committed the crime charged against him and his consent that judgment be entered without a trial of any kind. The plea usually subsumes both elements, and justifiably so, even though there is no separate, express admission by the defendant that he committed the particular acts claimed to constitute the crime charged in the indictment. Here Alford entered his plea but accompanied it with the statement that he had not shot the victim.

If Alford's statements were to be credited as sincere assertions of his innocence, there obviously existed a factual and legal dispute between him and the State. Without more, it might be argued that the conviction entered on his guilty plea was invalid, since his assertion of innocence negated any admission of guilt, which, as we observed last Term in *Brady,* is normally "[c]entral to the plea and the foundation for entering judgment against the defendant. . . ."

In addition to Alford's statement, however, the court had heard an account of the events on the night of the murder, including information from Alford's acquaintances that he had departed from his home with his gun stating his intention to kill and that he had later declared that he had carried out his intention. Nor had Alford wavered in his desire to have the trial court determine his guilt without a jury trial. Although denying the charge against him, he nevertheless preferred the dispute between him and the State to be settled by the judge in the context of a guilty plea proceeding rather than by a formal trial. Thereupon, with the State's telling evidence and Alford's denial before it, the trial court proceeded to convict and sentence Alford for second-degree murder.

State and lower federal courts are divided upon whether a guilty plea can be accepted when it is accompanied by protestations of innocence and hence contains only a waiver of trial but no admission of guilt. Some courts, giving expression to the principle that "[o]ur law only authorizes a conviction where guilt is shown," require that trial judges reject such pleas. But others have concluded that they should not "force any defense on a defendant in a criminal case," particularly when advancement of the defense might "end in disaster. . . ." They have argued that, since "guilt, or the degree of guilt, is at times uncertain and elusive," "[a]n accused, though believing in or entertaining doubts respecting his innocence, might reasonably conclude a jury would be convinced of his guilt and that he would fare better in the sentence by pleading guilty. . . ." As one state court observed nearly a century ago, "[r]easons other than the fact that he is guilty may induce a defendant to so plead, . . . [and] [h]e must be permitted to judge for himself in this respect."

This Court has not confronted this precise issue, but prior decisions do yield relevant principles. In *Lynch v. Overholser,* Lynch, who had been charged in the Municipal Court of the District of Columbia with drawing and negotiating bad checks, a misdemeanor punishable by a maximum of one year in jail, sought to enter a plea of guilty, but the trial judge refused to accept the plea since a psychiatric report in the judge's possession indicated that Lynch had been suffering from "a manic depressive psychosis, at the time of the crime charged," and hence might have been not guilty by reason of insanity. Although at the subsequent trial Lynch did not rely on the insanity defense, he was found not guilty by reason of insanity and committed for an indeterminate period to a mental institution. On habeas corpus, the Court ordered his release, construing the congressional legislation seemingly authorizing the commitment as not reaching a case where the accused preferred a guilty plea to a plea of insanity. The Court expressly refused to rule that Lynch had an absolute right to have his guilty plea accepted, but implied that there would have been no constitutional error had his plea been accepted even though evidence before the judge indicated that there was a valid defense.

The issue in *Hudson v. United States* was whether a federal court has power to impose a prison sentence after accepting a plea of nolo contendere, a plea by which a defendant does not expressly admit his guilt, but nonetheless waives his right to a trial and authorizes the court for purposes of the case to treat him as if he were guilty. The Court held that a trial court does have such power, and except for the cases which were rejected in *Hudson,* the federal courts have uniformly followed this rule, even in cases involving moral turpitude. Implicit in the nolo contendere cases is a recognition that the Constitution does not bar imposition of a prison sentence upon an accused who is unwilling expressly to admit his guilt but who, faced with grim alternatives, is willing to waive his trial and accept the sentence.

These cases would be directly in point if Alford had simply insisted on his plea but refused to admit the crime. The fact that his plea was denominated a plea of guilty rather than a plea of nolo contendere is of no constitutional significance with respect to the issue now before us, for the Constitution is concerned with the practical consequences, not the formal categorizations, of state law. Thus, while most pleas of guilty consist of both a waiver of trial and an express admission of guilt, the latter element is not a constitutional requisite to the imposition of criminal penalty. An individual accused of crime may voluntarily, knowingly, and understandingly consent to the imposition of a prison sentence even if he is unwilling or unable to admit his participation in the acts constituting the crime.

Nor can we perceive any material difference between a plea that refuses to admit commission of the criminal act and a plea containing a protestation of innocence when, as in the instant case, a defendant intelligently concludes that his interests require entry of a guilty plea and the record before the judge contains strong evidence of actual guilt. Here the State had a strong case of first-degree murder against Alford. Whether he realized or disbelieved his guilt, he insisted on his plea because in his view he had absolutely nothing to gain by a trial and much to gain by pleading. Because of the overwhelming evidence against him, a trial was precisely what neither Alford nor his attorney desired. Confronted with the choice between a trial for first-degree murder, on the one hand, and a plea of guilty to second-degree murder, on the other, Alford quite reasonably chose the latter and thereby limited the maximum penalty to a 30-year term. When his plea is viewed in light of the evidence against him, which substantially negated his claim of innocence and which further provided a means by which the judge could test whether the plea was being intelligently entered, its validity cannot be seriously questioned. In view of the strong factual basis for the plea demonstrated by the State and Alford's clearly expressed desire to enter it despite his professed belief in his innocence, we hold that the trial judge did not commit constitutional error in accepting it.

Relying on *United States v. Jackson,* Alford now argues in effect that the State should not have allowed him this choice but should have insisted on proving him guilty of murder in the first degree. The States in their wisdom may take this course by statute or otherwise and may prohibit the practice of accepting pleas to lesser included offenses under any circumstances. But this is not the mandate of the Fourteenth Amendment and the Bill of Rights. The prohibitions against involuntary or unintelligent pleas should not be relaxed, but neither should an exercise in arid logic render those constitutional guarantees counterproductive and put in jeopardy the very human values they were meant to preserve. . . .

Mr. Justice Brennan, dissenting . . .

Last Term, this Court held, over my dissent, that a plea of guilty may validly be induced by an unconstitutional threat to subject the defendant to the risk of death, so long as the plea is entered in open court and the defendant is represented by competent counsel who is aware of the threat, albeit not of its unconstitutionality. Today the Court makes clear that its previous holding was intended to apply even when the record demonstrates that the actual effect of the unconstitutional threat was to induce a guilty plea from a defendant who was unwilling to admit his guilt.

I adhere to the view that, in any given case, the influence of such an unconstitutional threat "must necessarily be given weight in determining the voluntariness of a plea." And, without reaching the question whether due process permits the entry of judgment upon a plea of guilty accompanied by a contemporaneous denial of acts constituting the crime, I believe that at the very least such a denial of guilt is also a relevant factor in determining whether the plea was voluntarily and intelligently made. With these factors in mind, it is sufficient in my view to state that the facts set out in the majority opinion demonstrate that Alford was "so gripped by fear of the death penalty" that his decision to plead guilty was not voluntary but was "the product of duress as much so as choice reflecting physical constraint." Accordingly, I would affirm the judgment of the Court of Appeals.

POSTSCRIPT

After *North Carolina v. Alford* (1970), the Supreme Court continued to provide strong support for the practice of plea bargaining even though many commentators demanded its reform or abolition. In *Santobello v. New York,* decided the year after *Alford,* Chief Justice Warren Burger described plea bargaining not only as "an essential component of the administration of justice" but also as "a highly desirable part" of the criminal justice process.

> It leads to prompt and largely final disposition of most criminal cases; it avoids much of the corrosive impact of enforced idleness during pretrial confinement for those who are denied release pending trial; it protects the public from those accused persons who are prone to continue criminal conduct even while on pretrial release; and, by shortening the time between charge and disposition, it enhances whatever may be the rehabilitative prospects of the guilty when they are ultimately imprisoned.[33]

According to the majority of Supreme Court justices, not only was it constitutional, but plea bargaining was also an admirable way to process the huge number of criminal cases. "Properly administered," it was "to be encouraged."[34] Many of the Court's plea-bargaining decisions after *Alford* were related to either of these two objectives: they either "encouraged" plea bargaining or defined the principle of "proper administration." Academic commentators have taken exception to what

---

[33]*Santobello v. New York,* 404 U.S. 257, 261 (1971).

[34]Idem, 260.

the Court has done in regard to both objectives, claiming that the Court has not done enough to ensure the proper administration of plea bargaining and that it is a practice that should be discouraged and strictly regulated, if not prohibited.

Plea bargaining, of course, could not flourish unless the bargains were kept. It made no sense for either party to engage in plea negotiation if the prosecutor could renege on the deal or if the defendant, at a later date, could easily overturn the guilty plea. The Court addressed the former issue in *Santobello v. New York* (1971). In this case, the prosecutor had promised to make no recommendation as to sentence in exchange for the defendant's plea to a less serious offense. However, when sentencing finally occurred, a different prosecutor recommended the maximum, which the defendant received, though the judge claimed that the prosecutor's recommendation had no effect on his sentencing decision. The Supreme Court's ruling was sharp and clear. When "a plea rests in any significant degree on a promise or agreement of the prosecutor, so that it can be said to be part of the inducement of consideration, such promise must be fulfilled."[35] The Court declined to say whether the state could rectify the situation by giving Santobello a sentence according to the terms of the bargain or whether it had to give Santobello the option of withdrawing his plea and going to trial. This particular issue was remanded to the lower court. Nevertheless, the decision recognized that a state had a constitutional duty either to sentence defendants according to the terms of their plea bargains or to give them the option of withdrawing their pleas.

In *Mabry v. Johnson* (1984), the Court explained what specifically triggered the state's obligation to respect the plea bargain. In this case, the prosecutor had withdrawn a plea-bargain offer after the defendant had accepted it. Johnson had been convicted of burglary, assault, and murder, but his murder conviction was set aside. At this point, before his retrial and while Johnson was serving concurrent twenty-one- and twelve-year sentences on the burglary and assault convictions, plea negotiations began anew on the murder charge. The prosecutor proposed that Johnson plead guilty to a reduced charge for a recommendation of a twenty-one-year sentence to be served concurrently with the burglary and assault sentences. Because this offer added no additional time to what Johnson was already serving for the less serious convictions, he accepted it. However, a day later, claiming that a mistake had been made, the prosecutor withdrew the offer and proposed instead that for a plea of guilty, he would recommend a twenty-one-year sentence to be served *consecutively* to Johnson's other sentences. Eventually, after his retrial had begun, Johnson accepted this later offer and was sentenced accordingly. He then attacked the lawfulness of his guilty plea, claiming that the state had an obligation to abide by the first offer he had accepted.

The Supreme Court decided against Johnson's claim. True, the state had violated its "promise" to Johnson, but the "Due Process Clause is not a code of ethics for prosecutors; its concern is with the manner in which persons are deprived of their liberty."[36] The Constitution required only that Johnson's plea be "voluntary and intelligent." If it was, it did not matter what happened prior to the plea during the process of negotiation. Plea negotiations are not over until they are over. Both

---

[35]Idem, 262.

[36]*Mabry v. Johnson*, 467 U.S. 504, 511 (1984).

the defendant and the prosecutor can withdraw offers accepted by the other side until the guilty plea is actually entered before a judge in open court. In effect, the guilty plea itself triggers the state's obligation to respect the terms of the bargain that induced the defendant to plead guilty. Until the plea is entered, the state has no constitutional duty to respect any of the bargains it has offered the defendant.

Though the prosecution had to respect the terms of the bargain that in fact induced a plea, the Court decided in *United States v. Benchimol* (1985) that its obligations extended no further. In this case, the defendant pleaded guilty to one count of mail fraud and agreed to restitution in exchange for the government's promise to recommend probation. At the sentencing hearing, the assistant United States attorney agreed with the defense counsel's claim that the government recommended probation with restitution but "left an impression with the court of less-than-enthusiastic support for leniency.[37] The district judge then sentenced Benchimol to six years of treatment and supervision under the Youth Corrections Act. The defendant claimed that the government had failed to comply with its plea bargain, but the Supreme Court dismissed his argument. The government was not obliged to do anything more than what was specifically promised in exchange for the guilty plea. Of course, the government could obligate itself to an "enthusiastic" recommendation of leniency, but the respondent had made no claim that the government had in fact made such a commitment in his case. Therefore, since the government had no duty to do anything beyond the specific terms of the plea bargain, the defendant's guilty plea withstood challenge.

By protecting the finality of plea bargains, *Santobello, Mabry,* and *Benchimol* encouraged the practice of exchanging leniency for guilty pleas. Plea bargaining had many advantages, both for the state and the defendant, but they could be secured "only if dispositions by guilty pleas are accorded a great measure of finality."[38] After these decisions, prosecutors and defense lawyers knew what legal consequences followed from their actions. Negotiations were nonbinding until the plea was entered, but both parties were obligated to respect the specific terms of the agreement—but only the specific terms—once the judge accepted the guilty plea.

The Supreme Court decisions following *Alford* encouraged plea bargaining, but they also recognized the possibility of abuse. The informal system of plea bargaining benefited all concerned only if it was "properly administered." The Court clarified the meaning of this requirement by analyzing what constituted a "voluntary and intelligent" waiver of constitutional rights. In *Henderson v. Morgan* (1976), the Court explored the requirement of an intelligent waiver. Morgan had been indicted for first-degree murder on the ground that he stabbed a woman repeatedly. After pleading guilty to second-degree murder, Morgan was sentenced, but he then attacked the validity of his guilty plea because he had never been informed that an intent to cause death was an element of second-degree murder. Neither his counsel nor the judge had told him about the requisite intent. He therefore argued that he had pleaded guilty "unintelligently," not knowing exactly

---

[37]*United States v. Benchimol,* 471 U.S. 453, 455 (1985).

[38]*Blackledge v. Allison,* 431 U.S. 63, 71 (1977).

to what he had pleaded. Since the waiver of his constitutional rights had been "unintelligent," he wanted once again to have the option of a trial.

In a majority opinion written by Justice John Paul Stevens, the Court agreed with Morgan. The fact that the evidence in the case clearly showed that Morgan intended to kill his victim made no difference. For the plea to be valid, it had to be an intelligent admission that he had committed the offense. But no such admission could be intelligent "unless the defendant received 'real notice of the true nature of the charge against him, the first and most universally recognized requirement of due process."[39] Accordingly, since Morgan had not been advised that he was admitting that he had intentionally killed his victim, the guilty plea was invalid. The Court's ruling was clear: before any plea was accepted, there should be "an explanation of the charge by the judge, or at least a representation by defense counsel that the nature of the offense has been explained to the accused."[40] The "proper administration" of plea bargaining required that this formal precaution be taken to ensure that the defendant's guilty plea was an intelligent one.

Henderson, along with the other cases considered here, indicates the degree to which the Supreme Court has relied on formal procedures at the plea hearing to obtain a "properly administered" system of plea bargaining. In accordance with the principles contained in these decisions, the Court has helped transform plea bargaining from a system of "secret covenants secretly arrived at" to a system of "open covenants secretly arrived at."[41] No longer was a plea agreement a confidential matter between the prosecutor and the defendant and his counsel. Instead, after the "secret" deal was struck, it was ratified in open court before a judge who was told of the plea bargain and who informed the defendant of the nature of the charge to which he was pleading guilty, the possible penalties attached to the offense, and the constitutional rights that he was waiving by pleading guilty. As plea bargaining has become, in this manner, more formalized, it is arguable that it has become less controversial and more of an accepted feature of the American criminal justice system.

However, the formalized procedures used by judges to ensure that guilty pleas are voluntary and intelligent may not be sufficient if the secret negotiations that precede them are left unregulated. *Bordenkircher v. Hayes* (1978) is a case in point. Paul Hayes was indicted for the forgery of a check in the amount of $88.30, punishable by a sentence of two to ten years. If Hayes would plead guilty, the prosecutor promised he would recommend a five-year sentence. However, if Hayes did not plead guilty to the offense, the prosecutor threatened that he would return to the grand jury and seek an indictment under Kentucky's Habitual Criminal Act, thereby exposing Hayes to a mandatory life sentence because he had two prior felony convictions (one for "detaining a female," the other for robbery) for which he had not been imprisoned (though he had spent five years in a reformatory). Hayes's options were a five-year sentence or, depending on the verdict, the possibility of acquittal or a life sentence. Despite the risk of life imprisonment,

[39]*Henderson v. Morgan,* 426 U.S. 637, 645 (1976).

[40]Idem, 647.

[41]Norval Morris, *The Future of Imprisonment* (Chicago: University of Chicago Press, 1974), p. 51.

Hayes decided to go to trial. A jury convicted him of forgery, and a judge sentenced him to life imprisonment. In his petition for a writ of *habeas corpus*, Hayes claimed that the prosecutor's threat to bring additional charges during plea bargaining amounted to "prosecutorial vindictiveness" in violation of due process.

Hayes won at the Court of Appeals, but the Supreme Court reversed that decision. According to Justice Potter Stewart's majority opinion, it was irrelevant that the prosecutor's motive for the new indictment was to discourage Hayes from exercising his right to a trial. That was the way plea bargaining worked. Prosecutors use the risk of a stiffer punishment to get defendants to give up their right to a trial. Therefore, to "hold that the prosecutor's desire to induce a guilty plea is an 'unjustifiable standard,' which, like race or religion, may play no part in his charging decision, would contradict the very premises that underlie the concept of plea bargaining itself."[42] It also did not matter that the indictment under the Habitual Criminal Act occurred during the plea negotiations after the original charge of forgery had been handed up by the grand jury. The chronology did not substantiate the claim that the prosecutor had "vindictively" punished the defendant for exercising his right to a trial. The prosecutor was only doing what he was legally entitled to do and, "in the 'give-and-take' of plea bargaining, there is no such element of punishment or retaliation so long as the accused is free to accept or reject the prosecution's offer."[43] Because Hayes, properly represented by counsel, had voluntarily made the decision to go to trial, his conviction and life sentence were valid.

Four justices dissented in *Hayes*. In general, they argued, first, that the prosecutor's admitted motive in bringing the second indictment constituted "prosecutorial vindictiveness" and, second, that adding charges for the same conduct during the course of plea negotiation penalized the defendant's right to a jury trial. A better approach would be to "hold the prosecution to the charge it was originally content to bring and to justify in the eyes of its public."[44] Plea bargaining would then reward those who pleaded guilty but would not penalize those who insisted on their constitutional right to a trial. Who has the better argument: the Court's majority or the dissenters? Is the majority correct that the prosecutor's tactics in this case are acceptable given the give-and-take nature of plea bargaining? Is the majority more or less admitting that plea bargains burden the exercise of constitutional rights when it acknowledges that the prosecutor's primary desire is to induce guilty pleas? If so, is plea bargaining nonetheless constitutional because it is necessary in our criminal justice system? If the prosecutor could add new charges to induce a defendant to plead guilty, what else could the prosecutor do? Could the prosecutor add additional *unwarranted* charges to increase the pressure on the defendant to plead guilty? Would such an option constitute "prosecutorial vindictiveness," even if the defendant is always free to accept or reject the offer? How do you compare the give-and-take character of plea bargaining to the more

---

[42]*Bordenkircher v. Hayes*, 434 U.S. 357, 364–365 (1978).

[43]Idem, 363.

[44]Idem, 368.

formal procedures by which the court accepts guilty pleas? Are the formalities enough to ensure that the defendant is indeed pleading guilty voluntarily? Is it possible that the formalities are a facade behind which prosecutors coerce defendants, not only to waive their constitutional rights but also to say in open court that their waivers were voluntary? Does the presence of defense counsel make the system defensible? What if it is a busy court-appointed lawyer?

Norval Morris has argued that the new form of plea bargaining—"open covenants secretly arrived at"—needs reform. His model is a system of "open covenants openly arrived at." He recommends a pretrial hearing (without a record) at which the defense counsel, the prosecutor, the judge (not the trial judge if the case goes to trial), the accused, and the victim "explore what might be feasible by way of settlement of all issues in dispute, acceptable to the state and the accused alike, including questions of compensation of victims, and everything that is now properly relevant to plea bargaining."[45] The presence of the judge and the victim would help eliminate irresponsibly weak negotiating on the part of either the defense counsel or the prosecutor. The judge would also not tolerate either prosecutorial overcharging or vindictiveness. In such a hearing, not only would the victim have full say, but the accused would also be treated more fairly than in the normal plea bargaining situation. Always retaining the right to go to trial if the result of the hearing was not to his satisfaction, the defendant would have no basis to object later to his sentence.

John Kaplan has argued that Morris's suggestions do not go far enough. Plea bargaining would still occur—guilty pleas would still be used to purchase leniency—and the result would be that equally culpable defendants will receive different sentences based on factors that should be irrelevant: for example, the prosecutor's backlog and the length of time the trial would take. Kaplan's suggestion is that we adopt a system of fixed sentences for various crimes. Each crime would be worth so many years, plus additional increments for aggravating circumstances. In such a system, a guilty plea could be viewed as a straightforward mitigating factor. Every criminal defendant would know beforehand both the length of his possible sentence (that prescribed for the crime plus any aggravating circumstances) and the fact that a guilty plea could reduce the sentence by a percentage established at the county level, whether by a legislative body or by the local district attorney's office. The beauty of such a system, according to Kaplan, is that it would sharply reduce bargaining, if not eliminate it entirely, and it would provide equitable treatment to equally culpable defendants.[46]

Stephen Schulhofer agrees with Kaplan that plea bargaining should be eliminated, but he takes a different approach. According to Schulhofer, guilty pleas should be neither negotiated nor discounted. In every case, the defendant must either plead guilty to the charge (and be sentenced accordingly) or the facts of guilt or innocence would be decided in a formal adversary bench trial before a

---

[45]Morris, *Future of Imprisonment*, p. 54. See pp. 51–55.

[46]See John Kaplan, "American Merchandising and the Guilty Plea: Replacing the Bazaar with the Department Store," *American Journal of Criminal Law* 5 (1977): 215–224.

judge. Such a system would efficiently permit "the expeditious but fair and accurate resolution of criminal cases on the basis of public testimony, tested and challenged with the traditional tools of American adversary procedure."[47] Philadelphia, Schulhofer points out, already has such a system, and it works. The city gives defendants a choice of a jury trial or a bench trial, and most choose the latter. These Philadelphia bench trials, Schulhofer insists, are not "slow guilty pleas." They are an efficacious means of determining guilt or innocence in a formal adversary proceeding. Bench trials for major crimes (excluding murder) were often completed in less than two hours; most trials for minor crimes took only one hour and twenty minutes, rather than the fifty-five minutes that it took for a judge to accept the normal guilty plea. The bottom line, according to Schulhofer, is that the elimination of plea bargaining is perfectly feasible. It is not a practice that is justifiable because it is inevitable.

Others doubt whether the bench trial is the solution for plea bargaining. One commentator notes, for example, that Philadelphia assigns its "toughest judges" to defendants who opt for jury trials.[48] Hence even if prosecutors do not bargain with individual defendants, the system structurally grants leniency in exchange for the defendant's right to a jury trial. In any case, if bench trials replaced plea bargaining, would it be necessary to abolish the right to a jury trial? Would such an option be worth the price? Would plea bargaining really disappear, or would it just become less visible?[49] Milton Heumann has argued that it is impossible to abolish plea bargaining.[50] In any system of criminal justice, someone will have to decide what criminal charges to bring against what defendants. Such discretion is intrinsic to the situation. The individual who exercises it, if only to resolve cut-and-dried cases and thereby save prosecutorial and judicial resources for cases that deserve more attention, will be tempted in particular cases to offer, openly or implicitly, leniency in exchange for guilty pleas. Heumann suggests that there is no practical way to avoid such implicit plea bargaining and that it differs only in degree from explicit plea bargaining. Is he right?

Hence the controversy about plea bargaining continues. For all practical purposes, the Supreme Court has settled the question of whether plea bargaining is constitutional. Though it remains an interesting theoretical question whether plea bargaining unconstitutionally penalizes a defendant's right to a fair trial, there is no reason to think that the Supreme Court will ever declare it unconstitutional. But even if plea bargaining is constitutional, has it become too widespread?

---

[47]Stephen Schulhofer, "Is Plea Bargaining Inevitable?" *Harvard Law Review* 97 (1984), 1107.

[48]John Kaplan, Jerome H. Skolnick, and Malcolm M. Feeley, *Criminal Justice* (Westbury, N.Y.: Foundation Press, 1991), p. 488.

[49]Several jurisdictions have tried, with limited success, to reduce or eliminate plea bargaining. The best-known attempt was Alaska's ban of prosecutorial bargaining in 1975 and judicial bargaining in 1977. However, later analysis of sentencing data showed that Alaskan defendants who went to trial received more severe sentences than equally culpable defendants who pleaded guilty. The impression is that an "implicit" system of leniency for those who pleaded guilty replaced the more explicit form of plea bargaining. See Schulhofer, "Is Plea Bargaining Inevitable?"

[50]Milton Heumann, *Plea Bargaining* (Chicago: University of Chicago Press, 1977), p. 166.

For more than two decades, the Court has encouraged plea bargaining as a system of "open covenants secretly arrived at." Some legal commentators have criticized the Court's handling of plea bargaining, claiming that it should be eliminated or at least subject to additional controls. Is the Court correct in its assessment of the value of plea bargaining? If "properly administered," does it "benefit all concerned"? Does it trouble you that the Court has done so much to encourage plea bargaining without establishing tough guidelines for the give-and-take process? What sort of standards would you suggest? Even if it is constitutional, would you favor abolishing plea bargaining? What about the costs of trials? The waste of resources on cut-and-dried cases? Is abolishing plea bargaining even possible?

CHAPTER 4

The Exclusionary Rule

UNITED STATES V. LEON
468 U.S. 902 (1984)

✦

The Fourth Amendment to the United States Constitution recognizes a substantive right to be free from "unreasonable searches and seizures." The police can engage only in "reasonable" searches, and judges can issue search warrants only if there is "probable cause." Such a substantive constitutional right, however, cannot enforce itself. If the substantive right is to have any meaning, the individual whose substantive *right* has been violated must have a *remedy*. In the case of the Fourth Amendment, the controversial remedy that the Supreme Court has developed is the well-known exclusionary rule. If and when a criminal prosecution occurs, a judge will remedy a violation of a person's right to be free from "unreasonable searches and seizures" by excluding any illegally seized evidence from the courtroom. The Court established this principle for federal courts in *Weeks v. United States* (1914) but did not apply it to the states until *Mapp v. Ohio* (1961).[1] Ever since this decision, public debate has raged over whether the exclusionary rule is the proper remedy for violations of Fourth Amendment rights. During the 1970s and 1980s, the Court has responded to this outcry by creating certain exceptions to the exclusionary rule. For example, in *United States v. Leon* (1984), a 6–3 decision, the Court recognized a "good faith" exception. Illegally seized evidence would not be excluded from a trial if the police who had engaged in the illegal search had, in "reasonable good faith," relied on an illegally issued search warrant.

---

[1]232 U.S. 383 (1914); 367 U.S. 643 (1961).

Leon is an important decision for a number of related reasons. First, the case provides a useful context to consider the merits of the exclusionary rule itself. Because the rule excludes evidence that is usually highly probative of guilt, it is not easy to justify. Why should a criminal court whose primary function is to determine guilt or innocence exclude evidence—even if it has been illegally seized— that could decisively establish the defendant's guilt? As New York Judge Benjamin Cardozo (who later became a Supreme Court justice) observed many years ago: "The criminal is to go free because the constable has blundered. . . . A room is searched against the law, and the body of a murdered man is found. . . . The privacy of the home has been infringed, and the murderer goes free."[2] Cardozo's point, of course, was that it made no sense to let the murderer go free because the state did something wrong. In his view, the violation of the Fourth Amendment should be remedied in some other way than by excluding probative evidence from the courtroom. What is your initial reaction? Is Cardozo right? This chapter will consider the reasons for and against the rule.

Besides providing a forum for a debate on the exclusionary rule's merits, *Leon* also uncovers the kind of relationship that exists between constitutional rights and remedies. The status and scope of any constitutional remedy depend on the character of its justification. If a justification of a remedy identifies it as a logical corollary of an underlying constitutional right, its status is assured and its scope broad. At one time, the Supreme Court gave the exclusionary rule a justification of this type. The rule was "part and parcel" of a right understood as a broad command to both the police and the courts not to search or seize unlawfully. However, as dissatisfaction with the exclusionary rule grew, the Court altered the rule's justification by adapting the meaning of the Fourth Amendment. Instead of viewing it as a broad command to the courts as well as to the police, the Court argued that the amendment was a restriction only on the police. Using illegally seized evidence at trial was therefore no longer a constitutional violation, only a judicially created means of deterring the police from engaging in unlawful searches and seizures.[3] Accordingly, because deterrence was the justification for the exclusionary rule, the Court narrowed its scope, announcing that the rule should be applied only in circumstances in which a cost-benefit analysis showed that it produced enough deterrence of unlawful police action to justify letting the guilty go free. *Leon* and the troubled history of the exclusionary rule will help uncover the vital but uneasy relationship that exists between constitutional rights and their remedies.

Finally, *Leon* poses the question of the value of legal consistency. It seems that whatever justification is offered for the exclusionary rule, there are troubling implications in regard to the scope of the rule, its constitutional status, and the Court's authority to enforce it. For example, if the rule is justified as a logical corollary of the Fourth Amendment, it should be applied uniformly without ex-

---

[2]*People v. De Fore*, 242 N.Y. 13, 21, 23–24, 150 N.E. 585, 586–588 (1926).

[3]A huge body of empirical literature exists concerning whether the exclusionary rule in fact deters police misconduct. For an overview, see Dallin Oaks, "Studying the Exclusionary Rule in Search and Seizure," *University of Chicago Law Review* 37 (1970): 665–757.

ceptions. The Constitution would logically compel compliance with the rule. But what if the consequences of such a broad and uniform application of the exclusionary rule are politically intolerable? Should the Court make the necessary exceptions to the rule, ignoring the problem of inconsistency, or should it change the rule's justification to one that would allow the Court to make exceptions to the rule? Historically, the Court took the latter course. It became a judicially created rule to deter unlawful police action, and the Court made a number of exceptions to it. However, to solve one problem of consistency, the Court unwittingly created another. If the exclusionary rule is a nonconstitutional rule, if it is merely a judicially created means of deterring unlawful searches and seizures, how could the Court impose it on the states? If using illegally seized evidence at trial is not itself a violation of the Constitution, what authority does the Supreme Court have to impose the rule on the states at all?

How should the Court respond to this situation? For the sake of consistency, should the Court abandon the exclusionary rule entirely? Should it return to the view of the exclusionary rule as a logical corollary of the Fourth Amendment and apply it broadly and uniformly? Or should the Court continue in its present course, applying the rule in some circumstances and not in others and not worrying unduly about legal consistency? *Leon* reveals how difficult it is at times to achieve legal consistency and thereby probes the value of legal consistency itself.

Early in the twentieth century, in *Weeks v. United States* (1914), Justice William Day articulated the justification of the exclusionary rule that presented it as a logical corollary of the Fourth Amendment. An admission of illegally seized evidence into a courtroom would, he argued, "affirm by judicial decision a manifest neglect, if not an open defiance, of the prohibitions of the Constitution." If illegally seized evidence could be admitted, then the "right to be secure" against unreasonable searches and seizures "is of no value, and . . . might as well be stricken from the Constitution." Accordingly, Day characterized the Fourth Amendment as a command not only to police but also to courts. "The effect of the 4th Amendment is to put the courts of the United States and Federal officials, in the exercise of such power and authority, and to forever secure the people, their persons, houses, papers, and effects, against all unreasonable searches and seizures under the guise of law."[4] In this way, Day gave the exclusionary rule a firm constitutional foundation by logically rooting the remedy in a broad understanding of the Fourth Amendment right. The amendment not only created an individual right of privacy but also implicitly prohibited any court from sanctioning unconstitutional searches and seizures.[5]

However, an alternative justification of the exclusionary rule arose even before the rule was applied against the states. In *Wolf v. Colorado* (1949), the Supreme Court held that the Fourth Amendment, which had heretofore only limited what the federal government could do, was "basic to a free society" and there-

---

[4]*Weeks v. United States*, 232 U.S. 383, 394, 393, 392 (1914).

[5]Justices Oliver Wendell Holmes and Louis Brandeis also endorsed the rationale of judicial integrity for the exclusionary rule in their dissents in *Olmstead v. United States*, 277 U.S. 438, 470, 485 (1928).

fore "enforceable against the states through the Due Process Clause" of the Four-teenth Amendment.[6] Every state therefore had a constitutional obligation to re-spect the right to be free from unreasonable searches and seizures. But Justice Felix Frankfurter, who wrote the majority opinion in *Wolf*, argued that the incor-poration of the Fourth Amendment did not mean that every state had to use the remedy of the exclusionary rule to enforce the underlying right. At the time, thirty states rejected the exclusionary rule, while only seventeen applied it. Hence, Frankfurter reasoned, the Court should not impose this controversial remedy on the states even though it was enforced in federal courts. The principle of federal-ism required the conclusion that state legislatures had the authority to decide how to remedy the unlawful searches and seizures that occurred within their borders.

The underlying premise of Frankfurter's federalism argument was that the exclusionary rule was not a logical corollary of the Fourth Amendment. If it were a logical corollary, it would, of course, have to be applied against the states along with the Fourth Amendment itself. Instead, Frankfurter described the exclusion-ary rule as merely "a matter of judicial implication" and not "an essential ingredi-ent of the right."[7] Frankfurter supported this reduction in the constitutional status of the exclusionary rule by shifting the meaning of the Fourth Amendment. De-spite what Day had said in *Weeks*, Frankfurter claimed that the right to be free from unreasonable searches and seizures pertained only to illegal seizures by po-lice. The sole question before the Court in *Wolf*, he insisted, was "whether the ba-sic right to protection against arbitrary intrusion by the police demands the exclu-sion of logically relevant evidence obtained by an unreasonable search and seizure"[8] By characterizing the Fourth Amendment right in this manner, by refus-ing to acknowledge it as a restriction on courts, Frankfurter undercut Day's earlier justification of the exclusionary rule remedy. No longer a logical corollary of the Fourth Amendment, the exclusionary rule became a judicially created rule of evi-dence. States could therefore decide for themselves whether to adopt the exclu-sionary rule or use some other alternative to protect the right of privacy.[9]

In *Mapp v. Ohio* (1961), Justice Tom Clark, endorsing the justification of the exclusionary rule given by Day in *Weeks*, called the exclusionary rule "part and parcel" of the Fourth Amendment, "an essential part of the right to privacy," and a "logical dictate of prior cases."[10] To some extent, the fact that *Mapp* compelled

---

[6]338 U.S. 25, 27–28 (1949).

[7]Idem, 28, 29.

[8]Idem, 28.

[9]Frankfurter was not very clear about how his opinion affected the status of the exclusionary rule in federal courts. He said: ". . . A different question would be presented if Congress under its legislative powers were to pass a statute purporting to negate the *Weeks* doctrine. We would then be faced with the problem of the respect to be accorded the legislative judgment on an issue as to which, in default of that judgment, we have been forced to depend upon our own." (Idem, 33.) In his concurring opin-ion, Justice Hugo Black was more clear. He concluded that "the federal exclusionary rule is not a com-mand of the Fourth Amendment but is a judicially created rule of evidence which Congress might negate." (Idem, 39–40.)

[10]*Mapp v. Ohio*, 367 U.S. 643, 650, 656, 657 (1961).

states to abide by the exclusionary rule dictated Clark's language. The only way that the Court could impose this particular remedy on the states was to argue that it was a logical corollary of the Fourth Amendment, itself applicable to the states by way of the due process clause of the Fourteenth Amendment. If the rule was just a judicially created rule of evidence, as Frankfurter had suggested in *Wolf*, perhaps the Court's general supervisory power over the lower federal courts would permit it to require the exclusionary rule in the federal system. But the Supreme Court had no supervisory role over the state courts. Hence in *Mapp*, legal consistency required that the Court base the exclusionary rule directly on the Constitution. The majority of the justices did so by endorsing the *Weeks* concept of the Fourth Amendment right to be free from unreasonable searches and seizures. It was a command to both the courts and the police. A judge's introduction of illegally seized evidence into a trial violated the amendment as much as an illegal police search or seizure. Therefore, at the time of *Mapp*, the constitutional status of the exclusionary rule seemed secure. The remedy was nothing less than a logical corollary of the substantive right itself.

The *Mapp* decision was quite a surprise if only because the parties in the case had not argued in favor of the exclusionary rule, either in their briefs or in oral argument. Dolly Mapp's main argument for the unconstitutionality of her conviction was that her free-speech rights had been violated, not that her Fourth Amendment rights had been violated by the admission of illegally seized evidence. The facts were as follows. On May 23, 1957, three Cleveland police officers, based on a tip, forcibly opened a door of the house of Mapp, who had refused to let them in without a search warrant. Mapp then grabbed what the police said was a warrant and placed it in her bosom. After forcibly retrieving the warrant and handcuffing her, the police searched the entire house, including a trunk in the basement. Though they had been looking for a person wanted for questioning in connection with a recent bombing, all that the police found was some obscene materials. They became the basis for Mapp's conviction of knowingly possessing obscene materials. At the trial, the state never produced a search warrant.

Since there was no inkling that *Wolf* was not good law, Mapp's attorneys argued her case in terms of free speech. Only one *amicus curiae* brief asked the Court to reconsider the *Wolf* rule, but here too no argument was made for the result. Therefore, no one knew beforehand that *Mapp* would be a landmark Fourth Amendment case. A memo written by Justice Potter Stewart indicates that Clark's opinion in *Mapp* even startled some of the members of the Court. According to this letter, the justices at the conference had voted to reverse Mapp's conviction on First Amendment grounds (see Box 4.1). If the implications of the letter are accurate, five justices decided after the conference to overrule *Wolf* without either full argumentation on the merits or perhaps even a formal conference discussion. In his dissent in *Mapp*, Justice John Harlan lamented the fact that five of his colleagues "reached out" to overturn *Wolf*.[11] What do you think? Did the five justices in the majority in *Mapp* act wisely? Did they abuse their power?

---

[11]*Mapp v. Ohio*, 367 U.S. 643, 674 (1961).

```
┌─────────────────────────────────────────────────────────────┐
│                      BOX 4.1                                 │
│                                                              │
│              Supreme Court of the United States              │
│                   Washington 25, D. C.                       │
│                                                              │
│   CHAMBERS OF                                                │
│  JUSTICE POTTER STEWART                      May 1, 1961      │
│                                                              │
│                                                              │
│                                                              │
│              No. 236 - Mapp v. Ohio                          │
│                                                              │
│                                                              │
│              Dear Tom,                                       │
│                                                              │
│                   As I am sure you anticipated, your proposed│
│              opinion in this case came as quite a surprise.  │
│              In all honesty, I seriously question the wisdom │
│              of using this case as a vehicle to overrule an  │
│              important doctrine so recently established and  │
│              so consistently adhered to.                     │
│   O/r of Wolf urged   Without getting into the merits, I     │
│   only in amicus -    point out only that the idea of        │
│   not discussed       overruling Wolf was urged in the brief │
│   at conference -     and oral argument only by amicus       │
│   Rev on 1st          curiae and was not even discussed at   │
│   amend -grounds      the Conference, where we all agreed,   │
│                       as I recollect it, that the judgment   │
│   If Wolf to be       should be reversed on First Amendment  │
│   reconsidered shored grounds. If Wolf is to be reconsidered,│
│   be only where required I myself would much prefer to do so │
│   + after argument by only in a case that required it, and   │
│   competent counsel + only after argument of the case by     │
│   full conference dis- competent counsel and a full          │
│   cussion             Conference discussion.                 │
│                                                              │
│                                      Sincerely yours,        │
│                                                              │
│                                          P.S.                │
│                                                              │
│                                                              │
│              Mr. Justice Clark                               │
└─────────────────────────────────────────────────────────────┘
```

Source: Tom C. Clark Papers, Tarlton Law Library, University of Texas at Austin, Box A115, Folder 6 (*Mapp v. Ohio*, October Term 1960, No. 236).

Since half of the states did not enforce the exclusionary rule in 1961, *Mapp* had a radical impact on police practices. Before then, police departments in twenty-five states could engage in illegal searches and seizures without worrying about whether the evidence would be ruled inadmissible. In the pre-*Mapp* era, there was therefore little incentive to train police in the intricacies of what constituted an illegal search. *Mapp* changed that. It forced New York City Police Commissioner Michael Murphy, in his own words, to adopt "new policies and new instructions. . . . Retraining sessions had to be held from the very top administrators down to each of the thousands of foot patrolmen and detectives engaged in the daily enforcement function."[12] *Mapp* therefore necessitated a huge allocation of funds for police training. Should the Court have imposed this administrative expense on the states without full constitutional argumentation? On the other hand, what does it say about the need for the exclusionary rule if the police in the pre-*Mapp* era were woefully ignorant and unconcerned about the meaning of the right to be free from unreasonable searches and seizures?

A *Wall Street Journal* editorial titled "The Right to Be Secure" appeared on June 21, 1961, just two days after *Mapp* was decided. It strongly endorsed the decision, claiming that it was "inconceivable to us that the authors of the Constitution meant to permit states . . . to invade individual privacy at the whim of a policeman." The editorial concluded with the observation that "overweening governmental powers" threatened individual liberty—"the overriding philosophy and political issue in this country today, as in the world" (see Box 4.2).

Does this editorial, published in a relatively conservative newspaper, surprise you? How can you explain it? Was it because Americans were not as worried about crime in 1961 as they were later to become? Perhaps the particular facts of *Mapp* had induced the newspaper to overlook the costs of the exclusionary rule. Do you think the *Wall Street Journal* would have published the same editorial if Dolly Mapp had been charged with first-degree homicide? In the same vein, would the Court have announced the *Mapp* rule if the case had involved a vicious murder? Is it possible or likely that the Court applied the exclusionary rule against the states in *Mapp*, even though the issue had not been argued, because the police's conduct in the case was much more outrageous than Dolly Mapp's trivial criminal act? Should the Court have acted in this fashion? Would the costs of the exclusionary rule have been clearer if the Court had applied the rule against the states in a serious drug or murder case?

After *Mapp*, the costs of letting dangerous criminals go free because of an illegal search, especially if the constitutional infraction was minor, became increasingly clear. As the crime rate rose during the 1960s, popular ambivalence about the exclusionary rule became outright opposition. The fact that, in the public's mind, so much violent crime was associated with the drug trade did not alleviate people's concerns about the exclusionary rule. Because claims of unlawful searches were most often raised in drug cases, the rule could be portrayed as an obstacle in the country's war against illegal drugs.

One way to gauge the shift in public opinion is to consider another *Wall Street Journal* editorial. On July 12, 1971, despite its strong endorsement of the exclusionary rule a decade earlier, this newspaper called on the Supreme Court to reexamine the exclusionary rule in an editorial titled "An Alternative Needed." After describing a case in which the cost of the exclusionary rule was painfully evi-

---

[12]Michael Murphy, "Judicial Review of Police Methods in Law Enforcement: The Problem of Compliance by Police Departments," *Texas Law Review* 44 (1966): 941. Cited by Yale Kamisar, "Is the Exclusionary Rule an 'Illogical' or 'Unnatural' Interpretation of the Fourth Amendment," *Judicature* 62 (1978), p. 72.

BOX 4.2

THE RIGHT TO BE SECURE

It may be that the Supreme Court majority, in ruling that the Constitution forbids the use of illegally seized evidence in state criminal trials, "reached out" to decide a Constitutional issue which the case before it did not primarily turn on. But the issue it reached for could hardly be more important.

According to Justice Harlan's dissenting opinion, the "pivotal" issue was not search and seizure but something else—whether an Ohio state law making the mere knowing possession of obscene literature a crime is consistent with Constitutional liberties. Instead, the Court majority chose to make this case the occasion for ruling that evidence—in this instance the obscene literature—obtained through unlawful search and seizure could not be used in state criminal trials. . . .

. . . Justice Clark, speaking for the majority, did rule on this fundamental issue of individual privacy versus government power, and he deserves to be listened to for what he said. And if we can put aside the technicalities for the moment, it seems to us that what he said is persuasive in its logic and in its concern for Constitutional guarantees.

The Fourth Amendment, after all, is as plain as could be: "The right of the people to be secure in their persons, houses, papers, and effects, against unreasonable searches and seizures, shall not be violated. . . ." Just as plainly, if this right is not secure, little else is. And if an accused can be convicted on the basis of evidence thus unlawfully obtained, the right can hardly be called secure.

. . . [I]t is inconceivable to us that the authors of the Constitution meant to permit states, any more than the Federal Government, to invade individual privacy at the whim of a policeman. For that is to make a mockery of the right of the people to be secure in their persons and homes.

. . . [T]he overriding philosophical and political issue in this country today, as in the world, is individual liberty and the threat posed to it by overweening governmental powers.

The Court having ruled at all, it is well that it ruled for the Constitution and the individual the Constitution was constructed to champion.

Source: Wall Street Journal, June 21, 1961, p. 14.

---

dent, the editorial insisted that there had to be a better way. Gone was the language about "overweening governmental powers" and the value of individual liberty. Taking its place was a recommendation that legislatures "ought to start looking for a less absurd way to discipline the police" (see Box 4.3). Taken together, these two *Wall Street Journal* editorials indirectly reflect the public's growing

BOX 4.3

An Alternative Needed

. . . No doubt . . . [the exclusionary] rule is an effective deterrent to over-reaching policemen. In extreme cases—for example, barring evidence gained by beating suspects—few would doubt its basic justice. But it does have the result of which Justice Cardozo long ago complained: "The criminal is to go free because the constable has blundered." As the courts have laid down increasingly detailed codes of police conduct, this has led to unto-ward rulings that cannot but sap public confidence that justice is being done.

In one of the cases in which Chief Justice Burger dissented, for example, a 14-year-old girl was lured from her home, apparently on promise of a baby-sitting job, and was found in a snowbank eight days later with her throat slit and a gunshot wound in her head. The suspect owned an automobile like one seen near the scene, and when his wife gave police some guns he owned, one of them was found to have fired the bullet that wounded the dead girl.

Upon this evidence a warrant was issued for the arrest of the suspect and seizure of his car. Vacuum sweepings from the car were introduced at the trial to prove they matched those from the dead girl's clothing. The warrant had been issued by the state attorney general, who had formal power to do so. However, he had personally assumed direction of this particular investigation, and therefore did not qualify as a "neutral and detached magistrate." The warrant was defective, the search "unreasonable" and the vacuum sweepings inadmissible. Conviction reversed.

Now obviously warrants will mean little if they are issued by the investigators themselves. Yet there simply must be a better way to enforce the requirement of neutral and detached magistrates than to exclude evidence and reverse a conviction in which a technically defective warrant played so minor a part.

. . . A good many liberal jurists and commentators, of course, are simply aghast at so radical a suggestion as replacing the exclusionary rule. Somehow they conceive of it as a cornerstone of fair jurisprudence. In fact, it became federal law only in 1914, and was applied to state courts as recently as 1961. Neither England nor Canada has such a rule, and few would consider their courts unfair. The Chief Justice is far nearer the truth when he views it as an "experimental step" with shortcomings that have now become apparent.

Given the decisions this rule tends to produce and the obvious need to bolster public confidence that courts do dispense justice, it's scarcely unreasonable to ask that it be reexamined. The Chief Justice's specific suggestions may not turn out to be the best ones, but he makes a convincing case that legislatures ought to start looking for a less absurd way to discipline the police.

Source: Wall Street Journal, July 12, 1971, p. 8.

concern about the rising crime rate and its hostility to an exclusionary rule that seemed to let clearly guilty criminals off.[13]

Critics proposed alternatives to the exclusionary rule almost as soon as the Supreme Court ruled that it was constitutionally required in *Weeks*. The application of the rule against the states in *Mapp* encouraged further consideration of the viability of these alternatives. Before the exclusionary rule had been imposed, the remedy had been a civil suit against the policeman who had violated the Fourth Amendment. This approach had the virtue of giving innocent victims of illegal searches a remedy, whereas the exclusionary rule paradoxically gave relief only to those who were prosecuted by the state. However, in reality, civil suits for Fourth Amendment violations were few and far between. The reason was simple: few police officers had sufficient monetary resources to make a suit worthwhile. Contemporary versions of this civil-liability approach to Fourth Amendment violations solve this problem by making the city, state, or federal government liable for the individual policeman's illegal act. Nonetheless, even with this modification, there is reason to doubt whether juries would bring many judgments against the police and whether a civil remedy against a government entity would deter police officers (who would not be personally liable) from engaging in unconstitutional searches. The fear is that absent a sanction against the offending officer, little or no deterrence of unlawful police conduct will be achieved.

Administrative sanctions are another alternative to the exclusionary rule, one that tries to protect the Fourth Amendment by punishing the police officer who violated it. Such sanctions can either complement or replace some version of the civil liability alternative. Disciplinary offices within law enforcement agencies would review complaints of unlawful searches and seizures and punish offenders by reprimands, fines, demotions, suspensions, and dismissals. Innocent victims of illegal searches would then have a sort of remedy, and the sanctions would be proportionate to the offense. If their credibility demanded it, these internal review boards could be staffed, in whole or in part, by persons outside the law enforcement community, by members of the executive branch, or even by judges. In any case, no matter how constituted, these review boards would punish police officers for their illegal actions. Instead of letting the exclusionary rule reward the criminal for the police officer's offense, review boards would increase the likelihood that both would receive their just deserts.

Of course, neither civil liability nor administrative sanctions could replace the exclusionary rule as long as the Supreme Court adhered to the *Mapp/Weeks* view that it was a logical corollary of the Fourth Amendment. However, the Court

---

[13]For a fine discussion of the political price of the exclusionary rule, see John Kaplan, "The Limits of the Exclusionary Rule," *Stanford Law Review* 26 (1974): 1035–1041. Kaplan insightfully explains why, if the police obey the law, the Fourth Amendment itself is the reason why many criminals are not caught. However, if a criminal who would not have been legally caught is caught because the police violated the Fourth Amendment, the exclusionary rule "rubs our noses in it.'" Kaplan's point is that the exclusionary rule has such a high political price because "it flaunts before us the costs we must pay for Fourth Amendment guarantees" (1037).

confronted issues that caused it to reconsider the status of the rule. In 1954, before the exclusionary rule was applied against the states, the Court had already
held that illegally seized evidence could be used to impeach the testimony of a
federal defendant who testified at his trial.[14] The justices created this exception to
the exclusionary rule because they would not let it become the means by which a
defendant could commit perjury and win an acquittal. If the government had evidence showing that the defendant was lying, even if it was illegally seized evidence, the government could introduce it at trial. Why the Court came to this result is obvious, but is it really consistent with the traditional justification of the
exclusionary rule? If the Fourth Amendment is, if only in part, a command to
courts not to participate in illegal searches and seizures, why should there be an
exception if the defendant is lying on the stand? If the government had respected
the Fourth Amendment, it never would have had the evidence to prove that the
defendant was committing perjury.

Similarly, soon after *Mapp* was decided, in *Linkletter v. Walker* (1965) the
Court considered whether the exclusionary rule had to be applied to all pre-*Mapp*
convictions that had involved illegally seized evidence. Consistency would seem to
require an affirmative answer to this question. After all, if the exclusionary rule
was "part and parcel" of the Fourth Amendment, the constitutional rights of defendants whose convictions had been obtained by the introduction of illegally
seized evidence had been violated. Retrials would seem to be required, with the
illegally seized evidence excluded from the courtroom. Many criminals would
have to be released because the state could no longer meet its burden of proof.
The illegally seized evidence would be excluded, and many of the witnesses who
had testified at the original trials would be either unavailable or unsure of their
memory.

Facing the issue of the retroactive application of *Mapp*, the Court retreated.
The price of consistently applying the exclusionary rule as a logical corollary of the
Fourth Amendment was just too high. Justice Clark, the very same justice who delivered the majority opinion in *Mapp*, wrote the opinion denying Linkletter's request for a new trial even though his conviction had been based on illegally seized
evidence. Clark defended the decision by abandoning the traditional justification
for the exclusionary rule and by revamping past precedents, especially *Mapp*. He
said that "all of the cases since *Wolf* requiring the exclusion of illegal evidence
have been based on the necessity for an effective deterrent to illegal police action." Since this was the justification for the rule, it made no sense, Clark argued,
to make the rule retroactive. "The misconduct of the police prior to *Mapp* has already occurred and will not be corrected by releasing the prisoners involved."[15]No
longer was the exclusionary rule a logical corollary of the right to be free from unreasonable searches and seizures. Instead, the rule had become a practical means
of deterring the police from engaging in such searches and seizures. Accordingly,

---

[14]*Walder v. United States*, 347 U.S. 62 (1954).

[15]*Linkletter v. Walker*, 381 U.S. 618, 636–637 (1965).

courts should apply the rule only when it served this purpose. The new justification therefore seriously undermined the status and scope of the exclusionary rule.

In a sharp dissent, Justice Hugo Black admonished the Court: "I have read and reread the *Mapp* opinion but have been unable to find one word in it to indicate that the exclusionary search and seizure rule should be limited on the basis that it was intended to do nothing in the world except to deter officers of the law."[16] According to Black, *Mapp* stood for the proposition that exclusion of illegally seized evidence was compulsory because courts as well as police fell within the Fourth Amendment's command. Black also noted a disturbing implication of the Court's new justification for the rule. Perhaps the new justification of the rule gave a consistent account of why retroactive application of *Mapp* was unnecessary, but it posed its own peculiar problem of consistency. If the exclusionary rule was not a remedy logically inferred from the Constitution, if it was rather a sort of "punishment against officers in order to keep them from depriving people of their constitutional rights," then, Black opined, "the Court's action in adopting it sounds more like law making than construing the Constitution."[17] In other words, if the exclusionary rule was not a logical corollary of the Fourth Amendment but a deterrent of police misconduct, the Court had no authority to impose the remedy on the states. Given its new justification for the exclusionary rule, if the Court wanted to be consistent, it should overrule *Mapp* and let the states decide whether to use the exclusionary rule or some other means to discourage police conduct that violated the Fourth Amendment.

What should the Court have done in *Linkletter?* Should it have been consistent? If so, how should it have ruled? Should it have decided in favor of retroactive application of the exclusionary rule, knowing that it would lead to the release of thousands of criminals? Or should the Court, since it now viewed the exclusionary rule as only a judicially created technique of discouraging unlawful police conduct, have reversed *Mapp,* letting the states decide whether to use the exclusionary rule or some other method of controlling police behavior? Or should the Court have done what it did: alter the justification for the rule, thereby reducing its constitutional status and narrowing its scope, yet insist on its authority to compel states to respect the exclusionary rule in all future criminal prosecutions? What does this last option imply about the value of legal consistency? Do you agree with this assessment?

Throughout the 1970s, the Court continued to pursue the approach taken in *Linkletter.* The exclusionary rule was no longer a constitutionally implied right of a defendant not to have illegally seized evidence used against him but rather a method of deterring the police from engaging in unlawful searches and seizures. Understanding the rule in this manner, the Court did not completely abandon it but narrowed its scope significantly.[18] In *United States v. Calandra* (1974), the

---

[16]Idem, 649.

[17]Idem.

[18]It should also be noted that after *Mapp,* the Court also restricted the use of the exclusionary rule as a means of enforcing the Fifth Amendment right to remain silent. See *Harris v. New York,* 401 U.S. 222 (1971); and *Oregon v. Haas,* 420 U.S. 714 (1975); also see Chapter 3.

Dick Wright. Reprinted by permission of United features Syndicate, Inc.

CARTOON 4.1.

Court ruled that the exclusionary rule did not apply to the grand jury.[19] The Court reasoned that it was doubtful that police practices would be significantly affected if grand juries had access to illegally seized evidence. Two years later, in *Stone v. Powell* (1976), the Court eliminated federal *habeas corpus* relief for state prisoners whose Fourth Amendment objections to their convictions had been reviewed and rejected by state appellate courts.[20] Even if such a prisoner's rights had been violated, even if the exclusionary rule should have been invoked at the trial, federal judges should not grant relief because the purpose of the exclusionary rule was only to deter police misconduct. Since federal *habeas corpus* decisions, coming long after the initial conviction, would have little or no deterrent impact on how the police went about their business, federal district courts should not grant relief. Again, *habeas corpus* relief was denied even though the illegal evidence should have been excluded at the trial.[21] Cartoon 4.1, insightfully captures the drift of this line of decisions as the Court viewed the exclusionary rule less as a log-

---

[19]414 U.S. 338 (1974).

[20]428 U.S. 465 (1976).

[21]The Court also narrowed the scope of the exclusionary rule in *United States v. Peltier,* 422 U.S. 531 (1975) (Supreme Court decisions on the Fourth Amendment need not be given retroactive effect); *United States v. Janis,* 428 U.S. 433 (1976) (illegally seized evidence may be used in a suit to recover unpaid federal income taxes); *Michigan v. De Fillippo,* 443 U.S. 31 (1979) (evidence from a search made in good faith that relied on an unconstitutional statute is admissible); and *United States v. Havens,* 446 U.S. 620 (1980) (illegally seized evidence may be used to impeach the testimony of an accomplice during cross-examination).

corollary of the Fourth Amendment and more as a judicially created means of deterring unlawful police conduct.

During the early 1980s, debate concerning the exclusionary rule centered on whether the Supreme Court should recognize a good faith exception. After all, if the purpose of the exclusionary rule was to deter the police from unconstitutional behavior, what sense did it make to exclude evidence when the police had acted in good faith? In such an instance, the search or seizure may have been unconstitutional, but the police thought they had been acting legally. Hence exclusion served no purpose. Obviously, exclusion could not deter the police from doing something that they thought they were empowered to do.

Political developments raised the temperature of the debate. The exclusionary rule remained an easy target for politicians wanting to capitalize on the public's fear of crime. A speech that President Ronald Reagan delivered before the International Association of Chiefs of Police in September 1981 was a good example of the kind of political ridicule that was heaped on the exclusionary rule (see Box 4.4). At about the same time, Attorney General William French Smith's Task Force on Violent Crime issued a report calling on Congress to create a good faith exception to the exclusionary rule. During late 1981 and early 1982, the Senate Judiciary Committee held hearings on a number of proposals to modify the exclusionary rule, including one that established a good faith exception. At these hearings (see Box 4.5), Professor Wayne La Fave, an expert on the Fourth Amendment from the University of Illinois Law School and a prominent defender of the exclusionary rule, argued that such an exception would "put a premium on the ignorance of the police officer," "stop dead in its tracks judicial development of Fourth Amendment rights," impose on judges "an exceedingly complex and difficult kind of judgment," create "a distinct anti–Fourth Amendment bias," and give the police "a license" to engage in illegal conduct.

Frank Carrington, executive director of Crime Victims Legal Advocacy Institute, Inc., expressed the police officer's point of view in his denial of La Fave's charges. The good faith exception would not reward police ignorance, he argued, because it would permit the introduction of illegally seized evidence only if the search and seizure passed an "objective test" of reasonableness. Since judges, including the justices on the Supreme Court, disagreed about what constituted a legal search, it made sense to establish such an exception. Police officers on the street, making tough quick decisions, could not be expected to know more about what the law required than the judges who, in their more "relaxed" surroundings, reviewed the lawfulness of what the police had done. The good faith exception would help rectify this situation. It would be the "opposite side of the same coin."

Finally, Steven R. Schlesinger, a professor from Catholic University, argued against the good faith exception despite his long-term opposition to the exclusionary rule. He claimed that the rule had to be abolished completely. Any "halfway house between retention and abolition," like the good faith exception, was an unsatisfactory outcome because it would remove the "necessary incentive to try serious alternatives" to the exclusionary rule. These arguments show the kind of constitutional and political debate that was occurring immediately prior to the Supreme Court's consideration of the good faith exception in *United States v. Leon*.

BOX 4.4

REAGAN CRITICIZES THE EXCLUSIONARY RULE

. . . We also support the reform of the exclusionary rule. I don't have to tell you, the people in this room, that this rule rests on the absurd proposition that a law enforcement error, no matter how technical, can be used to justify throwing an entire case out of court, no matter how guilty the defendant or how heinous the crime. The plain consequence of treating the wrongs equally is a grievous miscarriage of justice. The criminal goes free, the officer receives no effective reprimand, and the only ones who really suffer are the people of the community.

But I pause and interject here one incident, maybe known to a great many of you, because it is a famous case. But it occurred back while I was Governor of California, in San Bernardino. Two narcotics officers, with enough evidence to warrant a search, got a search warrant [and] entered a home where they believed heroin was being peddled. A married couple lived there. They searched. They found no evidence. As they were leaving, one of them, on a hunch, went over to the crib where the baby lay sleeping and removed its diapers, and there was the heroin. The case was thrown out of the court because the baby hadn't given its permission to be searched. [Laughter] It became known as the diaper case. I told that story once, and one of the Secret Service agents assigned to the Presidential detail came up later and said, "I was one of those narcotics officers. That's why I quit." [Laughter]

Source: Ronald Reagan, "Remarks at the Annual Meeting of the International Association of Chief of Police," September 28, 1981, in *Weekly Compilation of Presidential Documents,* vol. 17 (Washington, D.C.: U.S. Government Printing Office, 1981), p. 1041.

On August 18, 1981, a confidential informant told a Burbank, California, policeman that Armando Sanchez and Patsy Stewart were dealing drugs out of a house on Price Drive. The informant added that the two dealers usually kept only a small amount of drugs at this residence. The police immediately launched an investigation and on August 24 observed Ricardo Del Castillo, who had been arrested earlier for drug dealing, entering and leaving the Price Drive residence. By checking Del Castillo's probation records, the police came upon the name of Alberto Leon, whom Del Castillo had identified as his employer. In turn, when they reviewed Leon's arrest record, the police discovered two additional items of information. In 1980, one of Leon's companions had told the police that Leon imported drugs into the United States, and an informant had told the Glendale police that Leon had stored a large amount of drugs at his Glendale address. Once the Burbank police discovered that Leon had moved from Glendale to South Sunset Canyon Street in Burbank, he became a target of their investigation. On September 21, 1981, a California State Superior Court judge issued search

---

BOX 4.5

Congressional Hearings on the Good Faith Exception

WAYNE LA FAVE, Professor, University of Illinois School of Law:
. . . There are four adverse consequences I foresee [to the good-faith exception], and I would like to simply list them rather quickly.

First: It seems to me that adoption of the good-faith exception would stop dead in its tracks judicial development of Fourth Amendment rights. The reason for this is that if evidence is to be admitted in criminal trials in the absence of a clear precedent declaring the search to be unconstitutional, then, of course, the first duty of a court will be to deny the accused's motion to suppress if he cannot cite a case which is clearly in point. Indeed there is clear precedent supporting this notion that the Court is to avoid decision of a constitutional issue when the evidence will be admissible in any event.

Second: I believe that adoption of the good-faith exception would impose on suppression judges a heavy burden—indeed, I think it would be an intolerable burden—of making exceedingly difficult decisions on a regular basis.

For one thing, because the good-faith test has an important subjective element, it would be necessary for the suppression judge in each case to probe the subjective knowledge of the officer who made the arrest or the search.

. . . [W]e are talking about a task which would be unduly burdensome and a task which would intrude into the suppression process a factual issue on which evidence will be hard to come by apart from the officer's self-serving and generally uncontradicted testimony.

Indeed, I think it is well to note that our experience over the years tells us something on this point. What experience we have had in the Fourth Amendment exclusionary rule area, with inquiring into subjective states of mind, rather convincingly shows that the less frequently such inquiries are made the better off we will be. . . .

As some members of the Supreme Court said some years ago: "Sending courts on an expedition into the minds of police officers would produce a grave and fruitless misallocation of judicial resources."

Now, some proponents of the good-faith exception have attempted to blunt such arguments by noting that their test also contains an objective reasonableness component. But, of course, that is an additional requirement, not a substitute for an inquiry into the subjective state of mind, and it is an additional requirement which itself would be most troublesome.

The question again is: What kind of error concerning the law of search and seizure would be made by a reasonable officer? It seems to me that is an exceedingly complex and difficult kind of judgment to call upon a judge to make in case after case.

Third: I believe that adoption of the good-faith exception would likely result in a distinct anti–Fourth Amendment bias in suppression rulings. This is a natural consequence of making the suppression decision ride on a rather amorphous standard involving, as I have said, these exceedingly complex and unresolvable issues.

What I think it would mean in practice is that appellate courts would defer to trial courts and trial courts would end up deferring to the police.

Fourth: I believe that admission of illegally seized evidence under a good-faith exception would be perceived by the police, and indeed by the public at large, as giving the police a license to engage in the same kind of conduct in the future. . . .

The notion . . . is not that the police are inherently evil, but rather that because they are engaged in the often competitive enterprise of ferreting out crime, they are no less likely than the rest of us to equate admissibility with legality. . . .

For all these reasons, Mr. Chairman, I believe that a legislated good-faith exception to the exclusionary rule would not be a wise move for the Congress. . . .

FRANK CARRINGTON, *Executive Director, Crime Victims Legal Advocacy Institute, Inc.:*

. . . I submit to the subcommittee that in this country today, the law of search and seizure is so complex, so convoluted, so conflicting and confusing, that the policeman on the street, who is untrained in the law, as such, literally cannot know what it is he is supposed to do or what he is not supposed to do. . . .

. . . [W]hen the Justices of the Supreme Court of the United States not only can't agree on the holding of a given case, and they can't even agree about parts and subparts of the case, you have such a confusing situation that it is unrealistic to expect the policeman on the street to be able to draw any sort of finite guidelines.

The top constitutional interpretation is the Supreme Court, and then you multiply that by the factor of the interpretation of hundreds of appellate court judges, and thousands of trial judges, I submit to you that the question of what is or is not a legal or an illegal search is such a morass that the logical question that I propound to you comes into play: How does the policeman know what he is supposed to be deterred from doing? . . .

I think it also should be mentioned that the decisions made about search and seizure cases are made in very pleasant and relaxed surroundings, like this chamber or judicial chambers. The policeman is out there on the street. He may have minutes, perhaps even seconds, to make a decision. Should he stop the car? Does he have probable cause to stop the car? Should he stop somebody in an alley? . . .

A policeman, of course, could resolve the dilemma by simply never making an arrest or a search and seizure. But that is not what our society demands of him. He is out there to protect [members of] society, and they expect him to act. But if he acts in a vacuum of such conflicting rules all the way from the Supreme Court on down, . . . I really don't think he can logically be deterred [from engaging in unconstitutional searches by the exclusionary rule]. . . .

When I was a street policeman, . . . I did not know when I was making a [lawful] search and seizure. Even with a law degree and extensive study in the area, the facts and circumstances of each search and seizure are so volatile that except in extreme cases, one way or the other, where I knew that we did have probable cause, we did have a search warrant, or I knew that there was just no justification to make the search whatsoever. . . .

. . . [Y]ou still have this uncertainty as to every search and seizure you make, I would say, in approximately 80 percent of the cases.

So the premium on ignorance argument, I think, falls down. The ignorance is there, but it is not an ignorance created by the police officer. It is an ignorance created by the confusing and complex nature of the search and seizure. . . .

The current trend by some courts to carve out a "good faith" exception to the exclusionary rule seems to take this into consideration; the "opposite side of the same coin" as it were. . . .

STEVEN R. SCHLESINGER, *Professor, Catholic University:*
. . . [T]here are a number of specific reasons for preferring abolition of the rule to the course recommended by the Attorney General's task force.

First, the task force recommendation provides little or no deterrence for violations deemed by the courts to be in good faith. This fact could encourage a careless attitude on the part of law enforcement officials toward detail and might encourage them to see what can be gotten away with before the courts draw the line on what is an intentional violation.

Second, the task force recommendation virtually guarantees years of trial and appellate litigation focusing on what constitutes good and bad faith violation. The Supreme Court has already made so many fine distinctions in dealing with the question of when police may search and seize that a number of police departments, I'm sorry to have to tell you, have had to employ attorneys to explain the rules to officers. . . .

Third, the task force recommendation puts a substantial premium on the ignorance of law enforcement officers. In order to render legitimate a search or seizure under the task force's proposal the officer need only convince the judge that he did not know or fully understand the applicable legal requirements. Under the current rules, he must convince the judge that the search was indeed legal. Under the task force's proposal, as I understand it, he would need to convince the judge only that he thought it was legal. Ignorance may not be bliss, but it surely will have its uses in future search and seizure litigation if the task force recommendation becomes law.

As long as the exclusionary rule exists, even in modified form, . . . it is unlikely that we will try the kinds of alternatives to the rule that I and others have proposed: Police discipline imposed by an independent review board and a greatly improved civil remedy for innocent victims of illegal searches and seizures.

These alternatives would deter official misconduct, I believe, more effectively than does the [exclusionary] rule, would involve none of the costs and disadvantages of the rule discussed earlier, and would belatedly—and this is important—bring some serious redress to the innocent.

Let me conclude. The exclusionary rule is fundamentally unsound. The task force's recommended change in the rule would build an unsatisfactory half-way house between retention and abolition of the rule. Only a final end to the rule will produce the necessary incentive to try serious alternatives. As long as this country, which has adopted a more extensive exclusion policy than any other nation of the world, permits the rule to continue it may well deserve the unhappy consequences of its failure to abolish the [exclusionary] rule. . . .

Source: Hearings before the Subcommittee on Criminal Law, Committee on the Judiciary, Senate, 97th Cong., 1st and 2nd Sess., October 5 and 11, 1981; March 16 and 25, 1982, pp. 330–332; 115–118; 54–55.

warrants for Leon's South Sunset Canyon residence, the Price Drive address, and a condominium on Via Magdalena. The police searched the various houses and apartments and found a large quantity of drugs at Leon's South Sunset Canyon residence. Based on this evidence, a federal grand jury subsequently indicted Leon, who quickly moved to suppress the evidence.

The general rule is that if circumstances permit and the search is not incident to an arrest, the police must obtain a search warrant from a "neutral and detached magistrate" before a search can be made, especially if the search is of a private residence. In reviewing a search warrant application, the magistrate determines whether there is "probable cause" that contraband or instrumentalities of crime will be found.[22] The test is an objective one based on whether a "reasonable and prudent" person would think that the suspect had committed or was committing an offense.[23] To make this judgment, the magistrate considering the warrant application must consider the *reliability* of the information that the police are using as well as the *specificity* of the description of what is to be searched and the *par-*

---

[22]See *Wolf v. Colorado*, 338 U.S. 25 (1949); *Draper v. United States*, 358 U.S. 307 (1959); and *Spinelli v. United States*, 393 U.S. 410 (1969).

[23]*Beck v. Ohio*, 362 U.S. 309 (1960).

ticularity of what is to be seized.[24] In *Illinois v. Gates*, the Court ruled that reviews of probable cause in search warrant applications should be based on "the totality of the circumstances."[25] If, in the "totality of the circumstances," it could be determined that the informant knew what he was talking about, or if the police had reason to believe the informant, the magistrate could issue the warrant.

The federal district judge granted Leon's motion, ruling that the search was illegal and the evidence seized inadmissible. With one judge dissenting, the three-member Court of Appeals affirmed the lower court's ruling, arguing that probable cause had not existed for the search warrant because the informant's knowledge of Leon had been "fatally stale" and therefore inherently "unreliable." However, both the district judge and the Court of Appeals admitted that the police had acted in good faith. The Superior Court judge had made a mistake in issuing the search warrant, but the police had not consciously done anything wrong. Nevertheless, both courts refused to recognize a good faith exception to the rule excluding illegally seized evidence. The United States appealed to the Supreme Court, arguing that even if the search was illegal, the evidence should not be excluded because the police, in good faith, acted pursuant to a judicial warrant. Therefore, the specific question before the Court in *Leon* was whether a reasonable good faith exception was appropriate in circumstances in which the police had relied on a judicial warrant. In 1983, the Court had not yet recognized such a good faith exception, though individual members had indicated in earlier cases that the issue should be addressed.[26]

Based on the Supreme Court's exclusionary rule decisions of the 1970s, the brief filed by the United States in *Leon* assumed that the exclusionary rule was merely a judicially created technique to discourage illegal police conduct, not a logical corollary of the constitutional right to be free from unreasonable searches and seizures. Accordingly, the rule should be applied only when the benefits of excluding illegally seized evidence outweighed the costs. But when the police were acting in good faith, the government's brief contended, exclusion benefited no one but the criminal. The police could not be deterred from engaging in what they thought was a lawful search, especially if they were acting pursuant to a judicial warrant. Considering that judges presumably try, when they review warrant applications, to make the correct legal decision and that the exclusionary rule was not designed to restrict judges, exclusion advanced no Fourth Amendment interest. In contrast, the costs of exclusion were high: it let the guilty go free, provided no remedy for innocent victims, eroded the public's respect for the criminal justice system, reduced the effectiveness of the police, burdened unduly the judicial system, and encouraged judges to narrow Fourth Amendment rights. Given these

---

[24]*Jones v. United States*, 363 U.S. 309 (1960).

[25]462 U.S. 213 (1983).

[26]See Chief Justice Warren Burger's concurring opinion in *Stone v. Powell*, 428 U.S. 465 (1976); Justice Byron White's concurring opinion in *Illinois v. Gates*, 462 U.S. 213 (1983); Justice Lewis F. Powell's concurring opinions in *Brown v. Illinois*, 422 U.S. 590 (1975), and in *Schneckloth v. Bustamonte*, 412 U.S. 218 (1973); and Justice William Rehnquist's dissent from a denial of stay in *California v. Minjares*, 443 U.S. 916 (1979).

substantial costs and the lack of any clear benefits, the government's brief concluded that a good faith exception to the exclusionary rule should be created. Such an exception would not place a premium on police ignorance, burden the courts with time-consuming hearings, or remove the incentive to litigate Fourth Amendment rights.

The brief written by Norman Kaplan and Barry Tarlow on behalf of Alberto Leon disputed the government's contention that the good faith exception would have no detrimental consequences. According to their brief, the rule would encourage police ignorance, burden the courts, and decrease the opportunities for Fourth Amendment constitutional adjudication. However, the biggest problem with the exception, according to Kaplan and Tarlow, was that it directly violated the Fourth Amendment requirement that no search warrants be issued without "probable cause." Even if the prohibition of unreasonable searches and seizures pertained only to police actions, the warrant clause of the Fourth Amendment clearly restricted when judges and magistrates could issue search warrants. If the good faith exception were recognized, an ill-trained magistrate could issue a search warrant without probable cause, and any illegally seized evidence would nonetheless be used at the trial. Police would "shop around" for magistrates inclined to issue warrants, thereby producing a slow, steady deterioration of the Fourth Amendment. The underlying mistake of the proponents of the good faith exception was to assume that the Fourth Amendment substantively restricted only the police, not magistrates or courts. In fact, the exclusionary rule, whose costs the opposing side had completely exaggerated, only excluded evidence that the government would not have had if it had obeyed the Fourth Amendment. Accordingly, appellate judges must protect their own integrity and defend the Fourth Amendment by continuing to exclude illegally seized evidence from the courtroom. This was true even if police illegally seized evidence in good faith pursuant to a judicial warrant.

At oral argument, Rex Lee, solicitor general of the United States, defended the good faith exception from criticisms that the rule would encourage police ignorance and that it would make appellate review of Fourth Amendment issues more difficult. He also argued that since the purpose of the exclusionary rule was to deter police misconduct, it would be inappropriate to use this remedy against magistrates or judges, who were members of the judicial branch of government. In reaction, one justice pointed out that even such minor executive officials as city clerks could function as magistrates, implying that the exclusionary rule might be applicable to their actions. However, another justice came to Lee's assistance with the observation that the clerk's action fell outside of the normal scope of the exclusionary rule, even if the clerk was not a member of the judicial branch, because he was "in the particular setting" performing "a judicial function." Later in the oral argument, when a justice queried Lee about how magistrate's warrant decisions would be reviewed, Chief Justice Rehnquist reminded Lee that the issue before the Court was the police officer's action, not the magistrate's. Should justices come to the aid of an advocate in this fashion? Note that Leon's advocate, Barry Tarlow, did not receive such assistance in his debate with a justice as to whether twelve meetings with a known drug dealer would constitute probable cause for a search warrant.

In a 6–3 decision, the Supreme Court decided in favor of the government, thereby creating a good faith exception to the exclusionary rule in circumstances where the police relied on a judicial search warrant. Justice Byron White, who wrote the majority opinion, argued that the wrong prohibited by the Fourth Amendment was "fully accomplished" by the unlawful search and seizure. What prosecutors and courts did with the illegal seized evidence afterward was not a constitutional issue. Hence the exclusionary rule was not a constitutional right but rather a "judicially created remedy" to deter illegal police conduct. Accordingly, whether the rule should be applied in any particular context depended on a cost-benefit analysis. In regard to the relative costs and benefits of recognizing a good faith exception to the exclusionary rule, White's assessment, in the main, tracked the government's brief. The rule often produced disrespect for the judicial system, especially when serious felons went free because a search warrant contained small or technical violations. If the police were acting pursuant to a warrant, exclusion of evidence made no sense because the exclusionary rule was "designed to deter police misconduct rather than to punish the errors of judges and magistrates." Judges and magistrates, White added, have no inclination to "subvert the Fourth Amendment," and most important, exclusion would have no "significant deterrent effect on the issuing judge or magistrate" because these judicial officers "have no stake in the outcome of particular criminal prosecutions."

In addition, White continued, any argument that the police can be deterred from "magistrate shopping" by excluding evidence seized pursuant to a defective warrant was "speculative." Research had not been able to establish that the exclusionary rule deterred any police misconduct; hence the rule could not be expected to deter the police if they were reasonably relying on a warrant. Nor would the good faith exception prevent appellate courts from deciding Fourth Amendment issues. Judges could easily decide the Fourth Amendment issue before resolving whether the police had acted in good faith.

In his *Leon* dissent, Justice William Brennan rejected the deterrence-based rationale of the exclusionary rule favored by the majority and endorsed, once again, the view that the exclusionary rule was a logical corollary of the individual's right not to be subject to unreasonable searches and seizures. Hence, according to Brennan, the amendment restricted not only police actions but also what courts could do with what was unlawfully searched for and seized. This was so because "the evidence-gathering role of the police is directly linked to the evidence-admitting function of the courts." Police violate the Fourth Amendment for the purpose of convicting criminals. The initial unlawful search and seizure were therefore "directly linked" to the later admission of the seized evidence at trial. Hence by admitting illegally acquired evidence, "the judiciary becomes a part of what is in fact a single governmental action prohibited by the terms of the Amendment." For this reason, the exclusionary rule was not a "judicially created remedy" to deter police lawlessness but rather a logical corollary of the right to be free from unreasonable searches and seizures. Only if the exclusionary rule was understood in this fashion, as "part and parcel" of the Fourth Amendment, did the Supreme Court have any authority to enforce the rule against the states. But if understood in this way, the Court has not only the right to enforce the exclusionary rule against the states but also the duty to do so.

However, Brennan continued, even if one accepts the alternative view that the exclusionary rule was a judicially created means of deterring unlawful police conduct, the good faith exception was still not justified. The majority had completely miscalculated the costs of the exclusionary rule and the benefits of the exception. First, many of the costs that the majority ascribed to the exclusionary rule were in fact incurred because of the Fourth Amendment itself. If the government respected the amendment, some incriminating evidence would, of course, go undetected and some criminals would therefore escape punishment. But it was the amendment, not the exclusionary rule, that produced this result. Second, in its cost-benefit analysis, the majority used "faulty scales" to reach a "foreordained" result. Studies showed that the costs of the exclusionary rule were "quite low." Hence the costs of excluding illegally seized evidence when police have acted in good faith reliance on a search warrant "must necessarily be even smaller." Moreover, the majority grossly underestimated the benefits of excluding such evidence. Such exclusions "promote institutional compliance with Fourth Amendment requirements on the part of law enforcement agencies generally." A good faith exception would therefore "put a premium on police ignorance of the law" and remove a crucial incentive for magistrates "to continue performing the important task of carefully reviewing warrant applications." In effect, by recognizing a good faith exception to the exclusionary rule, the Court had taken the easy course of relaxing the Fourth Amendment as a way to satisfy "the public's demand for better law enforcement." There is, however, "a heavy price for such expediency." Once lost, Brennan noted, "rights are difficult to recover."

Justice John Paul Stevens also dissented in *Leon*. Though covering some of the same ground that Brennan did in his dissent, Stevens highlighted an implicit tension within the majority's justification for the good faith exception and the historical purpose of the Fourth Amendment's warrant clause. First, he claimed that the Court was using a "double standard of reasonableness." The Fourth Amendment authorizes a magistrate to issue a search warrant if there is probable cause, a standard that the Court has largely identified with a reasonable belief that a crime has been committed. In contrast, in circumstances involving judicial warrants, the good faith exception would be limited to warrants that the police could "reasonably" believe were valid. But how can a prospective search be simultaneously both "unreasonable," not justifying a warrant, and "reasonable," justifying a good faith exception? If a magistrate improperly issued a warrant, then the search was "unreasonable." The police cannot later argue that they had a "reasonable" belief that the search was legal because the magistrate approved the warrant. The specific purpose of the warrant clause was to address "the unreasonable issuance of warrants." For this reason, the exclusionary rule must apply if the search was based on an unconstitutional warrant.

The *Leon* litigation concerning the good faith exception places into sharp focus the tensions between the alternative rationales of the exclusionary rule. On the one hand, the warrant clause is the one part of the Fourth Amendment that seems clearly to be directed to the judiciary. A search warrant may not be issued without "probable cause." Accordingly, if the exclusionary rule is understood as a logical corollary to the Fourth Amendment, it would seem that evidence seized pursuant to a defective warrant would have to be excluded from courtrooms. It would not matter that the police had acted in good faith. Consistency would demand strict compliance with the exclusionary rule. On the other hand, if the exclusionary rule is merely a judicially created strategy to deter police misbehavior, the opposite conclusion seems unavoidable. Excluding evidence illegally seized by the police in good faith, especially if the police were acting pursuant to a search warrant issued by a magistrate, would have, at most, a negligible impact on illegal police behavior. If a legislature, after assessing the costs and benefits of the exclusionary rule and the good faith exception, opted in favor of creating the exception, courts would have little reason to second-guess the legislature's policy choice. In fact, it is arguable that if the exclusionary rule is merely a nonconstitutional rule of evidence, the Supreme Court has no authority whatsoever to compel the states to respect it in any circumstances, much less in those in which the police are acting reasonably in accordance with a judicial warrant.

Therefore, each of the options before the Court regarding the exclusionary rule has its problems. If the exclusionary rule is a logical corollary of the Fourth Amendment, none of the exceptions to it that have been created since *Mapp* seem to be consistent with this justification. Should the Court return to the interpretation of the Fourth Amendment that elevates the exclusionary rule to its former status as a logical corollary of the right to be free from unreasonable searches and seizures? Should the Court enforce strict compliance with the exclusionary rule? What about all the practical problems that would arise? What if the prosecution had illegally seized evidence that could prove that the defendant was committing perjury on the stand? What about the problem of retroactive application of the exclusionary rule? Conversely, if the Court reduces the constitutional status of the rule to a judicially created means of deterring police misconduct, what should the Court do? Has it undermined its authority to enforce the rule at all? Should the Court attain consistency by withdrawing from the field entirely, allowing legislatures to decide if and when the exclusionary rule is a cost-effective method for controlling the police? Would such a return to the pre-*Mapp* era be dangerous to Fourth Amendment values? Or, finally, should the Court continue its present course, deciding on a case-by-case basis when states must respect the exclusionary rule and when they need not? Is this option consistent with either of the Court's justifications for the exclusionary rule? Does it matter? These questions highlight that legal consistency is at times difficult to achieve, thereby posing the question of whether it is worth the price when a controversial remedy is used to enforce a substantive constitutional right.

BIBLIOGRAPHY

Bernardi, Frederick A. "The Exclusionary Rule: Is a Good Faith Standard Needed to Preserve a Liberal Interpretation of the Fourth Amendment?" *De Paul Law Review* 30 (1980): 51–108.

Kamisar, Yale. "*Gates,* 'Probable Cause,' 'Good Faith,' and Beyond." *Iowa Law Review* 69 (1984): 551–615.

Kaplan, John. "The Limits of the Exclusionary Rule." *Stanford Law Review* 26 (1974): 1027–1055.

La Fave, Wayne R. "'The Seductive Call of Expediency': *United States v. Leon,* Its Rationale and Ramifications." *University of Illinois Law Review* (1984): 895–931.

Oaks, Dallin. "Studying the Exclusionary Rule in Search and Seizure." *University of Chicago Law Review* 37 (1970): 665–757.

Schlesinger, Steven R. *Exclusionary Injustice.* New York: Dekker, 1977.

Wilkey, Malcolm R. *Enforcing the Fourth Amendment by Alternatives to the Exclusionary Rule.* Washington, D.C.: National Legal Center for the Public Interest, 1982.

BRIEFS

BRIEF FOR THE UNITED STATES

[1. Introduction.] . . . This Court first required the exclusion of evidence obtained in violation of the Fourth Amendment in *Weeks v. United States,* a case involving successive, warrantless searches by federal agents of an accused's home, which resulted in the seizure of letters and other personal documents. Later, in *Mapp v. Ohio,* the Court extended the application of the Fourth Amendment exclusionary rule to the states in the context of a case involving a forcible, warrantless entry into a suspect's home that was followed by an exploratory search through personal papers and effects. Since that time, however, the exclusionary rule has been increasingly criticized as "both conceptually sterile and practically ineffective in accomplishing its stated objective" of ensuring compliance with the Fourth Amendment by law enforcement officials. Accordingly, members of the Court have repeatedly urged a general reconsideration of the exclusionary rule and the situations in which it is applied.

The instant cases offer appropriate vehicles for such a reevaluation of the scope of the exclusionary rule. In *Leon,* the record establishes that the police officers obtained a search warrant after making a detailed submission to a state court judge based on both a tip and corroborating information obtained during a month-long investigation of the tip. Thereafter, the officers executed the warrant according to its terms. As was recognized by the district court and by Judge Kennedy in dissent, the officers "laid a meticulous trail" by conducting their investigation "with care, diligence, and good faith." Including the issuing judge, five judges have examined the officers' application for a warrant, and they have divided three to two on the existence of probable cause. Under such circumstances, it seems wholly unreasonable to suppose that the police can be deterred from making a similar "mistake" in the future. . . .

Thus . . . the officers' conduct [in *Leon*] stands on a far different footing from the palpably unlawful searches at issue in *Weeks* and *Mapp.* The suppression remedy does not meaningfully protect against the arbitrary invasion of privacy interests—the core value safeguarded by the Fourth Amendment—when, as in the instant cases, law enforcement officers have acted in the reasonable belief that their conduct complies with constitutional standards. Modification of the exclusionary rule to acknowledge this point is consistent with the fundamental purpose of the rule. . . .

[2. Purpose of the Exclusionary Rule.] . . . Any consideration of the extent to which the rule should be modified must begin with a clear understanding of its purpose.

Over time, the justifications advanced in support of the exclusionary rule have varied, but it is now clear that the principal, and certainly the only logical, purpose of the rule is to deter Fourth Amendment violations by law enforcement officers by removing the incentive to commit those violations. . . .

The rise to preeminence of the exclusionary rule's deterrent purpose reflects the abandonment of earlier justifications. Initially, the rule was justified as a remedy for the violation of an accused's personal Fourth Amendment right of privacy. This rationale has since been repeatedly and squarely rejected by the Court, and with ample reason. The exclusionary rule is fundamentally irrational as a remedy for unlawful invasions of privacy, both because it utterly fails to succor those most deserving of a remedy—the innocent victims of unreasonable searches—and because, as Judge Friendly has said in an observation particularly apt in cases like these of marginal illegality, "the benefit received [exclusion of evidence proving the defendant's guilt] is wholly disproportionate to the wrong suffered."

Another early rationale for the exclusionary rule was that it served to safeguard the purity of the courts' processes by forbidding the introduction of tainted evidence. But the "imperative of judicial integrity" has not in fact served as the basis for deciding cases. The Court has recognized that the strength of this rationale has been steadily eroded by a series of decisions permitting the collateral use of unlawfully seized evidence. Thus, preserving the courts' distance from tainted evidence has now been eclipsed by, and indeed subsumed within, the policy of deterrence: to the extent that the judicial integrity rationale was intended to insulate the courts from becoming partners in lawless government conduct, that function is fully served by the policy of deterrence.

But even if the "imperative of judicial integrity" had survived as an independent justification for the exclusionary rule, it would not be impugned by the "reasonable mistake" exception that we propose. As the Court recognized in *Peltier*, "the 'imperative of judicial integrity' is . . . not offended if law enforcement officials reasonably believed in good faith that their *conduct* was in accordance with the law even if decisions subsequent to the search or seizure have held that conduct of the type engaged in by the law enforcement officials is not permitted by the Constitution." Indeed, we suggest that judicial integrity is put in greater jeopardy by the rendition of erroneous verdicts caused by the suppression of dispositive evidence than it is by the admission of evidence that a reasonably well-trained police officer could not have been expected to know was being obtained in violation of the Fourth Amendment.

Recognition that the policy of deterrence is the only logical justification for the exclusionary rule has governed the Court's consideration of a multitude of applications of the rule. Because "the exclusion of evidence is not a personal constitutional right but a remedy," the judiciary "must be sensitive to the costs and benefits of its imposition." Indeed, this Court has long engaged in a cost-benefit analysis when it has confronted suggested expansions of the rule or has examined afresh the propriety of certain applications of the rule. . . .

. . . Preliminarily, however, we suggest that this weighing is not properly performed on scales that are evenly balanced. By excluding unquestionably reliable and relevant evidence, the exclusionary rule operates in precisely the opposite manner from what we generally demand of other rules of evidence. Thus, the rule's benefits should not simply be presumed; the rule's application to particular classes of cases requires more than an assumption that it *might* have the desired deterrent effect. As the Chief Justice observed in his concurrence in *Stone v. Powell:*

> To vindicate the continued existence of this judge-made rule, it is incumbent upon those who seek its retention . . . to demonstrate that it serves its declared deterrent purpose and to show that the results outweigh the rule's heavy costs to rational enforcement of the criminal law. . . . The burden rightly rests upon those who ask society to ignore trustworthy evidence of guilt, at the expense of setting obviously guilty criminals free to ply their trade. . . .

[3. Possible Benefits of the Exclusionary Rule.] The principal benefit claimed for the exclusionary rule is its deterrent effect. Unfortunately for the rule's proponents, however, its deterrent effect has never been proven, either in an absolute sense or relative to alternative, less costly means of enforcing the Fourth Amendment. The Court itself has acknowledged the lack of reliable empirical evidence to support the deterrent effect of the exclusionary rule. . . .

. . . Nevertheless, we accept as intuitively plausible (even if not empirically demonstrated) the premise that suppression of evidence in a criminal trial can to some extent or in some circumstances deter law enforcement officers from violations of the Fourth Amendment. What is pertinent to the present inquiry is how well, if at all, deterrence can operate in the "reasonable mistake" context. . . .

. . . In advancing the contention that exclusion of evidence is unjustified in such circumstances, we do not (and need not) go so far as to suggest that adoption of a reasonable mistake exception would have no effect at all on the presumed deterability of Fourth Amendment violations. Perhaps it is tenable to suppose that, if police are responsive to the suppression sanction, then the more sweeping and stringent the use of the sanction, the more cautious they will be in cases in which there is any room for doubt about the legality of a proposed search or seizure, a point the Court made in *United States v. Johnson.*

But the mere fact that some deterrence may be postulated plainly cannot control the inquiry here. . . . The question, in short, does not turn merely upon identification of some reasonable possibility of deterrence, but requires an evaluation of the substantiality of the anticipated deterrence. . . .

Experience teaches that Fourth Amendment violations vary greatly in their gravity and, we submit, in their amenability to deterrence. At one end of the spectrum, when officers have made Fourth Amendment intrusions under circumstances "so lacking in indicia of probable cause as to render official belief in its existence entirely unreasonable," or engaged in law enforcement activities that constitute "flagrantly abusive violation[s] of Fourth Amendment rights," "the deterrent value of the exclusionary rule is most likely to be effective." By contrast, when there is merely a "technical" violation of Fourth Amendment rights occasioned by actions that a reasonably well-trained police officer would not recognize as impermissible, "the deterrence rationale of the exclusionary rule does not obtain," and there is accordingly "no legitimate justification for depriving the prosecution of reliable and probative evidence.". . .

The "reasonable mistake" exception to the exclusionary rule that we advocate will be appropriate in a variety of factual settings, not all of which can or should be precisely mapped out at this stage of the development of the exception. But the facts in *United States v. Williams* . . . well illustrate two situations in which the exclusionary rule should be modified to accommodate the practical realities of police work. In *Williams,* the officer was required to make an on-the-spot decision concerning the scope of his arrest powers, a legal issue that had not been judicially resolved. Irrespective of what an appellate court might ultimately announce as the correct answer to that legal question, there can be no doubt that the officer was not unreasonable in believing that he had observed the commission of a crime in his presence. Society expects the police to act in such situations, and it cannot seriously be urged that society is benefitted, or that individual constitutional liberties are meaningfully advanced, by a rule of law that causes an officer to doubt the propriety of taking action when he observes what he reasonably believes to be an offense in progress. . . .

. . . [P]olicemen are not trained legal technicians; nevertheless, they are expected to make quick decisions, often involving complicated legal and factual analyses, "in the course of the difficult and often dangerous business of law enforcement." Thus, countless officers in the field must daily decide under rapidly-changing circumstances whether there exists the requisite probable cause to support an arrest or a search, reasonable suspicion to justify an investigative detention, or exigent circumstances permitting warrantless action. In such cases, "[i]nadvertent errors of judgment" and "honest mistakes" will "inevitably occur given the pressures inherent in police work having to do with serious crimes."

The uncertainties inherent in police work are exacerbated by a lack of coherent Fourth Amendment standards that are readily recognizable and can be predictably applied by officers in the field. Too often, courts leave police officers to resolve these difficult questions for themselves, and then feel free to second-guess what appeared at the time to have been reasonable judgments. The result is that the courts have engendered a "state of uncertainty" that is "intolerable" to the officer on the beat. Without the ability accurately to predict how courts will resolve Fourth Amendment questions, law enforcement officers will neither know the scope of their authority nor be sufficiently deterred from improper action to justify application of the exclusionary rule.

There is no basis for faulting an officer who has made a reasonable but incorrect assessment regarding the existence of reasonable suspicion or probable cause or the necessity of obtaining a warrant. Fourth Amendment adjudications inevitably leave "much room for disagreement among judges, each of whom is convinced that both he and his colleagues are reasonable men. Surely when this

Court divides five to four on issues of probable cause, it is not tenable to conclude that the officer was at fault or acted unreasonably in making the arrest.". . .

. . . Equally important, however, is the fact that *no* credible justification has ever been advanced for invoking the exclusionary rule when, as in *Leon*. . . the police have not engaged in any misconduct whatsoever, but a judicial officer has issued a search warrant that is subsequently held to be defective. "This court has never set forth a rationale for applying the exclusionary rule to suppress evidence obtained pursuant to a search warrant; it has simply done so without considering whether Fourth Amendment interests are advanced.". . .

In our submission, the exclusionary rule is an inherently inappropriate device for deterring Fourth Amendment violations that are the result of judicial miscalculation rather than police misconduct. As the Court observed in *Janis*, application of the exclusionary rule must be tied to the identity of those who are to be deterred and the nature of the conduct that is to be controlled. In the Fourth Amendment context, "the exclusionary rule was adopted to deter unlawful searches by police, not to punish the errors of magistrates and judges.". . .

Thus, even if one accepts the premise that the exclusionary rule is capable of affecting police behavior in some circumstances, there is no basis whatsoever for assuming that it can have any impact on magistrates. Magistrates are not part of the law enforcement "team"; as neutral judicial officers, magistrates have no stake in the outcome of any criminal prosecution, and the threat that evidence may be excluded from trial cannot logically be expected to have a significant deterrent impact on them. Instead, judicial officers considering warrant applications presumably are motivated—like judicial officers performing other duties—to reach a correct decision.

The suppression of evidence obtained pursuant to judicially-issued search warrants, even though an unintended extension of the exclusionary rule as originally conceived, might be justified if it furthered the rule's basic purpose of deterring police misconduct. But in fact it does no such thing. Rather, "[i]mposing an admittedly indirect 'sanction' on the police officer in that instance is nothing less than sophisticated nonsense," because law enforcement officers will never be deterred from executing a search warrant that a judge has told them is valid. . . .

Application of the exclusionary rule to the fruits of judicially-warranted searches is not only ineffective in terms of deterrence, but may well reduce incentives for police resort to the warrant procedure, which this Court has repeatedly held is the constitutionally preferred method for safeguarding individual privacy rights. Thus, a reasonable mistake exception to the exclusionary rule when a warrant has been obtained would provide a substantial incentive for law enforcement officers to utilize the preferred warrant procedure. Unlike instances in which the police have acted without judicial authorization and in which an exclusionary rule might, in limited circumstances, provide a deterrent to future misconduct, resort to the warrant procedure itself provides a substantial alternative barrier to unreasonable or otherwise defective searches and seizures. For this reason, the Court has recognized that errors of judgment by a magistrate should not necessarily be treated as severely as Fourth Amendment violations by law enforcement officers acting without judicial supervision and approval. . . .

We do not suggest that the exclusionary rule is never appropriate when a search has been conducted pursuant to a warrant, or that the mere issuance of a warrant wholly forecloses further inquiry into the existence of probable cause. Even when a warrant has been obtained, suppression of evidence may be justified if the factors relied on by the magistrate "were so lacking in indicia of probable cause as to render official belief in its existence entirely unreasonable," or if the warrant was procured in bad faith or on the basis of material misrepresentations. . . .

Manifestly, the rare circumstances that might justify exclusion of the fruits of a judicially-warranted search are not present in the cases now before the Court. In *Leon,* the police took meticulous care to ensure that their conduct at all times comported with constitutional requirements. First, rather than acting precipitously based on an informant's tip, the police independently investigated the allegations in the tip through extensive surveillance of respondents and their various residences. When their surveillance confirmed the accuracy of much of the information provided in the tip, the police did not act on their own initiative, but instead sought a warrant from a neutral judicial officer. Moreover, they provided the judicial officer with every bit of information they possessed that would assist him in making a reasoned, independent decision. And they executed the warrant properly and with no reason to be on notice that it was not valid. In turn, the judge issuing the warrant clearly had at least "reasonable cause to believe there was reasonable cause." In these circumstances, it would advance no Fourth Amendment policy to suppress the seized evidence. . . .

[4. Costs of the Exclusionary Rule.] Many of the costs of the exclusionary rule have been alluded to in previous sections of this brief. Nevertheless, in completing the cost-benefit analysis that we commend to the Court, it is appropriate to recapitulate briefly the most obvious costs and to elaborate more fully on some of the less evident ones.

First, the exclusionary rule excludes from consideration at trial the very evidence that is most relevant and trustworthy. The rule thus subverts the courts' paramount truth-finding function.

Second, the exclusionary rule directly benefits only those who are unquestionably guilty. In the now-famous words of Justice Cardozo, particularly apt to consideration of a reasonable mistake exception, the rule allows "[t]he criminal . . . to go free because the constable has blundered." The rule does nothing, however, to repair injury to innocent victims of unreasonable searches. While, judiciously applied, it may prevent future violations of constitutional rights, that objective can be accomplished by limiting use of the suppression sanction to cases in which substantial deterrence of future misconduct can realistically be expected.

Proponents of the exclusionary rule have argued that only a very small number of guilty defendants actually go free because of it, and that this is a small price to pay to safeguard the Fourth Amendment rights of all citizens. . . .

It is no doubt true, as Justice White observed, that "[w]e will never know how many guilty defendants go free as a result of the rule's operation," but still certain conclusions are possible:

The effects of the exclusionary rule are often felt before a case reaches trial. A recent study by the National Institute of Justices of felony arrests in California during the years 1976–1979 "found a major impact of the exclusionary rule on state prosecutions." The study found that 4.8% of the more than 4,000 felony cases declined for prosecution were rejected because of search and seizure problems. The exclusionary rule was found to have a particularly pronounced effect in drug cases; prosecutors rejected approximately 30% of all felony drug arrests because of search and seizure problems.

Moreover, in cases in which prosecutors elect to proceed to trial despite successful suppression motions, the resulting conviction rates are dramatically impaired. Although the systemic effects of the exclusionary rule have never been fully calculated, the limited studies available thus demonstrate that a definite relationship exists between the suppression of evidence and the prosecution's ability to obtain a conviction.

But even if the numerical impact of the exclusionary rule were to be discounted, the rule exacts an exceedingly high societal cost. This Court has noted that the exclusionary rule may well serve to lessen public respect for the judicial system. "Thus, although the rule is thought to deter unlawful police activity in part through the nurturing of respect for Fourth Amendment values, if applied indiscriminately it may well have the opposite effect of generating disrespect for the law and administration of justice." Moreover, indiscriminate application of the exclusionary rule may foster a public perception that the courts are simply unaware of reality.

In part, this problem of public perception arises because the exclusionary rule, as currently applied, lacks the vital ingredient of proportionality. As the Chief Justice observed in his concurrence in *Stone v. Powell:* "The disparity in particular cases between the error committed by the police officer and the windfall afforded a guilty defendant by application of the rule is contrary to the idea of proportionality that is essential to the concept of justice." This cost of the exclusionary rule is particularly evident in cases such as those now before the Court, in which it cannot seriously be urged that the police engaged in any misconduct. On the other hand, there can be little doubt that the suppressed evidence, if admitted, would conclusively establish the respondents' guilt.

The chilling effect on legitimate police activities is another less visible but equally important cost specifically associated with suppression of evidence garnered in good faith violations of the Fourth Amendment. As the circumstances surrounding a particular proposed course of action bring it closer to the indistinct line often separating lawful from unlawful searches or seizures, a relentless application of the exclusionary rule is increasingly likely to deter the former rather than the latter, since almost by definition this class of situations is as likely to involve legal as illegal police activity. "To the extent the rule operates to discourage police from reasonable and proper investigative actions, it hinders the solution and even the prevention of crime." Once application of the rule approaches the point at which it is as likely to chill legitimate police action as to discourage marginally improper action, powerful justifications indeed are needed to justify such results. . . .

A further cost of the exclusionary rule, often paid insufficient attention, is the burden it places on the judicial system. One-third of federal defendants going to trial file Fourth Amendment suppression motions, and 70% to 90% of these involve formal hearings. Although most of these motions are denied, the effect on judicial and prosecutorial resources is the same as if the motions were meritorious. Significantly, the result of this diversion of resources from criminal trials to pretrial motions may have its harshest impact on innocent defendants.

> . . . [W]e have come increasingly to rely on an informal system of negotiated settlements in the form of plea bargained arrangements between prosecutor and defendant. The results are woeful. Criminals guilty of grievous offenses routinely are permitted to escape with convictions for crimes far less serious carrying only wrist-slapping penalties. Meanwhile innocent defendants who might well have been vindicated at trial are coerced into settling for a conviction on a lesser charge. . . .
>
> It is against this background that we must measure the diversion of energy, talent and dollars from the central task of fairly determining the guilt and innocence of defendants into the work of adjudicating whether the police have blundered. . . . That function should be performed elsewhere and by others. The exclusionary remedy thus literally buys what little in the way of Fourth Amendment protection it affords at the cost of more trials for criminal defendants. Even if the rule did a fair job of promoting Fourth Amendment values, this would be at best a questionable bargain.

Finally, the exclusionary rule in the long run threatens the very Fourth Amendment values it is intended to safeguard. "If one were diabolically to attempt to invent a rule sure slowly to undermine the substantive reach of the Fourth Amendment, it would be hard to do better than the exclusionary rule." This is because of the obvious reluctance of judges to condemn questionable practices under the Fourth Amendment when they know that the result of their decision will be the freeing of a guilty defendant. . . .

. . . In addition, public support for the values served by the Fourth Amendment can too easily be undermined by a general perception that Fourth Amendment jurisprudence is bringing about the seemingly unjustified release into society of dangerous criminals. Thus, extravagant applications of the rule cannot help but threaten the substantive safeguards of the Fourth Amendment. . . .

[5. Criticisms of the Good Faith Exception.] Critics of a reasonable mistake exception to the exclusionary rule invariably argue that it would "put a premium on 'police ignorance.'" This is a palpable strawman. As the Fifth Circuit explained in *Williams*, the test for applying the exception is essentially objective:

> We emphasize that the belief, in addition to being held in subjective good faith, must be grounded in an objective reasonableness. It must therefore be based upon articulable premises sufficient to cause a reasonable, and reasonably trained, officer to believe that he was acting lawfully. Thus, a series of broadcast break-ins and searches carried out by a constable—no matter how pure in the heart—who had never heard of the Fourth Amendment could never qualify.

The objective standard we propose ensures that ignorance will not be rewarded. On the contrary, "[g]rounding the modification in objective reasonableness . . . retains the value of the exclusionary rule as an incentive for the law enforcement profession as a whole to conduct themselves in accord with the Fourth Amendment." Because such an objective standard requires individual officers to have a reasonable knowledge of what the law prohibits, the adoption of a reasonable mistake exception may actually enhance, but in any event certainly will not discourage, efforts to educate police officers about the extant principles of law. To avoid the risk of suppression through unreasonable ignorance, police departments can be expected (assuming validity in the hypothesis of deterrence by which the rule is justified in the first place) to ensure that individual officers are reasonably well trained, especially as the extent to which a police department takes seriously its duty of providing training and guidance to officers in the field might be considered in determining whether the exclusionary rule should be invoked. . . .

Because the focus of the inquiry will be objective reasonableness, rather than an officers' subjective intent, the reasonable mistake exception we propose is not likely to burden the courts unduly. Generally, it will be unnecessary for courts to engage in unwieldy and awkward inquiries into the subjective intent of arresting or searching officers. Instead, a reasonable mistake exception would require only an objective assessment of the officers' conduct in light of the factual circumstances of a particular case and the extent to which the governing legal principles had been predictably articulated. . . .

It is sometimes suggested that the exclusionary rule is needed to provide Fourth Amendment cases for the courts to adjudicate. "The risk [in modifying the exclusionary rule] is that our constitutional rights will atrophy."

This presumed risk should be placed in proper perspective. Assuming, arguendo, that adoption of a reasonable mistake exception to the exclusionary rule would substantially reduce the incentive for defendants to litigate substantive Fourth Amendment questions, the Court should bear in mind that the lost decisionmaking opportunities will be confined to the "grey, twilight area[s]" of Fourth Amendment law where the constitutional violation, if any, is minimal. In these areas at least, it would seem that our society would reap greater benefits from a more rational application of the exclusionary rule than from continued judicial resolution of every Fourth Amendment question that inventive lawyers can devise. Just as there is a point of diminishing returns in the application of the exclusionary rule, so too there is a point at which decisions of only marginal constitutional significance may be overpriced.

In any event, we are extremely skeptical about the validity of any assumption that defendants will lose their incentive to litigate meritorious substantive Fourth Amendment questions if confronted with a reasonable mistake exemption to the exclusionary rule. The overwhelming lack of success of most suppression motions does not seem to have had any effect on the number of such motions filed. Practical experience tells us that criminal defendants commonly assert suppression claims with little regard for their ultimate chances of success—in part, no doubt, because of the magnitude of the benefit to them if "lightning" should strike. While adoption of a reasonable mistake exception will tend to discourage presentation of substantively insubstantial Fourth Amendment suppression motions, it thus seems highly improbable that litigation of colorable Fourth Amendment issues will "atrophy" to any significant degree. . . .

Finally, both supporters and critics of the exclusionary rule have expressed reluctance about modifying it in the absence of an effective alternative.

. . . In our submission, the exclusionary rule must be evaluated on its own merits; if it fails to accomplish its objective, it should be appropriately modified, irrespective of the efficacy of the alternatives that might be substituted.

In any event, a number of alternatives have been suggested. Whether any of these alternatives will be effective cannot be known until they are tested; what should be obvious, however, is that the alternatives cannot possibly be any *less* effective than the exclusionary rule in its current form for cases like the ones now before the Court. Moreover, as has been noted by others, the continued existence of the exclusionary rule may itself actually inhibit experimentation with different approaches by the political branches of government. Accordingly, we submit that the presence of immediately available effective alternatives is simply not a controlling consideration in deciding whether the current rule requires the kind of modification that we propose. . . .

Respectfully submitted,
REX E. LEE,
Solicitor General of the United States.

LEON'S BRIEF

[1. Introduction.] . . . The essence of Petitioner's argument is that because: (1) the principal rationale for the exclusionary rule in any context is merely deterrence of the searching officer and (2) an officer who "reasonably" relies on a warrant cannot be deterred; the rule should not apply to searches conducted under a warrant unsupported by probable cause, in light of the overwhelming value of the seized evidence in the search for truth and the conviction of suspected criminals. Creating this unprecedented exception would inevitably be translated to the "reasonable, well trained" police officer as a new rule: by simply getting a magistrate's signature on a warrant, the search almost always will be "legal," and whatever evidence is discovered will be admissible. While this may increase incentives to utilize warrants, it will also eliminate any incentive to comply with the probable cause requirement.

The Court should not condone such violations of the Fourth Amendment. This exception would rest on an empty and unprecedented distinction between police conduct and constitutional violations by magistrates. In practice, it would nullify the purpose of the Warrant Clause, substantively denigrate the probable cause standard, cause increasingly complex and burdensome litigation, undermine the systemic deterrence function of the exclusionary rule and encourage unconstitutional searches. . . .

[2. Need for Appellate Review of Warrant Decisions.] . . . [T]he proposed exception to the exclusionary rule is actually an exception to the Warrant Clause, which would focus only upon the conduct or state of mind of the officer who executes the warrant. As a result, the broad discretion exercised by the magistrate who issues a search warrant would be virtually immune from judicial review.

Search warrant applications necessarily involve an *ex parte* proceeding without the benefit of adversary representation of Fourth Amendment interests. This process is generally marked with urgency and a heavy reliance upon untestable hearsay. In this context, the magistrate will tend to rely upon the initiative of the party presenting the application. . . . Despite the deference accorded to the magistrate's fact determination, and occasional disagreement regarding particular findings of probable cause, it appears that not a single Justice of this Court since *Weeks* has ever voted to decide a case on the ground that the magistrate's decision is immune from judicial review. The *ex parte* nature of warrant application proceedings can only be justified by the assurance of an opportunity for later judicial scrutiny in an adversary context.

The danger of an abuse of discretion in the context of the *ex parte* issuance of search warrants is incalculably increased by the minimal qualifications required to act as a magistrate with full authority to issue search and arrest warrants. "[I]t has never been held that only a lawyer or judge could grant a warrant, regardless of the court system or type of warrant involved." *Shadwick* approved issuance of an arrest warrant for violation of a city ordinance by a municipal court clerk whose job qualifications required no law degree or legal training. . . .

The specter of a warrant issued by a person with no meaningful legal training is a very real problem in the American judicial system. A recent study found approximately 14,000 non-attorneys acting as judges in the United States. The study found that most lay judges are elected, most are authorized to issue arrest and search warrants, and many had no formal training even after assuming the bench. Of the 44 states with non-attorney judges, 19 do not require any type of training program; a few merely require the judge to be a high school graduate, while others require that a judge be "literate."

. . . An independent survey and analysis of current state court systems by counsel for Respondent has verified that non-attorney magistrates are authorized by statute to issue search warrants in various court systems in at least 39 states as of this year. Moreover, in a number of states a search warrant may be issued by a non-attorney clerk. . . .

In *Illinois v. Gates*, the Court acknowledged that "probable cause is a fluid concept—turning on the assessment of probabilities in particular factual contexts—not readily, nor even usefully, reduced to a neat set of legal rules.". . .

In light of the unguided flexibility afforded magistrates of dubious qualifications, continued judicial review is now of paramount importance. Adoption of the proposed exception to the exclusionary rule, which would focus merely upon the police officer's reliance upon a warrant, would render this judicial review virtually impossible and meaningless at best. . . .

The tendency to succumb to law enforcement pressures is not limited to non-attorney magistrates.

[E]ven in the unusual case where law enforcement officials do seek a warrant, the judicial officer's participation is "largely perfunctory"—it is "notoriously easy" to obtain search warrants or court orders for electronic surveillance, and even easier to obtain warrants for arrest. Thus, almost always the first and only meaningful opportunity to decide the legality of a search or seizure arises [in appellate courts] after the fact.

The existence of "rubber stamp" magistrates has long been acknowledged. In a very recent study of the search warrant process conducted by the National Center for State Courts, the magistrate who received the most warrant applications in one subject city acknowledged that he had rejected only one search warrant application in 15 years as a judge. Rejections by surveyed judges ranged from about half to "almost never." The study found that "it was the nearly universal perception among police officers, prosecutors, and judges in all of our cities that very few applications are turned down by magistrates regardless of the [preapplication] screening procedures." Many interviewed officers felt judges "often just skim the affidavits looking for key words and phrases." In spite of the integrity and outstanding ability of many federal magistrates, it is unlikely that the "rubber stamp" approach is limited to the state court systems. In a related context, out of 5,563 federal and state wiretap authorization requests from 1969 through 1976, only 15 applications were rejected. . . .

In advocating what will amount to the end of judicial review of magistrates' decisions Petitioner asserts that judicial officers considering warrant applications are "presumably" motivated to reach a correct decision; that the training required for federal magistrates "enhance[s] the presumption of propriety"; and that this enhancement also applies to state court judges. As demonstrated above, the assumption that state court judges necessarily have any legal training is fallacious. Moreover, a law degree is no guarantee that a judge will properly make a delicate determination of probable cause under pressures from the police in an extremely limited amount of time and without any concern about future scrutiny of his decision. . . .

[3. Dilution of Probable Cause.] Adoption of a reasonable good faith exception where officers have procured a warrant would remove their current incentive to make sure the warrant will "hold up in court" by careful compliance with the requirements of probable cause. Professor Ball, a leading advocate of the good faith exception relied upon by Petitioner, concedes that a "signal from the Court that it is abating its aggressive enforcement of Fourth Amendment requirements is apt to evoke a consistent response from the police." An extensive study of the New York City Police Department yielded "substantial evidence that the police themselves would not respect courts which did not support constitutional standards by excluding any evidence which was unconstitutionally obtained. . . . [T]o the police, the imposition of the exclusionary rule is a prerequisite for the imposition of a legal obligation."

Retired Justice Stewart has recently expressed his agreement with this conclusion. In rejecting the proposed reasonable good faith exception, he states:

> [I]f this exception were adopted, police officers might shift the focus of their inquiry from "what does the Fourth Amendment require?" to "what will the courts allow me to get away with?" It seems inevitable in these circumstances that adoption of the proposed exception would result in more Fourth Amendment violations. . . .

Just as some magistrates apply a more lenient standard of probable cause than others, "[s]ome magistrates vary their requirements for a search warrant with the seriousness of the suspected offense." As a result of the variance in standards applied, police frequently engage in "magistrate shopping." "Empirical studies have shown that 'police "shop around" for a magistrate who is lenient' and that there is a 'substantial disparity between magistrates as to how much evidence is required to obtain a search warrant.'"

The fact that officers obtain a warrant demonstrates their desire to secure evidence which will be admissible at trial. With no threat of suppression due to a weak warrant application, any incentive to avoid an overly lenient magistrate would be removed.

> If a magistrate's issuance of a warrant were to be, as the government would have it, an all but conclusive determination of the validity of the search and of the admissibility of the evidence seized thereby, police officers might have a substantial incentive to submit their warrant applications to the least demanding magistrates, since once the warrant was issued, it would be exceedingly difficult later to exclude any evidence seized in the resulting search even if the warrant was issued without probable cause. . . . For practical purposes, therefore, the standard of probable cause might be diluted to that required by the least demanding official authorized to issue warrants, even if this fell well below what the Fourth Amendment required. . . .

The exception proposed by Petitioner takes the novel approach of focusing upon the reasonable belief of the police officer, instead of the magistrate, as to probable cause for the warrant. This focus puts a premium on police ignorance of the law, a consequence which has led a number of opponents of the exclusionary rule to oppose a "reasonable good faith" exception. With the assurance that evidence will be admissible where an officer has "reasonably" relied upon a warrant, police departments will invariably tend to train officers that if the warrant is signed, it is reasonable to rely on it. Absent the current danger of suppression, if there is any question about a warrant's validity police would have every reason to adopt the "let's-wait-until-it's-decided" approach recently condemned in *United States v. Johnson*. As a result, individual officers' beliefs and departmental policies will predictably shift toward institutionalized ignorance aimed at rendering "reasonable" an officer's reliance on an unreasonable warrant. . . .

[4. Burden on Courts.] In light of the insurmountable procedural and substantive problems created by the proposed "reasonable good faith" exception, it is understandable that Petitioner urges that "practical details" of the proposal would be "best left to future cases and initial resolution by lower courts." The problems raised in applying the proposed exception are far more than "practical details," and the wiser course is to consider the ramifications and the resulting inordinate expenditure of judicial resources before adopting such a sweeping proposal. The adoption of the exception would transform relatively limited hearings involving search warrant challenges into complex, time consuming evidentiary presentations.

Petitioner urges that the reasonable good faith exception should be an objective test, without spelling out how the test would work. While this proposal is doctrinally attractive, it is not workable or logically coherent. The essence of Petitioner's argument is that the exclusionary rule cannot deter an officer who believes in good faith that his conduct is within constitutional bounds. This assumes the officer's good faith belief; without it, he clearly can be deterred by the rule. It follows that the application of the proposal necessarily has a subjective component. . . .

The commentators cited by Petitioner as advocates of the proposed exception uniformly acknowledge that its application would require a subjective inquiry. As Professor Ball admits, "[u]nder the good faith exception, evidence would be suppressed as illegal unless the officer could establish *both* a good faith belief and a reasonable basis for that belief." Petitioner relies heavily upon the observations of Professor Kaplan, yet he ultimately rejects the proposed exception because it would necessarily include a subjective test, adding one more fact-finding function subject to police perjury and unreviewable and untrustworthy findings by lower courts opposed to applying the exclusionary rule. . . .

. . . The rationale for the exception is totally undermined by an officer who commits a sham mistake in bad faith which would nevertheless pass as "reasonable" under local standards. In that case, an officer may violate the Constitution and his own perceptions of what the Constitution requires, yet would Petitioner propose [that] his "mistake" would be excused under an arbitrary objective standard of something less than probable cause? This would occur in any number of contexts. For example, the officer may believe that a warrant application . . . lacks any substantial basis for probable cause and reviewing courts might agree if they reached that question; yet the fact that a magistrate signed the warrant and that it contained various irrelevant facts that could be understood as "corroboration" would presumably render the officer's bad faith reliance on the warrant "objectively reasonable."

The reasonable good faith exception would necessarily provide for subjective inquiry into issues of fraudulent behavior, such as intentional or reckless misstatements to the magistrate. Other areas similarly require subjective inquiry, such as where a reasonable warrant is obtained as a pretext for an overbroad search, or for purposes of harassment of the subject of the search. The premium on the "reasonableness" of the officer's reliance on a warrant would extend this subjective inquiry even further. Allegations of magistrate shopping would undermine an officer's good faith in relying on an "objectively reasonable" warrant. A warrant obtained in bad faith by one officer might be "reasonably relied upon" by another officer who executes the search and is subjectively unaware of how the warrant was obtained. . . .

Petitioner attempts to deal with these problems by defining them out of existence and blindly asserting that the proposed exception will simply focus on an objective test of reasonableness. As demonstrated above and acknowledged by virtually every court and commentator addressing the issue, a subjective inquiry is inherent to a good faith exception and simply unavoidable.

Justice White has observed that "[s]ending state and federal courts into the minds of police officers would produce a grave and fruitless misallocation of judicial resources." Any fact-finding test aimed at an officer's subjective state-of-mind would present impossible problems of proof and could easily be manipulated by the witness. There is evidence that police already engage in a "perjury routine" at suppression hearings. The potential for increased misrepresentations is enormous. As one commentator explains: "[I]t is unlikely that the 'good faith' exception would do anything to reduce police perjury. To the contrary, it is likely that adoption of the 'good faith' proposal would create *new* varieties of testimonial alteration." The problem of reliance upon self-serving, untrustworthy, and generally uncontradicted police testimony is yet another obstacle to accurate fact-finding under a "reasonable good-faith reliance" exception. It is doubtful that a police officer would ever testify he was not acting in good faith. . . .

[5. Ineffectiveness of Other Alternatives.] In the forty-eight years between *Weeks* and *Mapp*, states were free to devise an adequate disincentive to Fourth Amendment violations, but were unable to do so. As a result, the exclusionary rule is essential to keep the right of privacy secured by the Fourth Amendment from "remain[ing] an empty promise." No new remedies have appeared since *Mapp*. As observed by retired Justice Stewart, a number of alternative remedies exist in theory, but

> reality did not conform to theory. "Alternatives are deceptive. Their very statement conveys the impression that one possibility is as effective as the next. In this case their statement is blinding. For there is but one alternative to the rule of exclusion. That is no sanction at all."

Civil liability for damages has long been rejected as an adequate deterrent. As pointed out by Justice Murphy thirty-five years ago, the disadvantages of a tort remedy include the difficulty in obtaining punitive damages, variations in state rules limiting damages, and "judgment-proof" officers. Additional problems include the fear of reprisals from police, and the likelihood of jury prejudice in favor of officers. Generally, it is extremely difficult for the victim of an illegal search to finance or find a competent attorney to finance this type of litigation. The magistrate who issues an unconstitutional warrant is immune from suit. Where the reasonable good faith exception applies, it follows by definition that police officers would also have a good faith defense to civil liability for their misconduct, particularly where a search warrant is involved. Similarly, injunctive relief would be unavailable. A municipality would also be immune from suit unless the officer was implementing an official governmental policy by his unconstitutional conduct.

Civil litigation for damages or injunctive relief is a notoriously slow process which regularly drags on for years. Any alternative remedy must be swift if it is to act as a meaningful disincentive to improper police conduct.

Internal administrative discipline would also fail to prevent searches under warrants without probable cause. It is unrealistic to expect police departments to require a cross-check for the validity of every warrant obtained, or to order officers not to execute warrants which appear questionable. It is doubtful that law enforcement would seriously consider disciplining an officer who had been found to have "reasonably relied" on an unconstitutional warrant. It ignores the realities of the criminal justice system to believe that police will be criminally prosecuted for intentionally conducting unlawful searches and seizures.

To the extent any alternative remedy is available, it would only be invoked in cases of the most egregious misconduct which have generated significant publicity. Yet the exclusionary rule would presumably be left intact as a deterrent to such misconduct under a good faith exception. The misconduct to which it would not apply is the same misconduct that would be unremedied by alternative sanctions.

If civil or administrative remedies were available, they would function more as personal sanctions instead of systemic disincentives against illegal activity. This personal liability, whether in damages or professional reproval, would certainly intimidate police from legal conduct within constitutional bounds to a far greater extent than the threat of suppressed evidence.

Even if alternative remedies were available, it is unclear who would pursue them and to what end. Litigants would likely find little incentive for pursuing other remedies. A criminal defendant generally has limited resources, and more immediate concerns than litigation of collateral issues. . . .

[6. Fourth Amendment, not Exclusionary Rule, Restricts Police.] While the probable cause requirement impedes the gathering of evidence and apprehension of suspected criminals, it embodies a trade-off for the competing value of privacy protected by the Fourth Amendment. Each piece of evidence which is suppressed because it was seized in violation of the Fourth Amendment is evidence which the nation's founders determined should never have been seized by the government. Whatever evidence is lost by suppression (i.e., the "cost" of the exclusionary rule), and would presumably be saved by the proposed exception, is evidence that would not have been available if the government had complied with the law. As Professor La Fave has aptly explained:

> Those who drafted the Fourth Amendment may not have specifically contemplated the exclusionary sanction, but surely they expected the commands of the Amendment to be adhered to. "To the extent that the police obey the constitutional commands, the community forgoes such advantages as it might enjoy from evidence that can only be obtained illegally." It may fairly be said, then, as Justice Traynor once observed, that the cost argument was rejected when the Fourth Amendment was adopted.

To the extent [that] a reasonable good faith exception would reduce the "cost" of the exclusionary rule and "save" otherwise unavailable evidence, the "saved" evidence is presumed to be unavailable because of compliance with the Fourth Amendment, and is only available by its violation.

[7. Exaggerated Cost of Exclusionary Rule.] The "cost" of the exclusionary rule, measured in evidence suppressed and the inability to convict certain guilty defendants, has been substantially exaggerated. This is somewhat understandable, because the public can see evidence that is illegally seized and suppressed, yet is never aware of illegal police activities that are deterred by the rule, nor of undeterred police abuses which never come to the attention of the court. . . .

The expanding limitations on the scope of the exclusionary rule, and the nature of those limitations, strongly indicate that the cost of the rule is far less than Petitioner asserts. This conclusion is uniformly supported by the available empirical analysis of the rule's application.

According to a Government Accounting Office study of 2,904 cases handled in 38 U.S. Attorneys' offices in 1978, search and seizure problems accounted for only 0.4% of the arrests declined for prosecution by United States Attorneys, and evidence was suppressed in only 1.3% of the cases actually filed, half of which still resulted in convictions. A recent commentary indicates that these figures, *combined,* amount to a loss of only 0.8% of all federal arrests. Petitioner cites a 1982 study by the National Institute of Justice that found that 4.8% of California criminal cases declined for prosecution were rejected because of search and seizure problems. But the 4.8% figure is a percentage of *declined* arrests only, which is not a useful measurement.

A more valid measure of the exclusionary rule's effect is the percentage of all felony arrests that prosecutors reject because of illegal searches. The data reported in the NIJ [National Institute of Justice] study shows California prosecutors rejected only 0.8% of their total cases for search and seizure reasons. Moreover, this figure is significantly higher than the national average, because at the time of the study California recognized a broad vicarious standing rule that enabled defendants not personally victimized by an illegal search or seizure to gain the benefit of exclusion. . . .

Having failed to establish that the exclusionary rule has any substantial overall effect on failures to prosecute arrests generally, Petitioner claims that California prosecutors rejected 30% of all felony drug arrests because of search and seizure problems. This was based on samples of only a few hundred cases from two of 21 Los Angeles County prosecutors' offices with atypically high search-rejection rates and is totally unrepresentative of the state as a whole. The statewide figure, according to the statewide data source used by NIJ, is less than *three* percent. . . .

While the impact of the exclusionary rule on the successful prosecution of drug cases is small, its role in cases involving violent crimes is virtually nonexistent. Although the NIJ study does not report the percentages of violent crime arrests rejected because of illegal searches, it does show very small numbers of such rejections. . . .

In fact, evidence is very rarely suppressed in court at all. Suppression motions were [filed in only] 10.5% of all federal criminal cases surveyed. Of the motions filed, between 80% and 90% were denied. Evidence was actually excluded in only 1.3% of the 2,804 cases studied; only 0.7% of the cases resulted in acquittal or dismissal after evidence was excluded. A recent study of 7,500 felony prosecutions in Pennsylvania, Michigan, and Illinois found that suppression motions were filed in only 5% of the cases, and granted in only 0.7%. . . .

Finally, Petitioner asserts that the exclusionary rule "exacts an exceedingly high societal cost by lessening" public respect for the judicial system. The judiciary obviously should not be a barometer of public opinion. On the contrary, the exclusionary rule is a strong symbol of the judiciary's unwillingness to encourage official lawlessness by allowing the use of illegally seized evidence.

What does potentially lessen public respect for the judicial system is the systematic fanning of public sentiment by dissemination of misleading claims about the exclusionary rule's effect similar to those advanced by Petitioner. Compared to the immeasurable number of illegal searches and seizures deterred by the exclusionary rule, the number of prosecutions dropped or lost, the amount of judicial resources consumed in litigating suppression motions and the other alleged "costs" of the Fourth Amendment are not substantial. . . .

[8. Value of the Exclusionary Rule.] The exclusionary rule exception for reasonable good faith reliance upon a search warrant focuses on the belief of the officer executing the warrant, as opposed to the issuing magistrate. As a result, the operative determination on which a search is or is not invalidated will no longer be the requirement of probable cause; instead the issue turns upon what the officer reasonably believed. Professor La Fave recently observed that

> it is nothing short of nonsense to talk of a reasonable belief that there is probable cause, for the probable cause standard itself takes into account reasonable mistakes of fact. If mistakes of law were also to be taken into account, then the law becomes whatever the officer thinks it is.

Petitioner no doubt argues that this is not a problem, because the law would merely be what the officer *reasonably* thinks it is. But that is precisely the problem. Warrants will no longer require even a substantial basis for probable cause; all that would be required is a "reasonable belief" that there must be some basis for a finding of probable cause, or what Professor Kamisar has aptly described as a "double dilution" of the probable cause standard. In effect, reviewing courts would be sanctioning a "reasonably unreasonable" search based on the unprecedented and dangerous proposition that a reasonably well-trained police officer is not expected to obey the Fourth Amendment. . . .

The Fourth Amendment is not self-executing, in that it merely announces the right of the people to be secure from unreasonable searches and seizures. If its protections are to be enforced, they require a remedy which will guarantee the rights granted by its language. The mere issuance of a warrant is insufficient; the immediate concerns that motivated our founders to adopt the amendment was the use of general writs of assistance issued upon mere suspicion.

The obvious remedy, as provided in *Weeks v. United States,* is to render an unreasonable federal search a nullity by depriving the government of the primary use of its fruits—presentation of evidence in support of criminal charges in the case-in-chief at trial. This is consistent with the execution of other constitutional protections. While the Fifth Amendment does not mention coerced confessions, such evidence is excluded as a matter of course, even where circumstances show the confession is trustworthy. . . .

In proposing a good faith exception to the exclusionary rule, Petitioner asks the Court not merely to limit application of the rule, but to abolish it entirely in a set of circumstances involving an acknowledged violation of the Fourth Amendment. To the extent [that] the Warrant Clause remains intact under this exception, Petitioner would have the Court, for the first time, remove the only meaningful disincentive to its violation from application in any judicial context. In effect, the Fourth Amendment prohibition of warrants without probable cause would be reduced to a mere ideal. . . .

Petitioner reasons that the exclusion of evidence where an officer relies on a search warrant in good faith cannot deter misconduct because it imposes a sanction on the wrong party. This argument misconceives the deterrent function of the exclusionary rule. The rule is not designed to "punish" an individual officer, nor is its goal the imposition of sanctions. Instead, the rule is a disincentive to constitutional violations which acts upon the criminal justice system as a whole. This misconception derives from the unfortunate use of the term "deterrence." As Professor Kamisar points out:

> "Deterrence" suggests that the exclusionary rule is supposed to influence the police the way the criminal law is supposed to affect the general public. But the rule does not, and cannot be expected to, "deter" the police the way a criminal law is supposed to work. The rule does not inflict a "punishment" on police who violate the Fourth Amendment; exclusion of the evidence does not leave the police in a worse position than if they had never violated the Constitution in the first place.
>
> Because the police are members of a structural government entity, however, the rule influences them, or is supposed to influence them, by "systemic deterrence," i.e., through a department's institutional compliance with Fourth Amendment standards.

The underlying effect of the rule is not to repair damage done by a constitutional violation, but "to discourage law enforcement officials from violating the Fourth Amendment by removing the incentive to disregard it." Retired Justice Stewart, the author of the *Elkins* opinion, recently explained that

> the exclusionary rule is not designed to serve a "specific deterrence" function; that is, it is not designed to punish the particular police officer for violating a person's Fourth Amendment rights. Instead, the rule is designed to produce a "systematic deterrence": the exclusionary rule is intended to create an incentive for law enforcement officials to establish procedures by which police officers are trained to comply with the Fourth Amendment because the purpose of the criminal justice system—bringing criminals to justice—can be achieved only when evidence of guilt may be used against defendants. . . .

Proof of the effectiveness of the exclusionary rule as a systemic incentive for stricter compliance with the Fourth Amendment does not rest on logical assumption alone. It is demonstrated by law enforcement response to judicial announcement of Fourth Amendment standards.

For instance, as recently pointed out by retired Justice Stewart, Deputy Commissioner Leonard Reisman, the head of the New York City Police Department's legal bureau, explained at a post-*Mapp* training session:

> The *Mapp* case was a shock to us. We had to reorganize our thinking, frankly. Before this, nobody bothered to take out search warrants. Although the U.S. Constitution requires warrants in most cases, the U.S. Supreme Court had ruled that evidence obtained without a warrant—illegally, if you will—was admissible in state courts. So the feeling was, why bother?
>
> Well, once that rule was changed we knew we had better start teaching our men about it.

Commissioner Michael Murphy of New York echoed the same response:

> I can think of no decisions in recent times in the field of law enforcement which had such a dramatic and traumatic effect as this [application of the exclusionary rule]. . . . I was immediately caught up in the entire program of reevaluating our procedures, which had followed the *De Fore* rule, and modifying, amending, and creating new policies and new instructions for the implementation of *Mapp* . . . . Retraining sessions had to be held from the very top administrators down to each of the thousands of foot patrolmen.

Similarly, when California adopted the exclusionary rule Los Angeles Police Chief William Parker stated that "[a]s long as the exclusionary rule is the law of California, your police will respect it and operate to the best of their ability within the *framework of limitations imposed by that rule."* Stephen Sachs, the Attorney General of Maryland, testified that "[i]n my state, *Mapp* has been responsible for a virtual explosion in the amount and quality of police training in the last twenty years."

Response to the "framework of limitations" imposed by the exclusionary rule—i.e., the requirements of the Fourth Amendment—is evoked by each Fourth Amendment decision. FBI Director William Webster stated that "within 24 hours after a major case comes down affecting our right to do anything, the people in the field are informed of the significance of that case, with more details to follow.". . .

[9. Rationale of Judicial Integrity.] The imperative of judicial integrity, a major basis for the original adoption of the exclusionary rule, has never been repudiated by the Court. Instead, judicial integrity is now perceived to be vindicated by the exclusionary rule's discouragement of constitutional violations. As explained in *United States v. Janis:*

> The primary meaning of judicial integrity in the context of evidentiary rules is that the courts must not commit or encourage violations of the Constitution. . . .
> The focus therefore must be on the question whether the admission of the evidence encourages violations of Fourth Amendment rights. As the Court has noted in recent cases, the inquiry is essentially the same as the inquiry into whether exclusion would serve a deterrent purpose.

This formulation imposes a constitutional mandate on the Court to avoid any incentive or encouragement of constitutional violations. . . .

The intended impact of the exclusionary rule has never been explicitly limited to police officers. The Court states as early as *Weeks v. United States* that the "the 4th Amendment was intended to secure the citizen in person and property against unlawful invasion of the sanctity of his home by officers of the law, *acting under legislative or judicial sanction."*

Where a magistrate issues a warrant on less than probable cause, he has violated the Constitution just as surely as an officer who conducts an unreasonable warrantless search. . . .

Respectfully submitted,
NORMAN KAPLAN
BARRY TARLOW,
Counsel of Record.

ORAL ARGUMENT

❋   ❋   ❋

MR. LEE [Solicitor General of the United States]: ... [W]hether the magistrate's judgment in this case correctly assessed the presence of probable cause is not before the Court, but whether the totality of those circumstances did or did not amount to probable cause, it certainly could not be said that it should have been clear to officer Raumbach that there was no probable cause or that applying for a warrant would be improper in the circumstances.

He prepared his affidavit and presented it to a magistrate, so the decision whether to search or not to search was made as this Court has stated so frequently that it should be made, by a judicial officer, in this case a judge, rather than an executive officer.

I would invite the Court's attention to officer Raumbach's detailed, carefully prepared, 18-page affidavit, pages 34 to 52 of the joint appendix, which shows that the constable in this case was a cautious, highly trained, and experienced narcotics expert, who brought his experience and training to bear on his decision to apply for the warrant.

One of the strengths of the rule we propose is that it encourages that kind of high quality police work. Far from placing a premium on ignorance, as has been suggested, an objective, reasonable good faith exception, an exception which is keyed to the reasonably well trained officer, would place a premium on reasonableness and on training.

JUSTICE O'CONNOR: What does it do to encourage proper action by the magistrate?

LEE: Let me turn to that. Very little. And the reason is that whatever problem you have, Justice O'Connor, at the magistrate level is a problem that is simply outside the ambit of what the exclusionary rule was ever intended to accomplish and what it is by its very nature capable of accomplishing.

Magistrates are judicial officers. They are members of, if you will, the Article III branch, the judicial branch. In both the cases before the Court today they were judges, and the way—

THE COURT: If I may interrupt—

LEE: Yes.

THE COURT: —I assume that is usually the case. In the *City of Tampa* case 10 years ago we said it was all right for a city clerk to be a magistrate.

LEE: That is correct. But even there the Court clarified that there are two requirements that magistrates must meet. One of them is that they must be neutral and unbiased, and the other is that they have to be capable of making the probable cause judgment. Now, as long as those two requirements are met, those are the two requirements that are essential to the magistrate's job.

But regardless of the level of the training, as long as they are neutral and detached, and as long as they are capable of making the probable cause judgment, they are judges. They are part of the judicial branch. And the way our system—

THE COURT: Maybe it is enough, Mr. Solicitor General—

LEE: Excuse me.

THE COURT: —to say they are performing a judicial function in that particular setting.

LEE: That is absolutely right. That is absolutely right. They are performing as judges. And the way that our system corrects their past errors and prevents their future errors is to reverse their decisions on appeal.

Now, I recognize that it has been suggested by the respondents and the amici that reversal of magistrate decisions is not an adequate corrective, but however adequate it is or it is not to upgrade the quality of magistrates, it is certainly more closely linked to the magistrate function than is the exclusion of evidence, which imposes the remedy and its burden on another branch of government and on society as a whole.

THE COURT: How does one appeal from the finding of a magistrate? Are you talking now about the challenge to the admissibility of the evidence? Is that what you consider the appeal?

LEE: Well, whatever the system—

THE COURT: Well, but search warrants are issued ex parte. At least they always were in my experience.

LEE: That is correct. That is correct. But at a later point in time magistrates can be—their decision can be attacked in the trial.

THE COURT: I don't understand how that would come up. If the purpose of changing the exclusionary rule is to admit the evidence, I fail to see how you would ever have occasion to determine the propriety of the magistrate's action.

LEE: Well, on the later occasion when the evidence either is or is not admitted, then the decision of the magistrate would be reviewed in the normal course of events, but it is not simply a matter, we submit, of excluding the evidence.

CHIEF JUSTICE RHENQUIST: But the issue before us now is the conduct of the— not of the judicial officer, but of the police officer in acting in good faith on a presumptively valid warrant. Is that not the issue?

LEE: That is correct. Regardless of whether there would or would not be the opportunity to review what the magistrate has done, that is the issue, Mr. Chief Justice, as to whether the evidence should be excluded. The exclusionary rule is a remedy. As a remedy, it has its limitations. And it would simply be a mistake, I submit, every time there is some mistake somewhere in the criminal justice system to conclude that the solution is to exclude some probative evidence.

✣   ✣   ✣

MR. TARLOW [LEON'S ATTORNEY]:   . . . Magistrate shopping does in fact occur in our system. The police officer did not set out to get the most impartial opinion that he could find about whether the warrant was valid. He set out to get a magistrate who would sign his signature on a warrant that the police officer believed would hold up in court, and if we look at the—

THE COURT: How do we reach that conclusion?

TARLOW: Well, the realities—

THE COURT: Is there some testimony on that?

TARLOW: There is not testimony, Your Honor, but there is—

THE COURT: I mean, it is judge shopping the way prosecutors and defense counsel do it?

TARLOW: I think that the cases, at least *Karathanos* in the second circuit—the studies that have been done all recognize that—and no one is saying that all magistrates are rubber stamps. No one is saying that everyone magistrate shops. But the studies, particularly the Van Dusen study that was just prepared by the—with NIJ funding, involving 900 warrants in six cities across the country—establish that in 71 percent of [cases] warrants were signed in three minutes or less.

✣   ✣   ✣

MR. TARLOW: . . . [A]s to defendant Del Costello and as to my client, a reasonable magistrate would not have issued that warrant. Take Del Costello, Your Honor, which is the simplest of the fact patterns. All that—and my client becomes a little more complicated, but it still is nowhere near being sufficient. All they have on Del Costello is this. No informant. He was seen at the house. His car was seen at the house of a suspected narcotics dealer three times, and one of those times he was seen on the porch, and two years before he was arrested for marijuana. All that is mere association. It is nothing. There is—

THE COURT: Well, but all probable cause is a certain degree of association, and there is no magic cutoff point. . . . All the strands that go to make up probable cause are often just as consistent with innocence as they are with guilt.

TARLOW: Your Honor, mere association I didn't think was consistent with innocence as guilt.

THE COURT: Well, certainly association with a narcotics dealer, being seen with him, is some evidence that you may have some propensities of that kind yourself.

TARLOW: Well, I don't think that this Court has ever held, Your Honor, on any facts, anything close to this, you can get a warrant for a man's car or a man's house, and if that is the case, if this case comes within either *Gates* or within a supposed good faith exception, there is nothing left to the warrant clause. Only *Aguilar*—

THE COURT: Well, you could, on that basis, you could win, I suppose, win your case even with a good faith exception, because any—what you are submitting is that any fool would know you shouldn't get a warrant on these facts.

TARLOW: I am saying—we did argue in our brief as to my client that even within a good faith exception we would win, but that, as I was arguing—

THE COURT: Well, you could still win, right here, even if the government wins.

TARLOW: That might be, Your Honor, but it seems to me that there are overriding considerations. Of course, my primary responsibility is whether my client's—the outcome of my client's case.

THE COURT: Exactly. Exactly.

TARLOW: Nevertheless, as this Court speaks, it sends a message to law enforcement officers, to the public, about our constitutional rights. Enacting something such as good faith would seem to me to send out a message which would encourage police officers—

THE COURT: Well, what kind of a message would it send out if we said there is a good faith exception, but it doesn't do the government any good here? Anybody should have known there wasn't probable cause in connection with Mr.—what is it, Costello, Castillo?

TARLOW: Well, I said Mr. Del Costello. Mr. Leon is my client. But it was Mr. Leon and Mr. Del Costello. The message would be that instead of—as this Court has said, that the imperative of judicial integrity, which might be coextensive with the—

THE COURT: Well, it certainly wouldn't say—

TARLOW: —exclusionary—

THE COURT: It certainly wouldn't suggest you ought to be careless.

TARLOW: What it would say, though—

THE COURT: It would suggest that you ought to be careful.

TARLOW: You didn't make it this time, but if you have to make a mistake don't make it on the side of constitutional behavior, make that mistake on the side of unconstitutional behavior, because if you are wrong the evidence can still be admissible. Don't try to satisfy the Fourth Amendment. Just see if you can come close. . . .

THE COURT: If this gentleman had been seen on the porch of this dealer five times in seven days, how would that affect your position?

TARLOW: It wouldn't affect it at all.

THE COURT: Twelve days. Twelve times, twelve days.

TARLOW: Well, of course, I suppose, obviously—he was seen one time in one month, but I suppose—well, I don't—Your Honor, if he was seen 12 times in 12 days I don't think that means you could search his car. Maybe he lives there. Maybe he is a neighbor. Maybe he is dating the daughter. Any other thing. Being seen in the company of somebody and nothing more—

THE COURT: Let's make it 12 days at 12:00 noon, which would eliminate the daughter, probably.
[General laughter]

TARLOW: Maybe she has graduated from school and is in between things and is home at 12:00. But, no, I don't see how mere association could ever establish either probable cause or good faith.

THE COURT: With known drug dealers, you are talking about? Association with a known drug dealer is insignificant?

TARLOW: It is not probable cause or close to it, at least under any case that I have ever seen either from this Court or from any other court. . . .

THE OPINION

Justice White delivered the opinion of the Court . . . .

Language in opinions of this Court and of individual Justices has sometimes implied that the exclusionary rule is a necessary corollary of the Fourth Amendment. These implications need not detain us long. . . .

The Fourth Amendment contains no provision expressly precluding the use of evidence obtained in violation of its commands, and an examination of its origin and purposes makes clear that the use of fruits of a past unlawful search or seizure "work[s] no new Fourth Amendment wrong." The wrong condemned by the Amendment is "fully accomplished" by the unlawful search or seizure itself, and the exclusionary rule is neither intended nor able to "cure the invasion of the defendant's rights which he has already suffered." The rule thus operates as "a judicially created remedy designed to safeguard Fourth Amendment rights generally through its deterrent effect, rather than a personal constitutional right of the party aggrieved."

Whether the exclusionary sanction is appropriately imposed in a particular case, our decisions make clear, is "an issue separate from the question whether the Fourth Amendment rights of the party seeking to invoke the rule were violated by police conduct." Only the former question is currently before us, and it must be resolved by weighing the costs and benefits of preventing the use in the prosecution's case in chief of inherently trustworthy tangible evidence obtained in reliance on a search warrant issued by a detached and neutral magistrate that ultimately is found to be defective.

The substantial social costs exacted by the exclusionary rule for the vindication of Fourth Amendment rights have long been a source of concern. "Our cases have consistently recognized that unbending application of the exclusionary sanction to enforce ideals of governmental rectitude would impede unacceptably the truth-finding functions of judge and jury." An objectionable collateral consequence of this interference with the criminal justice system's truth-finding function is that some guilty defendants may go free or receive reduced sentences as a result of favorable plea bargains. Particularly when law enforcement officers have acted in objective good faith or their transgressions have been minor, the magnitude of the benefit conferred on such guilty defendants offends basic concepts of the criminal justice system. Indiscriminate application of the exclusionary rule, therefore, may well "generat[e] disrespect for the law and administration of justice." Accordingly, "[a]s with any remedial device, the application of the rule has been restricted to those areas where its remedial objectives are thought most efficaciously served."

Close attention to those remedial objectives has characterized our recent decisions concerning the scope of the Fourth Amendment exclusionary rule. The Court has, to be sure, not seriously questioned, "in the absence of a more efficacious sanction, the continued application of the rule to suppress evidence from the [prosecution's] case where a Fourth Amendment violation has been substantial and deliberate. . . ." Nevertheless, the balancing approach that has evolved in various contexts—including criminal trials—"forcefully suggest[s] that the exclusionary rule be more generally modified to permit the introduction of evidence obtained in the reasonable good-faith belief that a search or seizure was in accord with the Fourth Amendment.". . .

Because a search warrant "provides that detached scrutiny of a neutral magistrate, which is a more reliable safeguard against improper searches than the hurried judgment of a law enforcement officer 'engaged in the often competitive enterprise of ferreting out crime,'" we have expressed a strong preference for warrants and declared that "in a doubtful or marginal case a search under a warrant may be sustainable where without one it would fall.". . .

Deference to the magistrate, however, is not boundless. It is clear, first, that the deference accorded to a magistrate's finding of probable cause does not preclude inquiry into the knowing or reckless falsity of the affidavit on which that determination was based. Second, the courts must also insist that the magistrate purport to "perform his 'neutral and detached' function and not serve merely as a rubber stamp for the police." A magistrate failing to "manifest that neutrality and detachment demanded of a judicial officer when presented with a warrant application" and who acts instead as "an adjunct law enforcement officer" cannot provide valid authorization for an otherwise unconstitutional search.

Third, reviewing courts will not defer to a warrant based on an affidavit that does not "provide the magistrate with a substantial basis for determining the existence of probable cause." Sufficient information must be presented to the magistrate to allow that official to determine probable cause; his action cannot be a mere ratification of the bare conclusions of others.". . .

Only in the first of these three situations, however, has the Court set forth a rationale for suppressing evidence obtained pursuant to a search warrant; in other areas, it has simply excluded such evidence without considering whether Fourth Amendment interests will be advanced. To the extent that proponents of exclusion rely on its behavioral effects on judges and magistrates in these areas, their reliance is misplaced. First, the exclusionary rule is designed to deter police misconduct rather than to punish the errors of judges and magistrates. Second, there exists no evidence suggesting that judges and magistrates are inclined to ignore or subvert the Fourth Amendment or that lawlessness among these actors requires application of the extreme sanction of exclusion.

Third, and most important, we discern no basis, and are offered none, for believing that exclusion of evidence seized pursuant to a warrant will have a significant deterrent effect on the issuing judge or magistrate. Many of the factors that indicate that the exclusionary rule cannot provide an effective "special" or "general" deterrent for individual offending law enforcement officers apply as well to judges or magistrates. And, to the extent that the rule is thought to operate as a "systemic" deterrent on a wider audience, it clearly can have no such effect on individuals empowered to issue search warrants. Judges and magistrates are not adjuncts to the law enforcement team; as neutral judicial officers, they have no stake in the outcome of particular criminal prosecutions. The threat of exclusion thus cannot be expected significantly to deter them. Imposition of the exclusionary sanction is not necessary meaningfully to inform judicial officers of their errors, and we cannot conclude that admitting evidence obtained pursuant to a warrant while at the same time declaring that the warrant was somehow defective will in any way reduce judicial officers' professional incentives to comply with the Fourth Amendment, encourage them to repeat their mistakes, or lead to the granting of all colorable warrant requests.

If exclusion of evidence obtained pursuant to a subsequently invalidated warrant is to have any deterrent effect, therefore, it must alter the behavior of individual law enforcement officers or the policies of their departments. One could argue that applying the exclusionary rule in cases where the police failed to demonstrate probable cause in the warrant application deters future inadequate presentations or "magistrate shopping" and thus promotes the ends of the Fourth Amendment. Suppressing evidence obtained pursuant to a technically defective warrant supported by probable cause also might encourage officers to scrutinize more closely the form of the warrant and to point out suspected judicial errors. We find such arguments speculative and conclude that suppression of evidence obtained pursuant to a warrant should be ordered only on a case-by-case basis and only in those unusual cases in which the exclusion will further the purpose of the exclusionary rule.

We have frequently questioned whether the exclusionary rule can have any deterrent effect when the offending officers acted in the objectively reasonable belief that their conduct did not violate the Fourth Amendment. "No empirical researcher, proponent or opponent of the rule has yet been able to establish with any assurance whether the rule has a deterrent effect. . . ." But even assuming that the rule effectively deters some police misconduct and provides incentives for the law enforcement profession as a whole to conduct itself in accord with the Fourth Amendment, it cannot be expected, and should not be applied, to deter objectively reasonable law enforcement activity. . . .

This is particularly true, we believe, when an officer acting with objective good faith has obtained a search warrant from a judge or magistrate and acted within its scope. In most such cases, there is no police illegality and thus nothing to deter. It is the magistrate's responsibility to determine whether the officer's allegations establish probable cause and, if so, to issue a warrant comporting in form with the requirements of the Fourth Amendment. In the ordinary case, an officer cannot be expected to question the magistrate's probable-cause determination or his judgement that the form of the warrant is technically sufficient. "[O]nce the warrant issues, there is literally nothing more the policeman can do in seeking to comply with the law." Penalizing the officer for the magistrate's error, rather than his own, cannot logically contribute to the deterrence of Fourth Amendment violations.

We conclude that the marginal or nonexistent benefits produced by suppressing evidence obtained in objectively reasonable reliance on a subsequently invalidated search warrant cannot justify the substantial costs of exclusion. We do not suggest, however, that exclusion is always inappropriate in cases where an officer has obtained a warrant and abided by its terms. . . .

Suppression . . . remains an appropriate remedy if the magistrate or judge in issuing a warrant was misled by information in an affidavit that the affiant knew was false or would have known was false except for his reckless disregard of the truth. The exception we recognize today will also not apply in cases where the issuing magistrate wholly abandoned his judicial role in the manner condemned in *Lo-Ji Sales, Inc. v. New York;* in such circumstances, no reasonably well trained officer should rely on the warrant. Nor would an officer manifest objective good faith in relying on a warrant based on an affidavit "so lacking in indicia of probable cause as to render official belief in its existence entirely unreasonable." Finally, depending on the circumstances of the particular case, a warrant may be so facially deficient—i.e., in failing to particularize the place to be searched or the things to be seized—that the executing officers cannot reasonably presume it to be valid. . . .

. . . [We are also not] persuaded that application of a good faith exception to searches conducted pursuant to warrants will preclude review of the constitutionality of the search or seizure, deny needed guidance from the courts, or freeze Fourth Amendment law in its present state. There is no need for courts to adopt the inflexible practice of always deciding whether the officers' conduct manifested objective good faith before turning to the question whether the Fourth Amendment has been violated. Defendants seeking suppression of the fruits of allegedly unconstitutional searches or seizures undoubtedly raise live controversies which Art. III empowers federal courts to adjudicate. . . .

If the resolution of a particular Fourth Amendment question is necessary to guide future action by law enforcement officers and magistrates, nothing will prevent reviewing courts from deciding that question before turning to the good faith issue. Indeed, it frequently will be difficult to determine whether the officers acted reasonably without resolving the Fourth Amendment issue. Even if the Fourth Amendment question is not one of broad import, reviewing courts could decide in particular cases that magistrates under their supervision need to be informed of their errors and so evaluate the officers' good faith only after finding a violation. In other circumstances, those courts could reject suppression motions posing no important Fourth Amendment questions by turning immediately to a consideration of the officers' good faith. We have no reason to believe that our Fourth Amendment jurisprudence would suffer by allowing reviewing courts to exercise an informed discretion in making this choice. . . .

Justice Brennan, dissenting . . .

Ten years ago in *United States v. Calandra,* I expressed the fear that the Court's decision "may signal that a majority of my colleagues have positioned themselves to . . . abandon altogether the exclusionary rule in search-and-seizure cases." Since then, in case after case, I have witnessed the Court's gradual but determined strangulation of the rule. It now appears that the Court's victory over the Fourth Amendment is complete. That today's decisions represent the *pièce de résistance* of the Court's past efforts cannot be doubted, for today the Court sanctions the use in the prosecution's case in chief of illegally obtained evidence against the individual whose rights have been violated—a result that had previously been thought to be foreclosed.

The Court seeks to justify this result on the ground that the "costs" of adhering to the exclusionary rule in cases like these before us exceed the "benefits." But the language of deterrence and of cost/benefit analysis, if used indiscriminately, can have a narcotic effect. It creates an illusion of technical precision and ineluctability. It suggests that not only constitutional principle but also empirical data support the majority's result. When the Court's analysis is examined carefully, however, it is clear that we have not been treated to an honest assessment of the merits of the exclusionary rule, but have instead been drawn into a curious world where the "costs" of excluding illegally obtained evidence loom to exaggerated heights and where the "benefits" of such exclusion are made to disappear with a mere wave of the hand.

The majority ignores the fundamental constitutional importance of what is at stake here. While the machinery of law enforcement and indeed the nature of crime itself have changed dramatically since the Fourth Amendment became part of the Nation's fundamental law in 1791, what the Framers understood then remains true today—that the task of combating crime and convicting the guilty will in every era seem of such critical and pressing concern that we may be lured by the temptations of expediency into forsaking our commitment to protecting individual liberty and privacy. It was for that very reason that the Framers of the Bill of Rights insisted that law enforcement efforts be permanently and unambiguously restricted in order to preserve personal freedoms. In the constitutional scheme they ordained, the sometimes unpopular task of ensuring that the government's enforcement efforts remain within the strict boundaries fixed by the Fourth Amendment was entrusted to the courts. . . . If those independent tribunals lose their resolve, however, as the Court has done today, and give way to the seductive call of expediency, the vital guarantees of the Fourth Amendment are reduced to nothing more than a "form of words.". . .

At bottom, the Court's decision turns on the proposition that the exclusionary rule is merely a "judicially created remedy designed to safeguard Fourth Amendment rights generally through its deterrent effect, rather than a personal constitutional right." The germ of that idea is found in *Wolf v. Colorado,* and although I had thought that such a narrow conception of the rule had been forever put to rest by our decision in *Mapp v. Ohio,* it has been revived by the present Court and reaches full flower with today's decision. The essence of this view, as expressed initially in the *Calandra* opinion and as reiterated today, is that the sole "purpose of the Fourth Amendment is to prevent unreasonable governmental intrusions into the privacy of one's person, house, papers, or effects. The wrong condemned is the unjustified governmental invasion of these areas of an individual's life. That wrong . . . is *fully accomplished* by the original search without probable cause." This reading of the Amendment implies that its proscriptions are directed solely at those government agents who may actually invade an individual's constitutionally protected privacy. The courts are not subject to any direct constitutional duty to exclude illegally obtained evidence, because the question of the admissibility of such evidence is not addressed by the Amendment. This view of the scope of the Amendment relegates the judiciary to the periphery. Because the only constitutionally cognizable injury has already been "fully accomplished" by the police by the time a case comes before the courts, the Constitution is not itself violated if the judge decides to admit the tainted evidence. Indeed, the most the judge *can* do is wring his hands and hope that perhaps by excluding such evidence he can deter future transgressions by the police.

Such a reading appears plausible, because, as critics of the exclusionary rule never tire of repeating, the Fourth Amendment makes no express provision for the exclusion of evidence secured in violation of its commands. A short answer to this claim, of course, is that many of the Constitution's most vital imperatives are stated in general terms and the task of giving meaning to these precepts is therefore left to subsequent judicial decisionmaking in the context of concrete cases. . . .

A more direct answer may be supplied by recognizing that the Amendment, like other provisions of the Bill of Rights, restrains the power of the government as a whole; it does not specify only a particular agency and exempt all others. The judiciary is responsible, no less than the executive, for ensuring that constitutional rights are respected.

When that fact is kept in mind, the role of the courts and their possible involvement in the concerns of the Fourth Amendment comes into sharper focus. Because seizures are executed principally to secure evidence, and because such evidence generally has utility in our legal system only in the context of a trial supervised by a judge, it is apparent that the admission of illegally obtained evidence implicates the same constitutional concerns as the initial seizure of that evidence. Indeed, by admitting unlawfully seized evidence, the judiciary becomes a part of what is in fact a single governmental action prohibited by the terms of the Amendment. Once that connection between the evidence-gathering role of the police and the evidence-admitting function of the courts is acknowledged, the plausibility of the Court's interpretation becomes more suspect. Certainly nothing in the language or history of the Fourth Amendment suggests that a recognition of this evidentiary link between the police and the courts was meant to be foreclosed. It is difficult to give any meaning at all to the limitations imposed by the Amendment if they are read to proscribe only certain conduct by the police but to allow other agents of the same government to take advantage of evidence secured by the police in violation of its requirements. The Amendment therefore must be read to condemn not only the initial unconstitutional invasion of privacy—which is done, after all, for the purpose of securing evidence—but also the subsequent use of any evidence so obtained.

The Court evades this principle by drawing an artificial line between the constitutional rights and responsibilities that are engaged by actions of the police and those that are engaged when a defendant appears before the courts. According to the Court, the substantive protections of the Fourth Amendment are wholly exhausted at the moment when police unlawfully invade an individual's privacy and thus no substantive force remains to those protections at the time of trial when the government seeks to use evidence obtained by the police.

I submit that such a crabbed reading of the Fourth Amendment casts aside the teaching of those Justices who first formulated the exclusionary rule, and rests ultimately on an impoverished understanding of judicial responsibility in our constitutional scheme. For my part, "[t]he right of the people to be secure in their persons, houses, papers, and effects, against unreasonable searches and seizures" comprises a personal right to exclude all evidence secured by means of unreasonable searches and seizures. The right to be free from the initial invasion of privacy and the right of exclusion are coordinate components of the central embracing right to be free from unreasonable searches and seizures. . . .

. . . [N]o other explanation suffices to account for the Court's holding in *Mapp*, since the only possible predicate for the Court's conclusion that the States were bound by the Fourteenth Amendment to honor the *Weeks* doctrine is that the exclusionary rule was "part and parcel of the Fourth Amendment's limitation upon [governmental] encroachment of individual privacy."

Despite this clear pronouncement, however, the Court since *Calandra* has gradually pressed the deterrence rationale for the rule . . . to center stage. The various arguments advanced by the Court in this campaign have only strengthened my conviction that the deterrence theory is both misguided and unworkable. First, the Court has frequently bewailed the "cost" of excluding reliable evidence. In large part, this criticism rests upon a refusal to acknowledge the function of the Fourth Amendment itself. If nothing else, the Amendment plainly operates to disable the government from gathering information and securing evidence in certain ways. In practical terms, of course, this restriction of official power means that some incriminating evidence inevitably will go undetected if the government obeys these constitutional restraints. It is the loss of that evidence that is the "price" our society pays for enjoying freedom and privacy safeguarded by the Fourth Amendment. Thus, some criminals will go free *not,* in Justice (then Judge) Cardozo's misleading epigram, "because the constable has blundered," but rather because official compliance with the Fourth Amendment requirements make it more difficult to catch criminals. Understood in this way, the Amendment directly contemplates that some reliable and incriminating evidence will be lost to the government; therefore, it is not the exclusionary rule, but the Amendment itself that has imposed this cost. . . .

Even if I were to accept the Court's general approach to the exclusionary rule, I could not agree with today's result. There is no question that in the hands of the present Court the deterrence rationale has proved to be a powerful tool for confining the scope of the rule. In *Calandra,* for example, the Court concluded that the "speculative and undoubtedly minimal advance in the deterrence of police misconduct" was insufficient to outweigh the "expense of substantially impeding the role of the grand jury." In *Stone v. Powell,* the Court found that "the additional contribution, if any, of the consideration of search-and-seizure claims of state prisoners on collateral review is small in relation to the costs." In *United States v. Janis,* the Court concluded that "exclusion from federal civil proceedings of evidence unlawfully seized by a state criminal enforcement officer has not been shown to have a sufficient likelihood of deterring the conduct of state police so that it outweighs the societal costs imposed by the exclusion.". . .

Thus, in this bit of judicial stagecraft, while the sets sometimes change, the actors always have the same lines. Given this well-rehearsed pattern, one might have predicted with some assurance how the present case would unfold. First there is the ritual incantation of the "substantial social costs" exacted by the exclusionary rule, followed by the virtually foreordained conclusion that, given the marginal benefits, application of the rule in the circumstances of these cases is not warranted. Upon analysis, however, such a result cannot be justified even on the Court's own terms.

At the outset, the Court suggests that society has been asked to pay a high price—in terms either of setting guilty persons free or of impeding the proper functioning of trials—as a result of excluding relevant physical evidence in cases where the police, in conducting searches and seizing evidence, have made only an "objectively reasonable" mistake concerning the constitutionality of their actions. But what evidence is there to support such a claim?

Significantly, the Court points to none, and, indeed, as the Court acknowledges, recent studies have demonstrated that the "costs" of the exclusionary rule—calculated in terms of dropped prosecutions and lost convictions—are quite low. Contrary to the claims of the rule's critics that exclusion leads to "the release of countless guilty criminals," these studies have demonstrated that federal and state prosecutors very rarely drop cases because of potential search and seizure problems. For example, a 1979 study prepared at the request of Congress by the General Accounting Office reported that only 0.4% of all cases actually declined for prosecution by federal prosecutors were declined primarily because of illegal search problems. If the GAO data are restated as a percentage of *all* arrests, the study shows that 0.2% of all felony arrests are declined for prosecution because of potential exclusionary rule problems. Of course, these data describe only the costs attributable to the exclusion of evidence in all cases; the costs due to the exclusion of evidence in the narrower category of cases where police have made objectively reasonable mistakes must necessarily be even smaller. The Court, however, ignores this distinction and mistakenly weighs the aggregated costs of exclusion in *all* cases, irrespective of the circumstances that led to exclusion, against the potential benefits associated with only those cases in which evidence is excluded because police reasonably but mistakenly believe that their conduct does not violate the Fourth Amendment. When such faulty scales are used, it is little wonder that the balance tips in favor of restricting the application of the rule.

What then supports the Court's insistence that this evidence be admitted? Apparently, the Court's only answer is that even though the costs of exclusion are not very substantial, the potential deterrent effect in these circumstances is so marginal that exclusion cannot be justified. The key to the Court's conclusion in this respect is its belief that the prospective deterrent effect of the exclusionary rule operates only in those situations in which police officers, when deciding whether to go forward with some particular search, have reason to know that their planned conduct will violate the requirements of the Fourth Amendment. . . .

The flaw in the Court's argument, however, is that its logic captures only one comparatively minor element of the generally acknowledged deterrent purposes of the exclusionary rule. To be sure, the rule operates to some extent to deter future misconduct by individual officers who have had evidence suppressed in their own cases. But what the Court overlooks is that the deterrence rationale for the rule is not designed to be, nor should it be thought of as, a form of "punishment" of individual police officers for their failures to obey the restraints imposed by the Fourth Amendment. Instead, the chief deterrent function of the rule is its tendency to promote institutional compliance with Fourth Amendment requirements on the part of law enforcement agencies generally. . . .

If the overall educational effect of the exclusionary rule is considered, application of the rule to even those situations in which individual police officers have acted on the basis of a reasonable but mistaken belief that their conduct was authorized can still be expected to have a considerable long-term deterrent effect. If evidence is consistently excluded in these circumstances, police departments will surely be prompted to instruct their officers to devote greater care and attention to providing sufficient information to establish probable cause when applying for a warrant, and to review with some attention the form of the warrant that they have been issued, rather than automatically assuming that whatever document the magistrate has signed will necessarily comport with Fourth Amendment requirements.

After today's decisions, however, that institutional incentive will be lost. Indeed, the Court's "reasonable mistake" exception to the exclusionary rule will tend to put a premium on police ignorance of the law. Armed with the assurance provided by today's decisions that evidence will always be admissible whenever an officer has "reasonably" relied upon a warrant, police departments will be encouraged to train officers that if a warrant has simply been signed, it is reasonable, without more, to rely on it. Since in close cases there will no longer be any incentive to err on the side of constitutional behavior, police would have every reason to adopt a "let's-wait-until-it's-decided" approach in situations in which there is a question about a warrant's validity or the basis for its issuance.

Although the Court brushes these concerns aside, a host of grave consequences can be expected to result from its decision to carve this new exception out of the exclusionary rule. A chief consequence of today's decision will be to convey a clear and unambiguous message to magistrates that their decisions to issue warrants are now insulated from subsequent judicial review. Creation of this new exception for good faith reliance upon a warrant implicitly tells magistrates that they need not take much care in reviewing warrant applications, since their mistakes will from now on have virtually no consequence: If their decision to issue a warrant was correct, the evidence will be admitted; if their decision was incorrect but the police relied in good faith on the warrant, the evidence will also be admitted. Inevitably, the care and attention devoted to such an inconsequential chore will dwindle. Although the Court is correct to note that magistrates do not share the same stake in the outcome of a criminal case as the police, they nevertheless need to appreciate that their role is of some moment in order to continue performing the important task of carefully reviewing warrant applications. Today's decisions effectively remove that incentive. . . .

When the public, as it quite properly has done in the past as well as in the present, demands that those in government increase their efforts to combat crime, it is all too easy for those government officials to seek expedient solutions. In contrast to such costly and difficult measures as building more prisons, improving law enforcement methods, or hiring more prosecutors and judges to relieve the overburdened court systems in the country's metropolitan areas, the relaxation of Fourth Amendment standards seems a tempting, costless means of meeting the public's demand for better law enforcement. In the long run, however, we as a society pay a heavy price for such expediency, because as Justice Jackson observed, the rights guaranteed in the Fourth Amendment "are not mere second-class rights but belong in the catalog of indispensable freedoms." Once lost, such rights are difficult to recover. There is hope, however, that in time this or some later Court will restore these precious freedoms to their rightful place as a primary protection for our citizens against overwhelming officialdom. . . .

Justice Stevens, dissenting . . .

The Court assumes that the searches in these cases violate the Fourth Amendment, yet refuses to apply the exclusionary rule because the Court concludes that it was "reasonable" for the police to conduct them. In my opinion an unofficial search and seizure cannot be both "unreasonable" and "reasonable" at the same time. The doctrinal vice in the Court's holding is its failure to consider the separate purposes of the two prohibitory Clauses in the Fourth Amendment. . . .

Just last Term, the Court explained what probable cause to issue a warrant means:

> The task of the issuing magistrate is simply to make a practical, common-sense decision whether, given all the circumstances set forth in the affidavit before him, including the "veracity" and the "basis of knowledge" of persons supplying hearsay information, there is a fair probability that contraband or evidence of a crime will be found in a particular place.

Moreover, in evaluating the existence of probable cause, reviewing courts must give substantial deference to the magistrate's determination. In doubtful cases the warrant should be sustained. The judgment as to whether there is probable cause must be made in a practical and nontechnical manner. The probable-cause standard therefore gives law enforcement officers ample room to engage in any reasonable law enforcement activity. . . .

Thus, if the majority's assumption is correct, that even after paying heavy deference to the magistrate's finding and resolving all doubt in its favor, there is no probable cause here, then by definition—as a matter of constitutional law—the officers' conduct was unreasonable. The Court's own hypothesis is that there was no fair likelihood that the officers would find evidence of a crime, and hence there was no reasonable law enforcement justification for their conduct.

The majority's contrary conclusion rests on the notion that it must be reasonable for a police officer to rely on a magistrate's finding. Until today that has plainly not been the law; it has been well settled that even when a magistrate issues a warrant there is no guarantee that the ensuing search and seizure is constitutionally reasonable. . . .

The notion that a police officer's reliance on a magistrate's warrant is automatically appropriate is one the Framers of the Fourth Amendment would have vehemently rejected. The precise problem that the Amendment was intended to address was *the unreasonable issuance of warrants.* As we have often observed, the Amendment was actually motivated by the practice of issuing general warrants—warrants which did not satisfy the particularity and probable-cause requirements. The resentments which led to the Amendment were directed at the issuance of *warrants* unjustified by particularized evidence of wrongdoing. Those who sought to amend the Constitution to include a Bill of Rights repeatedly voiced the view that the evil which had to be addressed was the issuance of warrants on insufficient evidence. . . .

In short, the Framers of the Fourth Amendment were deeply suspicious of warrants; in their minds the paradigm of an abusive search was the execution of a warrant not based on probable cause. The fact that colonial officers had magisterial authorization for their conduct when they engaged in general searches surely did not make their conduct "reasonable." The Court's view that it is consistent with our Constitution to adopt a rule that it is presumptively reasonable to rely on a defective warrant is the product of constitutional amnesia. . . .

POSTSCRIPT

United States v. Leon established the rule that if the police reasonably relied on a search warrant, any evidence obtained could be admitted. Even if the search warrant was issued unlawfully, the prosecution could still use the illegally seized evidence.[27] In later cases, the Supreme Court expanded the scope of the good faith exception. In *Segura v. United States* (1984), the Court said that an illegal *warrantless* entry would not be grounds to exclude evidence if the police had acted in reasonable good faith.[28] The same rationale used in *Leon* reappeared in *Segura.*

---

[27]*Leon* involved a search warrant that a magistrate issued without probable cause. In a companion case, *Massachusetts v. Sheppard,* 468 U.S. 981 (1984), the Court also ruled that the exclusionary rule did not apply if the police reasonably relied on a search warrant that failed to identify correctly the items that were to be seized.

[28]468 U.S. 796 (1984).

Just as the exclusion of illegally seized evidence could not significantly deter un-lawful police action if the police had taken the precaution of getting a judicial war-rant, so also little deterrence could be achieved if the police reasonably believed that they had the authority to engage in a warrantless search. A few years later, in a 5–4 decision, the same argument convinced the Court to extend the good faith exception one step further.[29] If a police officer reasonably conducted a search pursuant to a statute, the evidence obtained was admissible even if the statute was later deemed unconstitutional. If exclusion could not have an appreciable deter-rent impact on the police when they reasonably relied on a warrant, it similarly could not deter police misconduct when they were reasonably relying on a legisla-ture's assessment of the constitutionality of a statute. In both instances, the Court concluded that the exclusionary rule did not apply because its purpose was only to deter police misconduct.

Leon and its progeny have produced some consternation among legal com-mentators.[30] Many wonder whether the good faith exception will destroy the in-tegrity of the exclusionary rule, thereby sacrificing important Fourth Amendment values. Is there any reason for this concern? Of course, illegally seized evidence will still be excluded if the police, with or without a warrant, act "unreasonably." But does this limited use of the exclusionary rule provide sufficient protection for the right to be free from unreasonable searches and seizures? What about in in-stances in which the police acted reasonably but nonetheless violated the Fourth Amendment rights of a defendant? In what way are these constitutional violations remedied if the good faith exception is recognized? Is the Constitution the supreme law of the land if such Fourth Amendment violations are not remedied? Do such unremedied constitutional violations concern you? If exclusion of any il-legally seized evidence is not the appropriate remedy, what remedy should be provided in cases of reasonable good faith constitutional violations of the Fourth Amendment? Should the individual police officers involved be subject to adminis-trative sanctions? Should victims be allowed to recover civil damages? Is the un-derlying constitutional right anything more than an ideal if violations of it go un-remedied?

Apart from the widening scope of the good faith exception, another important development is that the Court has created a totally different exception to the ex-clusionary rule: the "inevitable discovery" exception. According to this new modi-fication of the exclusionary rule, illegally seized evidence can be introduced at a trial if the police, acting legally, would have discovered it anyway. In other words, a judge who knows that the police, whether in good faith or bad, violated the con-stitution can nonetheless admit the evidence on the basis of a hypothetical judg-ment that the police would have eventually discovered the incriminating evidence

---

[29]*Illinois v. Krull,* 480 U.S. 340 (1987).

[30]See Abraham S. Goldstein, "The Search Warrant, the Magistrate, and Judicial Review," *New York University Law Review* 62 (1987): 1173–1217; Craig D. Uchida, Timothy S. Bynum, Dennis Rogan, and Donna Murasky, "Acting in Good Faith: The Effects of *United States v. Leon* on the Police and Courts," *Arizona Law Review* 30 (1988): 467–495; David Clark Esseks, "Errors in Good Faith: The *Leon* Exception Six Years Later," *University of Michigan Law Review* 89 (1990): 625–660; and other sources cited in these articles.

by lawful means. The Court handed down this ruling in *Nix v. Williams* (1984).[31] In this case, the police violated the defendant's right to be free from self-incrimination, yet the trial court permitted the prosecution to use evidence gained from the defendant's admissions. Any evaluation of *Williams* and the inevitable discovery exception requires some consideration of, first, the fruit-of-the-poisonous-tree doctrine and, second, the exclusionary rule's relationship to the Fifth Amendment right to be free from self-incrimination and the Sixth Amendment right to counsel.

The Court developed the substance of the fruit-of-the-poisonous-tree doctrine long ago in *Silverthorne Lumber Co. v. United States* (1920), a case involving the lawfulness of a subpoena of materials that the government had earlier illegally seized and then returned to the defendant.[32] Could the government violate the Fourth Amendment, rectify the wrong, and then proceed to obtain the incriminating evidence lawfully? The Court ruled that the federal government could not act in this fashion, arguing that the "essence of a provision forbidding the acquisition of evidence in a certain way is that not merely evidence so acquired shall not be used before the Court but that it shall not be used at all."[33] Government officials could not use the primary knowledge gained through unlawful means to obtain incriminating evidence through lawful secondary means. Such "derivative" evidence was "tainted" by the prior illegality. It was the "fruit of the poisonous tree."[34] The subpoena for the evidence in *Silverthorne* was therefore unlawful.

Though *Silverthorne* established the principle that the government could not use evidence derived from unlawful action, it also limited it. The government could not use its knowledge of the existence of incriminating evidence that it had gained by unlawful means, but that did not mean "that the facts thus obtained become sacred and inaccessible. If knowledge of them is gained from an independent source, they may be proved like any others."[35] Therefore, in *Silverthorne*, a subpoena would be lawful and appropriate, despite the government's earlier illegal actions, if an *independent* source could substantiate the relevant facts concerning the existence of the incriminating evidence. Notwithstanding the fact that certain evidence was the fruit of a poisonous tree, the government could use it if it were independently "nourished," that is, if it were also the "fruit of a nonpoisonous tree."

Silverthorne concerned the exclusion of evidence that was traceable to an unconstitutional search and seizure, but the scope of the exclusionary rule and the fruit-of-the-poisonous-tree doctrine was not confined to Fourth Amendment violations. Infractions of the Fifth and Sixth Amendments would have the same result. As early as *Brown v. Mississippi* (1936), the Supreme Court ruled that the Fourteenth Amendment's due process clause required states to exclude confessions that were physically coerced.[36] It was not until *Malloy v. Hogan* (1964), how-

---

[31]467 U.S. 431 (1984).

[32]251 U.S. 385 (1920).

[33]Idem, 392.

[34]The phrase "fruit of the poisonous tree" was crafted by Felix Frankfurter in *Nardone v. United States*, 308 U.S. 338 (1939).

[35]*Silverthorne Lumber Co. v. United States*, 251 U.S. 385, 392 (1920).

[36]297 U.S. 278 (1936).

ever, that the Court explicitly incorporated the privilege against self-incrimination into the due process clause of the Fourteenth Amendment.[37] This decision not only made the Fifth Amendment applicable to the states but also mandated the exclusionary rule as the means of its enforcement. Immediately thereafter, in *Murphy v. Waterfront Commission of New York Harbor* (1964), the Court imposed the fruit-of-the-poisonous-tree doctrine on state violations of the privilege against self-incrimination.[38] Not only could incriminating statements coerced from a defendant not be used at trial, but they also could not be used by the police to obtain, by seemingly lawful means, other evidence against the defendant. Courts were to exclude the fruit of Fifth Amendment violations just as they had excluded the fruit of Fourth Amendment violations.[39]

During the same period that the Supreme Court developed the rule that a coerced confession triggered the fruit-of-the-poisonous-tree doctrine, it also refined the criteria of what constituted a coerced confession. Physical beatings of prisoners were clearly beyond the pale. Any resulting confession would be "involuntary" if only because confessions elicited in this manner were inherently untrustworthy.[40] For many years, the Court struggled with the issue of what kind of psychological pressures produced coerced confessions. As the Court slowly became convinced that psychologically coerced confessions should also trigger the exclusionary rule, the Court shifted its justification for the rule. Physically coerced confessions were excluded because they were unreliable, while psychologically coerced confessions were excluded to discourage the police from using abusive interrogative tactics.[41]

One obvious way to ensure the voluntary character of confessions was to have the defendant's lawyer present during any interrogation. Because the Sixth Amendment guaranteed the right to counsel, the key issues were whether the police had to inform the defendant of this important right, whether the police had to honor a defendant's request to speak to an attorney before questioning, and whether the defendant had a right to have his attorney present during such interrogations. As discussed in Chapter 2 of this volume, these questions were settled in the groundbreaking cases of *Escobedo v. Illinois* and *Miranda v. Arizona.* [42] Describing the atmosphere of police interrogations as inherently coercive, the Court ruled that the police must tell the defendant that anything he says can be used against him and inform him of his rights to remain silent, to consult with a lawyer, and to have a lawyer present during interrogation. In effect, the Court had concluded that the best way to protect a defendant's right against self-incrimina-

---

[37]378 U.S. 1 (1964).

[38]378 U.S. 52 (1964).

[39]In *Kastigar v. United States,* 406 U.S. 441 (1972), the Court limited the fruit-of-the-poisonous-tree doctrine by the independent-source doctrine in the context of violations of the Fifth Amendment, just as it had earlier done in regard to the Fourth Amendment.

[40]See *Brown v. Mississippi,* 297 U.S. 278 (1936).

[41]See *Ashcraft v. Tennessee,* 322 U.S. 143 (1944); *Watts v. Indiana,* 338 U.S. 49 (1949); *Spano v. New York,* 360 U.S. 315 (1959); and *Massiah v. United States,* 377 U.S. 201 (1964).

[42]378 U.S. 478 (1964); 384 U.S. 436 (1966).

tion was to widen the scope of the defendant's right to counsel. Given the fruit-of-the-poisonous-tree doctrine, the decision meant that any evidence the police obtained through a violation of the *Miranda* rules was subject to the exclusionary rule.

In 1975, in *Brewer v. Williams,* the Supreme Court ruled that the state of Iowa had violated the *Miranda* rules in a case involving the murder of a ten-year-old girl from Des Moine.[43] Williams, for whom an arrest warrant had been issued, surrendered in Davenport, Iowa, which is 160 miles east of Des Moines. At this time, police were searching the countryside for the dead girl's body near Grinnel, a town halfway between Des Moines and Davenport. By telephone, Williams had spoken to a Des Moines attorney who had arranged for a lawyer from Davenport to meet Williams at the Davenport police station. The police informed counsel that they would transport Williams from Davenport to Des Moines without questioning him. However, one of the two detectives who picked Williams up said the following to him during the car ride back to Des Moines:

> I want to give you something to think about while we're travelling down the road. . . . They are predicting several inches of snow for tonight, and I feel that you yourself are the only person that knows where this little girl's body is . . . and if you get snow on top of it you yourself may be unable to find it. And since we will be going right past the area on the way into Des Moines, I feel that we could stop and locate the body, that the parents of this little girl should be entitled to a Christian burial for the little girl who was snatched away from them on Christmas eve and murdered. . . . I do not want you to answer me. . . . Just think about it. . . .[44]

Soon after this monologue, Williams directed the detectives to the body, located in a ditch next to a culvert beside a gravel road. The body was within the area around Grinnel that was going to be searched, but before Williams incriminated himself by guiding the officers to the dead body, the search party had suspended its operations for the day.

In a divided 5–4 decision, the Court ruled that the police had obtained incriminating information from Williams in violation of his right to counsel. Williams deserved a new trial from which all of his incriminating statements were to be excluded. The body's condition and location, the Court said, were another matter. Though the fruit-of-the-poisonous-tree doctrine would suggest that the body's location and condition would also have to be suppressed, the Court stated in a footnote that they "might well be admissible on the theory that the body would have been discovered in any event, even had incriminating statements not been elicited from Williams."[45] At Williams's retrial, the Iowa judge took the Supreme Court's hint and admitted evidence in regard to the location and condition of the victim's body. He reasoned that since the police would have "inevitably discovered" the body, such evidence was admissible even though it was, in fact,

---

[43]430 U.S. 387 (1975).

[44]Quoted in *Nix v. Williams,* 467 U.S. 431 (1984).

[45]*Brewer v. Williams,* 423 U.S. 387, 407, n. 12 (1977).

the fruit of unlawful police actions. On this basis, the jury reconvicted Williams. His case on appeal presented the Supreme Court with the explicit issue of whether it should draw another exception to the exclusionary rule.

In a 7–2 decision, the Supreme Court created the inevitable discovery exception to the exclusionary rule. Chief Justice Warren Burger wrote the majority opinion explaining why the new exception deserved recognition. First, the independent-source limitation of the fruit-of-the-poisonous-tree doctrine meant that unlawfully obtained evidence could be used if the police could establish the probable existence of the evidence from an independent source. The rationale for this limitation was that the fruit-of-the-poisonous-tree doctrine should not be allowed to put the police in a worse position than they would have been in without the unlawful activity. Burger continued:

> The independent source doctrine teaches us that the interest of society in deterring unlawful police conduct and the public interest in having juries receive all probative evidence of a crime are properly balanced by putting the police in the same, not a *worse,* position that they would have been in if no police error or misconduct had occurred."[46]

The same sort of principle ought to apply, Burger continued, in regard to evidence that the police would have inevitably discovered. If the police would have discovered the evidence by lawful methods, then the fact that they, in reality, discovered it as a result of unlawful means should not be a reason why the police should be put in a worse position than they would otherwise have been in. If evidence was going to be inevitably discovered, it should not be subject to the exclusionary rule, notwithstanding the fact that the police obtained it unlawfully.

It is important to note that in Burger's opinion, the police did *not* have to be acting in good faith to be entitled to the benefits of the inevitable discovery exception. Even if a police officer flagrantly and knowingly violated the constitution, the evidence obtained could be admitted if the police would have, in time, lawfully discovered it without the constitutional violation. The principle that the police should not be put in a worse position than they would have been in if no unlawful conduct had occurred outweighed the concerns about deterring police from deliberate constitutional violations. The deterrent benefits achieved by excluding illegally seized evidence if it would have been inevitably discovered through lawful means did not equal the costs of withholding truthful evidence from the jury. After all, Burger argued, a "police officer who is faced with the opportunity to obtain evidence illegally will rarely, if ever, be in a position to calculate whether the evidence sought would inevitably be discovered."[47] In other words, a police officer's decision as to whether to violate the constitution will rarely, if ever, be influenced by whether he thinks that the evidence will be inevitably discovered. It therefore follows that excluding evidence that would be inevitably discovered does not deter police illegality. "On the other hand," Burger continued, in the rare instances in which "an officer is aware that the evidence will inevitably be discovered, he will

---

[46]*Nix v. Williams,* 467 U.S. 431, 443 (1984).

[47]Idem, 445.

try to avoid engaging in any questionable practice. In that situation, there will be little to gain from taking any dubious 'shortcuts' to obtain the evidence."[48] Therefore, in either case, the exclusionary rule produced little or no deterrence of illegal police behavior. If the officer is unaware of the possibilities of inevitable discovery, exclusion will not deter; if the officer is aware, there is nothing to deter.

On the basis of this analysis, which balanced the cost of excluding the truth from courts against the benefits of deterrence of police misconduct, the Supreme Court created another exception to the exclusionary rule. It is now well established that if the police are acting in good faith or if the evidence would have been inevitably discovered, any illegally seized evidence can be used in a court of law. What do these developments say about the wisdom of resting constitutional rights or remedies on cost-benefit analysis? If it is the case, as this chapter has suggested, that the scope of any constitutional remedy will adapt to the nature and character of its justification, does a cost-benefit analysis provide an adequate foundation? Does the deterrence of police misconduct provide an adequate foundation for the exclusionary rule and the underlying Fourth Amendment right to be free from unreasonable searches and seizures? Should the Court continue to create new exceptions to the exclusionary rule? Should the rule be abandoned or reinvigorated? If the former, what sort of remedy should the law provide for Fourth Amendment violations? Internal police sanctions? Civil suits against the individual police officer? Against the city, state, or federal government? If the scope of the exclusionary rule should be broadened, what sort of justification for the exclusionary rule is required? What sort of rationale must the exclusionary rule have if the scope of the rule is to be broad enough to provide sufficient protection for Fourth Amendment values? How consistently should the Court apply a broad exclusionary rule?

---

[48]Idem, 445–446.

The Death Penalty

GREGG V. GEORGIA
428 U.S. 153 (1976)

✦

The death penalty raises dramatic questions that lie at the center of any system of criminal justice. What is the purpose of criminal punishment? Must a penalty be proportionate to the crime committed? Do independent principles of fairness or justice restrict how punishment can be applied? In regard to capital punishment, the questions are more specific: Why have the death penalty? What crimes, if any, should be punished with death? How should the death penalty be administered to ensure fairness? Over the past generation, the Supreme Court has responded to these issues through its interpretation of the Eighth Amendment's prohibition of "cruel and unusual punishments." In *Furman v. Georgia* (1972), a divided five-justice majority held that the death penalty was being applied in an "arbitrary" and therefore unconstitutional way.[1] Though two of the five concluded that the death penalty was unconstitutional as a penalty for any crime, the other three refused to go so far. Hence in *Furman*, the Court did not go beyond ruling on how the death penalty had to be administered. It left undecided the issue whether the Eighth Amendment had any bearing on the questions of why have the death penalty and for what crimes.

After the Supreme Court decided *Furman*, opponents of the death penalty demanded its complete and total abolition while proponents tried to formulate death penalty procedures that would survive constitutional scrutiny. The results of this political struggle were fairly decisive. Thirty-five states eventually enacted new statutes that purportedly solved the constitutional problem of the arbitrary administration of the death penalty. One of these statutes came before the Supreme Court in *Gregg v. Georgia* (1976). All of the potentially relevant argu-

---

[1]408 U.S. 238 (1972).

ments concerning the death penalty were once again before the Court. Why have it? For what crimes? How must it be administered?

The Court's effort to resolve these issues was complicated by the fact that it had earlier described the prohibition of cruel and unusual punishments as a "progressive standard," as one that had to "draw its meaning from the evolving standards of decency that mark the progress of a maturing society."[2] For example, the Eighth Amendment prohibited certain punishments—such as whipping and branding—that were commonplace in the founding era. But if the cruel and unusual punishments provision was to be interpreted in this fashion, it seemed arguable that popularly elected legislatures, not courts, should articulate its meaning. Considering that public opinion has more of a direct impact on legislatures than on courts, judges should defer to the legislative assessment of the "evolving standards of decency." *Gregg* therefore not only provides a useful context to consider the constitutional significance of the different aspects of the death penalty—the why, what, and how—but also raises the question of the role that public opinion and legislative will should have in regard to the meaning of the Eighth Amendment. Despite the fact that most of the amendments clearly limit and restrict legislative powers, is it arguable that the Eighth is a special amendment that expresses rather than limits popular will?

The primary justifications for the death penalty are deterrence and retribution. The former approach is a utilitarian one that assumes that punishment is not a good in itself but an evil that must be justified by its effects. The death penalty is therefore justifiable only because it deters others from engaging in illegal activity in the future. In contrast, rather than justifying punishment according to a forward-looking calculation of good versus bad consequences, the retributivist looks backward. The criminal act was a legal, if not a moral, wrong that deserves punishment for that reason alone, and the punishment must be of a type and an extent commensurate with the wrong. Wrongs must be righted by the imposition of the proper amount and kind of punishment. To punish a person for some other purpose is to use that person as a means to an end, which is itself an immoral act. Hence, according to the retributive view, punishments must be measured and applied purely for the sake of balancing the scales of justice.

In the eighteenth century, Immanuel Kant (1724–1804), a German philosopher, formulated a particularly strict version of the retributive approach to punishment in his justification for the death penalty. First, Kant condemned any attempt based on the "serpent-windings of Utilitarianism" to change the amount of punishment that any specific criminal act deserved. Any such effort treated the criminal "merely as a means." The "inherent personality" of the criminal precluded the legitimacy of any such treatment. The kind and degree of punishment depended on the principle of "Equality" and the "Right of Retaliation." One who steals thereby "falls for a time, or it may be for life, into a condition of slavery." The sanctions for theft may therefore vary to some degree, depending on the nature of the crime. But according to Kant, whoever murders another must die: taking a life requires that the murderer's life be taken in return. It is not that the state

---

[2]*Weems v. United States,* 217 U.S. 349, 378 (1909); *Trop v. Dulles,* 356 U.S. 86, 101 (1958).

may execute the murderer but rather that it *must*. Even if a political society is about to disband, it still has a duty to execute the last murderer in its prison. Such an execution would not serve any useful purpose, but according to Kant, it was nonetheless morally necessary. The cosmic scales of justice must be rebalanced (see Box 5.1).

Cesare Beccaria (1738–1794), an Italian criminologist and economist, rejected Kant's premises and conclusions concerning the death penalty. According to him, the state had no right to execute a criminal because the "aggregate" of political authority was composed only of the "smallest portions of the private liberty of each individual." And since the individual never had the right to kill himself, he could not give such a liberty to the state. The death penalty could not therefore be justified as a matter of right but only because it involved the least amount of suffering necessary to deter others. However, according to Beccaria, human beings were "more powerfully affected by weak but repeated impressions than by a violent but momentary impulse." Therefore "perpetual slavery" (or life imprisonment) was a better deterrent than the death penalty because the convicted person functioned as a lifelong example to others, while the fate of the executed person was quickly forgotten. Indeed, Beccaria continued, the death penalty was counterproductive because of "the example of barbarity it affords." Rather than deterring others, it exposed the state to charges of hypocrisy. By "murdering" the murderer, the state implicitly endorsed murder. Beccaria concluded that the death penalty was not only unnecessary but also "pernicious" (see Box 5.2).

Beccaria's rejection of retribution and his assessment of the disadvantages of the death penalty made him one of the first modern utilitarian critics of the death penalty. Not all utilitarians, however, accepted his arguments. During the nineteenth century, the most prominent utilitarian defender of capital punishment was the famous English philosopher and economist John Stuart Mill (1806–1873). Mill denied Beccaria's claim that life imprisonment was, from the point of view of the criminal, a less severe sanction than the death penalty. Even if most people incorrectly viewed it as a less rigorous sanction than the death penalty, a life of imprisonment at hard labor was a life in "a living tomb, there to linger out what may be a long life in the hardest and most monotonous toil." A sentence of life imprisonment therefore produced more suffering than deterrence. The death penalty had the opposite effect. It left a powerful impression on the popular imagination despite the fact that it was relatively free of suffering. It effected "its purpose at a less cost of human suffering than any other." The death penalty, according to Mill, was therefore a most efficacious form of punishment (see Box 5.3).

Which of these philosophers is the most persuasive? Is the retributive justification for capital punishment merely a disguised form of vengeance? What of the dispute between Beccaria and Mill? Which is the more efficient deterrent, life imprisonment or the death penalty? Is Beccaria correct that capital punishment leaves the state open to a charge of hypocrisy and brutality?

Notwithstanding the philosophical objections to the death penalty, it remained a popular form of punishment throughout the history of Western civilization. During the colonial period, some of the American colonies followed the English practice of mandating the death penalty for a vast number of crimes. By

---

BOX 5.1

IMMANUEL KANT ON CAPITAL PUNISHMENT

... Juridical Punishment can never be administered merely as a means for promoting another Good either with regard to the Criminal himself or to Civil Society, but must in all cases be imposed only because the individual on whom it is inflicted *has committed a Crime.* For one man ought never to be dealt with merely as a means subservient to the purpose of another, nor be classified with the objects of the law of property. Against such treatment his inherent Personality has a Right to protect him, even although he may be condemned to lose his Civil Personality. He must first be found guilty and *punishable,* before there can be any thought of drawing from his Punishment any benefit for himself or his fellow citizens. The Penal Law is a Categorical Imperative; and woe to him who creeps through the serpent-windings of Utilitarianism to discover some advantage that may discharge him from the Justice of Punishment, or even from the due measure of it.... For if Justice and Righteousness perish, human life would no longer have any value in the world....

But what is the mode and measure of Punishment which Public Justice takes as its Principle and Standard? It is just the Principle of Equality, by which the pointer of the Scale of Justice is made to incline no more to one side than the other. It may be rendered by saying that the undeserved evil which anyone commits on another is to be regarded as perpetrated on himself. Hence, it may be said: "If you slander another, you slander yourself; if you steal from another, you steal from yourself; if you strike another, you strike yourself; if you kill another, you kill yourself." ...

[Anyone who steals] ... must for this purpose yield his powers to the State to be used in penal labor; and thus he falls for a time, or it may be for life, into a condition of slavery. But whoever has committed Murder must *die.* There is, in this case, no juridical substitute or surrogate that can be given or taken for the satisfaction of Justice. There is no Likeness or proportion between Life, however painful, and Death; and therefore there is no Equality between the crime of Murder and the retaliation of it but what is judicially accomplished by the execution of the Criminal. His death, however, must be kept free from all maltreatment that would make the humanity suffering in his Person loathsome or abominable. Even if Civil Society resolved to dissolve itself with the consent of all its members—as might be supposed in the case of a People inhabiting an island resolving to separate and scatter themselves throughout the whole world—the last Murderer lying in the prison ought to be executed before the resolution was carried out. This ought to be done in order that everyone may realize the desert of his deeds, and that blood-guiltiness may not remain upon the people; for otherwise they might all be regarded as participators in the murder as a public violation of Justice....

Source: Immanuel Kant, *The Philosophy of Law,* trans. W. Hastie (Edinburgh: Clark, 1887), pp. 194–198.

BOX 5.2

CESARE BECCARIA ON THE DEATH PENALTY

. . . The laws, as I have said before, are only the sum of the smallest portions of the private liberty of each individual, and represent the general will, which is the aggregate of that of each individual. Did any one ever give to others the right of taking away his life? . . . If it were so, how shall it be reconciled to the maxim which tells us that a man has no right to kill himself, which he certainly must have, if he could give it away to another?. . .

A punishment, to be just, should have only that degree of severity which is sufficient to deter others. Now there is no man who, upon the least reflection, would put in competition the total and perpetual loss of his liberty, with the greatest advantages he could possibly obtain in consequence of a crime. Perpetual slavery, then, has in it all that is necessary to deter the most hardened and determined, as much as the punishment of death. I say it has more. There are many who can look upon death with intrepidity and firmness, some through fanaticism, and others through vanity, which attends us even to the grave; others from a desperate resolution, either to get rid of their misery, or cease to live: but fanaticism and vanity forsake the criminal in slavery, in chains and fetters, in an iron cage, and despair seems rather the beginning than the end of their misery. . . .

In all nations where death is used as a punishment, every example supposes a new crime committed; whereas, in perpetual slavery, every criminal affords a frequent and lasting example. . . .

I shall be told that perpetual slavery is as painful a punishment as death, and therefore as cruel. I answer that if all the miserable moments in the life of a slave were collected into one point, it would be a more cruel punishment than any other; but these are scattered through his whole life, whilst the pain of death exerts all its force in a moment. There is also another advantage in the punishment of slavery, which is, that it is more terrible to the spectator than to the sufferer himself; for the spectator considers the sum of all his wretched moments, whilst the sufferer, by the misery of the present, is prevented from thinking of the future. All evils are increased by the imagination, and the sufferer finds resources and consolations of which the spectators are ignorant. . . .

The punishment of death is pernicious to society, from the example of barbarity it affords. . . .

What must men think when they see wise magistrates and grave ministers of justice, with indifference and tranquillity, dragging a criminal to death, and whilst a wretch trembles with agony, expecting the fatal stroke, the judge, who has condemned him, with the coldest insensibility, and perhaps with no small gratification from the exertion of his authority, quits his tribunal, to enjoy the comforts and pleasures of life? They will say, "Ah! those cruel formalities of justice are a cloak to tyranny, they are a secret language, a solemn veil, intended to conceal the sword by which we are sacrificed to the insatiable idol of despotism. Murder, which they would represent to us as an horrible crime, we see practiced by them without repugnance or remorse. Let us follow their example. . . ."

Source: Cesare Beccaria, Essay on Crimes and Punishment (Philadelphia: Farrand, 1809), pp. 83–91.

the time of the American Revolution, however, most states confined its use to crimes of murder, treason, piracy, arson, rape, robbery, burglary, sodomy, counterfeiting, horse theft, and slave rebellion.[3] The number of crimes subject to the death penalty in the United States continued to decrease throughout the nineteenth and twentieth centuries. During this same period, American law created "degrees" of homicide, subjecting only people who engaged in premeditated homicide to capital punishment. In addition, legal reforms gave the jury the power to decide whether any particular person convicted of first-degree murder should receive the death penalty or life imprisonment. Motivated by a humanitarian desire to soften the harsh administration of mandatory capital punishment, this reform produced its own anomaly: one murderer would be executed while an equally culpable one would be sent to prison. Mandatory review of all death sentences by appellate courts also slowly developed.[4]

Reforms also had an impact on the public character of executions. Not too long ago, executions were public events. For instance, on August 14, 1936, twenty thousand people looked on as Rainey Bethea, an African-American convicted of the rape and murder of an elderly white woman, was hanged in Owensboro, Kentucky—one of the last public executions in the United States.[5] Soon thereafter, executions became private affairs between the state and the condemned person. This development has a direct bearing on the dispute that divided Beccaria and Mill. Were public executions a better deterrent than secret ones, as Mill implied, or did they brutalize the onlookers, as Beccaria suggests? Should executions be public? Would the possible gain in deterrence be worth the price of potential dehumanization? Are such utilitarian calculations morally relevant to the legitimacy of the death penalty? If executions are private, are they justifiable as deterrents, or can they only be justified on the ground of retribution?

Many of the legal reforms that reduced the number of executions in the United States were brought about by a growing abolition movement. In 1845, loosely affiliated antigallows societies organized the American Society for the Abolition of Capital Punishment. The organization's first major success occurred in 1846, when the territory of Michigan abolished capital punishment for all crimes but treason. Further progress was slow and sporadic, and there were numerous setbacks. Though nine states abolished the death penalty or radically restricted its

---

[3]Hugo Adam Bedau, The Death Penalty in America, 3rd ed. (New York: Oxford University Press, 1982), p. 7.

[4]These developments are discussed more thoroughly in ibid., ch. 1.

[5]Watt Espy, "The Death Penalty in America: What the Record Shows," Christianity and Crisis, June 23, 1980, p. 192.

BOX 5.3

John Stuart Mill on Capital Punishment

. . . Few, I think, would venture to propose, as a punishment for aggravated murder, less than imprisonment with hard labour for life; that is the fate to which a murderer would be consigned by the mercy which shrinks from putting him to death. But has it been sufficiently considered what sort of a mercy this is, and what kind of life it leaves to him? . . . What comparison can there really be, in point of severity, between consigning a man to the short pang of a rapid death, and immuring him in a living tomb, there to linger out what may be a long life in the hardest and most monotonous toil, without any of its alleviations or rewards—debarred from all pleasant sights and sounds, and cut off from all earthly hope . . . ?

. . . [I]t is characteristic of all punishments which depend on duration for their efficacy—all, therefore, which are not corporal or pecuniary—that they are more rigorous than they seem; while it is, on the contrary, one of the strongest recommendations a punishment can have, that it should seem more rigorous than it is; for its practical power depends far less on what it is than on what it seems. There is not, I should think, any human infliction which makes an impression on the imagination so entirely out of proportion to its real severity as the punishment of death. The punishment must be mild indeed which does not add more to the sum of human misery than is necessarily or directly added by the execution of a criminal. . . .

. . . [T]he most that human laws can do to anyone in the matter of death is to hasten it; the man would have died at any rate; not so very much later, and on the average, I fear, with a considerably greater amount of bodily suffering. Society is asked, then, to denude itself of an instrument of punishment which, in the grave cases to which alone it is suitable, effects its purpose at a less cost of human suffering than any other; which, while it inspires more terror, is less cruel in actual fact than any punishment that we should think of substituting for it. . . .

Much has been said of the sanctity of human life, and the absurdity of supposing that we can teach respect for life by ourselves destroying it. But I am surprised at the employment of this argument, for it is one which might be brought against any punishment whatever. It is not human life only, not human life as such, that ought to be sacred to us, but human feelings. The human capacity of suffering is what we should cause to be respected, not the mere capacity of existing. And we may imagine somebody asking how we can teach people not to inflict suffering by ourselves inflicting it. But to this I should answer—all of us would answer—that to deter by suffering from inflicting suffering is not only possible, but the very purpose of penal justice. Does fining a criminal show want of respect for property, or imprisoning him, for personal freedom? Just as unreasonable is it to think that to take the life of a man who has taken that of another is to show want of regard for human life. We show, on the contrary, most emphatically our regard for it, by the adoption of a rule that he who violates that right in another forfeits it for himself, and that while no other crime that he can commit deprives him of his right to live, this shall. . . .

Source: John Stuart Mill, *Parliamentary Debates* (April 21, 1868), 3rd ser., vol. 191, cols. 1047–1055. Paragraphs inserted by the editor.

use during the Progressive Era, seven of them reversed course during the "crime wave" of the Roaring Twenties and the Great Depression. Only five states (Michigan, Wisconsin, Minnesota, Rhode Island, and North Dakota) had either abolished or sharply restricted the death penalty for any length of time. During the 1960s, several more states joined the abolitionist fold, but legislative efforts to restrict or abolish the death penalty ground to a halt during the "law and order" crisis of 1968. By 1972, only ten states had formally abolished capital punishment.

Though only several states had abolished the death penalty for all crimes, the number of actual executions in the United States declined during the twentieth century, especially after 1940 and especially in the northern and western parts of the country. Throughout the post–World War II period, the South executed more convicts than all the other parts of the country put together.[6] This fact alone raised the question as to whether the death penalty was being administered in a racially discriminatory manner. However, after 1950, executions began to taper off even in the South. Whereas 199 persons had been executed nationwide in 1935, only 76 met this fate in 1955, and only 7 in 1965. In 1967, Hugo Adam Bedau, a dedicated abolitionist, described the death penalty as "in the twilight of its historical role."[7]

Before the 1960s, few commentators disputed the constitutionality of the death penalty. Attempts to abolish it or limit its use were therefore directed at legislatures. However, in a 1963 dissent, Justice Arthur Goldberg asked three questions: Did the punishment of death for the crime of rape violate "evolving standards of decency"? Was the death penalty for such a crime "excessive" or "disproportionate"? Was the death penalty unnecessary in cases of rape because the purpose of punishment could be achieved by a less severe sanction?[8] Goldberg's questions marked a turning point. They inspired the NAACP's Legal Defense Fund (LDF) to initiate a campaign of judicial litigation against the death penalty.[9] From then on, abolitionist efforts shifted from legislatures to the courts.

---

[6]William J. Bowers, *Legal Homicide* (Boston: Northeastern University Press, 1984), p. 28.

[7]Hugo Adam Bedau, *The Courts, the Constitution, and Capital Punishment* (Lexington, Mass.: Lexington Books, 1977), p. 9. The first chapter of this book consists of an article that Bedau wrote in 1967. In 1974, Bedau predicted that there would not be another execution in this century. See ibid., p. 90.

[8]Goldberg's dissent from the Supreme Court's decision not to review *Rudolph v. Alabama*, 375 U.S. 889 (1963).

[9]Other groups, particularly the American Civil Liberties Union, participated in the effort to have the death penalty declared unconstitutional.

As part of its strategy, the LDF in 1965 initiated a large research project to see if racial discrimination had an impact on who was sentenced to death. These studies were inconclusive in regard to people convicted of murder, but they showed that African-Americans who raped white women were more likely to be sentenced to death than blacks who raped blacks, whites who raped blacks, or whites who raped whites. Accordingly, the LDF argued that the statistics proved that the death penalty violated the state's Fourteenth Amendment obligation to provide "equal protection of the laws." Race was an "arbitrary" factor that should not have any impact on the capital sentencing process. By adding this argument concerning the "fair" administration of the death penalty (the "how" question) to other arguments that directly attacked the constitutionality of the death penalty, the LDF, in 1967, obtained a *de facto* national moratorium on executions. No executions could occur until the Supreme Court resolved all the constitutional issues that the LDF had raised in its coordinated campaign of litigation.[10]

In 1971, the year before *Furman,* the LDF suffered a sharp defeat in its effort to have the death penalty declared unconstitutional. In *McGautha v. California,* a 6–3 decision, the Court rejected the LDF's argument that death sentences imposed by juries or judges without any standards violated the due process clause of the Fourteenth Amendment.[11] In his majority opinion, Justice John Harlan II concluded that it was constitutionally proper for a state to give a jury or a judge absolute discretion over the question of whether a criminal guilty of a capital crime should be imprisoned or put to death. He deemed the effort to provide statutory guidance (by definitions of aggravating and mitigating circumstances) to sentencing juries and judges futile and probably counterproductive. Moreover, he added, a death sentence did not have to be decided at a separate proceeding, as the LDF had argued. The jury that determined guilt and innocence at the trial could at the same time decide whether death was the appropriate punishment. Hence in 1971, the future looked bleak for the LDF's campaign against the death penalty.

In the spring of 1972, while the Supreme Court was considering *Furman,* the LDF took its arguments to Congress. In hearings before the House Judiciary Committee, Anthony Amsterdam, a law professor from Stanford Law School deeply involved in the LDF's litigation campaign, and Jack Greenberg, director-counsel of the LDF, explained why the death penalty had to be abolished, if not by the Supreme Court, then by Congress. Their testimony focused primarily on how the death penalty was currently being administered. Amsterdam claimed that the "infrequency" of executions made capital punishment an ineffective sanction, whether for deterrence or retribution, and expressed his hope that the United States would be bold enough to abolish the death penalty now, before all of the convicts who had been placed on death row during the moratorium (more than five hundred) were executed. After a four-year moratorium, the country should

---

[10]For a full description of the LDF's campaign of litigation against the death penalty, see Michael Meltsner, *Cruel and Unusual: The Supreme Court and Capital Punishment* (New York: Random House, 1973).

[11]402 U.S. 183 (1971).

not "regress," at least not if it "aspires to be at the forefront of advancing civilization." Greenberg highlighted the problem of race. He noted, for example, that of the 372 convicts awaiting execution in the South, 230 were African-American. With such figures, he concluded, any resumption of capital punishment would be "an expression of racial genocide" (see Box 5.4).

One of the most articulate defenders of capital punishment who testified at the 1972 hearings was Ernest van den Haag, a professor of philosophy from New York University. First, he rejected the argument that the death penalty should be abolished because it was "more often and unfairly applied" to poor African-American convicts. Such unfairness or injustice, if it existed, concerned the "way in which the penalty is distributed, not the fairness or the unfairness of the penalty" itself. The solution was to apply the death penalty "fairly," not to abolish a sanction that was neither "unusual" nor "cruel." The American people had every right to act on their belief that the death penalty was an effective means for obtaining "justice" and "deterrence." Though van den Haag admitted that statistics could not prove the death penalty an effective deterrent, he insisted that they could not prove the reverse either. Accordingly, he argued, since we cannot be certain of the facts, it would be better to err on the side of capital punishment. The "vain sacrifice" of convicted murderers is a morally better option than the possibility that the abolition of capital punishment would result in an unknown number of innocent people being murdered (see Box 5.5).

Shortly after the hearings were over, despite the *McGautha* precedent from the year before, the Supreme Court handed down *Furman v. Georgia*, a 5–4 decision holding that how the death penalty was being administered violated the Eighth Amendment's prohibition against "cruel and unusual punishments." The majority in *Furman* was composed of the three dissenters in *McGautha* and two justices, Byron White and Potter Stewart, who had switched sides. Why did these two pivotal justices change their minds? Was it likely that they voted against the death penalty because by this time, after a five-year moratorium, more than five hundred convicts were then on death row? Should such a factor have affected a Supreme Court justice's deliberations concerning whether the death penalty was a cruel or unusual punishment? Was such an impact inevitable? One result of *Furman* was that almost all of the people then on death row were resentenced to life imprisonment. If you were a justice, could you sign the opinion that would send more than five hundred people to their deaths?

Each of the five justices in the *Furman* majority wrote separately, eliminating any chance that the decision would be a definitive stand against capital punishment. Justices William Brennan and Thurgood Marshall argued that the death penalty was an unconstitutional punishment for any crime, but the crucial swing votes—William Douglas, Potter Stewart, and Byron White—concluded that the "unfair" system of administering the death penalty made it a cruel or unusual punishment. Douglas claimed that the absolute discretion of the jury or the judge allowed "the penalty to be selectively applied, feeding prejudices against the accused if he is poor and despised, lacking political clout, or . . . a member of a suspect or unpopular minority."[12] In contrast, Stewart characterized the death

---

[12]*Furman v. Georgia*, 408 U.S. 238, 255 (1972).

BOX 5.4

AGAINST THE DEATH PENALTY

ANTHONY G. AMSTERDAM, Professor, Stanford Law School:

. . . In 1967, in the year of the National Crime Commission's report, a nationwide legal challenge to the constitutionality of the death penalty began in earnest, and brought with it a judicial moratorium of executions. As a result of that campaign, the last man executed in the United States died on June 2, 1967. We have now had a period of more than four and a half years without an execution in this country. . . .

There are now 582 persons awaiting execution in the United States. They are found in 34 States and the District of Columbia. . . .

Who are these people? They have been described by corrections officials, Governors, criminologists and other persons familiar with the death-row population. My own experience conforms to theirs. The men on the row are universally without funds; they are generally poorly educated; and many have no lawyers—are totally unrepresented. They tend to be friendless and abandoned by everybody outside the walls of their prisons. They have no resources—financial, intellectual or human—with which to carry their cases to courts, to commutation officials or to the public. . . .

The result, I think is a rather startling observation. There are probably fewer than 500 executions under legal authority in the entire world today, including the Communist nations and the underdeveloped nations. If the Supreme Court of the United States gave the go-ahead and we Americans in fact executed the 582 men now on our death rows, we would kill more people than are killed by all of the rest of the nations in the world in a year. Even if we killed one-fourth or one-fifth of them, we would be the largest single killer on the globe; for South Africa, the present world leader, only manages to kill a hundred people a year—as in the United States, most of them are black. That should be a sobering prospect to a Nation which aspires to be at the forefront of advancing civilization. . . .

The real question is whether, once we have come to the point where we can already historically perceive that the death penalty is going to be terminated by our society, we will have the guts to terminate it now, without killing the few poor remaining relics on death row, or whether, at this critical point in time—after we have had a $4\frac{1}{2}$ year moratorium, and at a point where communist Russia is commuting death penalties, and fascist Spain is commuting death penalties under the pressures of world opinion—we, the United States, are going to regress and take up executions on a scale unknown in this country for decades. That is the question. . . .

. . . It is not retribution to kill 19 men a year out of hundreds and hundreds of convicted murderers. These men are not being killed because they have committed murder. They are being killed because they are poor, or black, or ugly, or all of these things. As capital punishment is increasingly rarely applied, it is inevitably going to be increasingly arbitrarily applied as well. It is going to be increasingly discriminatory to fall only upon those who have no money to hire a good lawyer, who are poor and powerless, personally ugly and socially unacceptable. . . .

Jack Greenberg, Director-Counsel, NAACP Legal Defense Fund:
. . . I will confine myself in these remarks to the racial discrimination aspect of the capital punishment issue, which has affected me most deeply and signifies to me most dramatically the mockery that capital punishment makes of this society's promise of true equality and humane justice.

The evidence of racial discrimination was strongly suggested by the national execution figures kept since 1930 by the United States Department of Prisons. Of the 3,859 persons executed for all crimes since 1930, 54.6 percent have been black or members of other racial minority groups. Of the 455 executed for rape alone, 89.5 percent have been nonwhite. . . .

. . . Of the 582 persons now under sentence of death, 373 are in Southern States. Of these 373 awaiting execution in the South, it is known that at least 230 are black as against 115 white, or two black men for every white man. In Northeastern, Central, and Western States, 209 persons are condemned, at least 85, or 41 percent, are nonwhite.

. . . I believe that one need draw no more from these facts than the very limited and clearly irrefutable conclusion that there exists ample evidence justifying a moratorium and [a] Congressional inquiry. . . .

Were capital punishment to resume in this country without this minimal inquiry, the result must fairly be seen as an expression of racial genocide. We owe it to ourselves and this country to conduct a full and adequate inquiry during the proposed moratorium to avoid any possibility of that national spectacle. . . .

Source: Hearings before Subcommittee No. 3 of the Committee on the Judiciary, House of Representatives, 92d Cong., 2d Sess., 1972, pp. 57–72.

penalty as "wantonly and freakishly imposed."[13] Apart from whether racial prejudice was influencing capital sentencing decisions, convicts selected for death were not, in general, guilty of any crime more heinous than those sent to prison for life. The death penalty was cruel and unusual "in the same way that being struck by lightning is cruel and unusual."[14] White's rejection of the death penalty relied primarily on a somewhat different factor: the infrequency of executions. The death penalty was "pointless and needless" because it was applied so infrequently that it could no longer serve the goals of either retribution or deterrence.[15]

The four justices who dissented in *Furman* were Chief Justice Warren Burger and Justices William Rehnquist, Lewis Powell, and Harry Blackmun. In general,

---

[13]Idem, 310.

[14]Idem, 309.

[15]Idem, 312.

BOX 5.5

FOR THE DEATH PENALTY

PROFESSOR ERNEST VAN DEN HAAG, PROFESSOR, NEW YORK UNIVERSITY:

. . . It is suggested that the death penalty discrimination against the poor and the black [is unconstitutional], inasmuch as it is more often and unfairly applied to them.

If true—and I shall not deal with arguments for or against the allegation—the suggestion would be nonetheless wholly irrelevant. It concerns the unfair way in which the penalty is distributed, not the fairness or unfairness of the penalty.

Any penalty, a fine, imprisonment or the death penalty, could be unfairly or unjustly applied. The vice in this case is not in the penalty but in the process by which it is inflicted. It is unfair to inflict unequal penalties on equally guilty parties, or on any innocent parties, regardless of what the penalty is.

Hence, with the reasoning of the bills before you, Congress should suspend all penalties, or none. Or much more reasonably, you should try to correct the judicial processes by which, it is alleged, the penalties are unfairly inflicted on minority groups. . . .

The second suggestion in the bills before you is that the death penalty is unusual within the constitutional meaning of that term. Now obviously, the writers of the Constitution did not mean to exclude the death penalty, which certainly was usual in their day. . . .

To argue thereupon that the death penalty should be suspended or abolished is clearly to parody the intent of the Constitution. That intent was to exclude penalties that an eccentric judge might impose and which would not usually be imposed for the crime involved. Or, penalties which have not been imposed by common consent for a lengthy period. I find no such common consent in this country. Or, finally, penalties newly legislated which are contrary to our legal tradition. Certainly, this would not apply here either. . . .

It is also suggested that the death penalty is cruel in the constitutional meaning of that term. Standards of cruelty vary historically. There is, however, no evidence to my knowledge that the majority of Americans now regard the death penalty as cruel. . . .

The only question before this committee is whether the severity added by the death penalty adds enough deterrence to warrant inflicting it. In practical terms the question is whether potential murderers are deterred by the threat of the death penalty who would not be deterred by the threat of a life sentence. That is, I think, the basic and essential question. . . .

Since we do not know for certain whether or not the death penalty adds deterrence, we have in effect the choice of two risks.

Risk 1.—If we execute convicted murderers, without thereby deterring prospective murderers beyond the deterrence that could have been obtained by life imprisonment, we may have vainly sacrificed the life of the convicted murderers.

Risk 2.—If we fail to execute a convicted murderer whose execution might have deterred an indefinite number of prospective murderers, our failure sacrifices an indefinite number of victims of future murderers. The lives of these victims could have been spared had the convicted murderer been executed.

Let me paraphrase this once more. The statistics are such that we simply are confronted with two risks. We may execute without thereby adding to deterrence and vainly sacrifice the life of the executed murderer. But if we fail to execute, we may have failed to add the deterrent that might have prevented prospective murderers from engaging in murder. We may therefore have been sacrificing the lives of victims who might have been spared, had we executed the convicted man.

If we had certainty, we would not have risks. We do not have certainty. If we have risks, and we do, I would rather risk the life of the convicted man than risk the life of an indefinite number of innocent victims who might survive if he were executed.

So, I urge you neither to suspend [n]or to abolish the death penalty. . . .

Source: Hearings before Subcommittee No. 3 of the Committee on the Judiciary, House of Representatives, 92d Cong., 2d Sess., 1972, pp. 116–120.

the dissents argued that the Constitution clearly contemplated the death penalty (for example, the Fifth Amendment permitted the taking of life if due process of law was followed) and that public support for the death penalty made it impossible to say that it offended "evolving standards of decency" or that it was an ineffective sanction. In regard to the fairness of the administration of the death penalty, the dissents claimed that infrequency did not necessarily indicate unfairness and that (since the whole issue was a matter of due process) *McGautha* was the controlling precedent. It was constitutional for sentencing juries and judges to have complete discretion to decide when to impose the death penalty.

Opponents of the death penalty had hoped that *Furman* would result in the *de facto* abolition of the death penalty, but they were disappointed. In November, a California referendum restored the legislature's authority to enact death penalty statutes.[16] In the same month, a Gallup poll reported that 57 percent of the American people supported the death penalty for certain crimes.[17] More important,

---

[16]The California Supreme Court ruled that the death penalty violated California's constitution in *People v. Anderson,* 6 Cal. 3d 628, 493 P.2d 880, cert. denied, 406 U.S. 958 (1972). The constitutional amendment, in effect, negated this decision.

[17]See the useful chart on American attitudes toward the death penalty in Bedau, *Death Penalty in America,* p. 87. In the mid-1960s, only 42 percent of Americans favored the death penalty, 47 percent opposed it, and 11 percent had no opinion. By March 1972, before *Furman,* the percentages had approximately reversed: 50 percent pro and only 41 percent con. Eight months later, after *Furman,* 57 percent favored the death penalty and only 37 percent opposed it. By 1976, the numbers were 65 percent pro, 28 percent con. See ibid., p. 65, n. 1.

state after state reenacted statutes that kept the death penalty but changed the discretionary system of capital sentencing invalidated in *Furman*. One approach was to have legislatively mandated sentences for certain crimes. If a person was found guilty of one of these crimes, the judge or the jury had no choice but to sentence the person to death.[18] A more sophisticated tactic did not eliminate discretionary sentencing but purportedly reduced it by establishing statutorily defined guidelines that judges and juries were to use as they decided whether to sentence a convict to death or life imprisonment. These guidelines identified certain aggravating circumstances that, if present in a particular crime, were to incline the judge or jury to decide in favor of the death penalty and certain mitigating circumstances that were to have the opposite effect. By 1976, the year that the Supreme Court reconsidered the constitutionality of capital punishment, thirty-five states had reenacted these sorts of death penalty statutes.

One of the states to reenact a death penalty statute was Georgia, the state whose law had been declared unconstitutional in *Furman*. Its new system was a bifurcated one. In capital cases, after a judge or jury returned a verdict of guilty, a presentence hearing was conducted at which evidence of mitigation or aggravation of punishment was presented by the defense and the state, respectively. A jury or a judge could impose the death sentence only if one of ten aggravating circumstances defined by the statute was found to exist beyond a reasonable doubt. The aggravating factors listed in the statute addressed the nature of the offender (previous criminal record, motive for the murder), the character of the murder (did it involve torture or the risk of others' lives?), and the identity of the victim (was it a police or judicial officer?). Without one of these aggravating circumstances, no death sentence could be imposed; if one such circumstance was involved, a death sentence was not obligatory but was nevertheless within the jury's or the judge's discretion. In this way, the Georgia statute reduced but did not eliminate discretion in capital cases. Finally, the law established an automatic appeal for all death sentences to the Supreme Court of Georgia. The state's high court could reduce a death sentence to life imprisonment if it found that passion or prejudice had influenced the sentence, that the evidence did not support the finding of an aggravating circumstance, or that the sentence was either excessive or disproportionate to the punishment imposed in similar cases in Georgia.

The Supreme Court considered the constitutionality of the Georgia law in *Gregg v. Georgia* (1976), one of five death penalty cases before the Court.[19] Lawyers for the condemned men adapted the successful arguments used in *Furman* to the new legal context. G. Hughel Harrison, the attorney for Troy Leon Gregg, a condemned murderer who had killed two men in the commission of armed robbery, claimed that the new Georgia death penalty statute was just as arbitrary as the old one. It failed to reduce significantly the discretion inherent in Georgia's capital sentencing. First, the statute's standards of "aggravating" and "mitigating" circumstances were "extremely vague." In no way did they effectively

---

[18]The Supreme Court declared this option unconstitutional in *Woodson v. North Carolina*, 428 U.S. 280 (1976), a case decided at the same time as *Gregg v. Georgia*.

[19]The other cases were *Woodson v. North Carolina*, 428 U.S 280 (1976); *Proffitt v. Florida*, 428 U.S. 242 (1976); *Jurek v. Texas*, 428 U.S. 262 (1976); and *Roberts v. Louisiana*, 428 U.S. 325 (1976).

reduce the judge's or the jury's discretion. Second, the statute had no effect on other discretionary aspects of the criminal justice system that were no less pernicious than the sentencing process itself. For instance, even with the new statute, prosecutorial discretion and plea bargaining allowed many felons to escape the death penalty though they were no less culpable than those who were sentenced to death. Gregg's brief assumed that any system of capital sentencing that permitted such a result was constitutionally flawed. A system that put to death only some of the criminals who were equally culpable violated the Constitution's prohibition of cruel and unusual punishments.

Though Harrison, who was not affiliated with the LDF, relied primarily on his argument that Georgia's system of capital sentencing was arbitrary, he incorporated (in the form of an appendix) arguments from briefs that the LDF had filed in other death penalty cases, including Part III of the LDF's brief in *Fowler v. North Carolina*, a 1974 death penalty case that the Supreme Court had delayed and had not yet decided. Part III consisted of a frontal attack on the constitutionality of the death penalty. Written by a group including Jack Greenberg, Anthony Amsterdam, and James M. Nabrit, all prominent lawyers in the LDF, Part III argued that the death penalty violated the Eighth Amendment because it conflicted with "evolving standards of decency." The "cruelty" of the death penalty, they argued, resided in its peculiar characteristics: its irrevocability, its inability to serve the goals of either deterrence or retribution, and its repudiation by society. Calling on the Court to exercise "an independent perspective," the LDF *Fowler* brief claimed that the constitutionality of the death penalty depended on what "an enlightened public conscience will allow the law actually to do, not what it will permit a statute to threaten vaguely." Therefore, despite the fact that thirty-five state legislatures had voted in favor of retaining capital punishment, the Court should take the next step. Having already severely restricted how the death penalty could be applied in *Furman,* the Court should now explicitly abolish capital punishment.

The brief filed by Georgia disputed both of the main arguments made by Harrison and the LDF. First, it insisted that Georgia's new statute established a nonarbitrary system of administering the death penalty. Actual cases were cited to show that juries were capable of making distinctions based on the statutorily defined set of aggravating and mitigating circumstances. Mandatory review by Georgia's Supreme Court eliminated any likelihood that an arbitrary factor influenced a particular death sentence, that there was not sufficient evidence for the finding of the required aggravating circumstance, or that the death sentence was disproportionate. However, in regard to disproportionality, the state argued that it did not matter if a few criminals who were as culpable as those sentenced to death received only life imprisonment. A death sentence was disproportionate only if this sanction was "generally" not imposed for the type of crime committed. No constitutional problem arose if the death penalty was occasionally not imposed in such cases. In the same way, it was immaterial that certain criminals plea-bargained their cases or that certain condemned prisoners were given clemency. There was no evidence, Georgia claimed, that such discretion led to "arbitrary" results.

Georgia's brief also attacked the notion that the death penalty was unconstitutional *per se.* The very fact that thirty-five state legislatures modified their death penalty statutes without revoking them proved that capital punishment did not offend contemporary standards of decency. Courts had no authority to rule that death was either an "excessive" or a "disproportionate" punishment because the entire question as to whether the death penalty served legitimate legislative goals was a policy matter for the legislature, not for the courts. At a minimum, it was common sense that the death penalty deterred some individuals from committing capital crimes. In any case, it was up to the legislature to decide if the gain in deterrence justified the ultimate sanction. The Constitution therefore did not limit what crimes could be punished with death. Nor did it limit why the state punished with death. It was within the legislature's discretion to decide if death was the appropriate sanction for the purpose of retribution. "The people of Georgia do not agree" with the proposition that life imprisonment could satisfy this goal as well as the death penalty. Finally, the brief rejected the argument that the infrequency of actual executions showed that American society had repudiated the death penalty. The fact that legislatures had reenacted death penalty statutes after *Furman* and that juries continued to hand down death sentences for particularly vicious crimes indicated that the majority of Americans still believed that people who committed certain kinds of heinous offenses should be put to death.

In *Gregg*, the federal government filed an *amicus curiae* brief in favor of the constitutionality of the death penalty. Robert Bork, the solicitor general who wrote the brief, addressed all of the relevant issues, from the general problem of arbitrariness to the more specific objection concerning racial discrimination in death sentencing. However, a particularly striking passage of the brief, from which the following excerpt is taken, discusses the respective roles of courts and legislatures in interpreting the constitutional prohibition of cruel and unusual punishments. Bork argued that even if the clause was to be understood in light of "evolving standards of decency," legislatures were to have the final say concerning the constitutionality of the death penalty because they were far better able to reflect "the will of the people." Opponents of the death penalty must not be allowed "to seek a referendum among judges as a proxy for the 'true' will of the people." Since the legitimacy of the death penalty rested on "unsettled empirical and moral questions," popular will was the ultimate standard of whether death was a proportionate punishment for any type of crime.

In an interesting exchange at oral argument, during which Bork responded to Anthony Amsterdam's claim that "death was different," Bork returned to this theme of the constitutional primacy of the legislature's will in regard to the Eighth Amendment. Amsterdam claimed that the discretion that pervaded the criminal justice system was constitutionally flawed only when the death penalty was being applied. Only then did discretion constitute a cruel and unusual punishment because death was a unique punishment. Bork responded that death may be different from life imprisonment, but that did not mean that it was a constitutional difference. If a sufficient number of state legislatures decided to punish jaywalking with death, Bork concluded, judges were to defer. Because the "will of the people" was the ultimate standard of what constituted cruel and unusual punishment, courts had no authority to invalidate any form of punishment that was generally accepted by state legislatures.

During his presentation at oral argument, Harrison highlighted the main contentions of the brief he filed on behalf of Gregg: it was "unfair" and "cruel" to condemn Gregg to death. After all, he noted, Gregg's accomplice, Floyd Allen, was sentenced only to ten years in prison. The state should not be permitted to apply the ultimate sanction in this haphazard fashion. The cruelty of the death penalty resided in the fact that the state did not have an adequate justification for taking a human life. "Two wrongs don't make a right." In response, Georgia's attorney, G. Thomas Davis, pointed out that Allen was only sixteen years old at the time of the crime and that there was no evidence indicating that he had prior knowledge of Gregg's plan to kill the two men they had both robbed. The state's decision to seek the death penalty for Gregg, but not for Allen, was therefore completely justifiable. It coincided with the state's policy of making principled distinctions between criminal actions that deserved capital punishment and those that did not. Davis described other cases in which juries and judges had made similar principled decisions. The thrust of his comments were meant to convince the Court that the Georgia system of administering the death penalty did not produce arbitrary results. It was a system of limited discretion controlled by appropriate standards and a set of checks and balances.

On July 2, 1976, the Supreme Court affirmed Gregg's death sentence. Though there was no majority opinion in the case, seven of the justices concluded that the Georgia statute was constitutional. Stewart and White—two of the pivotal justices in *Furman*—wrote separate opinions upholding the law. Two justices joined Stewart's opinion, while three joined White's. The differences between those opinions and between those opinions and the dissents (written by William Brennan and Thurgood Marshall) revealed deep divisions on the Court in regard to the basic question presented in *Gregg*. The Court could find no consensus about the respective roles of the legislature and the courts in interpreting the Eighth Amendment.

Stewart's opinion openly admitted that the Eighth Amendment did change its meaning in accordance with "evolving standards of decency." However, he continued, since thirty-five states had enacted new death penalty statutes and since juries still returned death sentences, there was no basis for the conclusion that the death penalty violated contemporary standards of decency. But this fact alone, Stewart insisted, was not conclusive concerning the constitutionality of the death penalty. Even if contemporary standards of decency tolerated the death penalty, it could still be unconstitutional if it violated "the dignity of man," the "basic concept underlying the Eighth Amendment." A sanction violated the dignity of man if it was "excessive," that is, if it was either "unnecessary" or "out of proportion to the severity of the crime." In regard to the "necessity" of the death penalty, Stewart claimed that its opponents had not met the burden of proving that it did not serve legitimate goals of retribution and deterrence. And though a death sentence might be a disproportionate sentence for many crimes, its imposition in a case of premeditated murder was not. Therefore, according to Stewart, the Constitution restricted what crimes could incur the death penalty but did not bar it as a punishment for premeditated murder.

Stewart also concluded that Georgia's new system of administering the death penalty no longer suffered from the unconstitutional arbitrariness and capriciousness that had plagued its pre-*Furman* system. Georgia's bifurcated proceeding, its legislatively defined standards of aggravating and mitigating circumstances, and its mandated review by Georgia's Supreme Court satisfied "the concerns of *Furman*." The fact that prosecutors still had discretion to plea-bargain or that governors could offer clemency had no bearing on the *Furman* ruling. Mercy could be granted to certain offenders without lapsing into arbitrariness or capriciousness. The objection that the sentencing standards would not limit discretion because they were too vague was rejected on the ground that the Georgia Supreme Court need not construe them in such an open-ended manner. The role that the Georgia Supreme Court played in reversing death sentences for crimes in which Georgia juries did not generally impose them ensured that no jury could impose the ultimate sanction in a "freakish" way. The new procedures therefore satisfied the Constitution's requirements concerning how the death penalty was administered.

In his opinion, Justice White covered some of the same ground that Stewart had. For example, he accepted Stewart's argument that the Georgia statute had sufficiently alleviated the problem of arbitrariness that had tainted its administration of the death penalty in the pre-*Furman* era. However, by citing his dissent in *Roberts v. Louisiana*,[20] a 5–4 companion case in which the Supreme Court invalidated a statute that mandated the death penalty for all persons convicted of first-degree murder, White rejected Stewart's claim that the Court could abolish the death penalty on the ground that it violated the dignity of man. Stewart had argued that the Court could throw out capital punishment, even if it did not offend contemporary standards of decency, if it was "excessive." White disagreed. Referring to the "profound" fact that thirty-five states had reenacted death penalty statutes, White said that such a ruling was "foreclosed by recent events, which this Court must accept as demonstrating that capital punishment is acceptable to the contemporary community as just punishment for at least some intentional killings." What White seemed to be saying was that public opinion, reflected in the successful efforts to reenact the death penalty in thirty-five states, had a bearing not only on whether a judge could rule that the death penalty violated contemporary standards of decency but also on whether a judge could rule that death was an "excessive" or "disproportionate" crime. Judges were to accept the legislative assessment that the death penalty was neither excessive nor disproportionate. Hence, according to White but not Stewart, the Constitution limited what crimes could be punished with death only if public opinion supported the Court's judgment. In deciding whether any punishment was either excessive or disproportionate and therefore in violation of the Eighth Amendment, the Court could not act independently of public opinion.

Justices William Brennan and Thurgood Marshall dissented, but on slightly different grounds. In calling for the total abolition of the death penalty, both generally avoided the question as to whether Georgia's statute had solved the problem of arbitrariness. In their view, even if the death penalty was applied fairly, it was still unconstitutional. The two justices diverged, however, in how they justified their interpretation of the Eighth Amendment. By ignoring the fact that thirty-five states had reenacted death penalty statutes, Brennan implied that this development had no constitutional significance. According to him, the Supreme

---

[20] 428 U.S. 325 (1976). The exceprt is from White's dissent in this case.

Court alone, as "the ultimate arbiter of the meaning of our Constitution," had the duty of determining whether the death penalty violated "evolving standards of decency." Its evaluation of this question, therefore, should not depend on public opinion. Instead, the Court must ask whether the death penalty was compatible with the "primary moral principle that the State . . . must treat its citizens in a manner consistent with their intrinsic worth as human beings—a punishment must not be so severe as to be degrading to human dignity." Applying this "moral concept," Brennan claimed that the Eighth Amendment required the elimination of capital punishment because it prohibited the "pointless infliction of excessive punishment when less severe punishment can adequately achieve the same purposes." Life imprisonment could achieve the goals of deterrence or retribution as well the death penalty. In short, since the "moral concept" of the Eighth Amendment restricted what punishments could be inflicted, the death penalty was unconstitutional *per se,* regardless of the desires and beliefs of the American people.

Marshall agreed with Brennan that capital punishment was unconstitutional because it was not needed for deterrence, but he rejected retribution as a constitutionally permissible goal. A "purely retributive justification for the death penalty," one that imposed the death sentence "because the taking of the murderer's life is itself morally good," constituted a "total denial of the wrongdoer's dignity and worth." Retributive punishment was therefore incompatible with the "core" of the Eighth Amendment. This conclusion went beyond what Brennan had said. According to Marshall, the Constitution not only restricted what crimes could be punished with death but also limited why any punishment could be imposed.

In regard to the separate question as to whether the death penalty violated "evolving standards of decency," Marshall admitted that he "would be less than candid" if he did not concede that the legislative trend in favor of capital punishment had "a significant bearing on a realistic assessment of the moral acceptability of the death penalty to the American people." However, he continued, the only public opinion that had constitutional significance was that "of an *informed* citizenry." If judges were convinced that the American people, if they knew what the death penalty entailed and how it was being arbitrarily applied, would find the death penalty offensive, they should invalidate the death penalty even if most Americans currently supported it.

Is there any real difference between Brennan's and Marshall's approaches to the role of public opinion in determining whether the death penalty violated "contemporary standards of decency"? Brennan said that a judge can apply evolving moral principles that are embodied in the Constitution's Eighth Amendment without considering public opinion. Marshall claimed that public opinion must be considered, but only after it has been "informed." Would a judge's estimate of what "an informed citizenry" would think be so heavily influenced by personal moral commitments that such an exercise would be indistinguishable from allowing the judge to decide the constitutionality of the death penalty by consulting his own interpretation of a "moral concept"? Of course, the other justices in *Gregg* objected to how Brennan and Marshall went about identifying contemporary standards of decency. Though some of the other justices said that the death penalty might be unconstitutional on the ground that it was an excessive punishment for certain crimes, no other justice claimed that capital punishment offended contemporary standards of decency. In their view, after thirty-five state legislatures had reenacted the death penalty, it was impossible and illegitimate for a judge to rule that it offended contemporary standards of decency. Which of these approaches is most defensible? What role should courts and legislatures play in applying the contemporary-standards-of-decency branch of the Eighth Amendment?

The *Gregg* opinion also covered the full spectrum concerning whether the death penalty was unconstitutional on Eighth Amendment grounds other than the one that it offended contemporary standards of decency. Marshall denied that pure Kantian retribution could be a constitutionally valid purpose of capital punishment, implying that the Constitution restricted why a state could punish. According to him, the Constitution precluded the legitimacy of Kant's justification for capital punishment even though Kant believed that the state treated the murderer as "an end in himself" only if it executed him. In contrast, Brennan claimed that despite what many state legislatures thought, the death penalty was unnecessary to obtain the ends of either deterrence or retribution and that it was for this reason unconstitutional. The Constitution restricted what sanctions could be imposed on what crimes. Judges were to make these determinations apart from public opinion. Stewart and two other justices accepted Brennan's principle that the Constitution, apart from public opinion, restricted what sanctions could be imposed on what crimes but ruled that the death penalty for premeditated murder was permissible. Capital punishment might be excessive or disproportionate for other crimes, but it was not for first-degree murder. Presumably, according to these three justices, public opinion was not the decisive factor in making this judgment of whether the death penalty was excessive.

The three justices who joined White's opinion, in contrast, implied that the whole question of whether a particular crime deserved the death penalty, whether to obtain deterrence or retribution, should be determined by public opinion through legislative deliberation. The issue of what crimes deserved capital punishment might implicate the Constitution, but judges should resolve such a question with a proper respect for the legislature's decision. Their view, it would seem, was that only if the legislature's policy diverged from public opinion could the Court rule that the Constitution restricted what crimes could be punished with death. In general, White thought that as long as the system of administering the death penalty was not "arbitrary" or "capricious," the courts should stay out. Apart from public opinion, the Constitution restricted only how states administered the death penalty; it did not restrict why a state imposed the death penalty or for what crimes.

Which of the foregoing approaches is the most defensible? The basic question concerns whether courts or legislatures are the appropriate forums in which to decide why death is the most appropriate punishment and for what crimes. What features of courts and legislatures are relevant to your opinion concerning which branch of government should make these decisions? If the Eighth Amendment embodies "evolving standards," which branch should decide whether the death penalty offends "contemporary standards of decency"? If the amendment prohibits "excessive" or "disproportionate" sentences, which branch should decide whether the death penalty is appropriate for what crimes? If your view is that the legislature should make these determinations, in what way does the Eighth Amendment limit legislative power? Does it trouble you that your interpretation suggests that the Eighth Amendment is more of a grant of legislative power than a restriction on it?

Of course, in *Gregg*, the Court did not question that how the death penalty was being administered was a constitutional issue that the Court should evaluate apart from public opinion. How the death penalty must be applied was therefore a constitutional issue independent of the questions of why it might be used and for what crimes. The controversy in regard to the "how" question is whether the Supreme Court was correct when it ruled that Georgia's new system had remedied the earlier problems of arbitrariness and capriciousness. What is your view? Does the statutory list of aggravating circumstances (included in the brief) provide meaningful guidance to judges and juries? Does review by the Georgia Supreme Court solve the problem? What if it does not? Is the whole criminal justice system not rife with discretion and arbitrariness? Can the death penalty be declared unconstitutional on this ground without declaring the whole system unconstitutional? Is death different?

BIBLIOGRAPHY

Bedau, Hugo Adam. *The Death Penalty in America.* 3rd ed. New York: Oxford University Press, 1982.

Berns, Walter. *For Capital Punishment: Crime and the Morality of the Death Penalty.* New York: Basic Books, 1979.

Black, Charles L. *Capital Punishment: The Inevitability of Caprice and Mistake.* 2nd ed. New York: Norton, 1978.

Haag, Ernest van den, and John P. Conrad. *The Death Penalty: A Debate.* New York: Plenum, 1983.

Meltsner, Michael. *Cruel and Unusual: The Supreme Court and Capital Punishment.* New York: Random House, 1973.

Polsby, Daniel. "The Death of Capital Punishment? *Furman v. Georgia.*" *Supreme Court Review* (1972), ed. Philip B. Kurland, pp. 1–40.

B R I E F S

GREGG'S BRIEF

[1. Arbitrariness.] . . . In response to *Furman*, the Georgia legislature passed, and the Governor of Georgia signed into law on March 28, 1973, a new capital punishment statute for Georgia, and it is under the new statute that Petitioner has been condemned to die. The question presented here is whether the modifications to the capital punishment statute wrought by the Georgia legislature are substantial enough to meet the minimum requirement of *Furman v. Georgia*—that the most extreme penalty known to contemporary man not be imposed arbitrarily.

The arbitrary infliction of death which this Court condemned in *Furman* and companion cases arose from various procedures whereby juries (or judges) were given the option to sentence convicted capital offenders to life (or term) imprisonment or death. Certainly *Furman* and the Eighth Amendment are to be extended beyond the specific procedures invalidated in *Furman* so as to forbid *any* arbitrarily selective imposition of the "unique penalty" of death, whatever the source or mechanism of the arbitrariness. The particular *method* of selecting some men to die while others in like cases live with "no meaningful basis for distinguishing" among them cannot be thought constitutionally decisive. For the Federal Constitution is not ordinarily concerned with the forms of state procedure, but with their result. It "nullifies sophisticated as well as simple-minded modes" of producing unconstitutional consequences. Federal constitutional guarantees cannot—as Justice Holmes wrote in another context—"be evaded by attempting a distinction" of form without a difference in substance. . . .

The new Georgia Law provides a bifurcated trial for the administration of the death penalty. . . . After the jury or judge returns a verdict or finding of guilty or after a plea of guilty to one of these crimes, a sentencing hearing is conducted before the jury or judge, and at this hearing, "the jury or judge shall hear additional evidence in extenuation, mitigation and aggravation of punishment, including the record of any prior criminal convictions and pleas of guilty or pleas of nolo contendere of the defendant, or the absence of such prior convictions and pleas." The State may present only such evidence in aggravation as it has made known to the defendant.

The judge is to consider or to include in his instructions to the jury "any mitigating circumstances or aggravating circumstances otherwise authorized by law and . . . statutory aggravating circumstances which may be supported by the evidence." The "statutory aggravating circumstances" for which the death penalty may be imposed in murder and armed robbery cases are [as follows]:

1. The offense of murder . . . [or] armed robbery . . . was committed by a person with a prior record of conviction for a capital felony, or the offense of murder was committed by a person who had a substantial history of serious assaultive criminal convictions.
2. The offense of murder . . . [or] armed robbery . . . was "committed while the offender was engaged in the commission of another capital felony, or aggravated battery, or the offense of murder was committed while the offender was engaged in the commission of burglary or arson in the first degree.
3. The offender by his act of murder [or] armed robbery . . . knowingly created a great risk of death to more than one person in a public place by means of a weapon or device which would normally be hazardous to the lives of more than one person.
4. The offender committed the offense of murder for himself or another for the purpose of receiving money or any other thing of monetary value.

5. The murder of a judicial officer, former judicial officer, district attorney, or solicitor or former district attorney or solicitor during or because of the exercise of his official duty.
6. The offender caused or directed another to commit murder or committed murder as an agent or employee of another person.
7. The offense of murder . . . was outrageously or wantonly vile, horrible or inhuman in that it involved torture, depravity of mind, or an aggravated battery to the victim.
8. The offense of murder was committed against any peace officer, corrections employee or fireman while engaged in the performance of his official duties.
9. The offense of murder was committed by a person in, or who has escaped from, the lawful custody of a peace officer or place of lawful confinement.
10. The murder was committed for the purpose of avoiding, interfering with, or preventing a lawful arrest or custody in a place of lawful confinement, for himself or another. . . .

The discrepancy between the regularity and evenhandedness constitutionally required in capital sentencing and the unpredictable arbitrariness which results from the modified Georgia procedures can only be appreciated after analysis of the various selective mechanisms which operate before, during, and after sentencing of defendants charged with crimes potentially punishable by death. For the imposition of a death sentence in Georgia remains an extraordinarily rare and fortuitous event not only because judges and juries so often seize the opportunity for mercy offered in sentencing discretion, but also because a death sentence signifies that a defendant has missed each of the many opportunities for a lesser disposition. . . .

The impact of the district attorney's discretion on the administration of criminal justice in Georgia is enormous and is unaffected by the new capital punishment statute: "Whom he chooses to prosecute, what he charges them with, whether he charges them at all, whether he later drops the charges or recommends a lower sentence at the time of trial are all within the prosecutor's exercise of discretion." In Georgia, the decision to prosecute and the choice of charges for which indictment will be sought are left to the district attorney's absolute, unguided discretion. . . .

Furthermore, the district attorney's discretion to plea bargain—a process by which an estimated ninety percent of all criminal cases are resolved—is utterly unfettered by the new capital punishment statute, or by any other significant restriction. The fact that capital cases are likely to take up a great deal of time in preparation and trial makes them particularly likely to be settled by plea bargaining. . . .

Once a Georgia defendant has been convicted of a capital crime, the sentencer has absolute discretion to impose a sentence of life imprisonment, since the procedure of finding "aggravating" and "mitigating" circumstances at the second stage of a bifurcated proceeding does not—and was not intended to—confine the unfettered power of the sentencer to spare the life of a sympathetic capital defendant. . . .

The particular "aggravating circumstances" specified in the statute are extremely vague, all-encompassing, and open to different interpretations in like cases, depending upon the subjective judgment of the sentencer. Terms like "substantial history of serious assaultive criminal convictions," creation of a "great risk of death to more than one person," and use of a "weapon or device which would normally be hazardous to the lives of more than one person" are extremely imprecise and leave great freedom to the trial judge or jury to define their content. In addition to the great vagueness of these phrases, their coverage is extraordinarily broad. To allow the sentencer to impose a death penalty if the crime of murder or armed robbery is "outrageously or wantonly vile, horrible or inhuman in that it involved torture, depravity of mind, or an aggravated battery to the victim" is potentially to authorize capital punishment for *any* murder or armed robbery. Furthermore, the list of statutory "aggravating circumstances" is not exclusive or exhaustive, so that even if the foregoing "aggravating circumstances" did somehow curb the sentencer's discretion, the sentencer is still free to consider any "aggravating circumstances otherwise authorized by law." Exactly what this phrase means is obscure but it is clear that there is very little limitation on the nature or scope of evidence in aggravation which may be heard or considered. While the statute sets forth certain factors in aggravation for the jury to consider, it nowhere directs that the jury may not consider other factors in aggravation. The statute does "no more than suggest some subjects for the jury to consider during its deliberations."

The statute does not define "mitigating circumstances," and the sentencer is therefore free in any case to consider *anything* a mitigating factor which should justify mercy. There is thus *no case at all* in which the sentencer might not conclude that some factual element was present which entitled the defendant to a lesser sentence than death.

The deficiencies of the statute, and particularly the imprecision, lack of objective guidelines and arbitrariness in the sentencing state engendered by the specified "statutory aggravating circumstances" are glaringly illustrated in petitioner's case. After petitioner was convicted on two counts of murder and two counts of armed robbery, a sentencing hearing was held and the trial court charged the jury on the possible "aggravating circumstances" it might consider. The jury recommended death on all four counts, conveniently using the armed robbery counts in aggravation of the murder counts and the murder counts in aggravation of the armed robbery counts pursuant to the circumstance that the capital offenses were committed "while the offender was engaged in the commission of another capital felony." In further aggravation of the armed robbery counts, the jury was instructed by the trial court that it could find that the robberies were "outrageously or wantonly vile, horrible and inhuman in that they involved the depravity of the mind of the defendant." How the armed robberies could possibly have involved the "depravity of the mind" of the petitioner is nowhere stated, nor does the statute require that it be stated. Instead all that is required of the jury in its finding of "aggravating circumstances" is the affixation of certain conclusory labels to the defendant's conduct and the incantation of certain magical phrases in the words of the statute.

In short, under the sentencing provisions of the new Georgia capital punishment statute, any case becomes a possible one for the death penalty or for life imprisonment, and total discretion is left to jurors and trial judges to determine whether any particular defendant shall be put to death. . . .

. . . [The] review process whereby the Supreme Court of Georgia is asked to determine "[w]hether the sentence of death was imposed under the influence of passion, prejudice, or any other arbitrary factor," "[w]hether . . . the evidence supports the . . . finding of a statutory aggravating circumstance," and "[w]hether the sentence of death is excessive or disproportionate to the penalty imposed in similar . . . cases, considering . . . both the crime and the defendant" in fact exacerbates the arbitrariness of capital sentencing.

First, the vagueness and breadth of the statutory "aggravating circumstances" means that the death penalty can be imposed in virtually any capital case, while the fact that "mitigating circumstances" are undefined means that the jury can find a reason to afford mercy to any capital defendant. Given this enormous statutorily-authorized sentencing discretion, it is difficult to see how the Georgia Supreme Court can determine whether "any . . . arbitrary factor" influenced the sentencing deliberations.

Second, the Georgia Supreme Court's reliance on cases that are appealed as a standard for determining whether a "sentence of death is excessive or disproportionate to the penalty imposed in similar cases, considering both the crime and the defendant," will provide no reliable guide to whether the death penalty is being uniformly imposed under similar factual circumstances. A comparative sample consisting only of cases appealed to the Georgia Supreme Court is drastically skewed in two ways. Otherwise eligible cases are ignored which were disposed of by various selective mechanisms described above. No account is taken of those capital crime convictions where a life sentence is imposed and no appeal is taken. The myopia inherent in this scheme will prevent ascertainment of the penalties normally imposed in particular circumstances. . . .

The capital defendant who fails to escape the death penalty during the charging, plea bargaining, guilt determination, and sentencing processes is subjected to a final lottery in which the Executive Department (the three members of the Board of Pardons and Paroles acting with the consent of the Governor) has absolute discretion to spare his life or permit his execution. There are no standards whatsoever for the exercise of the commutation power, and the state courts have "no jurisdiction" to review the grant or denial of a commutation in a death case. In the eighteen years between 1946 and 1963, 41 of 187 condemned prisoners (22%) were spared by executive clemency. In view of the precipitous decrease in the number of executions over the past few decades, it appears reasonable to assume that under the new Georgia death penalty statutes, a significant number of those defendants condemned to die will be spared through the exercise of the freakish mercy of executive clemency.

The preceding view of the post–*Furman v. Georgia* modifications in Georgia's capital procedures reveals that discretionary opportunity for imposition or avoidance of the penalty are, in fact, as numerous and as unregulated as in the pre–June 29, 1972, period. The arbitrariness present in all stages of the procedural system thus insures "that there is no meaningful basis for distinguishing the few cases in which ... [the death penalty] is imposed from the many cases in which it is not." ... It is submitted that Georgia's modified capital punishment procedures are no more consistent with the Eighth and Fourteenth Amendments to the United States Constitution than were the capital punishment procedures invalidated in *Furman,* and the Georgia legislature's attempt to evade the meaning of *Furman* should be recognized as nothing more than the exaltation of form over substance and should be brought to an immediate halt by this Court. ...

Part I of this brief demonstrated that the imposition of the death penalty remains arbitrary, random and occasional under Georgia's modified capital punishment procedure because that procedure involves a series of uncontrolled discretionary judgments that operate to spare the lives of some defendants while other in similar circumstances are sentenced to die. Part II of this brief will now attempt to demonstrate that the punishment of death is on its face violative of the Eighth Amendment because it is excessive and affronts the principle of human worth embodie[d] in the prohibition of cruel and unusual punishments as defined in the light of contemporary human knowledge.

To avoid burdening this Court with repetitive matter, petitioner adopts and incorporates the argument set forth in Part III of the Brief for Petitioner ... [in *Fowler v. North Carolina*].

Respectfully submitted,
G. HUGHEL HARRISON

Appendix
Part III of the LDF's Brief in
Fowler v. North Carolina

❖   ❖   ❖

[2. Excessive Cruelty.] ... [I]n the present case, additional considerations arising from the unique nature of the punishment of death require [a] uniquely stringent standard of judicial review under "the evolving standards of decency that mark the progress of a maturing society."

First, "[t]he basic concept underlying the Eighth Amendment is nothing less than the dignity of man." The Amendment stands to assure that respect for individual human life and dignity restricts the state's responses to even the most culpable criminal conduct. Yet the decision to use capital punishment on a man implies a judgment that his dignity and worth may be denied absolutely, that his "'life ceases to be sacred when it is thought useful to kill him.'" Such a judgment deliberately to extinguish human life—to employ a sanction that necessarily denies the very value upon which the Eighth Amendment rests—imperatively calls upon "the obligations [of] ... the judiciary to judge the constitutionality of punishment" from an independent perspective.

Second, the death penalty bears an awesome and irrevocable finality incomparable with other punishments. This Court has said of sterilization that "[t]here is no redemption for the individual whom the law touches." That is *literally* true of capital punishment. No eloquence can embellish, nor human mind entirely conceive, death's utter irreversibility. New knowledge, second thought, calmer passions, lessons of experience—every known corrective for the inevitable errors of judgment in penological, political, and constitutional experimentation comes too late.

Third, any balancing process which sets out to weigh the penalty of death in the pans of the Eighth Amendment must begin with the proposition that capital punishment is self-evidently cruel within every meaning of that word which a civilized, Twentieth-Century society can accept. . . .

It is not an overstatement to describe confinement under sentence of death as exquisite psychological torture. With the commendable motive—and under the inescapable obligation—of striving to avoid erroneous or illegal executions, Twentieth-Century American justice has prolonged that torture. Of 608 persons under sentence of death at the end of 1970, 302 had been on Death Row for more than three years, 165 for more than five years, 81 for more than seven years, and 67 for more than eight years. "[C]ontemporary human knowledge" of the nature of suffering and its effects upon the human mind teaches that over such extended periods the familiar manifestations of immediate terror cease as the extraordinary anxiety and pain of condemnation find other outlets. Anguish can no longer be conceived as some enormous multiple of the pain of a broken bone or a crushed fingernail, because human beings cannot tolerate many such multiplications without severe personality distortions such as the denial of reality. The effects of these coping mechanisms observed in Death Row prisoners are acute; the alternative is emotional breakdown.

The torture is perhaps more nearly comprehensible in the words of those who have suffered it:

> My feeling toward being on death row is unlimited. I can go on and on telling you the different feelings I experience being on death row. But I'm going to make it brief, because I can take the 68,634,000 square miles of the Pacific Ocean and put it into ink, and take all the trees in America and put them into pencils and paper, and still, it won't be enough material to express my feeling towards being on death row. My feeling being on death row is like no tomorrow. When I go into deep meditation, I can see life and feel the freedom that the universe has to offer, but when I come out of it, it's like being in the middle of a nightmare. So you can see why my thoughts has no end.
>   I feel as tho' the world is caving in on me.

The physical and psychological pain of execution itself—whether life is destroyed by gas, by electrocution, or by other means—is, of course, unmeasurable. It is one of the questions to which capital punishment cuts off an answer, leaving only such scant comfort or nagging doubt as speculation may provide.

. . . Here again, the ordinary deference due to legislative judgment encounters the objection that legislators, in common with all other men, simply *cannot* know significant facts on which advised, dispassionate judgment ought to turn at least in part. The decision to kill a human being is intractably a decision to do an act whose most immediate major consequences are unknowable. No amount of legislative inquiries or knowledge can close up that gap and all a legislature's "groping efforts" at experimenting with the penalty of death will not provide its members or mankind more information on the subject.

Fourth, the compatibility of the death penalty with Eighth Amendment values is called into question by its *de jure* or *de facto* abandonment among civilized nations. Capital punishment has been abolished by most of the countries of Western Europe and the Western Hemisphere, and is now in virtual disuse throughout the world. . . .

Finally, in suggesting that . . . [the Court should give the death penalty close scrutiny], we ask no more of the Court than society itself demands. Other punishments—even punishments of extreme severity—are and have long been accepted without the extraordinary controversy, the collective soul-searching, and the parade of elaborate justifications and rationalizations that have accompanied the peculiar institution of capital punishment. Despite the relatively minuscule number of its victims, the justifiability of the death penalty has been the subject of continuing and heated debate in religious, academic, legislative and law enforcement circles and among the general public. It is surely the case that "[a]t the very least . . . contemporary society views this punishment with substantial doubt." . . .

Agonizings of this sort that can neither be resolved nor stilled suggest a widespread perception that there is something fundamentally questionable about the penalty of death. In view of the extreme infrequency of its use, the troubled concerns which the punishment invariably arouses can only be explained by its uniquely and profoundly problematic aspects: its dissonance with the basic values of our society. . . . [T]he problematic aspects of capital punishment have not stayed state and federal legislatures from enacting it. But those aspects particularly warrant independent and stringent examination of the death penalty by this Court at a moment when the Nation, which has not executed a man or woman for seven and a half years, agonizes once again upon the brink.

Such an examination requires that the Court determine whether the manifest cruelty of taking human life is or is not "justified by the social ends it [is] . . . deemed to serve." Because of the unique character of the death penalty, those justifications must be real and substantial; and they must conform to the fashion in which the penalty is applied in fact. If "less drastic means for achieving the same basic purpose" are available, the State must use them rather than indulge in the "pointless and needless extinction of life with only marginal contributions to any discernible social or public purposes." This much is implied in "the duty of [the] . . . Court to determine whether the action [of killing people] bears a reasonable relationship to the achievement of the governmental purpose asserted as its justification," or whether, conversely, the punishment of death is excessive and therefore unconstitutional.

. . . [T]he question of how far retribution, standing alone, is a legitimate goal of the criminal law in the mid-1970's is a complex one; but this case does not present that question for decision, since the death penalty . . . is not retributive in any meaningful way:

> [T]he issue . . . is not . . . whether it is fair or just that one who takes another person's life should lose his own. Whatever you think about that proposition it is clear that we do not and cannot act upon it generally in the administration of the penal law. The problem rather is whether a small and highly random sample of people who commit murder or other comparably serious offenses ought to be

despatched, while most of those convicted of such crimes are dealt with by imprisonment.

The concept of retribution requires both a factual equivalency and a procedural regularity in the imposition of punishment which are simply not present in the administration of the death penalty for first degree murder. . . .

The most frequently voiced justification for the death penalty is the deterrence of capital crimes. However, . . . there is no credible evidence—despite the most exhaustive inquiry into the subject—that the death penalty is a deterrent superior to lesser punishments. . . . Official and scholarly inquiries have concluded overwhelmingly that use or disuse of the death penalty has no effect upon the frequency of criminal homicide. This conclusion is based on the following statistical evidence.

> Death penalty jurisdictions do not have a lower rate of criminal homicide than abolition jurisdictions.
>
> Given two states otherwise similar in factors that might affect homicide rates, and differing in that one employs capital punishment while the other does not, the abolition state does not show any consistently higher rate of criminal homicide.
>
> In jurisdictions which abolish the death penalty, abolition has no influence on the rate of criminal homicide.
>
> Jurisdictions which reintroduce the death penalty after having abolished it do not show a decreased rate of criminal homicide after reintroduction.
>
> Prisoners and prison personnel do not suffer a higher rate of criminal assault and homicide from life-term prisoners in abolition jurisdictions than in death penalty jurisdictions.

The same conclusion has been reached with regard to the "mandatory" death penalty; "no indication" has been found "that the mandatory death penalty [is] . . . a more effective deterrent" of homicide than discretionary capital punishment.

Against the background of this evidence that the death penalty is excessive and unserviceable in terms of the legitimate goals of the criminal justice system, we ask the Court to look again at the use society has made of it. For although the facts warrant a judicial judgment of excessiveness, the Court need not rely solely on its own appraisal of them. Society itself has pronounced a judgment, by its actions if not by its words. That judgment is that the penalty of death is both excessive and unacceptable.

To be sure, thirty jurisdictions have enacted death penalty legislation since *Furman* (narrower, in all but two cases, than their pre-*Furman* authorizations of capital punishment). But, in every case, the legislature has preserved or created a wide range of selective mechanisms by which the death penalty can be avoided in most cases. . . . In this setting at least, the number of legislative authorizations is not—as *Furman* properly held—an appropriate test of acceptability of a harsh punishment. For acceptability is measured by what an enlightened public conscience will allow the law actually to do, not what it will permit a statute to threaten vaguely. And the authors of even purportedly "mandatory" legislation—

legislation written to be administered through discretionary judgments of prose-cutors, judges, juries, and the Governor—can hardly be unaware that they are not in fact ordaining death except in a fraction of the cases covered by the statute. . . .

We are left, then, with the history of the past as prelude to the future. What that history shows is a rejection of the death penalty that "could hardly be more complete without becoming absolute." Given a choice of punishing "capital" of-fenders by death or something less, American systems of criminal justice have chosen against death for all but a scant handful of offenders. . . .

This reluctance "to impose or authorize the carrying out of a death sentence" is the more eloquent because of the context in which it has occurred. For it is fair to say that the conditions of administration of capital punishment during the past several decades have been such as to promote its public acceptability to the fullest extent consistent with its nature and the tenor of the public conscience. In the first place, every American execution since 1936 has taken place in secret, isolated by law from the public eye and conscience. . . .

The rarity and secrecy of executions account for the fact that, although it is everywhere agreed that the cruelty of a death sentence is such that its imposition requires extraordinary justification, the wealth of research and theoretical debate on the subject of capital punishment is largely ignored. The often noted fact that "American citizens know almost nothing about capital punishment" reflects two circumstances: we are protected by disuse and by official secrecy from its reality; and, as a consequence, there is no incentive to examine rigorously its justifiability.

But the death penalty also knows a different and less innocent kind of isola-tion from public consciousness and conscience. It is a fact of human nature that we respond more readily to wrongs committed against those with whom we iden-tify—those most like ourselves in appearance, background and mores. Con-versely, wrongs we would not tolerate when done to our own kith or kind are tol-erable when inflicted on those we despise or can ignore. The strong extant evidence and observations that the death penalty has been disproportionately ap-plied to racial minorities and to the poor therefore cannot be ignored in assessing the quality of such acceptance as the penalty has had. For present purposes, it matters little whether these disproportions are the result of discrimination, pas-sive lack of empathy, inadequacy of defense resources, or some more benign ex-planations. The very fact of the disproportion means that public response to the enormity of the decision to kill a fellow human being is blunted. To the average citizen and the citizen of influence, death remains a penalty for *them,* not for *us.*

At this point, description of the acceptance of capital punishment by contem-porary society becomes appropriately cyclical. For infrequent, racially and socially disproportionate application of the death penalty is maintained by the very atti-tudes it has helped to create. A harsh penalty, unacceptable in general application, is inflicted on the powerless and the unpopular while more sympathetic and at-tractive classes of defendants are spared. Thus applied, the residue of the penalty is acceptable to the public, which feels no pressure to restrict its broad availability on the statute books. The broad availability of the penalty in turn creates consis-tent pressure upon prosecutors, jurors, judges, and Governors, to take advantage of a variety of selective mechanisms to avert the punishment from all but an impotent and anonymous few.

This pattern of use, in turn, makes the justifications of capital punishment even more hollow. Reluctant, unpredictable and spotty application of the death penalty deprives it of the least capacity to serve its supposed penal functions. As a deterrent, it is wholly incredible;. . . as an instrument of retribution, it is inadequate, haphazard, and unjust. The few men whom it kills die for no reason; they are executed "in the name of a theory in which the executioners do not believe." Distaste for the penalty grows, and fewer men are killed as society "watch[es] without impatience its gradual disappearance." . . .

Respectfully submitted,
JACK GREENBERG
JAMES NABRIT
ANTHONY G. AMSTERDAM

GEORGIA'S BRIEF

[1. Arbitrariness.] . . . After *Furman,* the elected General Assembly of Georgia retained a discretionary death penalty but under controlled conditions. The statute provides for a meaningful exercise of discretion by adding to the checks and balances, which already characterized Georgia procedure in any criminal case.

The General Assembly itself continues to determine when a death penalty may never be imposed. To the necessity of finding a defendant guilty of a capital crime, there is now added a requirement in all capital cases except treason and aircraft hijacking, that a statutorily-defined, aggravating circumstance be present beyond reasonable doubt. Together, these definitions of crime and punitive circumstance limit capital punishment to only the most outrageous crimes (manifesting democratic abhorrence and condemnation of such acts), and to crimes which especially need to be thwarted by the ultimate threat (e.g., treason and murder of public servants, whose duties place them in great danger).. . .

The most frequently applied statutory aggravating circumstance has been the commission "of murder, rape, armed robbery, or kidnapping . . . while the offender was engaged in the commission of another capital felony." Of these, the most common instance has been callous elimination of a witness to a crime of greed or selfishness, usually armed robbery.

While not applied as frequently, the other statutory aggravating circumstances also have served already to control discretionary death penalty imposition in a rational, understandable way. Jury decisions and Supreme Court of Georgia review have added content to the statutory format. . . .

For example, Marcus Wayne Chenault entered a church on Sunday morning and sprayed the congregation with pistol shots in an act of terrorism, killing Mrs. Martin Luther King, Sr., and another person. The Supreme Court of Georgia had no difficulty in affirming a jury's determination that Chenault had "knowingly created a great risk of death to more than one person in a public place by means of a weapon or device which would normally be hazardous to the lives of more than one person." In contrast, the State argued in the case of David Jarell that his kidnapping of Mala Still at pistol point in a shopping center parking lot, without more, satisfied the same criterion. In holding that no evidence supported the determination, the Supreme Court lent credence to the proposition that the statutory aggravating circumstances are meant to be applied as confining agents, in a straightforward manner, and in consideration of their context as well as common understanding.

In a typical case, juries understand the concepts easily. . . . [A] jury has only to draw on its common human experience to understand the confining role and meaning the General Assembly intended when it authorized death for murders, rapes, kidnapping, and armed robbery, which are "outrageously or wantonly vile, horrible or inhuman in that [they] involved torture, depravity of mind, or an aggravating battery to the victims." . . .

Amicus contends . . . that "torture" in this same aggravating circumstance has "no perceptible boundaries" and cites *Floyd v. State.* Overlooked in this contention are the events which occurred in the William Lloyd Martin home in Atlanta when defendant Floyd and his cohorts arrived on December 12, 1973.

Floyd and his companions came to get money they believed to be in the home, but they did not stop at that. Young Ginger Martin, and apparently her mother also, were gagged by having thick socks stuffed in their mouths. At times, they were marched up and down stairs as if to harass them. They were subjected to the terror of being isolated from each other, and while they were apart, Mrs. Martin was told by defendant that he would cut off her daughter's fingers if Mrs. Martin did not tell him where the money was. The elimination murders were accomplished in a taunting manner. Defendant Floyd later laughed in recalling how Mrs. Martin put her hands up as if to hide from the pistol aimed at her, and how before he killed Ginger Martin, he bent over and kissed her.

In affirming the determination that this aggravating circumstance was present, the Supreme Court of Georgia correctly declined to hold that the moments of terror in the Martin home were not torture and in doing so did not render the meaning of torture in any way imperceptible. . . .

In summary, the "statutory aggravating circumstances" do operate in a rational way to confine jury discretion to impose the death sentence. They limit the imposition to the most outrageous cases, along straightforward guidelines, and in doing so, they also implement sound legislative policy determinations.

The 1973 death penalty procedures provide for "automatic and swift appellate review." . . . [T]he sentence review requires the Supreme Court to determine whether the statutory imposition of the death penalty is unconstitutional as applied in each given case.

Thus, on sentence review, the Supreme Court is required to determine:

(1) Whether the sentence of death was imposed under the influence of passion, prejudice, or any other arbitrary factor, and
(2) Whether, in cases other than treason or aircraft hijacking, the evidence supports the jury's or judge's finding of a statutory aggravating circumstance . . . , and
(3) Whether the sentence of death is excessive or disproportionate to the sentence imposed in similar cases, considering both the crime and the defendant. . . .

The first two criteria of sentence review, the search for arbitrariness and the presence of an aggravating circumstance, are meant to insure fairness within the context of the immediate case. The search for disproportionality in the sentence is meant to insure fairness when the case is compared to other, similar cases. Traditionally, the focus has been on the nature of the crime and, more recently, the nature of the criminal himself—the latter explored through pre-sentence investigations and bifurcated trials. Now, there is concern, not limited to capital cases, with the interrelationships among sentences of different offenders, considering the defendant and his crime and other defendants and their crimes. . . .

However, the existence of one "similar" case in which a life sentence was imposed does not by itself mean that a death penalty defendant's sentence is "disproportionate." To the contrary, the Georgia Supreme Court has said:

> As we view the court's duty in light of the *Furman* and *Jackson* cases and the statutory provisions designed by the Georgia legislature to meet the objections to those cases, this court is not required to determine that less than a death sentence was never imposed in a case with similar characteristics. On the contrary, we view it to be our duty under the similarity standard to assure that no death penalty is affirmed unless in similar cases throughout the state the death penalty has been imposed generally and not "wantonly and freakishly" imposed. . . .

Petitioner Gregg complains that he is the victim of capricious sentencing. Yet the reported cases under the 1973 Act now clearly establish the proposition that he is a member of an abhorrent but nevertheless coherent group. It is not at all unusual or freakish, and, in fact, frequently occurs, that a Georgia judge or jury imposes the death sentence, when a murder is committed in the course of an armed robbery or other capital felony for the purpose of callously eliminating witnesses. . . .

It is also said that the pool of similar cases is skewed by the absence of cases which were plea bargained, or were not appealed. . . . The assumption should be that prosecutors plea bargain in cases of the least culpability and the least conclusive evidence of guilt. In other words, the plea bargained cases are not similar cases to be selected for comparison. . . .

Nor does it skew the sample that there will be convictions of capital crimes, from which no appeal is taken. The problem has not been that isolated members of a well-defined group escaped death. The problem has been that isolated members did not escape it. Under the sentence review procedures of the Supreme Court of Georgia, as prescribed by the 1973 Act, each sentence is affirmed if, and only if, it can be demonstrated from records available to the Court that the sentence is frequently imposed in similar cases. . . .

Thus, the death penalty procedures passed in 1973 by the Georgia General Assembly serve several functions. They confine trial courts to considerations of the death penalty only in the most abhorred circumstances. They require careful appellate review of each sentence to insure its constitutionality. The sentence must be in an authorized category; it cannot be arbitrary; and it cannot be disproportionate to the punishments imposed in similar cases upon similar defendants. As implemented, the act has been accomplishing its goals and also has served to warn persons like petitioner that punishment of death will consistently be applied to those who take the lives of others in callous, selfish ways. . . .

Obviously, the role of the prosecutor is one where a large degree of discretion is employed. However, there should be a presumption that the exercise of that discretion is like that of a judge and implies "conscientious judgment, not arbitrary action." For the district attorney in Georgia who abuses his office, in addition to facing the electorate and the State Bar, he must contend with . . . the prosecution of a district attorney for misfeasance or malfeasance in office. . . .

Against the district attorney's oath, ethical directions and presumption that he is not performing his duties improperly or arbitrarily, what does the petitioner present to show arbitrariness? Only the bald assertion, based on a statement obtained from an assistant district attorney in another state in another region of the country, contained in a law review, that capital cases are particularly likely to be settled by plea bargaining because of the amount of time they consume in preparation and trial.

Can the same be said for prosecutors in Georgia? I think not. It has been this writer's observation that those cases in which the district attorney would seek the death penalty are no more likely for plea bargaining than any other case. But certainly a finding of arbitrariness cannot rest on bald assertions nor upon observations. . . .

The briefs written on behalf of petitioner describe the role of executive clemency in Georgia as a "final lottery," "an absolute discretion," [a matter that] "is not and cannot be constrained by any bounds or principles of regularity," and "freakish mercy."

Apparently, the petitioner should be informed as to the policy of the State Board of Pardons and Paroles. . . .

In Georgia the State Board of Pardons and Paroles may act on the commutation of a death penalty *only* when the Governor has suspended said penalty. In addition, any such action must be reported to the General Assembly at its next regular session. Thus, action by the executive branch of Sate government in commuting a death penalty sentence requires affirmative action by the Governor, a majority of the State Board of Pardons and Paroles, with an overview by the State legislature. In addition, for any abuse of his duties, a member of the Board may be removed for cause by unanimous vote of the Governor, Lt. Governor, and Attorney General. Therefore, actions in the area of executive clemency are well regulated. . . .

[2. Excessive Cruelty.] The Amendment to the United States Constitution basically involved in the present case is, of course, the Eighth Amendment. This Amendment by its nature suggests a more prominent role for the State legislature than any other Amendment to the Constitution. It is doubtful if anyone would seriously argue that the legislature is not presumed to embody the basic standards of decency prevailing in the society. Such must be presumed in a democracy. And, indeed, the petitioner has presented nothing that would suggest that the General Assembly has lost touch with the current social values of the citizens of this State. To invalidate Georgia's legislative enactments providing for a death penalty would have this Court encroaching upon an area squarely within the historic prerogative of the legislative branch, i.e., its duty to protect its citizens through the designation of penalties for prohibitable conduct. . . .

. . . [T]he petitioner urges that in this case the ordinary deference due to legislative judgment should be ignored because the imposition of a death sentence is fundamentally contrary to the basic values of our society. It would be interesting to determine how petitioner arrived at such a conclusion since as we have already seen the legislature is more likely to reflect the basic standards of decency prevailing in our society. The petitioner appears to be posturing that he is in better communication with society than the *elected* representatives of that society. The error in such a posture is apparent on its face. Since *Furman v. Georgia,* 35 state legislatures have enacted statutes providing for the death penalty. . . .

It is clear that what the petitioner seeks is that this Court hold constitutionally impermissible a punishment clearly permissible under the Constitution at the time of its adoption and accepted as such by every member of the Court until *Furman v. Georgia.* One must ask what has happened so suddenly as to cause the particular punishment to become so cruel as to become unconstitutional under the Eighth Amendment. . . .

. . . Upon what does the petitioner base his conclusion that capital punishment is not a deterrent? Apparently, upon various studies of crime rates of states with capital punishment as opposed to those states without such punishment and similar studies. The conclusion of such studies, that capital punishment is not a deterrent, is explained by the petitioner with the proposition that people who commit such violent crimes as would qualify them for capital punishment are irrational people who do not respond as rational people would expect. Such an argument begs the question. . . .

How can it possibly be said that the death penalty does not act to deter would-be crime perpetrators from carrying out their schemes? In *Powell v. Texas,* the Court presumed that the very existence of criminal sanctions serves to reinforce condemnation of murder, rape and other anti-social conduct. It cannot, on the other hand, be presumed that the threat of death has not stayed the hand and saved the life, simply because the penalty has failed to deter those who commit capital felonies. Statistics probably could never be gathered to positively prove how many capital crimes were averted by the existence of the death penalty, for no census gatherer or polltaker could persuade even one person to admit that he would have committed a murder but for the knowledge that he might have received the death penalty. . . .

. . . [T]he more reasonable view is that except for the insane (not punishable) and those fanatics who would welcome martyrdom, men generally weigh the costs or risks of the acts they contemplate. When the risk or the cost of an act is too high, men usually do not do it.

Even the Royal Commission found that there was some evidence to support the conclusion that the penalty of death is likely to have a stronger effect as a deterrent than any other form of punishment.

If human life is sacred (on this petitioner and respondent would probably agree) and if the threat of capital punishment deters *some* murders, then capital punishment should be retained. At the cost of some lives, more may be saved—the lives of those who would have been the victims of murderous assaults and the lives or liberties of those who have been deterred. If there is a genuine reverence for human life, there must at least be as much concern for the lives of those who are innocent victims of capital crimes as for those who have been convicted of a capital crime. The assailant is often seen as an object of pity, as a victim of circumstance beyond his control. However, pity for the defendant should not be permitted to misguide us into disregard for his victims and future victims. . . .

Although recognizing that one member of the Court has branded retribution as having been roundly condemned as an intolerable aspiration for a government in a free society, it is . . . [necessary] to address the concept of retribution. . . .

Contrary to what the petitioner would have us accept, there is a widespread view that justice requires that no man should be allowed to gain by his misdeeds; that an individual who commits a crime should "pay his debt to society," regardless of whether he is reformed by having to do so and regardless of the deterrent effects such payment may have on others. Such a view has deep roots in history. This concept, so deeply rooted in our past, has to a degree come to us in the present and thus should be understood. Mr. Justice Marshall in his concurring opinion in *Furman v. Georgia* noted that "[p]unishment as retribution has been condemned by scholars for centuries." However, Immanuel Kant, the 19th Century philosopher, should not be completely ignored. Kant has stated:

> Judicial punishment can never be used as a means to promote some other good for the criminal himself or for civil society, but instead it must in all cases be imposed on him only on the ground that he has committed a crime.

While Kant's view may represent the other extreme, certainly it may not be said that retribution is no longer a legitimate reason for punishment and thus constitutionally impermissible. It is submitted that retribution is a vital part of mankind's concept of justice. It is difficult for people to understand that in our "system of criminal justice" the victim should be compelled to suffer more than the attacker. . . .

How does the petitioner confront the concept of retribution? By the bold and singular assertion that "[w]ith these constitutional limitations, it cannot be asserted that any particular penalty is more supportable by a retributive purpose than any other penalty." The people of Georgia do not agree. . . .

Petitioner has alleged in his brief, by incorporation of other briefs, the contention that the public has repudiated capital punishment and attempts to support the contention by arguing that because all of those who are convicted of crimes for which the law authorizes a capital sentence as the maximum sentence do not receive that maximum.

Petitioner urges that if capital punishment were uniformly applied to all persons liable to it, it would be unacceptable to "the people." Such an argument would undoubtedly render all maximum penalties unconstitutional, because while it's true that contemporary society would probably not accept the imposition of current maximum penalties for every offender for murder or rape, the same is true for any other crime (such as 20 years for every burglary and every burglar, 10 years for every aggravated assault, 10 years for every first degree forgery and every such forger).

The argument is nothing more than a demand that we revert to a system of mandatory penalties fixed for narrowly-categorized crimes so that regardless of mitigating circumstances or the personal history of the defendant, the death penalty (or any other penalty for that matter) would be automatic once guilt was determined. It is difficult to see how such a wooden approach would be constitutionally mandated, particularly when the discretion of the jury has been regarded as the intervention of the voice of society against which the crime was committed. . . .

What the fatal degree of infrequency is the petitioner does not inform us. Nor does he inform us of the specific infrequency of imposition of the death penalty by Georgia juries. Yet he postulates that such unknown infrequency subjects an enactment of the General Assembly of Georgia to a finding of unconstitutionality. Certainly such blatant self-serving generalities will not suffice in a constitutional court.

Petitioner makes the mistake of looking only at the convicted criminal, with respect to punishment, and not to society as a whole and to the victim and to future victims:

> But justice, though due to the accused, is due to the accuser also. The concept of fairness must not be strained till it is narrowed to a filament. We are to keep the balance true.

The picture is askance if it is viewed only from the point of view of the condemned criminal. The Court must look at the penalty from the point of view also of society, of the victims in these cases and future victims of violent crimes, of the capabilities of current law enforcement as well as the capabilities of current penal systems.

The death penalty is a means of self-defense for the members of society. Capital crimes violate the imperative of social preservation. The contest is not between the State and the individual; it is wholly between competing rights of the individual—the right to be protected from criminal attack and the several rights in the amendments. A basic, if not the first, right of the individual is to be protected from attack. That is why we have government. Retention of the death penalty insures a greater fear in the potential criminal and thereby contributes to a more civilized society wherein citizens may live and move with a diminished apprehension of criminal attack. Forbidding the imposition of the penalty can do no more than foster social permissiveness among law-breakers at the cost of social permissiveness among law-abiding citizens.

It has *not* been demonstrated that the death penalty as provided for under Georgia law is excessive or disproportionate to a constitutional degree, barbaric, contrary to commonly-held notions of human decency, unnecessarily or inherently cruel. Petitioner has not met the burden of proving that the legislatively-provided penalties are contrary to the constitutional principles invoked.

The Constitution does not demand the abolition of forfeiture of life as a penalty for crime and as a weapon against crime by way of its existence as a threat; the Constitution does not demand that the balance of fear weigh more heavily on the citizen than on the potential capital criminal.

Respectfully submitted,
ARTHUR K. BOLTON,
Attorney General of Georgia.

BRIEF FOR THE UNITED STATES AS *AMICUS CURIAE*

. . . [E]ven if the cruel and unusual punishments clause must also be considered in light of the evolving standards of decency that mark a maturing society, the history of the amendment provides guidance to the understanding of how contemporary standards are to be evaluated, and how they are to be weighed against competing social goals. . . .

When a penalty is enacted by a legislature and imposed only by a unanimous jury, the sanction is very unlikely to be outside the bounds of social tolerance. In our form of democracy the will of the people is expressed through their representatives. Since this Court's decision in *Furman v. Georgia* at least 35 states and the United States have enacted new statutes providing for the death penalty. We submit that it is utterly implausible that so many legislatures can, time and again, fail to reflect the will of the people concerning capital punishment. Were this Court to hold the death penalty unconstitutional, it would have to conclude that it—whose justices are not elected and have been given life tenure in order to insulate them from popular and political opinion—is more conscious of and more responsive to the will of the people than are the representatives directly elected by and responsible to those people. Petitioners seek a referendum among judges as a proxy for the "true" will of the people. But if the people are to give their verdict of what is cruel and unusual, the people—through their elected representatives and through juries—must sit in judgment.

To the extent [that] the constitutionality of capital punishment depends not only on the limits of current social tolerance, but also on the nature of the purposes served by the sanction, we submit that capital punishment serves important and legitimate purposes. Because capital punishment is society's "ultimate" sanction, it is likely to have a stronger effect as a deterrent than do alternative sanctions. . . . This alone is sufficient to satisfy any constitutional requirement that the death penalty serve important social purposes.

Capital punishment of course has other purposes as well. The death penalty serves a vital function as society's expression of moral outrage, and marks off some crimes as so repulsive that they are to be avoided by those individuals with even a trace of social responsibility. Some crimes, too, are so vicious, so offensive to society's standards of decency, that they call out for an ultimate sanction in order to reinforce the social feeling of revulsion to acts of that character. This response—retribution perhaps, although without vindictiveness—has been endorsed by respected commentators and seems an essential ingredient of a healthy society.

Finally, capital punishment incapacitates some individuals who, if allowed to remain alive, would be so immune to normal forms of social control that they would continue to commit murders even if sentenced to life imprisonment without possibility of parole. The federal prison system now confines at least one man who, since his incarceration for murder, has committed and been convicted of murders within prison on three separate occasions. This man, and others like him, will find opportunities to kill again, regardless of the care taken to guard them, and we submit that the Eighth Amendment does not compel society to grant them those opportunities.

Although there may be legitimate differences of opinion regarding capital punishment's propriety and utility in modern society, its value as a deterrent, and society's need for it to reinforce social values and incapacitate dangerous offenders, those differences of opinion are to be resolved by the legislature. The legislative judgment on these matters should be accepted by the judicial arm. Once the Court has satisfied itself that there is support for the legislature's decision, its role has been exhausted. An omniscient observer might conclude that all legislatures were mistaken in believing that capital punishment is ever appropriate, but the data such an observer would use, and the standards he would apply when weighing the moral values implicated in the death penalty, are beyond the ken of courts and perhaps beyond the ken of mankind. The judgment of a legislature that capital punishment is necessary and appropriate is based on its evaluation of unsettled empirical and moral questions, and its resolution of those questions should not be cast aside. . . .

Respectfully submitted,
ROBERT H. BORK,
Solicitor General of the United States.

ORAL ARGUMENT

MR. AMSTERDAM[21] [Legal Defense Fund Attorney]: . . . What *Furman* said was that when a procedure of that sort resulted in an arbitrary dispensation of death across the total range of those cases in which it was authorized, so that the infliction of the death penalty on a particular individual was senseless—his case being indistinguishable from that of others who were spared—the imposition of that death penalty only on him was cruel and unusual in a constitutional sense because he was being selected out of an indistinguishable group for no reason to suffer a penalty inordinately greater than that suffered by others—no rhyme or reason, no justification.

This arbitrariness defeated the penological justifications for capital punishment; this arbitrariness made the death penalty unusual in a constitutional sense; and it is our submission that it doesn't matter whether one device or another is used to achieve that result. The Federal—

JUSTICE STEWART: Mr. Amsterdam, doesn't your argument prove too much? In other words, in our system of adversary criminal justice, we have prosecutorial discretion; we have jury discretion, including jury nullification, which is known; we have the practice of submitting to the jury the option of returning verdicts of lesser included offenses; we have appellate review; and we have the possibility of executive clemency. And that is true throughout our adversary system of justice. And if a person is sentenced to anything as the end product of that system, under your argument, his sentence, be it life impris-

---

[21]Amsterdam presented the arguments for the petitioners in *Jurek v. Texas* and *Roberts v. Louisiana*, two cases that the Supreme Court considered along with *Gregg v. Georgia*.

onment or five years imprisonment, is a cruel and unusual punishment because it is the product of this system. That is your argument, isn't it?

AMSTERDAM: No.

STEWART: And why not?

AMSTERDAM: It is not. Our argument is essentially that death is different. If you don't accept the view that for constitutional purposes death is different, we lose this case, let me make that very clear. There is nothing that we argue in this case that will touch imprisonment, life imprisonment, any of those things.

Now, why do we say death is different? One, because this Court in *Furman* said it was different. It seems to me that there is no doubt that this Court did not mean to strike down in *Furman* sentences of life imprisonment, twenty years, ten years, although courts have just as broad discretion to sentence to those things or less as they did for life and death under the system invalidated in *Furman*.

. . . Our legal system, as a whole, has always treated death differently. We allow more peremptory challenges; we allow automatic appeals; we have indulging requirements, unanimous verdict requirements in some jurisdictions, because death is different.

And, finally, death is factually different. Death is final. Death is irremediable. Death is unnullable; it goes beyond this world; it is a legislative decision to do something and we know not what we do. Death is different because even if exactly the same discretionary procedures are used to decide issues of five years versus ten years or life versus death, the result will be more arbitrary on the life or death choice.

Now, why do I say the result will be more arbitrary on the life or death choice? It will be more arbitrary on the life or death choice because the magnitude of what is at stake. . . . [T]o kill somebody or spare him dwarfs the factual differences on which the decision is to be made; renders them . . . demeaningly trivial, compared to the stakes in a way that no such other decision is unrelated to the factual basis on which it is made.

The decision is different, the discretion is different, and the result is different, Mr. Justice Stewart, in a death case than in a case where lesser penalties are issued, because, as the history of capital punishment, under the discretionary system struck down in *Furman* shows, the death penalty has become so repugnant, so abhorrent to those who must actually apply it in particular cases, as distinguished in the abstract question of having it on the books, that in order for a jury and a judge and a prosecutor and a governor to condemn a defendant, an intense *ad hominem* condemnatory judgment has to be made, which is very different from the kind of judgment applied when it is applied with the ten-year question; which is a judgment that is uniquely difficult to control, uniquely difficult to rationalize or regularize.

Now, that, combined with the breadth of discretion which is in the system, some of which is like the discretion involved elsewhere and some of which is not, create[s] a total pattern whose result is that the infliction of death on specific defendants condemned to die is cruel and unusual.

❊   ❊   ❊

CHIEF JUSTICE BURGER: What you are saying, I take it, is that the frequency or infrequency has nothing to do with the term "unusual" as used in the Eighth Amendment?

MR. BORK [Solicitor General of the United States]:   I think that is right, Mr. Chief Justice. I think it is the infrequency of the type of punishment. That is, in *Weems,* we had *cadena temporal,* an extraordinary Spanish punishment, unknown to our jurisprudence, and that is why it was unusual, and not because it was only rarely inflicted. . . .

Now, I think "cruel," as the Court suggested in *Weems,* means a punishment which is amazing in its lack of proportion to the offense. I don't think the Court defines . . . whether there is an exact proportion. I think it has to be so wildly out of proportion that it becomes cruel.

JUSTICE WHITE: It means that, perhaps, but it doesn't mean only that. I mean, in other words, you would concede, I would suppose, that if a state imposed and inflicted capital punishment for jaywalking, it would be cruel and unusual punishment, even though, as you submitted to us, capital punishment per se is not cruel and unusual? But it means—and that is your point now—but also what if a state said that for the most heinous kind of first degree murders we are going to inflict breaking a man on the wheel and then disemboweling him while he is still alive and then burning him up: What would you say to that?

BORK: I would say that that practice is so out of step with modern morality and modern jurisprudence that the state cannot return to it. That kind of torture was precisely what the framers thought they were outlawing when they wrote the cruel and unusual punishment clause.

WHITE: So it is not just disproportionality, is it?

BORK: No, no. It is also that it is foreign to our jurisprudence, but has become for some time completely out of step with our morality—which that has become—so the state could not revert to those kinds of punishments.

WHITE: So you also accept judging the cruelty in the light of contemporary morality?

BORK: I do indeed, Mr. Justice White. . . . [H]owever, . . . once we have thirty-five [states] . . . adopting a penalty, it is impossible to say that it is in conflict with current morality, because I think there is no other source of current morality to which a court may properly look; that is, it may not look to the writings of the more enlightened professors.

WHITE: And do you say the same as to the question of proportionality, or do courts have some independent input into that question?

BORK: I think the proportionality would have to be judged on objective standards as well; that is, . . . proportionality would be judged by the frequency with which legislatures choose. If one jurisdiction only suddenly imposed death for jaywalking, or flogging for jaywalking, I think, looking across the spectrum of the American commonwealths and seeing that that was wildly out of proportion with every other jurisdiction would be one way of judging proportionality.

WHITE: So if enough legislatures pass a law, you would say the courts have no basis to say that the penalty is disproportionate?

BORK: I doubt very much, Mr. Justice White, whether a court could—disproportionateness depends in great part upon the moral understanding of the community. If the moral understanding of the community in a very widespread way views the punishment as proportionate, I don't know what independent source a court would have to look to.

✿   ✿   ✿

MR. BORK: These arguments that are made against the death penalty could be made against any other form of punishment. There is not one of them that does not apply to life imprisonment. Now, the sole answer that counsel gives to this is that capital punishment is unique, it is different. Of course, it is different. Life imprisonment is different from a year imprisonment. Life imprisonment is different from a fine.

JUSTICE STEWART: But it is different in kind from any term of imprisonment, is it not, in two or three different respects? At least it is wholly irretrievable, for one thing— . . .

BORK: Mr. Justice Stewart, I don't know how a life spent in prison is—

STEWART: Well, if you made a mistake, you can cancel it—

BORK: Oh, I see.

THE COURT: —and undo it.

BORK: You can undo it to the extent you set him free when you discover the mistake, but the years are gone.

STEWART: That's right. And it wholly discards any notion of rehabilitation, of course. It is different in that respect.

BORK: It does that.

STEWART: And it is different in other respects, is it not, not in degree but in kind, it is, and—

BORK: Well, I would suggest as to that, Mr. Justice Stewart, there is only one respect in which it is not different, and that is in contemplation of the Constitution, because the Constitution provides for it, with imprisonment. It draws no line between them. A legislative line can be drawn between them, but I don't think a constitutional line can be drawn between them.

Capital punishment is also different in one other respect, which I would like to come to, if I have time. It is different in that it deters more than any other punishment. There are some categories of criminals who cannot be deterred any other way. For example, the man serving life imprisonment, and he knows it is a real life term, has no incentive not to kill, and some of them have done so. A man who has committed an offense which carries life imprisonment, but who has not yet been apprehended, has no incentive not to kill to escape and to commit other crimes, except the prospect of a death penalty. So that, as the ultimate sanction, capital punishment is unique; it is different in the sense that it deters more and thereby saves more innocent lives; and it is unique in that it upholds the basic values of our society symbolically and internalizes them for us more than any other punishment.

So its uniqueness, I think, is something that has to be weighed in favor of the punishment as well. But I return to my point that I don't think it is unique in the constitutional sense. In fact, the argument for its uniqueness that was made yesterday was that we recognize it is unique because we surround it by so many precautions and procedural safeguards that other punishments don't have. Well, I think that is true, although I don't see why the very existence of precautions makes it unconstitutional. . . . Presumably the same thing would happen if we began to add the same precautions to life imprisonment: It would become unconstitutional, because we recognize its uniqueness.

❖   ❖   ❖

MR. HARRISON [Attorney for Gregg]:   . . . There were two people who were involved in an incident, two people, one suffering the death sentence and one going away with ten years, for no reason, no explainable reason. Gregg [had] no prior record. He admitted he killed the people, but he said he did it in self-defense. The jury rejected it and that apparently is the end of it. He is still suffering the death penalty and he is under it today. . . .

Your Honor, we submit that the 1973 law was an attempt to meet *Furman,* and it hasn't done it. It still leaves that discretion, both in the prosecution. I submit to you, whether it's right or wrong—and I would be the first to admit that some discretion must be vested in a prosecuting attorney. We must have it. But is that to be unlimited, and is it to have the right to carry with it, "You live, you die."

❖   ❖   ❖

MR. HARRISON: . . . Your Honor, we submit that under these circumstances, that in this case we do not have to go to the ultimate question of the death penalty under the Eighth Amendment, even though we say that even there we question the sufficiency of proof to justify the taking of human life. Two wrongs don't make a right. . . .

. . . [T]his Court can take and can consider any punishment imposable under the judicial system in this country today, and . . . [ask] "Does it meet the

test of the Eighth Amendment?" without any apologies to anyone anywhere
. . . . The bottom line is: Is it justified, or has the Government proven that it is
such a punishment, has it proven that there is such a deterrent that in 1976
we will continue to impose the death penalty under such conditions when we
don't know for sure[?]

✾   ✾   ✾

MR. DAVIS [Attorney for Georgia]:   Briefly at the beginning I wish to address a
few of the comments made by Mr. Harrison as to the facts of this case. . . .
　　The jury determined beyond a reasonable doubt that Mr. Gregg was guilty
of two murders with malice while in the commission of an armed robbery.
Mr. Harrison has intimated that another man involved in the crime was somehow arbitrarily and capriciously not sentenced to death, but given a sentence
in years. Mr. Harrison has failed to point out that the other man—Mr.
Allen—involved, was sixteen years of age and could not have been punished
by death in Georgia. Additionally, there was no evidence to indicate that he
had any prior knowledge of Mr. Gregg's planning to kill these two men.

✾   ✾   ✾

MR. DAVIS: A number of these aggravating circumstances have been attacked—
either by petitioner or *amicus* on behalf of petitioner—as being overly broad,
as being meaningless. . . .
　　. . . [One] statutory aggravating circumstance they attack as being meaningless and overbroad is number (7), which involves torture and depravity of
mind. In the case of *McCorkadale v. State,* where McCorkadale tortured a
young woman for hours by use of acid, fire, surgical scissors, kept her alive—
it's amazing the woman lived as long as she did—finally breaking her limbs
and stuffing her into a trunk, the jury found statutory aggravating circumstance number (7). There was no problem in affirming that. That would be
torture to anyone.
　　Petitioner, in brief of *amicus*—and I may refer to the petitioner when I
mean the Legal Defense Fund [which] submitted a brief in his behalf—cites
the case of *Floyd v. State* as an obvious inappropriate use of statutory aggravating circumstance number (7)—torture again. The question—it's overly
broad—what is torture? In the case of *Floyd,* Floyd entered the home, forced
the mother and the daughter . . . to march up and down the stairs, trying to
force from them the location of money; separated them, threatened the
mother with cutting fingers off the daughter; brought them together, knelt
them down, put the gun to the daughter's head, kissed her good-bye and blew
her brains out in her mother's presence and then, turning to the mother, blew
her brains out, laughing that she put up her hand to shield from the bullet.
He thought that was humorous. The jury found torture, aggravating circumstance number (7). . . .

THE OPINION

Mr. Justice Stewart . . .

. . . [T]he Eighth Amendment has not been regarded as a static concept. As Mr. Chief Justice Warren said, in an oft-quoted phrase, "[t]he Amendment must draw its meaning from the evolving standards of decency that mark the progress of a maturing society." Thus, an assessment of contemporary values concerning the infliction of a challenged sanction is relevant to the application of the Eighth Amendment. . . .

But our cases also make clear that public perceptions of standards of decency with respect to criminal sanctions are not conclusive. A penalty also must accord with "the dignity of man," which is the "basic concept underlying the Eighth Amendment." This means, at least, that the punishment not be "excessive." . . . [T]he inquiry into "excessiveness" has two aspects. First, the punishment must not involve the unnecessary and wanton infliction of pain. Second, the punishment must not be grossly out of proportion to the severity of the crime. . . .

Of course, the requirements of the Eighth Amendment must be applied with an awareness of the limited role to be played by the courts. This does not mean that judges have no role to play, for the Eighth Amendment is a restraint upon the exercise of legislative power. . . .

Therefore, in assessing a punishment selected by a democratically elected legislature against the constitutional measure, we presume its validity. We may not require the legislature to select the least severe penalty possible so long as the penalty selected is not cruelly inhumane or disproportionate to the crime involved. And a heavy burden rests on those who would attack the judgment of the representatives of the people.

This is true in part because the constitutional test is intertwined with an assessment of contemporary standards and the legislative judgment weighs heavily in ascertaining such standards. "[I]n a democratic society legislatures, not courts, are constituted to respond to the will and consequently the moral values of the people." . . .

In the discussion to this point we have sought to identify the principles and considerations that guide a court in addressing an Eighth Amendment claim. We now consider specifically whether the sentence of death for the crime of murder is a per se violation of the Eighth and Fourteenth Amendments to the Constitution. We note first that history and precedent strongly support a negative answer to this question.

The imposition of the death penalty for the crime of murder has a long history of acceptance both in the United States and in England. . . .

It is apparent from the text of the Constitution itself that the existence of capital punishment was accepted by the Framers. At the time the Eighth Amendment was ratified, capital punishment was a common sanction in every State. . . .

For nearly two centuries, this Court, repeatedly and often expressly, had recognized that capital punishment is not invalid per se. . . .

Four years ago, the petitioners in *Furman* and its companion cases predicated their argument primarily upon the asserted proposition that standards of decency had evolved to the point where capital punishment no longer could be tolerated. . . .

The petitioners in the capital cases before the Court today renew the "standards of decency" argument, but developments during the four years since *Furman* have undercut substantially the assumptions upon which their argument rested. Despite the continuing debate, dating back to the 19th century, over the morality and utility of capital punishment, it is now evident that a large proportion of American society continues to regard it as an appropriate and necessary criminal sanction.

The most marked indication of society's endorsement of the death penalty for murder is the legislative response to Furman. The legislatures of at least 35 States have enacted new statutes that provide for the death penalty for at least some crimes that result in the death of another person. And the Congress of the United States, in 1974, enacted a statute providing the death penalty for aircraft piracy that results in death. . . .

The jury also is a significant and reliable objective index of contemporary values because it is so directly involved. . . . It may be true that evolving standards have influenced juries in recent decades to be more discriminating in imposing the sentence of death. But the relative infrequency of jury verdicts imposing the death sentence does not indicate rejection of capital punishment per se. Rather, the reluctance of juries in many cases to impose the sentence may well reflect the humane feeling that this most irrevocable of sanctions should be reserved for a small number of extreme cases. . . .

As we have seen, however, the Eighth Amendment demands more than that a challenged punishment be acceptable to contemporary society. The Court also must ask whether it comports with the basic concept of human dignity at the core of the Amendment. Although we cannot "invalidate a category of penalties because we deem less severe penalties adequate to serve the ends of penology," the sanction imposed cannot be so totally without penological justification that it results in the gratuitous infliction of suffering.

The death penalty is said to serve two principal social purposes: retribution and deterrence of capital crimes by prospective offenders.

In part, capital punishment is an expression of society's moral outrage at particularly offensive conduct. This function may be unappealing to many, but it is essential in an ordered society that asks its citizens to rely on legal processes rather than self-help to vindicate their wrongs.

> The instinct for retribution is part of the nature of man, and channeling that instinct in the administration of criminal justice serves an important purpose in promoting the stability of a society governed by law. When people begin to believe that organized society is unwilling or unable to impose upon criminal offenders the punishment they "deserve," then there are sown the seeds of anarchy—of self-help, vigilante justice, and lynch law.

"Retribution is no longer the dominant objective of the criminal law," but neither is it a forbidden objective nor one inconsistent with our respect for the dignity of men. Indeed, the decision that capital punishment may be the appropriate sanction in extreme cases is an expression of the community's belief that certain crimes are themselves so grievous an affront to humanity that the only adequate response may be the penalty of death.

Statistical attempts to evaluate the worth of the death penalty as a deterrent to crimes by potential offenders have occasioned a great deal of debate. The results simply have been inconclusive. . . .

. . . We may nevertheless assume safely that there are murderers, such as those who act in passion, for whom the threat of death has little or no deterrent effect. But for many others, the death penalty undoubtedly is a significant deterrent. There are carefully contemplated murders, such as murder for hire, where the possible penalty of death may well enter into the cold calculus that precedes the decision to act. And there are some categories of murder, such as murder by a life prisoner, where other sanctions may not be adequate. . . .

In sum, we cannot say that the judgment of the Georgia legislature that capital punishment may be necessary in some cases is clearly wrong. Considerations of federalism, as well as respect for the ability of a legislature to evaluate . . . the moral consensus concerning the death penalty and its social utility as a sanction, require us to conclude, in the absence of more convincing evidence, that the infliction of death as a punishment for murder is not without justification and thus is not unconstitutionally severe.

Finally, we must consider whether the punishment of death is disproportionate in relation to the crime for which it is imposed. There is no question that death as a punishment is unique in its severity and irrevocability. . . . But we are concerned here only with the imposition of capital punishment for the crime of murder, and when a life has been taken deliberately by the offender, we cannot say that the punishment is invariably disproportionate to the crime. It is an extreme sanction, suitable to the most extreme of crimes. . . .

. . . [T]he concerns expressed in *Furman* that the penalty of death not be imposed in an arbitrary or capricious manner can be met by a carefully drafted statute that ensures that the sentencing authority is given adequate information and guidance. As a general proposition these concerns are best met by a system that provides for a bifurcated proceeding at which the sentencing authority is apprised of the information relevant to the imposition of sentence and provided with standards to guide its use of the information. . . .

We now turn to consideration of the constitutionality of Georgia's capital-sentencing procedures. . . .

In short, Georgia's new sentencing procedures require as a prerequisite of the imposition of the death penalty, specific jury findings as to the circumstances of the crime or the character of the defendant. Moreover to guard further against a situation comparable to that presented in *Furman,* the Supreme Court of Georgia compares each death sentence with the sentences imposed on similarly situated defendants to ensure that the sentence of death in a particular case is not disproportionate. On their face these procedures seem to satisfy the concerns of *Furman.* No longer should there be "no meaningful basis for distinguishing the few cases in which [the death penalty] is imposed from the many cases in which it is not."

The petitioner contends, however, that the changes in the Georgia sentencing procedures are only cosmetic, that the arbitrariness and capriciousness condemned by *Furman* continue to exist in Georgia—both in traditional practices that still remain and in the new sentencing procedures adopted in response to *Furman.*

First, the petitioner focuses on the opportunities for discretionary action that are inherent in the processing of any murder case under Georgia law. He notes that the state prosecutor has unfettered authority to select those persons whom he wishes to prosecute for a capital offense and to plea bargain with them. Further, at the trial the jury may choose to convict a defendant of a lesser included offense rather than find him guilty of a crime punishable by death, even if the evidence would support a capital verdict. And finally, a defendant who is convicted and sentenced to die may have his sentence commuted by the Governor of the State and the Georgia Board of Pardons and Paroles.

The existence of these discretionary stages is not determinative of the issues before us. At each of these stages an actor in the criminal justice system makes a decision which may remove a defendant from consideration as a candidate for the death penalty. *Furman,* in contrast, dealt with the decision to impose the death sentence on a specific individual who had been convicted of a capital offense. Nothing in any of our cases suggests that the decision to afford an individual defendant mercy violates the Constitution. *Furman* held only that, in order to minimize the risk that the death penalty would be imposed on a capriciously selected group of offenders, the decision to impose it had to be guided by standards so that the sentencing authority would focus on the particularized circumstances of the crime and the defendant.

The petitioner further contends that the capital-sentencing procedures adopted by Georgia in response to *Furman* do not eliminate the dangers of arbitrariness and caprice in jury sentencing that were held in *Furman* to be violative of the Eighth and Fourteenth Amendments. He claims that the statute is so broad and vague as to leave juries free to act as arbitrarily and capriciously as they wish in deciding whether to impose the death penalty. . . .

[For example,] . . . [t]he petitioner attacks the seventh statutory aggravating circumstance, which authorizes imposition of the death penalty if the murder was "outrageously or wantonly vile, horrible or inhuman in that it involved torture, depravity of mind, or an aggravated battery to the victim," contending that it is so broad that capital punishment could be imposed in any murder case. It is, of course, arguable that any murder involves depravity of mind or an aggravated battery. But this language need not be construed in this way, and there is no reason to assume that the Supreme Court of Georgia will adopt such an open-ended construction. . . .

The provision for appellate review in the Georgia capital-sentencing system serves as a check against the random or arbitrary imposition of the death penalty. In particular, the proportionality review substantially eliminates the possibility that a person will be sentenced to die by the action of an aberrant jury. If a time comes when juries generally do not impose the death sentence in a certain kind of murder case, the appellate review procedures assure that no defendant convicted under such circumstances will suffer a sentence of death.

The basic concern of *Furman* centered on those defendants who were being condemned to death capriciously and arbitrarily. Under the procedures before the Court in that case, sentencing authorities were not directed to give attention to the nature or circumstances of the crime committed or to the character or record of the defendant. Left unguided, juries imposed the death sentence in a way that could only be called freakish. The new Georgia sentencing procedures, by contrast, focus the jury's attention on the particularized nature of the crime and the particularized characteristics of the individual defendant. While the jury is permitted to consider any aggravating or mitigating circumstances, it must find and identify at least one statutory aggravating factor before it may impose a penalty of death. In this way the jury's discretion is channeled. No longer can a jury wantonly and freakishly impose the death sentence; it is always circumscribed by the legislative guidelines. In addition, the review function of the Supreme Court of Georgia affords additional assurance that the concerns that prompted our decision in Furman are not present to any significant degree in the Georgia procedure applied here. . . .

Mr. Justice White . . .

Petitioner's argument that there is an unconstitutional amount of discretion in the system which separates those suspects who receive the death penalty from those who receive life imprisonment, a lesser penalty, or are acquitted or never charged, seems to be in [the] final analysis an indictment of our entire system of justice. Petitioner has argued, in effect, that no matter how effective the death penalty may be as a punishment, government, created and run as it must be by humans, is inevitably incompetent to administer it. This cannot be accepted as a proposition of constitutional law. Imposition of the death penalty is surely an awesome responsibility for any system of justice and those who participate in it. Mistakes will be made and discriminations will occur which will be difficult to explain. However, one of society's most basic tasks is that of protecting the lives of its citizens and one of the most basic ways in which it achieves the task is through criminal laws against murder. I decline to interfere with the manner in which Georgia has chosen to enforce such laws on what is simply an assertion of lack of faith in the ability of the system of justice to operate in a fundamentally fair manner.

For the reasons stated in dissent in *Roberts v. Louisiana,* neither can I agree with the petitioner's other basic argument that the death penalty, however imposed and for whatever crime, is cruel and unusual punishment. . . .

Excerpts from Justice White's dissent in Roberts . . .

. . . I also cannot agree with the petitioner's other basic argument that the death penalty, however imposed and for whatever crime, is cruel and unusual punishment. . . . It is plain enough that the Constitution drafted by the Framers expressly made room for the death penalty. . . . In *Trop v. Dulles,* four Members of the Court—Mr. Chief Justice Warren and Justices Black, Douglas, and Whittaker—agreed that "[w]hatever the arguments may be against capital punishment, both on moral grounds and in terms of accomplishing the purposes of punishment—the death penalty has been employed throughout our history, and, in a day when it is still widely accepted, it cannot be said to violate the constitutional concept of cruelty."

Until *Furman v. Georgia*, this was the consistent view of the Court and of every Justice who in a published opinion had addressed the question of the validity of capital punishment under the Eighth Amendment. In *Furman*, it was concluded by at least two Justices that the death penalty had become unacceptable to the great majority of the people of this country and for that reason, alone or combined with other reasons, was invalid under the Eighth Amendment, which must be construed and applied to reflect the evolving moral standards of the country. That argument, whether or not accurate at that time, when measured by the manner in which the death penalty was being administered under the then prevailing statutory schemes, is no longer descriptive of the country's attitude. Since the judgment in *Furman*, Congress and 35 state legislatures re-enacted the death penalty for one or more crimes. All of these States authorize the death penalty for murder of one kind or another. With these profound developments in mind, I cannot say that capital punishment has been rejected by or is offensive to the prevailing attitudes and moral presuppositions in the United States or that it is always an excessively cruel or severe punishment or always a disproportionate punishment for any crime for which it might be imposed. These grounds for invalidating the death penalty are foreclosed by recent events, which this Court must accept as demonstrating that capital punishment is acceptable to the contemporary community as just punishment for at least some intentional killings. . . .

The widespread re-enactment of the death penalty, it seems to me, answers any claims that life imprisonment is adequate punishment to satisfy the need for reprobation or retribution. It also seems clear enough that death finally forecloses the possibility that a prisoner will commit further crimes, whereas life imprisonment does not. This leaves the question of general deterrence as the principal battleground: does the death penalty more effectively deter others from crime than does the threat of life imprisonment?

The debate on this subject started generations ago and is still in progress. Each side has a plethora of fact and opinion in support of its position, some of it quite old and some of it very new; but neither has yet silenced the other. I need not detail these conflicting materials, most of which are familiar sources. It is quite apparent that the relative efficacy of capital punishment and life imprisonment to deter others from crime remains a matter about which reasonable men and reasonable legislators may easily differ. In this posture of the case, it would be neither a proper [nor a] wise exercise of the power of judicial review to refuse to accept the reasonable conclusions of Congress and 35 state legislatures that there are indeed certain circumstances in which the death penalty is the more efficacious deterrent of crime.

It will not do to denigrate these legislative judgments as some form of vestigial savagery or as purely retributive in motivation; for they are solemn judgments, reasonably based, that imposition of the death penalty will save the lives of innocent persons. This concern for life and human values and the sincere efforts of the States to pursue them are matters of the greatest moment with which the judiciary should be most reluctant to interfere. The issue is not whether, had we been legis-lators, we would have supported or opposed the capital punishment statutes presently before us. The question here under discussion is whether the Eighth Amendment requires us to interfere with the enforcement of these statutes on the grounds that a sentence of life imprisonment for the crimes at issue would as well have served the ends of criminal justice. In my view, the Eighth Amendment pro-vides no warrant for overturning these convictions on these grounds. . . .

The . . . reason offered [by the plurality of Justices Stewart, Powell, and Stevens] for invalidating the Louisiana statute . . . [is that] the concept of the mandatory death sentence has been rejected by the community and departs so far from contemporary standards with respect to the imposition of capital punish-ment that it must be held unconstitutional. . . .

. . . [T]he plurality overreads the history upon which it so heavily relies. Nar-rowing the categories of crime for which the death penalty was authorized re-flected a growing sentiment that death was an excessive penalty for many crimes, but I am not convinced, as apparently the plurality is, that the decision to vest dis-cretionary sentencing power in the jury was a judgment that mandatory punish-ments were excessively cruel rather than merely a legislative response to avoid jury nullifications which were occurring with some frequency. That legislatures chose jury sentencing as the least troublesome of two approaches hardly proves legislative rejection of mandatory sentencing. States legislatures may have pre-ferred to vest discretionary sentencing power in a jury rather than to have guilty defendants go scot-free; but I doubt that these events necessarily reflect an affir-mative legislative preference for discretionary systems or support an inference that legislatures would have chosen them even absent their experience with jury nullification. . . .

Louisiana and North Carolina have returned to the mandatory capital punish-ment system for certain crimes. Their legislatures have not deemed mandatory punishment, once the crime is proven, to be unacceptable; nor have their juries rejected it, for the death penalty has been imposed with some regularity. Perhaps we would prefer that these States had adopted a different system, but the issue is not our individual preferences but the constitutionality of the mandatory systems chosen by these two states. I see no warrant under the Eighth Amendment for re-fusing to uphold these statutes.

Indeed, the more fundamental objection than the plurality's muddled reason-ing is that in *Gregg v. Georgia* it lectures us at length about the role and place of the judiciary and then proceeds to ignore its own advice, the net effect being to suggest that observers of this institution should pay more attention to what we do than what we say. The plurality claims that it has not forgotten what the past has taught about the limits of judicial review; but I fear that it has again surrendered to the temptation to make policy for and to attempt to govern the country through a misuse of the powers given this Court under the Constitution. . . .

Mr. Justice Brennan, dissenting . . .

The Cruel and Unusual Punishments Clause "must draw its meaning from the evolving standards of decency that mark the progress of a maturing society." The opinions of Mr. Justice Stewart, Mr. Justice Powell, and Mr. Justice Stevens today hold that "evolving standards of decency" require focus not on the essence of the death penalty itself but primarily upon the procedures employed by the State to single out persons to suffer the penalty of death. . . .

In *Furman v. Georgia,* I read "evolving standards of decency" as requiring focus upon the essence of the death penalty itself and not primarily or solely upon the procedures under which the determination to inflict the penalty upon a particular person was made. I there said:

> From the beginning of our Nation, the punishment of death has stirred acute public controversy. Although pragmatic arguments for and against the punishment have been frequently advanced, this longstanding and heated controversy cannot be explained solely as the result of differences over the practical wisdom of a particular government policy. At bottom, the battle has been waged on moral grounds. The country has debated whether a society for which the dignity of the individual is the supreme value can, without a fundamental inconsistency, follow the practice of deliberately putting some of its members to death. In the United States, as in other nations of the western world, "the struggle about this punishment has been one between ancient and deeply rooted beliefs in retribution, atonement or vengeance on the one hand, and, on the other, beliefs in the personal value and dignity of the common man that were born of the democratic movement of the eighteenth century, as well as beliefs in the scientific approach to an understanding of the motive forces of human conduct, which are the result of the growth of the sciences of behavior during the nineteenth and twentieth centuries." It is this essentially moral conflict that forms the backdrop for the past changes in and the present operation of our system of imposing death as a punishment for crime.

That continues to be my view. For the Clause forbidding cruel and unusual punishments under our constitutional system of government embodies in unique degree moral principles restraining the punishments that our civilized society may impose on those persons who transgress its laws. Thus, I too say: "For myself, I do not hesitate to assert the proposition that the only way the law has progressed from the days of the rack, the screw, and the wheel is the development of moral concepts, or, as stated by the Supreme Court . . . , the application of 'evolving standards of decency.'. . . "

This Court inescapably has the duty, as the ultimate arbiter of the meaning of our Constitution, to say whether, when individuals condemned to death stand before our Bar, "moral concepts" require us to hold that the law has progressed to the point where we should declare that the punishment of death, like punishments on the rack, the screw, and the wheel, is no longer morally tolerable in our civilized society. My opinion in *Furman v. Georgia* concluded that our civilization and the law had progressed to this point and that therefore the punishment of death, for whatever crime and under all circumstances, is "cruel and unusual" in violation of the Eighth and Fourteenth Amendments of the Constitution. I shall not again canvass the reasons that led to that conclusion. I emphasize only that foremost among the "moral concepts" recognized in our cases and inherent in the Clause is the primary moral principle that the State, even as it punishes, must

treat its citizens in a manner consistent with their intrinsic worth as human beings—a punishment must not be so severe as to be degrading to human dignity. A
judicial determination whether the punishment of death comports with human
dignity is therefore not only permitted but compelled by the Clause.

. . . Death for whatever crime and under all circumstances "is truly an awesome punishment. The calculated killing of a human being by the State involves,
by its very nature, a denial of the executed person's humanity. . . . An executed
person has indeed 'lost the right to have rights.'" Death is not only an unusually
severe punishment, unusual in its pain, in its finality, and in its enormity, but it
serves no penal purpose more effectively than a less severe punishment; therefore
the principle inherent in the Clause that prohibits pointless infliction of excessive
punishment when less severe punishment can adequately achieve the same purposes invalidated the punishment.

The fatal constitutional infirmity in the punishment of death is that it treats
"members of the human race as nonhuman, as objects to be toyed with and dis-
carded. [It is] thus inconsistent with the fundamental premise of the Clause that
even the vilest criminal remains a human being possessed of common human dignity." As such it is a penalty that "subjects the individual to a fate forbidden by the
principle of civilized treatment guaranteed by the [Clause]." I therefore would
hold, on that ground alone, that death is today a cruel and unusual punishment
prohibited by the Clause. "Justice of this kind is obviously no less shocking than
the crime itself, and the new 'official' murder, far from offering redress for the offense committed against society, adds instead a second defilement to the first." . . .

Mr. Justice Marshall, dissenting . . .

. . . My sole purposes here are to consider the suggestion that my conclusion in
Furman has been undercut by developments since then, and briefly to evaluate
the basis for my Brethren's holding that the extinction of life is a permissible form
of punishment under the Cruel and Unusual Punishments Clause.

In Furman I concluded that the death penalty is constitutionally invalid for
two reasons. First, the death penalty is excessive. And second, the American people, fully informed as to the purposes of the death penalty and its liabilities, would
in my view reject it as morally unacceptable.

Since the decision in Furman, the legislatures of 35 States have enacted new
statutes authorizing the imposition of the death sentence for certain crimes, and
Congress has enacted a law providing the death penalty for air piracy resulting in
death. I would be less than candid if I did not acknowledge that these developments have a significant bearing on a realistic assessment of the moral acceptability of the death penalty to the American people. But if the constitutionality of the
death penalty turns, as I have urged, on the opinion of an *informed* citizenry, then
even the enactment of new death statutes cannot be viewed as conclusive. In *Furman*, I observed that the American people are largely unaware of the information
critical to a judgment on the morality of the death penalty, and concluded that if
they were better informed they would consider it shocking, unjust, and unacceptable. A recent study, conducted after the enactment of the post-*Furman* statues,

has confirmed that the American people know little about the death penalty, and that the opinions of an informed public would differ significantly from those of a public unaware of the consequences and effects of the death penalty.

Even assuming, however, that the post-*Furman* enactment of statutes authorizing the death penalty renders the prediction of the views of an informed citizenry an uncertain basis for a constitutional decision, the enactment of those statutes has no bearing whatsoever on the conclusion that the death penalty is unconstitutional because it is excessive. An excessive penalty is invalid under the Cruel and Unusual Punishments Clause "even though popular sentiment may favor" it. The inquiry here, then, is simply whether the death penalty is necessary to accomplish the legitimate legislative purposes in punishment, or whether a less severe penalty—life imprisonment—would do as well.

The two purposes that sustain the death penalty as nonexcessive in the Court's view are general deterrence and retribution. . . .

. . . The evidence I reviewed in *Furman* remains convincing, in my view, that "capital punishment is not necessary as a deterrent to crime in our society." The justification for the death penalty must be found elsewhere.

The other principal purpose said to be served by the death penalty is retribution. The notion that retribution can serve as a moral justification for the sanction of death finds credence in the opinion of my Brothers Stewart, Powell, and Stevens, and that of my Brother White in *Roberts v. Louisiana.* It is this notion that I find to be the most disturbing aspect of today's unfortunate decisions. . . .

. . . Some of the language of my Brothers Stewart, Powell, and Stevens . . . appears positively to embrace this notion of retribution for its own sake as a justification for capital punishment. They state:

> [T]he decision that capital punishment may be the appropriate sanction in extreme cases is an expression of the community's belief that certain crimes are themselves so grievous an affront to humanity that the only adequate response may be the penalty of death.

The plurality then quotes with approval from Lord Justice Denning's remarks before the British Royal Commission on Capital Punishment:

> The truth is that some crimes are so outrageous that society insists on adequate punishment, because the wrong-doer deserves it, irrespective of whether it is a deterrent or not.

Of course, it may be that these statements are intended as no more than observations as to the popular demands that it is thought must be responded to in order to prevent anarchy. But the implication of the statements appears to me to be quite different—namely, that society's judgment that the murderer "deserves" death must be respected not simply because the preservation of order requires it, but because it is appropriate that society make the judgment and carry it out. It is this latter notion, in particular, that I consider to be fundamentally at odds with the Eighth Amendment. The mere fact that the community demands the murderer's life in return for the evil he has done cannot sustain the death penalty, for as the plurality reminds us, "the Eighth Amendment demands more than that a challenged punishment be acceptable to contemporary society." To be sustained under the Eighth Amendment, the death penalty must "[comport] with the basic concept of human dignity at the core of the Amendment"; the objective of imposing it must be "[consistent] with our respect for the dignity of [other] men." Under these standards, the taking of life "because the wrongdoer deserves it" surely must fall, for such a punishment has as its very basis the total denial of the wrongdoer's dignity and worth.

POSTSCRIPT

Since *Gregg v. Georgia,* the Supreme Court has continued to struggle with the constitutionality of how the death penalty should be applied to what crimes. [22] Less attention has been given to whether the Constitution limits why a state can impose the death penalty. Correct or not, the dominant view is that the Constitution does not preclude executions for the purpose of retribution. The Court's performance in regard to the two other basic questions concerning the constitutionality of the death penalty has been marked by inconsistency and increasing passivity. Though the Court has ruled that executions for rape are unconstitutional, it did so on the ground that the American people opposed inflicting the ultimate sanction for this particular offense. Nor did the Court presume any authority to engage in an independent calculation of proportionality in regard to the execution of murderers who were children or mentally retarded.

In the years immediately following *Gregg,* the Court continued its tradition of imposing constitutional restrictions on how the death penalty was applied. Its more recent decisions, however, have inclined in the opposite direction. Despite the objection that the murderers who are currently being selected for executions are selected "arbitrarily," the Court has increasingly adopted a hands-off attitude. The result may well be that the United States will soon execute more criminals per year than any other country in the world.

At the same time that the Court decided *Gregg,* it invalidated statutes that imposed mandatory death sentences in *Woodson v. North Carolina* (1976) and *Roberts v. Louisiana* (1976).[23] There was no majority opinion in the 5–4 decision, but Justice Potter Stewart's pivotal plurality opinion explained that the finality of an execution constitutionally required an opportunity for mercy. In Stewart's view, since the Constitution restricted how the death penalty could be administered, a judge or jury had to have the option of sentencing a murderer to life imprisonment. Capital crimes required "individualized" consideration of the criminal and the circumstances of the crime. Two years later, in *Lockett v. Ohio* (1978), the Court extended this reasoning by rejecting an attempt by a state to limit the

---

[22]For a critical review of the Supreme Court's recent *habeas corpus* decisions, especially in regard to how they effect death penalty cases, see Jeffrey Rosen, "Bad Noose," *New Republic,* October 4, 1993, pp. 13–15. Also see *New York Times,* July 4, 1993, IV, p. 1.

[23]428 U.S. 280 (1976); 428 U.S. 325 (1976).

kinds of mitigating factors that a jury could consider in a capital case.[24] The Court concluded that the Constitution gave the jury the latitude to consider any aspect of the case as a mitigating factor. It is arguable that this ruling to some extent qualified the import of the *Gregg* decision. Standards and guidelines in capital sentencing were constitutionally required, but they were not to operate in a way that prevented a jury from exercising mercy as it saw fit. In any case, *Lockett* continued the trend of decisions holding that the Constitution limited how the death penalty could be administered.[25]

In the year following *Gregg*, the Court also affirmed the principle that the Eighth Amendment restricted what crimes could be punished by the death penalty. In *Coker v. Georgia* (1977), the Court held that capital punishment was disproportionate to the crime of rape, at least the rape of an adult woman.[26] Justice Byron White, who wrote the plurality opinion, supported the Court's ruling by referring, first, to the fact that Georgia was the only state after *Furman* to reauthorize capital punishment for rape of an adult woman and, second, that Georgia juries had declined to hand down death sentences in 90 percent of rape convictions. Therefore, Justice White insisted, the Court's judgment as to proportionality was based not on "the subjective views of individual justices" but instead on "objective factors" concerning contemporary values.[27] In effect, true to what he had said in *Gregg*, White determined that death was a constitutionally "disproportionate" sentence for certain kinds of rapes only because he felt that public opinion supported this ruling. Judges could limit what crimes were punished with death only in accordance with social consensus, not in opposition to it.

In response, Chief Justice Warren Burger wrote a dissent accusing the plurality of "disingenuousness." By ignoring the experience from 1900 to 1970, during which time one-third of all American jurisdictions punished rape with death, and by focusing on the experience of the past five years, during which time the Court's decisions had cast considerable doubt on the constitutional status of the death penalty in general, the justices in the majority had allowed their subjective preferences to shape their assessment of contemporary values.[28] The Court should apply contemporary standards only after it has filtered out the effects the *Furman* decision had had on state legislatures. Burger concluded that, given the ambiguous character of contemporary standards in the post–*Furman* period, the Court should defer to Georgia's legislative judgment that death was a proportionate punishment for rape—a crime that the plurality agreed was second only to murder in its character as an "ultimate violation of self."[29]

Is Justice White's or Chief Justice Burger's argument more credible? Both justices place a great deal of significance on contemporary values as an objective

[24]438 U.S. 586 (1978).

[25]In *Blystone v. Pennsylvania*, 110 S.Ct. 1078 (1990), the Court qualified the *Lockett* rule somewhat. It upheld a Pennsylvania law that mandated the death penalty if the jury found no mitigating factors and at least one aggravating circumstance.

[26]433 U.S. 584 (1977).

[27]Idem, 592.

[28]Idem, 614.

[29]Idem, 620.

basis for determining if and when death is a disproportionate punishment in violation of the Eighth Amendment. However, White is much more willing to overrule a state legislature's judgment based on his assessment of American contemporary standards, while Burger believes that states should have more latitude to experiment with the death penalty, to discover if and when it is an effective deterrent, and that judges should be more deferential to the legislature's decision. Which approach coincides more with your understanding of how courts should interpret the standards of decency implicit in the Eighth Amendment? Should they more or less automatically defer to the legislature's interpretation of contemporary standards, or should they act on their own independent assessment?

Similar questions arose in regard to the nature of the offender rather than that of the crime. If it violated contemporary standards of decency to execute a rapist, did it also violate these same standards to execute a murderer who is a child or who is mentally retarded but not insane? In *Thompson v. Oklahoma,* the Court addressed the first issue in a case involving a condemned murderer who was under sixteen years of age when he participated in a brutal homicide.[30] Of the eight justices participating in the decision, four said that such an execution would violate contemporary standards of decency, three said that such an execution would not *necessarily* violate the standards, and one justice, Sandra Day O'Connor, argued that it was too early for the Court to tell. Although fourteen states had abolished the death penalty entirely, and eighteen had specifically restricted capital punishment to offenders over the age of sixteen, O'Connor noted that the federal government and nineteen states had authorized the use of the death penalty without setting any age limits. In this context, O'Connor was unwilling to conclude that the execution of criminals under sixteen years of age violated contemporary standards "as a matter of constitutional law without better evidence than we now possess."[31]

In *Penry v. Lynaugh* (1989), the Court addressed whether a state could execute a mentally retarded person who was not insane.[32] In a majority opinion written by Justice O'Connor, the Court ruled that the jury had to be told that it could consider Penry's mental retardation as a mitigating factor but that contemporary standards of decency did not preclude the possibility of a death sentence for a mentally retarded murderer. O'Connor observed that a recent poll in Texas had found that 73 percent of Texans opposed applying the death penalty to the mentally retarded but found such evidence to be an "insufficient" basis for a constitutional ruling. "The public sentiment expressed in these and other polls and resolutions may ultimately find expression in legislation, which is an objective indicator of contemporary values upon which we can rely."[33]Accordingly, since at that time only one state had explicitly banned the execution of retarded persons, the Court could not rule that such was a violation of the Eighth Amendment.

---

[30]487 U.S. 815 (1988).

[31]Idem, 849.

[32]109 S.Ct. 2934 (1989).

[33]Idem, 2955.

What do you think of the Court's decisions in *Thompson* and *Penry?* Is it permissible to execute a fifteen-year-old? What if the murder was particularly vicious and cold-blooded and the defendant showed no remorse? How do our standards of decency apply to a mentally retarded murderer who was not insane—in other words, someone who knew that murder was wrong and had the capacity to conform to the law? What is your opinion of Justice O'Connor's approach? Does it coincide more with the views of Justice White or those of Chief Justice Burger? Was there enough evidence for the Court to rule in *Thompson* that the execution of a fifteen-year-old violated contemporary standards? Should the Court have based its decision in *Penry* on the poll? Should the Court rely on polls in other areas of constitutional adjudication? If polls are inappropriate elsewhere, why use them in regard to the Eighth Amendment? If the Court must wait until the American people's evolving sentiments of decency are expressed into legislation, what is the purpose of the Eighth Amendment? Does it limit legislative power? Is it a grant of power?

In 1987, the Court adopted a more passive attitude toward the death penalty when it declined to interfere with how states were racially administering the death penalty. The 5–4 decision in *McCleskey v. Kemp,* a case coming once again from Georgia, rejected the constitutional significance of an empirical study (the Baldus study, conducted by David C. Baldus, George Woodworth, and Charles Pulaski), which established that persons who were charged with killing white victims in Georgia were 4.3 times more likely to be condemned to death than defendants charged with killing African-Americans.[34] Justice Lewis Powell, who wrote the majority opinion, did not question the validity of the study's conclusions but held that they were insufficient to make out a valid constitutional objection to how Georgia administered the death penalty. Powell emphasized that even if McCleskey were black and his victim white, the Baldus study did not "prove" that he was racially discriminated against at the sentencing stage of *his* trial. "[In] light of the safeguards designed to minimize racial bias in the process, the fundamental value of jury trial in our criminal justice system, and the benefits that discretion provides to criminal defendants," Powell added, "the Baldus study does not demonstrate a constitutionally significant risk of racial bias affecting the Georgia capital-sentencing process."[35] Accordingly, since the defendant could not prove that actual racial discrimination had occurred in his case, the Court would not say that the risk of discrimination outweighed the virtues of Georgia's system of capital sentencing.

Justice William Brennan, in his dissent, pointed out that the Court had never before required that defendants challenging their death sentences show that racial prejudice had actually influenced their own sentencing decisions. All that such de-

---

[34]The Baldus study also showed that the death penalty was applied in 22 percent of the cases involving black defendants and white victims, 8 percent of the cases involving white defendants and white victims, 1 percent of the cases involving black defendants and black victims, and 3 percent of the cases involving black defendants and black victims.

[35]*McCleskey v. Kemp,* 481 U.S. 279, 313 (1987).

fendants had to show was "that the system under which they were sentenced posed a significant risk of such an occurrence."[36] Moreover, Brennan continued, what constituted a "significant" risk of such an impermissible occurrence had to "be informed by awareness of the fact that death is irrevocable."[37] In this context, Brennan insisted, the Baldus study more than met the burden of proof. Since in plea-bargain negotiations, Georgia lawyers advising African-American clients who had killed white victims would not underestimate the significance of the Baldus study, the Court should not either. Therefore, according to Brennan, by not compelling Georgia to eliminate the arbitrary factor of race from its capital sentencing process, the Court was not fulfilling its constitutional duty of monitoring how states administered the death penalty.

Do you agree with Brennan? If you do, what should the Court do if it were established that defendants who victimized whites were sentenced to longer prison terms than those who victimized African-American? Is race discrimination in capital sentencing more constitutionally intolerable than race discrimination in other kinds of sentencing? If you support Justice Powell's reasoning—if you think it is not constitutionally "significant" that the killers of whites in Georgia are 4.3 times more likely to be executed than killers of African-Americans—at what point would the risk of racial discrimination in capital sentencing become constitutionally "significant"? Moreover, it seems that to require a condemned person to prove, above and beyond statistical disparities, that racial prejudice actually occurred in his case is a very difficult burden of proof to meet. How would a person on death row go about proving that racism influenced the jury or judge that sentenced him to death?

Though *Gregg* opened the door for states to begin executing the more than five hundred people then on death row, no execution occurred because of the availability of federal writs of *habeas corpus*. These writs allowed condemned persons to attack their convictions and sentences even if they were upheld by the state's highest court and by the Supreme Court. After all such direct appeals had failed, convicts on death row could *indirectly* attack their convictions by petitioning their local federal district court for a writ of *habeas corpus*. If their petitions were successful, their executions would be stayed (delayed) until after the district court had ruled on the constitutional objections to their convictions or to their death sentences. If the federal district court ruled against a condemned person, further delay was possible because the case could be appealed to the federal Court of Appeals and to the Supreme Court. And if all these appeals failed to overturn a prisoner's conviction or to reduce his sentence to life imprisonment, the process could perhaps be started all over again, with new petitions for writs of *habeas corpus* at the federal district court level.

With this system of *habeas corpus* in operation, the first person since 1967 to be executed in the United States was a condemned man who refused to appeal his conviction. Gary Gilmore was shot by a Utah firing squad on January 17, 1977. He preferred death to a life behind bars. The first person executed while still trying to

---

[36]Idem, 324.

[37]Idem, 335.

appeal his sentence was John Spenkelink, who died in Florida on May 23, 1979. No one was executed in 1980 and only one person in 1981. By 1983, only eleven executions had taken place, though the number of people on death row had increased radically. In 1985, about seventeen hundred prisoners were under "active sentences of death."[38] Clearly, many prisoners on death row were able to delay their executions indefinitely by taking advantage of the system of *habeas corpus*.

Partly in response to this situation, the Supreme Court, under the leadership of Chief Justice William Rehnquist, took the controversial step of limiting the availability of *habeas corpus* relief. For example, before 1986, if a lawyer of a condemned murderer failed to raise a constitutional objection on direct appeal because he mistakenly believed that it would be futile, the defendant could still raise the issue in a *habeas corpus* petition if he could show cause as to why he failed to raise the issue at the state level and if he could show that the constitutional error had probably produced a "miscarriage of justice." However, in *Smith v. Murray* (1986), the Court ruled that the lawyer's mistake in not raising the constitutional issue was "a procedural default."[39] Even if there was a chance that Smith's death sentence would have been overturned on direct appeal if his attorney had raised the issue, it made no difference. The lawyer had "defaulted," and the issue could not be raised in a *habeas corpus* petition. Smith was executed on July 31, 1986.

In *Smith,* the Court said that the defendant's procedural default should not bar *habeas corpus* relief if it had produced "a fundamental miscarriage of justice,"[40] but the justices declined to apply this exception to Smith. The Court refused to invoke this exception, though it did not deny that Smith's death sentence might have been overturned on direct appeal if his lawyer had made the proper constitutional objection. Does it trouble you that Smith may have been executed only because his lawyer made a mistake? How do you balance this possibility against the problem of clever attorneys using the system of *habeas corpus* to cause undue delay of executions? Which issue is more important? What should the Supreme Court have done in *Smith?*

One reason why lawyers for death row inmates were able to delay executions in the post-*Gregg* era was because they were permitted to apply retroactively new Supreme Court decisions to death sentences that had already been upheld on appeal.[41] A person convicted and sentenced in 1980 could seek *habeas corpus* relief under a 1985 Supreme Court decision, even though his conviction and sentence had been upheld on appeal in 1983. The Court sharply limited this practice in *Teague v. Lane* (1989).[42] It ruled that, apart from certain exceptions, "new constitutional rules of criminal procedure will not be applicable to those cases which

---

[38]Franklin E. Zimring and Gordon Hawkins, *Capital Punishment and the American Agenda* (Cambridge: Cambridge University Press, 1986), p. 95.

[39]477 U.S. 527 (1986). Our discussion of *habeas corpus* and the death penalty relies heavily on Welsh S. White, *The Death Penalty in the Nineties* (Ann Arbor: University of Michigan Press, 1991), pp. 14–25.

[40]Idem, 538.

[41]A brief filed by the LDF in a death penalty case claimed that since 1976, fully 70 percent of defendants had prevailed in federal *habeas corpus* cases. See White, *Death Penalty in the Nineties*, p. 19.

[42]109 S.Ct. 1060 (1989).

have become final before the new rules are announced."[43] In effect, the Supreme Court would not normally reverse death sentences imposed and upheld by state courts, even if mistakes of federal constitutional rights had occurred in these cases, as long as the state had interpreted the existing precedents "reasonably" and in "good faith."[44] The troubling implication was that improvements in criminal procedure that were thought to be constitutionally compelled would not save people condemned under procedures now thought to be constitutionally inadequate.

Are the Supreme Court's decisions in regard to *habeas corpus* justifiable? Have they altered the purpose of the writ of *habeas corpus* from one of ensuring that states respect the constitutional rights of prisoners to one of ensuring only that states *try* to respect the constitutional rights of convicts, including those sentenced to death? Have they allowed an indefensible arbitrariness to creep into how states choose who is to be executed and who is not? For instance, is it not arbitrary if a lawyer's failure to raise a constitutional claim on appeal is the reason why one defendant is executed while another is not? Why should one murderer be executed and another not, merely because the former's attorney was tired, busy, or incompetent? Do the Supreme Court's new rules concerning *habeas corpus* permit such a possibility? Do they encourage it? Do these decisions mean that the Supreme Court is retreating from its constitutional function of monitoring how the states apply the death penalty? Should it retreat?

All of these questions reveal the deep paradoxes underlying the Supreme Court's role in regard to the death penalty. If the old *habeas corpus* system had not been modified, it is likely that very few people sentenced to death would have been executed. Can such a system of capital punishment be justified? What if, on average, only one out of five hundred condemned prisoners is executed? Would such an execution be "arbitrary"? Can executions be so infrequent that they serve no purpose? On the other hand, it has been estimated that if the Supreme Court maintains its generally passive attitude toward the death penalty, it is likely that the number of executions in the United States will climb to more than three hundred per year—"twice as many as the peak year of executions in the United States in this century and more than three times as many as the annual total reported by South Africa."[45] In late 1992, the number of convicts on death row was 2,636.[46] Should the Court try to stop the so-called leader of the free world from becoming the world's leading executioner? If it should, on what grounds should it base its decision? Is the death penalty a "cruel and unusual" punishment because of how it is applied, because of what kind of punishment it is, or because the Constitution limits why states can punish? And what role do "evolving standards of decency" play in your argument? In what way can the Supreme Court act on standards of decency when 90 percent of the American people support the death penalty?[47]

---

[43]Idem, 1075.

[44]See *Butler v. McKellar*, 110 S.Ct. 121 (1990).

[45]Zimring and Hawkins, *Capital Punishment*, p. 96.

[46]*New York Times*, November, 18, 1992, p. A16.

[47]*U.S. News & World Report*, March 26, 1990, cited by Welsh, *Death Penalty in the Nineties*, p. 32, n. 147.

Index

✦